Brian Street's edited volume, *Cross-cultural approaches to literacy*, investigates the meanings and uses of literacy in different cultures and societies. In contrast to previous studies, where the focus of research has been on aspects of cognition, education and on the economic 'consequences' of literacy, these largely ethnographic essays bring together anthropological and linguistic work written over the last ten years by anthropologists and sociolinguists. Accounts of literacy practices in a variety of locations, including Great Britain, the United States, Africa, and South Pacific and Madagascar, illustrate how these practices vary from one context to another, and challenge the traditional view that literacy is a single, uniform skill, essential to functioning in a modern society. The conclusions reached will be crucial for future researchers, and of interest to educators, developers and practitioners in the field.

Cambridge Studies in Oral and Literate Culture 23

CROSS-CULTURAL APPROACHES TO LITERACY

Cambridge Studies in Oral and Literate Culture

Edited by PETER BURKE and RUTH FINNEGAN

CROSS-CULTURAL APPROACHES TO LITERACY

EDITED BY
BRIAN STREET
School of Social Sciences, University of Sussex

CAMBRIDGE
UNIVERSITY PRESS

Published by the Press Syndicate of the University of Cambridge
The Pitt Building, Trumpington Street, Cambridge CB2 1RP
40 West 20th Street, New York, NY 10011–4211, USA
10 Stamford Road, Oakleigh, Victoria 3166, Australia

First published 1993

Printed in Great Britain at the University Press, Cambridge

A catalogue record for this book is available from the British Library

Library of Congress cataloguing in publication data

Cross-cultural approaches to literacy / edited by Brian V. Street.
  p.   cm. – (Cambridge studies in oral and literate culture : 23)
  Includes index.
  ISBN 0–521–40167–4 ISBN 0–521–40964–0 pb
1. Literacy. 2. Intercultural education. I. Street, Brian V. II. Series.
LC149.C74   1993
302.2'244–dc20   92–4500   CIP

ISBN 0 521 40167 4 hardback
ISBN 0 521 40964 0 paperback

CONTENTS

FIGURES AND TABLES

Figures

ix

(All figures in chapter 10 from A. Shuman, *Storytelling rights*, Cambridge University Press, 1986)

Tables

CONTRIBUTORS

MIKE BAYNHAM, Faculty of Adult Education, University of Technology, Sydney

NIKO BESNIER, Department of Anthropology, Yale University

CAROLINE H. BLEDSOE, Department of Anthropology, Northwestern University

MAURICE BLOCH, Department of Anthropology, The London School of Economics and Political Science

MIRIAM CAMITTA, Graduate School of Education, University of Philadelphia

DON KULICK, Department of Linguistics, Research School of Pacific Studies, Australian National University

I. M. LEWIS, Department of Anthropology, The London School of Economics and Political Science

PETER PROBST, Berlin

STEPHEN REDER, Literacy, Language and Communication Program, Northwest Regional Educational Laboratory, Portland, Oregon

KENNETH M. ROBEY, Department of Anthropology, University of New Mexico

KATHLEEN ROCKHILL, Department of Adult Education, Ontario Institute for Studies in Education, Toronto

AMY SHUMAN, Department of English, Ohio State University, Columbus

BRIAN STREET, School of Social Sciences, University of Sussex

CHRISTOPHER STROUD, Centre for Research on Bilingualism, University of Stockholm

GAIL WEINSTEIN-SHR, School of Education, University of Massachusetts, Amherst

KAREN REED WIKELUND, Literacy, Language and Communication Program, Northwest Regional Educational Laboratory, Portland, Oregon

ACKNOWLEDGEMENTS

The author and the publishers gratefully acknowledge permission to publish revised versions of the following material:

D. Kulick and C. Stroud, 'Conceptions and uses of literacy in a Papua New Guinean village', from *Man*, n.s., 25 (1990), 286–303.

N. Besnier, 'Literacy and feelings: the encoding of affect in Nukulaelae letters', from *Text*, 9: 1 (1989), 69–92.

C. Bledsoe and K. Robey, 'Arabic literacy and enlightenment amongst the Mende of Sierra Leone', from *Man*, n.s., 21: 2, (1986), 202–206.

I. Lewis, 'Literacy and cultural identity in the Horn of Africa: the Somali case', from G. Baumann (ed.), *The written word*, Clarendon Press, 1986.

K. Rockhill, 'Gender, language and the politics of literacy', from *British Journal of the Sociology of Education*, 8: 2 (1987), 153–67.

S. Reder and K. Green (now publishing as Karen Reed Wikelund), 'Contrasting patterns of literacy in an Alaskan fishing village', from *International Journal of the Sociology of Language*, 42 (1983), 9–39.

P. Probst, 'The letter and the spirit: literacy and religious authority in the history of the Aladura movement in Western Nigeria', from *Africa* (1989), 471–95.

A. Shuman, 'Collaborative writing: appropriating power or reproducing authority?', from *Storytelling rights: the uses of oral and written texts by urban adolescents*, Cambridge University Press, 1986.

INTRODUCTION: THE NEW LITERACY STUDIES

BRIAN STREET

The field of literacy studies has expanded considerably in recent years and new, more anthropological and cross-cultural frameworks have been developed to replace those of a previous era, in which psychologistic and culturally narrow approaches predominated (as they arguably still do in much educational and development literature). Where, for instance, educationalists and psychologists have focused on discrete elements of reading and writing skills, anthropologists and sociolinguists concentrate on literacies – the social practices and conceptions of reading and writing. The rich cultural variation in these practices and conceptions leads us to rethink what we mean by them and to be wary of assuming a single literacy where we may simply be imposing assumptions derived from our own cultural practice onto other people's literacies. Research in cultures that have newly acquired reading and writing draws our attention to the creative and original ways in which people transform literacy to their own cultural concerns and interests. Research into the role of literacies in the construction of ethnicity, gender and religious identities makes us wary of accepting the uniform model of literacy that tends to be purveyed with the modern nation state: the relationship of literacy and nationalism is itself in need of research at a time when the dominant or standard model of literacy frequently subserves the interests of national politics. Research into 'vernacular' literacies within modern urban settings has begun to show the richness and diversity of literacy practices and meanings despite the pressures for uniformity exerted by the nation state and modern education systems. Whilst in the last decade a number of researchers have made these points separately, there is now a need to bring the arguments together in one place, and to make the rich array of supporting data accessible to a wider audience. This volume, then, presents a series of papers which illustrate what is now a developing and influential trend in anthropological and sociolinguistic approaches to the analysis of literacy – but one as yet represented in rather scattered publications and for this reason not always as well known as it deserves.

The authors all take an ethnographic perspective on literacy, that is they assume that an understanding of literacy requires detailed, in-depth accounts of actual practice in different cultural settings. It is not sufficient, however, to extol simply the richness and variety of literacy

1

practices made accessible through such ethnographic detail: we also need bold theoretical models that recognise the central role of power relations in literacy practices. I elaborate below on the ideological model of literacy that, I suggest, enables us to focus on the ways in which the apparent neutrality of literacy practices disguises their significance for the distribution of power in society and for authority relations: the acquisition, use and meanings of different literacies have an ideological character that has not been sufficiently recognised until recently. Most of the contributions to this volume, though to varying degrees, show a broad commitment to the new theoretical approaches to literacy generated by the ideological model. They all, distinctively, illustrate the theoretical implications of these recent shifts in perspective through one or more specific case studies. They argue that the key questions that have concerned literacy scholars – the uses, consequences and meanings of literacy; the differences and similarities between written and spoken registers and inter-register variation within spoken and written modes; and the problem of what is culture specific and what universal in literacy practices – must be answered with reference to close descriptions of the actual uses and conceptions of literacy in specific cultural contexts. The experimental methods or the broad conjectures of previous scholars in this field have not provided satisfactory answers to these questions.

Besnier, for instance, criticising traditional approaches, finds it 'surprising' that 'little research has focused on the run-of-the-mill written registers' (such as personal letters) and argues that as a result the kinds of research question in which he is interested cannot be answered. Wishing to explore the relationship between writing and affect, he finds that previous research in this area has focused mainly on western literary genres, such as the essay. Shuman similarly argues that not all writing belongs to the genre of the essay – that deemed most consequential according to the autonomous model – and that not only literacy – the channel of communication in Hymes' sense – but also genre can be an important way of distributing knowledge and attitudes towards texts in a community. For Besnier, the lack of attention to the 'day-to-day written output of members of the speech communities' and to their local genres, means that 'we do not have a basis on which to compare the role of affect in spoken and written communication'. Not only have variationists and discourse analysts focused almost exclusively on western literacy situations, but they have also used highly biased data bases on literacy processes and products in western settings, namely the literate activities and output of the intellectual elite. Typically discourse produced by academics is what they have studied and compared across registers and modes (Besnier 1988). Both Shuman and Camitta in this volume demonstrate the variation of genres and literacies within a western context and provide the beginnings of a new and less restricted data basis for cross-cultural comparison of the kind Besnier is seeking.

Similarly, Kulick and Stroud, interested in the consequences of literacy acquisition in previously non-literate cultures, find that previous research has failed to take account of how the people themselves 'actually think about literacy and how they apply their literacy skills in their day-to-day lives'. 'Lack of this fundamental knowledge' has led those interested in the transition to literacy to 'downplay the creativity and cultural concerns of the people being taught to read and write'. As a result the emphasis has been on the 'impact' of literacy on supposedly passive recipients and on the apparently neutral and universal character of the providers' models of literacy. Trapped within approaches such as this, it is difficult to learn anything new or to see anything different in the world of literacy since we see only our own reflections when we look at others, our own literacy when we look at the literacies of other people.

As a result of these limitations in traditional approaches to literacy, 'ethnographic' perspectives have become popular in a number of disciplines in recent years: amongst for instance progressive educators in the United States, within the sociology of education in the United Kingdom and in some branches of sociolinguistics. The papers collected here mainly derive their conception of ethnography from the discipline of social anthropology, although a number of the pieces also owe much to recent developments of discourse analysis in sociolinguistics and many are conscious of the challenging educational implications of these approaches. In an earlier paper I suggested that it is at the interface between sociolinguistic and anthropological theories, on the one hand, and between discourse and ethnographic method on the other, that I envisaged future research in the field of literacy studies being conducted (Street 1988). These papers share that distinctive theoretical and methodological focus. The collection aims to represent a state-of-the-art sample of the most promising current research in these areas. The object, then, is not simply to provide a student reader but – more ambitiously – a programmatic document of the new literacy studies. Having criticised the generalisations of previous eras (Goody, Ong, Olson and others), it is now timely to try to develop some new generalisations about literacy, with the benefit of these new approaches.

The papers have been selected to provide a balance of Third World and 'Western' ethnography; of material focused upon urban and upon rural areas; of previously unpublished work by young scholars deserving of a wider audience; and of articles by established scholars that have been published in journals not always accessible to non-specialist readers. This introduction attempts to put their broad aims and aspirations into perspective, by outlining the state of literacy studies at the end of the 1980s and charting the shifts in theory and method that lie behind the research presented here.

The new literacy studies

During the early 1980s there appeared a number of collections of academic papers that claimed to represent the relationship between literacy and orality as a 'continuum' rather than, as in much of the previous literature, as a 'divide' (see Coulmans and Ehlich 1983; Frawley 1982; Nystrand 1982; Tannen 1982; Wagner 1983; Whiteman 1981; Olson et al 1985). It appeared that the differences between literate and oral channels of communication had been overstated in the past and that scholars were now more concerned with overlap, mix and diverse functions in social context. A number of books appeared whose titles deliberately signalled this perspective: *The social construction of literacy* edited by J. Cook-Gumperz; *Literacy in social context* by K. Levine; *Literacy and society* edited by K. Schousboe and M. T. Larsen; *The logic of writing and the organisation of society* by J. Goody. I have argued that the supposed shift from 'divide' to 'continuum' was more rhetorical than real: that, in fact, many of the writers in this field continued to represent literacy as sufficiently different from orality in its social and cognitive consequences, that their findings scarcely differ from the classic concept of the 'great divide' evident in Goody's earlier work (1977). This was to be explained by reference to the methodological and theoretical assumptions that underlay their work: in particular a narrow definition of social context; the reification of literacy in itself at the expense of recognition of its location in structures of power and ideology, related to assumptions about the 'neutrality' of the object of study; and, from the point of view of linguistics, the restriction of 'meaning' to the level of syntax. Besnier further points out that the concept of a 'continuum' is inadequate because spoken and written activities and products do not in fact line up along a continuum but differ from one another in a complex, multidimensional way both within speech communities and across them. The criticism of 'continuum' approaches is, therefore, even more fundamental than saying their proponents do not practice what they preach (Besnier 1988).

An alternative approach, which would avoid some of the problems generated by these assumptions begins with the distinction between 'autonomous' and 'ideological' models of literacy that I proposed some years ago (Street 1985) and that I would now like to clarify and extend in the light of subsequent comments and criticisms.

The 'autonomous' model of literacy

The exponents of an 'autonomous' model of literacy conceptualise literacy in technical terms, treating it as independent of social context, an autonomous variable whose consequences for society and cognition can be derived from its intrinsic character. The writers I characterise in this way do not necessarily themselves use the phrase 'autonomous model of literacy' but I nevertheless found the term model useful to describe their perspective as it draws attention to the underlying coherence and relationship of ideas which on the surface might appear unconnected and haphazard. No one practitioner necessarily adopts all of the characteristics of the model, but the use of the concept helps us to see what is entailed by adopting particular positions, to fill in gaps left by untheorised statements about literacy and to adopt a broader perspective than is apparent in any one writer. The term autonomous itself appears in many of the authors I cite, and is closely linked in their minds with writing. Goody and Watt, for instance, in their seminal article to which much subsequent literature refers, maintain that writing is distinctive because it is, at least potentially, 'an autonomous mode of communication' (in Goody 1968: 40). Walter Ong, probably the most influential writer on literacy in the United States, develops this idea more fully: 'By isolating thought on a written surface, detached from any interlocutor, making utterance in this sense autonomous and indifferent to attack, writing presents utterance and thought as uninvolved in all else, somehow self-contained, complete' (1982: 132). David Olson has perhaps been the most explicit exponent of the 'autonomous' model, arguing that 'there is a transition from utterance to text both culturally and developmentally and that this transition can be described as one of increasing explicitness with language increasingly able to stand as an unambiguous and autonomous representation of meaning' (1977: 258). Where Goody has recently denied that his argument involves technological determinism or 'autonomy' (see Goody 1986 and 1987, especially the preface), Olson holds enthusiastically to the strong version of the autonomous model, repeating in a recent article the claim that 'the media of communication, including writing, do not simply extend the existing structures of knowledge; they alter it' (Olson 1988: 28). For him it is writing itself that has these major consequences: 'writing did not simply extend the structure and uses of oral language and oral memory but altered the content and form in important ways'. He represents the consequences of literacy not only in terms of social development and progress but also in terms of individual cognitive processes: 'when writing began to serve the memory function, the mind could be redeployed to carry out more analytic activities such as examining contradictions and deriving logical implications. It is the availability of an explicit written record and its use for representing thought that impart to literacy its distinctive properties' (Olson 1988: 28). Hill and Parry (forthcoming) note further extensions of this claim that literacy has distinctive, 'autonomous' properties:

> That text is autonomous is the basic premise of this model of literacy, but we have found the word 'autonomous' used in other ways as well. Goody (1986), for example, applies it to both institutions and individuals. As an anthropologist, he is particularly interested in institutions and so it is to institutional autonomy that he generally refers. In writing about religion he claims: 'Literate religions have some kind of autonomous boundary. Practitioners are committed to one alone and may be defined by their attachment to a Holy Book, their recognition of a Credo, as well as by their practice of certain rituals, prayers, modes of propitiation ... Contrast the situation in societies without writing. You cannot practise Asante religion unless you are an Asante: and what is Asante religion now may be very different from Asante religion one hundred years ago'.
>
> (Goody 1986: 4–5; quoted in Hill and Parry, forthcoming)

Probst's analysis of the Aladura movement in western Nigeria in this volume suggests, contra Goody, that literacy is not necessarily an autonomous factor in differences between local and central religions and that the distinction between oral and literate is overstated here as in other domains. For Probst as for other contributors, the concept of an autonomous literacy is unhelpful with regard to both the social nature of literacy itself and to its relationship with other institutions. Goody, however, has recently extended the argument about the autonomy of literate religions to other kinds of organisation, to law, and bureaucracy: 'writing has tended to promote the autonomy of organisations that developed their own modes of procedure, their own corpus of written tradition, their own specialists and possibly their own system of support' (1986: 90). Again many of the authors included here address these claims and find them wanting with respect to the specific ethnographic contexts that they know in detail (Lewis, Bledsoe and Robey).

Hill and Parry also note Goody's extension of the concept of autonomy to the literate individual and cite his recent comments on the relationship between literacy and development: 'If we take recent moves to expand the economies of countries of the Third World, a certain rate of literacy is often seen as necessary to radical change, partly from the limited standpoint of being able to read the instructions on the seed packet, partly because of the increased autonomy (even with regard to the seed packet) of the autodidact' (Goody 1986: 46). This idea frequently lies behind characterisations of literate individuals as more 'modern', 'cosmopolitan', 'innovative' and 'empathetic' than non-literates (Oxenham 1980: 15; Clammer 1976: 94; Lerner 1958). Lerner, for instance, interviewed some 300 individuals in middle eastern countries and found that 'those who rated high in empathy were also more likely to be literate, urban, mass media users and generally non-traditional in their orientations' (in Rogers 1969: 45). Literacy, then, has come to be associated with crude and often ethnocentric stereotypes of 'other cultures' and represents a way of perpetuating the notion of a 'great divide' between 'modern' and 'traditional' societies that is less acceptable when expressed in other terms. The recognition of these problems was a major impulse behind the development of an alternative model of literacy that could provide a more theoretically sound and ethnographic understanding of the actual significance of literacy practices in people's lives.

The 'ideological' model of literacy

Researchers dissatisfied with the autonomous model of literacy and with the assumptions outlined above, have come to view literacy practices as inextricably linked to cultural and power structures in society, and to recognise the variety of cultural practices associated with reading and writing in different contexts. Avoiding the reification of the autonomous model, they study these social practices rather than literacy-in-itself for their relationship to other aspects of social life. A number of researchers in the new literacy studies have also paid greater attention to the role of literacy practices in reproducing or challenging structures of power and domination. Their recognition of the ideological character of the processes of acquisition and of the meanings and uses of different literacies led me to characterise this approach as an 'ideological' model (Street 1985).

I use the term 'ideological' to describe this approach, rather than less contentious or loaded terms such as 'cultural', 'sociological' or 'pragmatic' (see Hill and Parry 1988) because it signals quite explicitly that literacy practices are aspects not only of 'culture' but also of power structures. The very emphasis on the 'neutrality' and 'autonomy' of literacy by writers such as Goody, Olson and Ong is itself 'ideological' in the sense of disguising this power dimension. Any ethnographic account of literacy will, by implication, attest its significance for power, authority and social differentiation in terms of the author's own interpretation of these concepts. Since all approaches to literacy in practice will involve some such bias, it is better scholarship to admit to and expose the particular 'ideological' framework being employed from the very beginning: it can then be opened to scrutiny, challenged and refined in ways which are more difficult when the ideology remains hidden. This is to use the term 'ideological' not in its old-fashioned Marxist (and current anti-Marxist) sense of 'false consciousness' and simple-minded dogma, but rather in the sense employed within contemporary anthropology, socio-linguistics and cultural studies, where ideology is the site of tension between authority and power on the one hand and resistance and creativity on the other (Bourdieu 1976; Mace 1979; Centre for Contemporary Cultural Studies 1977; Asad 1980; Strathern 1985; Grillo 1989; Fairclough 1989; Thompson 1984). This tension operates through the medium of a variety of cultural practices, including particularly language and, of course, literacy. It is in this sense that it is important to approach the study of literacy in terms of an explicit 'ideological' model.

Individual writers do not always employ the term to describe their own work, nor do they necessarily subscribe to all of the positions with which I associate the ideological model: but the use of the term model is a useful heuristic for drawing attention to a cluster of concepts and assumptions that have underlying coherence where on the surface they may appear disconnected. It helps us to see what is involved in adopting particular positions, to fill in gaps left by untheorised statements about literacy and to adopt a broader perspective than is apparent in any one writer. Lewis, for instance, writing about the meanings and uses of literacy in Somalia and Ethiopia, does not employ the concept of an ideological model of literacy, but his work does fit with this new direction in literacy studies in a number of ways: he rejects the 'great divide' between literacy and orality intrinsic to the autonomous model of literacy; he demonstrates the role of mixed literate and oral modes of communication in local politics, in the assertion of identity and in factional struggles; and he relates the particularities of local literacies to wider issues of nationalism and religion in the Horn of Africa. Similarly, Rockhill's account of the politics of literacy among Hispanic women in Los Angeles, with its focus on literacy as power, is implicitly located within the ideological model of literacy. She sees her research as demonstrating the multiple and contradictory ways in which ideology works. Women adopt new literacy genres that they hope will open up new worlds and identities and overcome their oppressive situations but these genres also reproduce dominant gender stereotypes – for instance, of the magazine or TV secretary/receptionist. Their faith in the symbolic power of literacy and education represents a threat to their male partners and to traditional domestic authority relations: but it also represents a threat to the women themselves as they abandon local relations and networks to enter the alienating world of middle class America. These complex examples, Rockhill argues, demonstrate that 'the construction of literacy is embedded in the discursive practices and power relations of everyday life – it is socially constructed, materially produced, morally regulated and carries a symbolic significance which cannot be captured by its reduction to any one of these'.

Reading through dense and theoretically sophisticated ethnographies of literacy such as this, it becomes apparent that literacy can no longer be addressed as a neutral technology as in the reductionist 'autonomous' model, but is already a social and ideological practice involving fundamental aspects of epistemology, power and politics: the acquisition of literacy involves challenges to dominant discourses (Lewis), shifts in what constitutes the agenda of proper literacy (Weinstein-Shr; Carmetti; Shuman) and struggles for power and position (Rockhill, Probst). In this sense, then, literacy practices are saturated with ideology.

Some critics have taken the distinction between ideological and autonomous models to involve an unnecessary polarisation and would prefer a synthesis. However, I take the 'ideological' model to provide such a synthesis, since it avoids the polarisation introduced by any attempt to separate out the 'technical' features of literacy, as though the 'cultural bits' could be added on later. It is those who have employed an 'autonomous' model, and who have generally dominated the field of literacy studies until recently, who were responsible for setting up a false polarity between the 'technical' and 'cultural' aspects of literacy. The ideological model, on the other hand, does not attempt to deny technical skill or the cognitive aspects of reading and writing, but rather understands them as they are encapsulated within cultural wholes and within structures of power. In that sense the 'ideological' model subsumes rather than excludes the work undertaken within the 'autonomous' model.

Other critics have objected that my resistance to the assumption of a 'great divide' between literacy and orality has led me to underplay the real differences between these media. Miyoshi, for instance, claims that 'by denying or underplaying the distinction between orality and literacy, Street collapses the social variables into a single model or oral and literate mix, thereby licensing clearly against his intent the universalist reading of cultures and societies' (Miyoshi 1988: 17). Commenting on this discussion in a recent edition of *Literacy and Society* Mogens Trolle Larsen asserts: 'The proper balance in our evaluation of such high-level questions must be based on a series of informed analyses which scrutinise the empirical evidence in the light of the theoretical discussion' (Larsen 1989: 10). The present volume represents, I believe, a distinctive contribution to such empirical scrutiny, based in the kind of theoretical development outlined above. However, the papers in this volume should make it clear that challenging the great divide in favour of an oral/literate 'mix' does not necessarily entail naive universalism: what I had in mind, and what I believe many of these accounts demonstrate, is that the relation of oral and literate practices differs from one context to another. In that sense the unit of study is best not taken as either literacy or orality in isolation, since the values associated with either in our own culture tend to determine the boundaries between them.

Weinstein-Shr's comparison of the different literacies, or rather the different oral/literate mixes, of two Hmong refugees in Philadelphia brings out both the theoretical and methodological points involved here. She is concerned to demonstrate, like Kulick and Stroud, that newcomers to school literacy are not necessarily passive 'victims' but take an active role in employing it as a 'resource'. The question that this forces us to ask is what precisely is the 'resource' under consideration? It turns out not simply to be school literacy itself, but nor is it simply traditional 'oral' skills. For one Hmong refugee in Philadelphia that resource begins from the uses and meanings of literacy constructed in an educational context (what we have referred to elsewhere as 'pedagogised' literacy, Street and Street 1991), whilst for another it derives from cultural assumptions about the representation – in the form of scrap books, pictures and text – of history and the role of great men. In the one case the oral/literate 'resource' that a young man has acquired in school enables him to act as a broker between the host society and some of the Hmong around him; in the other the resource is derived from traditional cultural norms regarding authority and history, adapted through forms of literacy that are often at variance with that purveyed through formal classes. In this context it makes little sense to talk of 'literacy', when what is involved are different literacies: and equally it makes little sense to compare the two subjects by distinguishing between their oral and literate practices when what is involved are different mixes of orality and literacy. The concept of oral/literate practices provides us with a unit of study that enables more precise cross-cultural comparison than when we attempt to compare literacy or orality in isolation. This is not quite the 'universalism' that Miyoshi fears, although in the long run all of the authors here are interested in more than just local description and I would hope that we can begin to make some useful generalisations, of the kind Weinstein-Shr proposes in her conclusion, as data of this quality begin to amass.

Research implications of the two models of literacy

The development of an alternative approach to literacy study during the 1980s, then, involving a move towards an ideological model, rejection of the great divide and attention to an oral/literate mix, has I believe, opened up the possibility of different kinds of account than those which previously dominated the field. From the point of view of research, the autonomous model of literacy had generated two main strands of inquiry, one concerned with questions about the consequences of reading and writing for individual and cognitive processes, the other considering the functional operation of literacy within specific modern institutions. Both approaches failed to pay sufficient attention to the social and ideological character of literacy. Educationalists, linguists and psychologists conceptualised literacy as a universal constant whose acquisition, once individual problems can be overcome by proper diagnosis and pedagogy, will lead to higher cognitive skills, to improved logical thinking, to critical inquiry and to self-conscious reflection. The distinction of myth from history, of science from illusion, of democracy from autocracy, of elaborated from restricted code have all variously been attributed to such literacy as though it were a single, autonomous thing that had these consequences irrespective of context. Whilst anthropologists and folklorists (Finnegan 1989; Opland 1983; Parry 1989; Street 1987) have demonstrated that members of 'oral' cultures – however defined – share all of the cognitive qualities attributed to literacy within the 'autonomous' model, their attention to these questions in itself has meant that the study of literacy has remained embedded within the narrow confines of the debate about rationality, cognition and relativism. Relativist anthropologists have argued that absence of literacy, whether for individuals or for societies, did not necessarily mean lack of critical thinking and so on, rehearsing the arguments of Levy-Bruhl and Evans-Pritchard, McIntyre and Winch and, more recently, Lukes and Hollis, about open and closed societies and minds, primitive and modern thought, bricoleurs and engineers (Bloch 1989; Street 1985). In doing so they accepted the terms of reference of the debate and focused the study of literacy narrowly, so that the potential for richer and broader analysis of the subject was understated.

Where the social context of literacy has been addressed, the premises of the 'autonomous' model have directed attention away from its significance for power relations in specific social conditions. With regard to bureaucracy and the social organisation of the modern state, for instance, literacy has been seen as a 'neutral' mechanism for achieving functional ends, a *sine qua non* of the state whatever its ideological character, a technology to be acquired by sufficient proportions of the population to ensure the mechanical functioning of its institutions (Gellner 1983; Goody 1986). Again the ideological character of the processes of acquisition and of the meanings and uses of literacy in specific cultural contexts have been understated: the 'naturalisation' of ideologies, as though they were universal necessities rather than institutions for reproduction of the cultural and power bases of particular interests and groups, has been reinforced by the academic community as much as by those whose interests it serves.

In contrast, then, to the study of literacy as either an individual cognitive tool or as a neutral function of institutions, the conceptualisation of literacy as ideological practice opens up a potentially rich field of inquiry into the nature of culture and power, and the relationship of institutions and ideologies of communication in the contemporary world. For the discipline of anthropology, currently disillusioned with the frameworks and questions of the post-war era and looking to make some contribution to the analysis of ideology and power in contemporary societies, there is much of interest here. For those working within sociolinguistics and concerned to address language in social context, in contrast with the reified and a-social models employed by formal linguists, the study of literacy practices in ethnographic context also opens up new research possibilities. It is no surprise, then, that the vast increase in collections of articles and books on literacy to which I referred at the outset have tended to come from these fields. I would now like to consider recent developments in linguistic and anthropological theory and methodology as providing the context from which both the ideological model of literacy and the papers in the present volume have emerged.

Linguistics and anthropology: discourse and ethnography

Within linguistics there has recently been a shift towards 'discourse' analysis, which takes as the object of study larger units of language than the word or sentence (see Coulthard 1977; Stubbs 1985; Benson and Greaves 1985; van Djik 1990). I would like to suggest that this trend towards 'discourse' analysis in linguistics could fruitfully link with recent developments of the 'ethnographic' approach within anthropology, that take fuller account of theories of power and ideology. With respect to research in orality and literacy, this merging of disciplines and methodologies, within an 'ideological' as opposed to an 'autonomous' model of literacy, provides a means to replace the concept of the 'great divide' with richer, and less ethnocentric concepts. Some of the key terms in the new literacy studies derive from these approaches: the concepts of 'literacy events' (Heath 1983), 'literacy practices' (Street 1984), and 'communicative practices' (Grillo 1989). I begin with a brief account of these terms before elaborating on the notion of 'discourse' and of 'context' within which they are situated.

Heath defines a 'literacy event' as 'any occasion in which a piece of writing is integral to the nature of participants' interactions and their interpretive processes' (Heath 1982). I employ 'literacy practices' as a broader concept, pitched at a higher level of abstraction and referring to both behaviour and conceptualisations related to the use of reading and/or writing. 'Literacy practices' incorporate not only 'literacy events', as empirical occasions to which literacy is integral, but also 'folk models' of those events and the ideological preconceptions that underpin them (Street 1987). Grillo has extended this notion still further to the notion of 'communicative practices' in general, which obviously owes much to Hymes' work on the 'ethnography of communication' (Hymes 1974 and passim). Grillo construes the concept of 'communicative practices' as including 'the social activities through which language or communication is produced', 'the way in which these activities are embedded in institutions, settings or domains which in turn are implicated in other, wider, social, economic, political and cultural processes' and 'the ideologies, which may be linguistic or other, which guide processes of communicative production' (Grillo 1989: 15). For Grillo, then, 'literacy is seen as one type of communicative practice', within this larger social context, moving the emphasis away from attempts to attribute grand consequences to a particular medium or channel.

'Context' in linguistics and anthropology

Central to development of this conceptual apparatus for the study of literacy is a re-evaluation of the importance of 'context' in linguistic analysis. Sociolinguists, with some justification, have been reluctant to allow the floodwaters of 'social context' to breach defences provided by the rigour and logic of their enterprise. They sense that such 'context' is so unbounded and loose that it would swamp their own very precise and bounded studies. Within linguistics and its sub-disciplines, therefore, 'context' has tended to be excluded altogether from consideration. Grillo, Pratt and Street point out, in an article on 'Anthropology and linguistics' that 'although it is often stressed that language is, amongst other things, a social fact, the importance of this dimension is diminished by the way the levels of "semantics" have been constructed, in particular the claim (made by Lyons, amongst others, 1981: 28) that word and sentence meaning are "to a high degree context independent"' (cited in Grillo, Pratt and Street 1987: 11). Even when they have paid attention to 'social context', it has been in terms of a narrow definition. In sociolinguistics, for instance,

> the term 'social' tends to be reserved for personal interaction, whereas most anthropologists would want to emphasise that even the native speaker intuiting is a social being ... (Furthermore) when in the analysis of utterance meaning, attention is turned to the social context, the main focus of enquiry has been pragmatics, doing things with words. This is undoubtedly an important area of enquiry, and at least one anthropologist (Bloch) has recently made extensive use of the concept of illocutionary force. However, this should not diminish the attention paid to social

context in the analysis of the use of language to make propositions about the world, since this is also fundamentally a social process.

(Grillo, Pratt and Street 1987: 11)

When they do turn to sociology, for instance in the analysis of 'context', sociolinguists have tended to borrow mainly from 'network' theory, or from Goffman-inspired 'interactionism', which refers only to those aspects of 'context' that are directly observable and to such immediate links between individuals as their 'roles', obligations, 'face-to-face encounters' and so on. In his recent book on pragmatics, for instance, Levinson explicitly and self-consciously excludes wider interpretations of 'context' and admits: 'a relatively narrow range of contextual factors and their linguistic correlates are considered here: context in this book includes only some of the basic parameters of the context of utterance, including participants' identity, role and location, assumptions about what participants know or take for granted, the place of an utterance within a sequence of turns at talking and so on' (1983: x). He does acknowledge the existence of wider interpretations of 'context': 'We know, in fact, that there are a number of additional contextual parameters that are systematically related to linguistic organisation, particularly principles of social interaction of various sorts of both a culture-specific kind (see, for example, Keenan 1976) and universal kind (see, for example, Brown and Levinson 1978).' But he excludes them because his aim is to faithfully represent the philosophico-linguistic tradition in the United States and Britain, rather than, for instance that on the continent, where the tradition he notes is 'altogether broader' (p. ix). (See also Dillon 1985 and Bailey 1985 for explorations of recent developments in post-Firthian linguistics, particularly with regard to discourse analysis and pragmatics.)

I would like to argue that the analysis of the relationship between orality and literacy requires attention to the 'wider parameters' of 'context' largely underemphasised in Anglo-American linguistics. Within social anthropology, for instance, these would be taken to include the study of kinship organisation, conceptual systems, political structures, economic processes and so on, rather than simply of 'network' or 'interaction'. There is little point, according to this perspective, in attempting to make sense of a given utterance or discourse in terms only of its immediate 'context of utterance', unless one knows the broader social and conceptual framework that gives it meaning. This involves not just 'commonsense', but the development of theories and methods as rigorous as those employed in other domains. It is these theories and methods that provide some guarantee that attention to social context need not swamp or drown the precise aspects of language use selected for study within linguistics and its sub disciplines.

It is to the broader meaning of the term 'context', for instance, that Bledsoe and Robey refer when they argue in this volume for understanding literacy in its 'cultural context'. In Sierra Leone writing is absorbed by Mende secret societies into a tradition of secrecy and exclusion, where hierarchies of access to knowledge maintain successive degrees of power and control over others. We cannot really claim to make sense of script produced within this framework if we attend only to the meaning of the 'words on the page' and to the lexical devices for encoding meaning. These represent only one aspect, they argue, of the potential of writing: writing is used also as a means of establishing secrecy and maintaining control of, or as they put it 'managing', knowledge. This is to be understood not simply in terms of the immediate context of utterance or production but of broader features of social and cultural life, such as the secret societies and their institutional control and definition of hierarchies of power.

'Discourse' in linguistics and anthropology

In recent years the methods and theories employed by anthropologists to study social life in cross-cultural perspective have been subject to rigorous criticism. In contrast with the static, functionalist approach implied in, for instance, Malinowski's 'context of situation', recent approaches within the discipline have emphasised the dynamic nature of social processes and the broader structure of power relations. This has frequently taken the form of exploration of the concept of ideology and of 'discourse' (see Asad 1980; Parkin 1985; Grillo et al. 1987; Grillo 1989; Bloch 1975; Agar 1986; Agar and Hobbs 1983; Strathern 1985; Fardon 1990). In this sense 'discourse' refers to the complex of conceptions, classifications and language use that characterise a specific sub-set of an ideological formation. For Sherzer discourse refers to 'the nexus, the actual and concrete expression of the language- culture- society relationship. It is discourse which creates, recreates, modifies and fine-tunes both culture and language and their intersection' (Sherzer 1987: 296; quoted in Grillo 1989: 18). Grillo, as an anthropologist, wishes to stress that analysis 'must always be concerned with the practice of discourse – *inter alia* the social activity through which discourse is produced and in which it is located'. Asad employs the term as a means of challenging traditional static accounts of culture by his anthropological colleagues. He criticises accounts that assumed 'an integrated set of cultural meanings', a 'total culture', notions owing something to formal linguistic models. For him the crucial question is how a given discourse comes to define what is correct and what 'meaningless'. The definition of what is on the agenda, of which discourse is appropriate, is constructed, he asserts, out of specific political conditions 'which make certain rhetorical forms objectively possible and authoritative' (Asad 1979). Social change involves challenging a given form of (dominant) discourse and the production and assertion of other discourses within new material conditions. He would like to use the concept of discourse, then, not at the level of abstract philosophical enquiry but in terms of the real social relations between historical forces and relations on the one hand and forms of discourse sustained or undermined by them on the other. Parkin sees the anthropologist's contribution as providing 'detailed micro-historical cases of ideological discourse in action' (Parkin 1984: 28). His account at times almost merges with those of some sociolinguists: anthropologists, he claims, are showing 'increasing interest in figurative speech': they 'now examine forms of rhetoric, tropes and oratory for evidence of internal cultural debate'. Anthropological usage, however, remains rather broader than within linguistics, where 'discourse' frequently indicates simply chunks of language larger than the sentence. The boundaries between the senses of the term in the different disciplines remain unclear and can frequently overlap. Far from being a source of confusion, however, this ambiguity may be turned to constructive use, providing a means to pursue issues that are perhaps harder to grasp within the language and definitions of either discipline separately.

Travelling from a different direction from the anthropologists, sociolinguists such as Brown and Yule have recently arrived at a similar point: they are concerned to 'link thickly described discourse to larger patterns of action and interaction' (quoted in Dillon 1985), to provide a method which can be more sensitive to language in use than traditional ethnography has been. Where the new anthropological interest in language as discourse needs to take some account of the detailed micro-linguistic studies available in sociolinguistics, Brown and Yule recognise the need for their sociolinguist colleagues to develop a linguistic theory that conceives of language as essentially a social process, and which takes full account of more sophisticated theories of discourse relations than simple interactionalism, network analysis or 'commonsense'. The methods employed by anthropologists do not on their own guarantee theoretical sophistication: it is possible, for instance, for 'ethnographic' accounts of literacy to be conducted within the 'autonomous' model, with all the problems and flaws that entails. However, when ethnographic method is allied to contemporary anthropological theory, emphasising ideological and power processes and dynamic rather than static models, then it can be more sensitive to social context than either linguistics in general or discourse analysis in particular have tended to be. It is at the interface between these linguistic and anthropological theories on the one hand, and between discourse and ethnographic method on the other, that the papers in this volume may be located.

The contributions

The papers fall into three sections: 'The incorporation of literacy into the communicative repertoire'; 'Local literacies and national politics; ethnicity, gender and religion'; and 'Literacy variation in urban settings'. I explain the classification and describe the contributions in a short introduction at the beginning of each section.

References

Agar, M. 1986. *Independents declared.* Washington: Smithsonian Institution Press.
Agar, M. and Hobbs, J. 1983. 'Natural plans: using AI planning in the analysis of ethnographic interviews', *Ethos*, 11: 33–48.
Apple, M. (ed.), 1982. *Cultural and economic reproduction in education.* London: Routledge and Kegan Paul.
Asad, T. 1980. 'Anthropology and the analysis of ideology', *Man*, n.s., 14 (4): 604–27.
Bailey, R. W. 1985. 'Negotiation and meaning: revisiting the "Context of Situation"', in J. D. Benson and W. S. Greaves (eds.), 1985.
Barber, K. and de Moraes Farias, P. F. (eds.), 1989. *Discourse and its disguises: the interpretation of African oral texts.* Birmingham: Centre of West African Studies.
Barton, D. and Ivanic, R. (eds.), 1991. *Writing in the community.* London: Sage.
Baumann, G. (ed.), 1986. *The written word.* Oxford: Clarendon Press.
Benson, J. D. and Greaves, W. S. (eds.), 1985. *Systemic perspectives on discourse.* Norwood, NJ: Ablex.
Besnier, N. 1988. 'The linguistic relationship of spoken and written Nukulaelae registers', *Language*, 64: 707–36.
Bhola, H. S. 1984a. *Campaigning for literacy.* Paris: Unesco.
  1984b. Letter to *Unesco Adult Information Notes*, no. 3. Paris: Unesco.
Blank, M. 1982. 'Language and school failure: some speculations on the relationship between oral and written language', in L. Feagans and D. Farran (eds.), *The language of children reared in poverty*, pp. 75–93. New York: Academic Press.
Bledsoe, C. and Robey, K. 1986. 'Arabic literacy and secrecy among the Mende of Sierra Leone', *Man*, n.s., 21 (2): 202–26.
Bloch, M. (ed.), 1975. *Political language and oratory.* New York: Academic Press.
  1989. 'Literacy and enlightenment', in K. Scousboe and M. T. Larsen (eds.).
Bloome, D. (ed.), 1989. *Classrooms and literacy.* Norwood, NJ: Ablex.
Bourdieu, P. 1976. 'Systems of education and systems of thought', in J. Dale, G. Esland and M. MacDonald (eds.), *Schooling and capitalism.* London: Open University/Routledge and Kegan Paul.

Bourdieu, P. & Passeron, J.-C. 1977. *Reproduction in education, society and culture*. London: Sage.

Brown, P. and Levinson, S. 1978. 'Universals in language usage: politeness phenomena', in E. Goody (ed.), *Questions and politeness: strategies in social interaction*. Cambridge: Cambridge University Press.

Butler, C. 1985. *Systemic linguistics: theory and applications*. London: Batsford.

Centre for Contemporary Cultural Studies. 1977. *On ideology*. London: Methuen.

Clammer, J. 1976. *Literacy and social change: a case study of Fiji*. Leiden: Brill.
  1980. 'Towards an ethnography of literacy: the effect of mass literacy on language use and social organisation', *Language Forum*, 4 (3): 24–52.

Cook-Gumperz, J. (ed.), 1986. *The social construction of literacy*. Cambridge: Cambridge University Press.

Coulmas, F. and Ehlich, K. (eds.), 1983. *Writing in focus*. New York: Mouton.

Coulthard, M. 1977. *An introduction to discourse analysis*. London: Longman.

Craig, R. and Tracy, K. 1983. *Conversational coherence: form, structure and strategy*. London: Sage.

Dillon, G., Coleman, L., Fahnestock, J. and Agar, M. 1985. Review article of discourse analysis and pragmatics in *Language*, 61 (2): 451–8.

Fairclough, N. 1989. *Language and power*. London: Longman.

Fardon, R. (ed.), 1990. *Localising strategies: regional traditions in ethnographic writing*. Edinburgh: Scottish University Press and Washington: Smithsonian Institution Press.

Feagans, L. and Farran, D. (eds.), 1982. *The language of children reared in poverty*. New York: Academic Press.

Fingeret, A. 1983. 'Social network: a new perspective on independence and illiterate adults', *Adult Education Quarterly*, 33 (3): 133–4.

Finnegan, R. 1973. 'Literacy versus non-literacy: the Great Divide', in R. Finnegan and R. Horton (eds.), *Modes of thought*, pp. 112–44. London: Faber.
  1969. 'Attitudes to speech and language among the Limba of Sierra Leone', *Odu*, n.s., 2: 61–76.
  1988. *Literacy and orality*. Oxford: Blackwells.

Frawley, W. (ed.), 1982. *Linguistics and literacy*. Proceedings of the Delaware Symposium on Language Studies. New York: Plenum.

Gellner, E. 1983. *Nations and nationalism*. Oxford: Blackwell.

Goelman, H., Oberg, A. and Smith, F. (eds.), 1983. *Awakening to literacy*. Cambridge: Cambridge University Press.

Goody, J. (ed.), 1968. *Literacy in traditional societies*. Cambridge: Cambridge University Press.
  1977. *The domestication of the savage mind*. Cambridge: Cambridge University Press.
  1986. *The logic of writing and the organisation of society*. Cambridge: Cambridge University Press.
  1987. *The interface between the written and the oral*. Cambridge: Cambridge University Press.

Grillo, R. 1989. 'Anthropology, language, politics', introduction to *Social anthropology and the politics of language*. Cambridge: Cambridge University Press.
  1989. *Dominant languages*. Cambridge: Cambridge University Press.

Grillo, R., Pratt, G. and Street, B. 1987. 'Linguistics and anthropology', in J. Lyons et al. (eds.), 1987.

Hak, T., Haafkens, J. and Nithof, G. 1985. Working Papers on Discourse and Conversational Analysis, *Konteksten*, 6. Rotterdam.

Hall, S., Hodson, D., Lowe, A. and Willis, P. (eds.), 1980. *Culture, media, language*. London: Hutchinson.

Hamilton, M. and Barton, D. 1985. 'Social and cognitive factors in the development of writing', in A. Lock and C. Peters (eds.), *The handbook of human symbolic evolution*. Oxford: Oxford University Press.

Heath, S. B. 1982a. 'What no bedtime story means: narrative skills at home and at school', *Language in Society*, 11 (2): 49–76.

1982b. 'Protean shapes in literacy events', in D. Tannen (ed.), (1982).

1983a. *Ways with words*. Cambridge: Cambridge University Press.

1983b. 'The achievement of pre-school literacy for mother and child', in Goelman et al. (eds.), 1983.

Hill, C. and Parry, K. 1988. 'Ideological and "pragmatic" models of assessment', Columbia University, Teachers' College, *Occasional Papers*, no. 1.

forthcoming. *The test at the gate: ethnographic perspectives on the assessment of English language*.

Hodges, N. 1988. *Literacy and graffiti: alternative reading and writing in Milton Keynes*. Centre for Language and Communication, Open University Occasional Papers, no. 16. Milton Keynes.

Hymes, D. (ed.), 1964. *Language in culture and society*. New York: Harper and Row.

1974. *Foundations in sociolinguistics: an ethnographic approach*. Philadelphia: University of Pennsylvania Press.

Keenan, E. L. 1976. 'The universality of conversational implicature', *Language in Society*, 5: 67–80.

Larsen, M. T. 1989. 'Introduction', in K. Scousboe and M. T. Larsen (eds.), 1989.

Lerner, D. 1958. *The passing of traditional society*. New York: Glencoe Free Press.

Levine, K. 1980. *Becoming literate*. London: Social Science Research Council.

1986. *The social context of literacy*. London: Routledge and Kegan Paul.

Levinson, S. 1983. *Pragmatics*. Cambridge: Cambridge University Press.

Lyons, J. 1981. *Language, meaning and context*. London: Fontana.

Lyons, J., Coates, R., Deuchar, M. and Gazdar, G. (eds.), 1987. *New horizons in linguistics – 2*. London: Penguin.

Mace, J. 1979. *Working with words*. London: Chameleon.

Meek, M. 1991. *On being literate*. London: Bodley Head.

Miyoshi, M. 1988. 'The "great divide" once again: problematics of the novel and the Third World', in *Culture and History 3*. Copenhagen: Museum Tusculanum Press.

Nyystrand, M. (ed.), 1982. *What writers know: the language, process and structure of written discourse*. New York: Academic Press.

Olson, D. 1977. 'From utterance to text: the bias of language in speech and writing', *Harvard Educational Review*, 47 (3): 257–81.

1988. 'Mind and media: the epistemic functions of literacy', *Journal of Communications*, 38 (3): 254–79.

Olson, D., Torrance, N. and Hildyard, A. (eds.), 1985. *Literacy, language and learning*. Cambridge: Cambridge University Press.

Ong, W. 1982. *Orality and literacy*. London: Methuen.

Opland, J. 1983. *Xhosa oral poetry*. Cambridge: Cambridge University Press.

Oxenham, J. 1980. *Literacy: reading, writing and social organisation*. London: Routledge and Kegan Paul.

Parkin, D. 1984. 'Political language', *Annual Review of Anthropology*, 13: 345–65.

Parkin, D. (ed.), 1982. *Semantic anthropology*. London: Academic Press.

Parry, J. 1989. 'The Brahmanical tradition and the technology of the intellect', in K. Scousboe and M. T. Larsen (eds.), 1989.

Rogers, E. M. 1969. *Modernisation among peasants. The impact of communications*. New York: Rinehart.

Saljo, R. (ed.), 1988. *The written world: studies in literate thought and action*. Berlin and New York: Springer-Verlag.

Scousboe, K. and Larsen, M. T. (eds.), 1989. *Literacy and society*. Copenhagen: Akademsig Forlag.

Sherzer, J. 1987. 'Language, culture and discourse', *American Anthropologist*, 89: 295–309.

Shuman, A. 1983. 'Collaborative literacy in an urban, multi-ethnic neighbourhood', in D. Wagner (ed.), *Literacy and ethnicity*. International Journal for the Sociology of Language 42. New York: Mouton.

Strathern, M. 1985. 'Feminism and anthropology'. Unpublished MS.

Street, B. 1984. *Literacy in theory and practice*. Cambridge: Cambridge University Press.

1986. 'Walter Ong on literacy', *Accents*. Journal of the Language Society of the University of Sussex, 1 (1): 1–5.

1987. 'Literacy and orality as ideological constructions: some problems in cross-cultural studies', in *Culture and History 2*. Copenhagen: Museum Tusculanum Press.

1987. 'Literacy and social change: the significance of social context in the development of literacy programmes', in D. Wagner (ed.), *The future of literacy*. Oxford: Pergamon Press.

1988. 'Literacy practices and literacy myths', in R. Saljo (ed.), 1988.

Street, B. and J. 1991. 'The schooling of literacy', in D. Barton and R. Ivanic (eds.), *Writing in the community*. London: Sage.

Stubbs, M. 1980. *Language and literacy*. London: Routledge and Kegan Paul.

1983a. *Discourse analysis*. Chicago: University of Chicago Press.

1983b. 'Can I have that in writing please?: some neglected topics in speech act theory', *Journal of Pragmatics*, 7: 479–94.

Tannen, D. 1982. 'The myth of orality and literacy', in W. Frawley (ed.), 1982.

Tannen, D. (ed.), 1982. *Spoken and written language: exploring orality and literacy*. Norwood, NJ: Ablex.

Thompson, J. B. 1984. *Studies in the theory of ideology*. London: Polity Press.

van Djik, T. (ed.), 1990. *Discourse and society*, vol. 1. London: Sage.

Wagner, D. (ed.), 1983. *Literacy and ethnicity*. International Journal of the Sociology of Language, no. 42. New York: Mouton.

Wagner, D., Messick, B. and Spratt, J. 1986. 'Studying literacy in Morocco', in

B. B. Schieffelin and P. Gilmore (eds.), *The acquisition of literacy: ethnographic perspectives.* Norwood, NJ: Ablex.

Wertsch, J. (ed.), 1985. *Culture, communication and cognition: Vygotskyan perspectives.* Cambridge: Cambridge University Press.

Whiteman, M. (ed.), 1981. *Writing: the nature, development and teaching of written communication,* vol. 1, 'Variation in Writing: functional and linguistic and cultural differences'. Hillsdale, NJ: Lawrence Erlbaum.

Willinsky, J. 1990. *The new literacy.* London: Routledge.

PART 1

The incorporation of literacy into the communicative repertoire

During the last century a number of societies that previously had little or no acquaintance with literacy have come to use reading and writing as part of their communicative repertoire. Questions about the 'impact' of literacy on such peoples, or its 'consequences' for cognition and social development have tended to assume a single literacy – that of the imparters – and a single predictable process – that of transformation of passive 'illiterates' into literates. Kulick and Stroud found, in reading the literature on literacy transfer, that 'it is often difficult to escape the conclusion that human beings are basically passive objects who become affected by literacy in ways they are not fully aware of or can control'. Those responsible for imparting literacy have tended to treat the people as they would school pupils, debating whether they are 'ready' for literacy and whether they should have access to it. From a pedagogic point of view, the process is seen as the acquisition of specific technical skills and the learning of those conventions and assumptions about literacy held by the teachers.

The contributors to this section take a less paternalistic and less narrowly pedagogic view of the process. As Kulick and Stroud state: 'rather than stress how literacy affects people, we want to take the opposite tack and examine how people affect literacy'. They want to demonstrate 'how individuals in a newly literate society, far from being passively transformed by literacy, instead actively and creatively apply literate skills to suit their own purposes and needs'. An ethnographic perspective enables us to see how literacy is incorporated into the receiving culture's already existing conventions and concepts regarding communication – the 'subjects' are not 'tabula rasa' as many development literacy campaigns appear to assume (Street 1987). It also reveals how literacy processes cannot be understood simply in terms of schooling and pedagogy: they are part of more embracing social institutions and conceptions. Literacy practices are altered by and themselves may serve to change ideas about self and language (Kulick and Stroud), about body, gender and maturation (Bloch), about the expression of affect and identity (Besnier), about secrecy and hierarchy (Bledsoe and Robey). It is this contextualising of the processes by which literacy is added to the communicative repertoire that distinguishes the ethnographic approach adopted here.

Kulick and Stroud analyse the adaptations to literacy they observed in a rural, newly literate Papua New Guinean village by contextualising it, in relation to local notions of Christianity, the self and language. They argue that the villagers' interpretations of the relationship between Catholicism and the written words is based on their Cargo-oriented world view and on their pre-Christian beliefs about language as a powerful means by which individuals could bring about transformations in their world. They demonstrate how local ideals of the self and others are articulated and reinforced through an emphasis on particular dimensions of oral language use. Many of the conventions employed in oral discourse, particularly in speech making, carry over into written forms: the avoidance of 'hed' – of appearing pushy and self-oriented – and the emphasis on 'save' – a complex concept indicating both openness to knowledge and sensitivity to others' interests. Some of the new written forms that emerged under missionary influence were obliged to come to terms with these values and conventions, leading to outcomes not necessarily envisioned by the missionaries themselves. The form and character of the communicative repertoire prior to the introduction of literacy, then, has consequences for the uses to which literacy is put, the structure of the writing the villagers produce and the ways in which the villagers attribute meaning to written texts.

Besnier's paper demonstrates both the assimilation of new literacies to pre-existing communicative conventions, as in the New Guinea case, and the ways in which the repertoire may expand and alter local forms of communication. Again, the introduction of literacy by missionaries into a Central Pacific Atoll involved the adaptation of their purposes to those of the islanders. The paper provides both detailed ethnography of the particular uses and meanings of literacy on Nukulaelae and a challenge to traditional western assumptions regarding the use of writing for detached and unemotional purposes rather than to convey feeling. The primary purpose of literacy production on Nukulaelae is to write letters. Nukulaelae letters are sent to relatives on neighbouring atolls, and serve a variety of functions: monitoring economic reciprocity; informing kin of family events; and admonishing younger people. Permeating every aspect of letters is a heavy emphasis on the overt expression of affect, of a nature not found in any other area of Nukulaelae social life. The new literacy, then, facilitated an expansion of the communicative repertoire in this social context. The paper describes the way in which affect is encoded in the text of letters, and shows how the topics addressed in letters are emically defined as affectively charged. A content and historical ethnographic analysis of letter writing on the atoll indicates that letters have been defined as cathartic events from the very introduction of literacy. It is suggested that the metaphorical affiliation of letter-writing with parting is to a large extent responsible for letters having become affect-display contents. The overt expression of certain types of affect in letters, whilst in oral communication islanders normally express affect through covert means, suggests that traditional assumptions about the association of the medium of communication with particular expressions of emotion or detachment cannot easily be generalised. The ways in which affect is encoded in the communicative repertoire varies across culture and across media and we cannot assume that as people acquire literacy so they will acquire the conventions for using the repertoire expected in the imparting culture.

Bloch's paper exposes the problems with such assumptions as they affect our view of the spread of western education systems. He describes and analyses the introduction of both secular and religious education institutions to a Zafimaniry village in remote eastern Madagascar. The role of literacy in these processes is to be understood in terms of a 'wider notion of context' than generally employed by either missionaries or developers. This includes not only the socio-economic and functional aspects of the environment usually considered in the development education literature, but also implicit cultural theories of knowledge. Amongst Zafimaniry the uses and meanings of literacy are bound up with beliefs about the body, about maturation and about the nature of the living world, issues at first apparently unconnected with literacy at all. The very remoteness and unusualness of the village he describes is intended to bring home to western readers how culturally specific are their expectations about the role and significance of schooling and of literacy. For here the response to the development of government and church schooling is quite different from the norm in western educational environments. Bloch describes in close detail the daily practices associated with schooling in the village of Mamolena, where there is an apparent contradiction between the evident irrelevance for daily life of what is taught and yet the strength of respect for learning and regard for the value of literacy. The explanation, he suggests, lies in the association of different types of knowledge with different stages of life, with different communicative codes and with broader cultural concerns regarding the body, gender and maturation. School knowledge is assimilated to these local conceptions rather than simply having an 'impact' on them.

The notion of elders' wisdom as fixed, non-functional, above and beyond everyday practical concerns and therefore worthy of respect but in many ways irrelevant, provides a framework for conceptualising the new school knowledge: this too is practically irrelevant for local purposes but worthy of the status of elders' knowledge. Problems occur when the young are taught it rather than the old, but Bloch shows how such difficulties are overcome through a series of subtle local adjustments. Letters, for instance, are mainly written by young men, but the authority associated with them is 'taken over' by the elders, who treat young men as simply scribes, channels through which elders continue their authoritative discourses. As in the examples provided by Kulick and Stroud and by Besnier, local communicative conventions determine how the processes and techniques associated with literacy and schooling are actually employed. Bloch concludes that, in contrast with expectations embedded in the autonomous model of literacy, 'neither writing nor schooling have made any significant difference to the basic organising principles governing the evaluation of knowledge among Zafimaniry, rather literacy and schooling have been put to use to reinforce existing patterns'. This is not to say that such societies are always simply conservative and that new literacies do not also alter existing conventions, as Besnier's data illustrate: indeed this is the case in other parts of Madagascar, as Bloch notes. But such differences have to be explained in terms of local conditions and require a fuller sense of 'context' than is evident from most discussions of schooling and literacy.

Bledsoe and Robey similarly point out that, whilst great efforts and expenses go into spreading literacy, these have 'been poorly matched by social scientists' attempts to understand it'. Like other contributors to this section, they see literacy as a 'resource that people may use to achieve certain goals that do not necessarily correspond to those posited by the 'autonomous' model of literacy. Amongst the Mende of Sierra Leone, literacy may to some extent be viewed as a way to aid memory and long-distance communication, as the traditional literature expects, but the Mende's main interest in it is as a mode of access to other secret domains of knowledge whose meanings are dangerous without legitimate and ritual qualifications'. Literacy, then, is incorporated into other indigenous practices regarding the nature of knowledge and power, not simply borrowed unchanged from its sources. In this case there are two potential sources of literacy, Arabic and English, and in both cases the issue for the Mende is how it can be used 'for secrecy and segregation'. Bledsoe and Robey show that those Mende who are competent in Arabic literacy use their skills much like indigenous elites who used traditional secret knowledge to gain the labour and allegiance of dependants. In contrast with the paradigm that views literacy as a mode of facilitating communication, they show that those Mende who are learned in Arabic construe the knowledge to which literacy gives access as dangerous and therefore secret. Communication is controlled and restricted rather than enhanced and spread by the uses to which literacy may be put, an insight that might also fruitfully be applied in many western societies.

They also challenge the view expressed by Goody and others that writing in some way replaces oral communication, an assumption that lies behind much of the attempt to evaluate the two media and to demonstrate the superiority of literacy. Like the other contributors to this section, Bledsoe and Robey see writing 'as one component of the total pool of potential knowledge that the Mende strive to attain and manipulate in competition with others'. Literacy is part of the communicative repertoire and like other parts, including oral discourses, registers, codes and dialects with which it interacts and frequently merges, it is a social construction not a neutral technology: it varies from one culture or sub-group to another and its uses are embedded in relations of power and struggles over resources. When we have further ethnographic studies of this variation we may begin to make some useful generalisations about the uses and meanings of such literacy practices in society: these papers will, I hope, make a helpful contribution towards that process.

1

CONCEPTIONS AND USES OF LITERACY IN A PAPUA NEW GUINEAN VILLAGE

DON KULICK AND CHRISTOPHER STROUD

Among certain scholars, educators and missionaries working in the Pacific, there is a debate currently brewing about the consequences of vernacular literacy for traditional societies. On the one hand, the missionary-linguists of the Summer Institute of Linguistics/Wycliffe Bible Translators (SIL) increasingly justify their continued existence in countries like Papua New Guinea by de-emphasising their evangelistic goals and by accentuating instead the role they play in furthering vernacular literacy. These missionary-linguists stress the importance of literacy in the promotion of the 'dignity of the indigenous people and their languages' (Franklin 1975: 139). There is an oft-unstated assumption in all that they write about their work that vernacular literacy a priori strengthens the position of the vernacular.

This view of literacy has begun to be challenged by others. In a number of recent papers,[1] the linguist Peter Mühlhäusler has argued that vernacular literacy, far from leading to the preservation of local languages and cultures, in fact has the opposite effect. 'Vernacular literacy', he writes, 'is potentially as powerful an agent of social change and decline of traditional modes of expression and life as literacy in a metropolitan language' (1990: 203).

Even though the overt focus of this debate is on vernacular literacy, what is really at issue are the pros and cons of any type of literacy, as Mühlhäusler's statement makes clear. The basic point of contention between the SIL missionary-linguists and researchers like Mühlhäusler is whether or not the effects of literacy on small-scale societies are desirable. The missionaries, who believe in the power of the Word to 'transform' people into Christians (see, for example, Townsend 1963: 8; Renck 1990), consider that literacy, the ability to read the Word, is unquestionably positive. Indeed, translating the Christian gospel into local languages is the *raison d'être* of the SIL. Mühlhäusler, who draws attention to the proselytising motives of the SIL, and who appears to regard all literacy as an 'agent of decline' of traditional lifestyles, considers that the overall effects of literate skills on small-scale societies are dubious.

Regardless of whether they can be said to be for or against the acquisition of literacy by such societies however, those engaged in this debate appear to accept without much reflection the view that literacy constitutes a kind of potent, active force in itself, and that it acts as an 'agent' of 'linguistic, religious and social change' (Mühlhäusler 1990: 203). This is a position underlying most of the scholarly work that has been done on literacy since the 1960s. Indeed, this work can largely be seen as a grand attempt to demonstrate the ways in which literate skills transform cognitive processes, social institutions and historical consciousness (Goody 1977, 1986; Ong 1982; Olson 1977; Havelock 1976).

In reading through this literature, it is often difficult to escape the conclusion that human beings are basically passive objects who become affected by literacy in ways they are neither fully aware of nor able to control. One of the more unfortunate practical consequences of a position which assumes that people become changed in predictable ways by literacy is that debates like the one referred to above can easily assume a tone of paternalistic wrangling over whether or not 'the natives' are ready for, or should have, access to literate skills.

In this paper, rather than stress how literacy affects people, we want to take the opposite tack and examine how people affect literacy. We are going to demonstrate how individuals in a newly literate society, far from being passively transformed by literacy, instead actively and creatively apply literate skills to suit their own purposes and needs. In pursuing this argument, we are not claiming that the acquisition of literacy might not in itself have consequences for social groups. We are suggesting, however, that these consequences should not be simply assumed, nor should they be exaggerated. Like an increasing number of researchers in disciplines such as social psychology (Cole and Scribner 1981), history (Clanchy 1979), linguistics (Stubbs 1980; Cook-Gumperz 1986) and anthropology (Finnegan 1988; Heath 1983), we have come to the conclusion that literacy has been and continues to be unjustifiably reified in discussions and debates around the world. By analysing empirical data in a way that shows how literacy is bound up with 'quite profound levels of belief and the fundamental concepts through which a society creates order and design in the world' (Street 1984: 114), we hope in this paper to contribute to what appears to be a growing consensus that literacy is shaped by a group's social organisation and cultural concerns in much more far-reaching and subtle ways than has formerly been appreciated.

The uses of literacy

The data on which we will base our discussion come from a small, rural village located in the lower Sepik region of Papua New Guinea. The village is called Gapun, and it is populated by about 100 people who are largely self-supporting through a combination of swidden agriculture, hunting and sago processing.

When discussing literacy in Gapun, or anywhere else in Papua New Guinea, it is first necessary to understand the rather complicated linguistic situation into which reading and writing skills become embedded. In Gapun, two languages dominate the verbal repertoire of the villagers. These are the vernacular language, Taiap, and Tok Pisin. Taiap is an isolate non-Austronesian language, probably belonging to what in the linguistic literature is called the Sepik–Ramu Phylum of Papuan languages (Kulick and Stroud in press; Laycock and Z'graggen 1975). It is spoken only in Gapun and it is not a written language. Tok Pisin is an English-based creole. It is the most widely spoken language in Papua New Guinea today.

A few members of Gapun village have been minimally literate in Tok Pisin since the late 1950s. In 1967, a government-run grammar school was opened in a nearby village, and since that time the majority of children in Gapun have attended school for three to six years. In addition to the two languages spoken in the village, the children who attend grammar school are confronted with yet another tongue: English. For a variety of social, historical and political reasons, English is the language of instruction in Papua New Guinea, and it is used in classrooms from the very first day of school.[2] Gapun children thus acquire literacy skills in a language they almost never hear or use outside the classroom. Despite the fact that the children learn very little during the first two or three years of school, due in large measure to their inability to cope with instruction in English, most of them leave school having acquired some literacy skills. The children are able, without any formal instruction, to transfer those skills to Tok Pisin, thus becoming functionally literate in that language.

Outside of school, however, literacy skills are almost never used. Most boys and virtually all girls who become literate in school make almost no use of their reading and writing abilities outside the classroom, and after they leave school at ages fourteen to fifteen, many of these young people may never read and will almost certainly never write again. There are few opportunities in the course of normal village life to read or write. The only type of literature that regularly enters the village, for example, is the *Sydney Morning Herald*, but this is purchased in loose sheets by the villagers and is used to roll cigarettes; it is never read.

Nevertheless, most households do contain some printed matter which is occasionally looked at, and a few villagers do sometimes write. But the ways in which Gapun villagers have incorporated literacy skills into their community differ from the ways in which the written word is often assumed to be used in literate societies. Noticeably absent from Gapun are those types of reading and writing which are stressed in Western societies and educational systems. Gapuners do not read to gain information about people they do not know or about events which do not directly concern them. Nobody in the village considers that one can become better informed or more competent in any way by reading (although there is the belief that an intensive reading of a text might cause one to understand its hidden message – we return to this below). Consequently, there is no notion in the village that everyone *should* read. The act of reading in itself has no value apart from accomplishing some immediate goal like confirming the words to a hymn, preparing to recite a prayer, reading a note one has been given, deciding to discover a heretofore concealed truth in a religious text, or checking the hand of cards one has just been dealt in a game with friends.

Writing too has particular, circumscribed uses in the village. Despite the fact that children do some expository writing in school, none of this is carried over to a village context: villagers do not keep diaries or write letters to friends in distant villages to maintain contact. Instead, the single most common type of writing done in Gapun is short notes that villagers write to one another requesting a favour or a loan such as the use of a hunting dog or a gun. Other uses of writing include the habit of a few villagers of recording the dates of deaths in the village, and sometimes the writing of lists of villagers' names by men elected to positions of nominal importance instituted by the national government (the listing of these names serves no other purpose than giving these men occasion to tell the villagers, in dark tones, that their names have been recorded 'in the book'). Like reading, writing in Gapun is never talked about or evaluated in terms of aesthetics, and there is no notion that everyone should know how to write.

While the people of Gapun use their literacy skills in a variety of ways (see Kulick and Stroud 1990a for a more detailed description), two general characteristics stand out. First, a great deal of the villagers' literate activity is directed towards Christianity. This is especially true of the reading that occurs in Gapun, which is primarily concerned with religious material. Second, the great bulk of the villagers' writing concerns aspects of their relationships with one another. Messages requesting favours, lists of names and notes recording deaths are all part of the general flow of communication that villagers have with and about one another.

These characteristics of the uses of literacy in the village lead us to pose certain questions. Why, we wonder, is so much of the villagers' literate activity concerned with Christianity? And what aspect of village interpersonal relationships is being addressed when, for example, a villager sends a note to his mother's brother asking for a chicken?

We will attempt to answer those questions by demonstrating that Gapun villagers use their literacy skills in the ways they do because of the meanings they have attached to the written word. That is, they have creatively adapted reading and writing activities to pursue certain goals and achieve particular effects which have been generated from larger cultural concerns. Using the two characteristic features of Gapun literacy as rubrics, we will examine the ways in which local conceptions of Christianity, and of interpersonal relations have influenced how the villagers structure, use and evaluate literacy.

We begin by arguing that the villagers' interpretation of the relationship between Christianity and literacy is based upon their pre-Christian notions of language as a powerful means by which knowledgeable men and women could bring about transformations in their world. Following this, we then go on to discuss how local ideas about the self and others are articulated and reinforced through a pronounced emphasis on particular dimensions of oral language use. We will show how this emphasis has consequences for the uses to which literacy is put, the structure of the writing that the villagers produce, and the ways in which the villagers attribute meaning to written texts.

Getting the word to work

Historically, literacy in Gapun, like virtually everywhere else in the Pacific region, was introduced by missionaries. The first village man to acquire literacy skills did so on a Catholic mission station in the mid-1950s. This man, Kruni Aiarpa, worked hard to learn how to read and write. He learned these skills by sitting in on lessons that the missionaries and nuns held for local children:

> I learned my A B Cs and after a while I could read and write now. I knew now. I went and read the Bible, the prayer book, the hymn book...

The social setting in which Kruni became literate and the uses to which he subsequently applied his literacy skills illustrate the tight connection that has existed between literacy and Catholicism ever since villagers first began acquiring the written word. When Kruni returned to Gapun from the mission station, he used his newly acquired literacy skills in Tok Pisin to say a simple mass on Sundays. He shared his knowledge of letters with other village men, and a few of these learned enough to follow along in hymn booklets and perhaps write their names. In the early 1960s, several of the village men and women who are now in their forties were sent by their parents to another mission station for schooling. Harsh punishment drove these boys and girls to run away before acquiring any literacy skills beyond perhaps learning the alphabet.

In any case, from the introduction of literacy in Gapun in the mid-1950s, until the late 1960s, any villager who became literate did so in a context directly associated with the Catholic Church, be this through Kruni, the village prayer leader, or on a mission station. This link between literacy and the Church was reinforced even more by the fact that there was a total absence of any literature except booklets and pamphlets addressing Catholic beliefs and liturgy. When villagers learned to read, they did so in order to be able to read Christian literature.

Catholicism and Cargo

The establishment of Catholicism in Gapun had occurred in the years immediately following the Second World War. It coincided with and was in all probability reinforced by a period of Cargo cult activity in the area. The first of these was a typical Cargo cult, involving ecstatic prayer, promiscuous sex and expectations that money would materialise in the village graveyard. It was inspired by stories of the Rai Coast cult led by the well-known cult leader Yali (Lawrence 1964; Morauta 1974). This cult, which lasted several months, was soon followed by another spate of millenarian activity, inspired this time by the teachings of a man named Ninga, who came from the lower Sepik village of Bien. This movement was based on a combination of intensive prayer and the imitation of plantation work routines and military drills, and lasted perhaps as long as a year.

From its very beginnings, then, Catholicism in Gapun has been closely linked with notions of Cargo. Since the 1950s there have been two more outbreaks of overt Cargo cultism in the village: once in 1965–6, and the other as recently as 1987.

The millenarian activity in 1987 is particularly interesting from the perspective of the study of literacy, because it was directly sparked off by rumours that the villagers of Bogia (about one and a half days' walk from Gapun along the coast) had received a letter from God informing them of the exact time at which the world would end. For weeks, Gapun villagers talked excitedly about travelling to Bogia to see this letter for themselves. Although no one actually ever made that trip, bits of information contained in the letter from God did leak out and eventually reach Gapun: the world, it was said, would end at 'three o'clock' on 'day ten'. This would be a Thursday, in 'year thirteen'.

Nobody in Gapun understood what 'year thirteen' possibly could mean, but many of the villagers began to 'ready themselves' for the End anyway, expecting it to arrive at any moment. They constructed an elaborate altar which they decorated with flowers, large, bulbous orange seeds, sago fronds and eight inch plastic statues of the Virgin Mary. And every evening for several weeks they held prayer meetings, sometimes lasting most of the night. Several times these meetings resulted in many of those present falling into convulsive *extase*.

That this latest bout of Cargo activity was directly related to a written product, from the pen of no one less than God Almighty Himself, testifies to the extremely salient and vigorous associations that exist in Gapun between Christianity, Cargo and literacy. The strength of these associations is further illustrated by the type of literature that the villagers possess.

Types of literature in the village

To discover what literature actually existed in Gapun, a survey was conducted by going from household to household and asking the villagers to show all the books and papers they possessed. Discounting loose pages and the vaccination booklets that the nurse who occasionally comes to the village sometimes gives to parents for their children, eighty-four specimens of printed matter were found in Gapun.

Of these eighty-four specimens, all but two were directly connected with Christianity. One of those two items was an automobile maintenance manual in English that the sons of one couple had somehow come by during a trip to the Provincial capital of Wewak. The other item was a small booklet called *Daisy Sing-Along*. It contained a number of ever-green songs like 'Yellow Rose of Texas' and 'O Du Lieber Augustin'. The automobile maintenance manual was frequently passed around in the household which owned it, as adults and children enjoyed tracing their fingers along the line drawings of gears and sockets and wondering how they all fit together and made a car run. The *Daisy Sing-Along* booklet was never read.

All the rest of the literature in Gapun was religious. The most common printed item in the village is the small paperbound hymn booklet called *Niu Laip* (New Life). If a household possesses only one item of literature, this will be it. The next most common item is the soft covered *Nupela Testamen na Ol Sam* (New Testament and the Psalms), which several households keep in a plastic rice bag up in the rafters of their roof. The remainder of the religious matter consists of various booklets and calendars containing Bible stories, prayers and liturgical instructions, always in Tok Pisin.

With the exception of the hymn booklet, which the villagers take with them to mass and sometimes look in while singing, most of this literature is almost never read. Only printed matter containing pictures or line drawings is ever really looked at. Nobody ever actually reads the Bible, for example, but school children or an adult and several school children sometimes page through it together and comment to each other about the abstract line drawings of figures they find there. This paging through printed material and commenting to one another about the pictures there is how villagers most often 'read' such material.

Figure 1.1 'The death of a sinner.'

One extremely popular item of literature in the village is a single copy of an old soiled booklet without a cover called '*Bel Bilong Man*' (Man's Heart; literally Man's Stomach) by the villagers. It contains line drawings of various animals, which the Tok Pisin text explains personify different sinful behaviours: a bird of paradise represents vanity and '*bikhet*' (big-headedness, wilfulness); a dog symbolises '*pasin bilong pamuk*' (promiscuity); a cassowary is meant to stand for aggression, and so on. The story that the booklet tells is that men must work to drive these sinful

Figure 1.2 'The death of a believer.'

ways from their heart and replace them with Christian qualities, symbol-
ised iconographically by a smiling mouth (for a Christian conscience), an
open eye (for seeing the Light), an open book (symbolising the Bible), a
burning bush, and a crucifix. If one does not replace sinful ways with
Christian ways, the text warns, then one's soul will be dragged to Hell.
This fate is rather dramatically illustrated in a drawing from the booklet
reproduced in figure 1.1.

Village schoolchildren have added to this drawing, writing *sinman* (sinner) on the soul destined for the Flames, and labelling the horned figures as *seten* (Satan). An interesting iconographic detail of the drawing is the appearance of a book, in the hand of the man who is standing near the centre of the picture. This book, even though it has no label, is immediately understood by every villager to be the bible, in a manner which suggests that the very concept 'Book' is essentially Christian in nature. The man holding this book, neatly dressed in a button down shirt and standing poignantly apart from the dead sinner, is understood by every villager as representing the village prayer leader.

Another drawing later on in the booklet represents the death of another man – possibly this same prayer leader (figure 1.2). The text on the page opposite this illustration explains that it depicts 'The death of a believer' (*Indai bilong man i bilip*). There are several interesting details in this picture, such as the European-style window in the man's house, but what is most relevant for us here is to note the prominence, once again, of a book. The book in this drawing is again unlabelled, but it is clearly not representing a *Daisy Sing-Along* book or a car repair manual. This picture is an uncommonly apt and powerful encoding of what the villagers in Gapun believe to be the relationship between literacy and Christianity. Note also the colour of the rising spirit's hair (and, by association, of his skin). In illustrations such as this, the villagers continually find proof that they are correct in believing things such as that they 'change' and become white when they die.

The power of the Word

We are now in a position to ask ourselves why the villagers of Gapun maintain such a tight link between Christianity and literacy. Scholars who have addressed the issue of literacy in Papua New Guinea in recent years (for example Mühlhäusler 1977, 1990; Gilliam 1984; Lynch 1979) have frequently put forward the argument that the almost total absence of any literature in Tok Pisin other than religious material has shaped rural Papua New Guineans' perception of what literature is and what literacy is for. While it would certainly be possible to present such a case for Gapun, an argument phrased in such language implies that the villagers are merely passively moulded in their conceptions by the availability of a certain kind of literature. We want to emphasise instead that the villagers of Gapun *actively* maintain and elaborate this link between literacy and Christianity because they are convinced that they can get that link to work for them.

Gapuners strongly believe that Christianity is the key to obtaining the Cargo. They anticipate that the Cargo will arrive as reward for their pious Christianity. In this sense, the whole idea of Cargo is an expression of a strong emic notion of agency. The villagers believe that the Cargo will materialise as a result of their actions; it is they themselves who can bring about the change. They are therefore always on the lookout for a 'road' which they can manipulate to obtain the money and the factories they want. And it is at this juncture that the villagers' literacy skills fit into their scheme of things.

Like numerous other Melanesian societies described in the ethnographic literature (for example Lawrence 1964; Meggitt 1968), Gapun villagers consider that words have power; words have always been associated with the ability to directly influence spirit powers to make things come about. Village men and women possessed (and some still possess) magic chants that they used for a variety of reasons, from making dogs able to hunt better, to curing illness, to killing someone through sorcery.

Personal names are also imbued with power, and certain relatives, such as in-laws, cannot be called by name, lest one bring down ancestral wrath upon oneself or one's close matrilineal relatives. Likewise, mythical figures usually have many names: 'big names' that can be said aloud, and 'little names' or 'inside names', that if uttered anywhere near Gapun would cause the entire village to perish.

So in Gapun, certain words uttered in certain contexts are seen by the villagers to have the power to bring about certain outcomes. Words constitute direct links to spiritual powers, who will respond in desired ways if the proper words are said in the proper manner. The power of words is thus a creative power; those who have obtained verbatim knowledge of a chant, for example, can utilise the power of those words for their own purposes. Words are, in themselves, 'roads': ways of obtaining desired results.

It appears to be the case that the Christian Word of God has been interpreted by the villagers in precisely this manner. Gapuners were certainly not slow to notice the strikingly prominent role played in the Catholic religion by particular words uttered in specific ways. In order to demonstrate their devotion to God, villagers had to learn to recite prayers, sing hymns, and respond with the appropriate formulaic phrases during Sunday mass. Such a stress on words and on proper formulae for the saying of those words must have seemed unremarkable to the villagers. What was remarkable, on the other hand, was the effect that those Christian words had on the Christian God. Whereas their own words to their ancestors or cult deities (*trambaran*/*marip*) could only cure a sickness or make a dog kill more pigs, the words of the priests linked them to a much more potent Being – one who rewarded His devotees with outboard motors, aeroplanes, money and white skin.[3]

As soon as they discovered that 'God's talk' was marked on paper and actually accessible to anyone who could learn to decipher the marks, enterprising villagers like Kruni Aiarpa in the 1950s seized upon literacy as the 'road' they had been searching for. Why the villagers still have been unable to obtain the Cargo, even though they can now read the Word, is a point to which we shall return below. But even though they have not been able to make literacy work for them yet, the villagers have not given up. Gapuners are ingenious people forever on the lookout for some new clue that might reveal to them how they can *really* get the Cargo, and all recent innovations in village life have come to be seen in this light. The opening of a government-run grammar school in a nearby village in 1967, for example, gave the villagers their first access to non-religious reading material. But schooling is interpreted by Gapun villagers in terms of their millenarian world view, and they believe that the ultimate purpose of schooling is to reveal to their children the secret of the Cargo.[4] What this means is that even the secular literature read by children in school is conceptualised in what is essentially a religious framework. In addition to this, literacy in school, as noted earlier, is acquired in English, a language which the village children almost never encounter in any form outside the classroom. The esoteric and mysterious nature of this language, together with a growing realisation that English, and not Tok Pisin, is the white man's true *tok ples* (vernacular) further fires the villagers' suspicions that the 'meaning' of school is to reveal millenarian secrets to their children.

The power of the word thus persists in Gapun, and the villagers are busy trying to get that power to work for them in Christian contexts. This is why they accept some types of literature into their lives and reject others. Although it is still scarce, secular literature in Tok Pisin, such as the weekly newspaper *Wantok*, does exist today. But none of this interests anyone in Gapun. The only non-religious literature ever actively read by the villagers is glossy, brightly coloured brochures from American mail order companies that have been passed into Gapun from friends in other villages. Even though they are secular, however, these brochures are invariably interpreted by the villagers within a religious framework. Men and women pore over them in excited groups and marvel at the abundance of goods that the brochures seem to be offering. Proclaiming triumphantly that they have finally found the 'road' they have been seeking, young men sit down and write brief letters to the addresses they find in the front of the brochures, requesting that the Cargo be sent to them forthwith.

Writing, the self and others

The idioms of Christianity and Cargo receive a tremendous amount of elaboration in Gapun, and, as we have just seen, they are a major factor shaping the way in which the villagers choose to think about and use literacy.

But Gapuners do not only use their literacy skills to read hymn booklets or to write to foreign companies asking for steamliners. They also write notes to one another. In order to understand why they do this, and how, we believe that it is necessary to examine the villagers' notions of self, and their ideas about how different selves most appropriately relate to one another through language.

The maverick hed

Gapuners have very strong and very definite notions of self. An essential aspect of the self is referred to by the Tok Pisin word *hed* and in the vernacular by *kɔkir*. Both these words mean, exactly, 'head'. Each individual, the villagers believe, 'has *hed*', which means that each individual has a strong will and sense of personal autonomy.

From the moment of birth, babies in the village are treated as stubborn, big-headed individualists. Pre-verbal infants are frequently shaken lightly by their mothers and chastised playfully that their *heds* are too 'strong' and 'big', and that they 'never listen to talk'. When children begin to make babbling noises and sounds, these are commonly interpreted by caregivers as expressions of anger or dissatisfaction. Thus a baby cooing softly in its mother's lap is likely to suddenly be shaken and asked: '*Ai! Yu belhat long wanem samting? Ah?*' (Ai! What are you mad about? Ah?). Similarly, a child's first word is generally held to be *ɔki* (go + IRREALIS), a vernacular language word meaning, approximately, 'I'm getting out of here'. This word, which adults attribute to infants as young as two months, reflects the village notion that children are born with *hed*, and that they will go where they want and do what they want, regardless of the wishes of anyone else.

In anyone but small children, *hed* is officially condemned. Village rhetoric uses the term *hed* to mean egoism, selfishness and maverick individualism. *Hed* is bad. It is anti-social and stubbornly autonomistic. It is held up in stark contrast to 'development' (*kamap* [literally 'come up']), which is portrayed as a group pursuit: development and change will only occur in Gapun if everyone joins together, becomes truly Christian and makes the village into a *kristen komuniti*. That this has not yet happened is blamed in part on the *heds* of fellow villagers. Other villagers' *hed*, especially the 'big' *heds* of women, is what is preventing the village from 'coming up', everybody agrees. It is the plug blocking the metamorphosis that one day will occur and change their village, their material living conditions and even their physical selves.

But even though the villagers harshly deplore the *heds* of each other in their talk and rhetoric, they spend much of their time defending their own personal autonomy. Furthermore, in a myriad of different ways, from their political institutions to their notions of provocation, Gapuners make it clear that a person's *hed* is inviolate in their community.

Like most Papua New Guinea societies, Gapun is acephalous and politically anarchistic. There are 'big men' (*bikpela man*/*munje suman*) in the village, but these are not leaders in the usual sense of the word. Men are 'big' because of their strong personalities, their age and experience, their skills in hunting and oratory (and, traditionally, in warfare) and their ability to maintain a wide range of social relationships. There are no formal or hereditary underpinnings to the big man role, and people listen to these men to the extent that they want to. For their part, big men cannot order anyone to do anything. They can suggest and cajole and harangue, but they cannot command. To do so would be considered to be the grossest provocations, and it would almost certainly result in violence.

This type of relationship permeates the entire society. No relationship, not even that between adult and child, is understood by the villagers to legitimately involve the power to order another person to do something against his or her will. Any attempt to do this is regarded by the villagers as provocation. Provocation (*pusim* [literally 'to push']/*kɔkɨr ikru* [literally 'to give head']) is considered to be any action by an individual which causes somebody else to feel put out, exploited, insulted, wronged, violated or mistreated. To 'push' somebody, to 'give them head', is to challenge them, and among adults this will almost inevitably result in an argument or a fight, sooner or later.

Villagers' abhorrence of any type of provocation has led them to develop a number of dramatic ways of announcing it and dealing with it. The most common consequence of perceived provocation in Gapun is what the villagers call a *kros*. *Kros*es are public proclamations of conflict in which villagers – especially women – assert themselves and their autonomy by sitting in their houses and shouting through the village that these have been violated in some way. *Kros*es occur almost daily in Gapun, and they are often scathing and bitterly vituperative (see Kulick 1992 for a detailed discussion). Another, even more flamboyant way in which villagers deal with what they consider to be provocation by another person is by ostentatiously destroying their own possessions – their betel palms, their cooking utensils, their hunting spears, even their entire houses – in fits of rage. Whenever this happens, villagers are usually unhesitant in laying the blame for the destruction not on the person who wrought it, but rather on the person or persons seen as having provoked the destruction.

This kind of notion of provocation both reflects and reinforces the villagers' conceptions of themselves and others as fiercely individualistic. Any attempt to influence the behaviour of another person is risky, because that person may react against such an attempt with violence. In this kind of social climate, almost any kind of social interaction contains the potential for conflict.

One might justifiably wonder at this point how villagers ever actually cooperate and work or live together if everybody is always on guard against violations of their personal autonomy. The answer to that is partly that villagers do not, in fact, work together very often, despite a great deal of talk in the men's house that they should cooperate and work together to repair rotting bridges or clear overgrown footpaths. Also, it is as though the villagers have decided they can live together as long as they can make sure that everyone else is constantly aware of their rights. And so these get proclaimed in a *kros* or through the destruction of one's own possessions whenever a violation of some sort provides the opportunity for self assertion.

The consensual self

Yet another reason why the villagers do not leave the village forever and move away with their families into the jungle, as most of them periodically threaten to do, is the fact that in addition to having *hed*, the self in Gapun is also considered to possess *save* (knowledge; the vernacular equivalent is <u>numbwan</u>). In its most basic sense, *save* signifies knowledge: the knowledge of facts and being able to learn from experience and through doing. But it also means more than that. *Save* is knowledge about appropriate behaviour and speech, awareness of social obligations and roles, cognisance of the consequences that one's own or someone else's actions or words can have. *Save* is a metaphor often used in Gapun to mean social sensitivity and solidarity. When the old Kruni Aiarpa in the middle of a tirade about not getting his dinner screams at his ancient wife from his men's house, shouting that she '*nogat save*' (has no knowledge), he means that she is not fulfilling her role as his wife and as a good Christian; he means that she is 'showing *hed*', flaunting her autonomy, being selfish. *Save*, the knowledge that one sometimes must 'suppress *hed*' (*daunim hed*), compromise and fulfil social obligations even if one doesn't want to, is the existential quality which villagers consider most clearly separates adults from children. Adults have, or should have, *save*. Children don't.

Attaining *save*, coming to know, is not something that the villagers think children can be taught. Children can be taught certain things, like the names of objects and of relatives, but *save* itself is not taught: *save*, in the villagers' view, 'breaks open' (*bruk/krarara ɔ-*) inside the child, like an egg. Children begin to show evidence of *save* when they start, at between about twenty to thirty months, to use language by themselves to engage others in verbal interactions. Villagers thus view language used in interactions with others as both an indication and a result of *save* 'breaking open'. This conceptual tie between verbal interaction and *save* suggests that villagers see language as one of the chief means through which an individual can express his or her social competence.

Talking consensus

In informal interactions, this belief is expressed through the work that villagers do to accommodate others verbally. Speakers are considered to be demonstrating their *save* when they accommodate others in language choice and in the opinions they express, for example.

The most powerful and archetypical expression of the villagers' concern with displaying social awareness and knowledge through speech, however, is the verbal genre of oratory. Oratories are delivered frequently in Gapun. They occur whenever groups of men gather together in the men's house for any specific reason. These gatherings, which nowadays usually concern the need to organise communal labour or large-scale cooperation in preparation for events such as funerary feasts, provide the men with occasion to engage in speeches that downplay tension, smoothe over disagreement, emphasise consensus and, in doing so, create contexts in which they and others may publicly demonstrate their *save*.

However, as is commonly the case in Melanesian societies (Lederman 1984; Brison 1989; Lindstrom 1990; McKellin 1990), any consensus reached as a result of oratory is essentially only cosmetic. Villagers know this, since they have all at one time or another found it expedient to express agreement with opinions that have been completely antithetical to their own. The prominence in village life of oratory and the values associated with it indicates, though, that village men ascribe importance to the appearance of consensus even when it does not necessarily mean anything in practical terms. The villagers, to put it another way, like to agree, even when they disagree.

One consequence of the strong link between oratory and consensus is that talk during formal village meetings is expected to be and is interpreted as being consensus oriented. Unlike the *kros*, which overtly announces conflict, open disagreement is not possible within the framework of oratorical speech. The only way of truly disagreeing in a social situation dominated by oratory is to say nothing at all. Meetings such as the yearly parent-teacher meeting in the nearby village of Wongan, which are always pockmarked with long silences on the part of the villagers and by anxious urgings of one or two men to '*Toktok! Toktok!*' (Talk! Talk!) are meetings in which most of the participants are very much opposed to the general direction that the talk is taking.

Another result of the villagers' stress on consensus in oratory is that the

particular facts under di~   ..? points made by speakers
in their speeches are   ~ine creation of a general feeling
of agreement. O~   ~greement – or, at least, the absence of
open disagreem~   ~ved in village oratories is by structuring talk
so that the speaker u~ ~n expresses and simultaneously dissociates himself
from controversial statements. This strategy of rhetorical dissociation has
strongly influenced the villagers' literacy patterns. In order to see clearly
how this is so, we can begin by briefly examining a short extract from the
beginning of a forty minute long speech by Kem, a forty-five year old man
who is one of the most skilful orators in the village.

Kem's speech was delivered near the end of a meeting held in the men's
house to discuss the status of the village's *yut grup* (youth group). *Yut* is a
government-instituted village work force to which, despite its name, all
villagers ideally belong. *Yut* is supposed to provide an organisational
basis for the villagers to cooperate in performing communal labour such
as repairing broken bridges and cutting grass along footpaths. It is also
intended to serve as a labour pool which enterprising villagers with coffee
crops or coconut trees can hire to harvest crops or collect and prepare
coconuts for drying into copra. In Gapun, the village *yut* group had been
inactive for quite a while, due to conflicts among villagers. It is this
situation which Kem begins his speech by addressing:

> Yes thank you
> And
> I'm going to tell you all a little talk.
> Sorry true, it's not a big talk.
>
> 5 Talk/Your work is good.
> Good now,
>   there aren't any complaints.
> The work you're doing now is good.
> The way of *yut*, you've understood it.
>
> 10 And
> A little problem arose
> Last month.
> This little problem is here
> I haven't straightened it out.
>
> 15 And
> Maybe that's why there are a few complaints around.
>
> And
> So I'm saying this:
> A sickness has got [my] wife

20 And
    <u>So I'm still getting ready.</u>
    I don't know what time what day I'll be able look
    after this problem from earlier ...[5]

Kem's speech is typical of the majority of oratories that get produced in the men's house. Several specific characteristics of his speech are especially relevant here.

First, there is the formal structure of the talk. Kem begins with the formulaic marker '*yes*'. *Yes, plis* (please) and *tenk yu* (thank you) are oral markers of formality that men habitually use to begin their speeches. They are usually followed by phrases announcing that the speaker has 'a little talk' or 'a little worry' to deliver to his audience. These opening phrases are discourse framing devices which function partly to mark what follows as a formal speech and partly to announce the speaker's intention to assume the floor. Notice also the use Kem makes of the conjunction 'And' (Tok Pisin *Na*). In oratorical speech, this conjunction is used to maintain the floor and to structure information into bounded units. Kem uses 'And' as a means of segmenting his talk and as a way of signalling the introduction of new information.

The second important feature of Kem's speech is his use of indirection and reneging to dissociate himself from the talk he is producing. After announcing his intention to make a speech, Kem hurries to stress that the work of the village's youth group is 'good', and that 'there aren't any complaints'. Once he has established this, Kem then goes on to reveal that there are, in fact, 'a few complaints' about the youth group after all. Kem uses extreme indirection here, and he is careful not to assign blame to anyone but himself. Furthermore, he doesn't criticise. Nothing in Kem's speech could possibly be interpreted by any villager as aggressive or 'pushy'. By first saying there are no complaints and by then leaving unstated who has the complaints, Kem is indicating that he is not accusing anyone of being anti-social and harbouring complaints; he is merely noting the fact that complaints 'are around'. Such a discursive strategy conveys the impression that the speaker's words have been generated from a source outside the speaker and that the speaker is merely reporting something.

This dissociative strategy is tied to the third relevant aspect of Kem's talk. Throughout this entire stretch of speech, Kem displays a guise of self-effacement. He consistently tones down his status and role as a big man. The speech is delivered in a placating tone which suggest 'I really have nothing to say and perhaps shouldn't be wasting your time talking at all'. His consistent use of diminutives emphasises this: he explains that his talk is not 'a big talk'; he speaks of a 'little problem' and 'a few complaints'.

Kem's self-effacement is purposeful. One of the things that he is doing with his talk is reaffirming his intention to sponsor a large conciliatory feast to compensate another village man, who had been injured in a fight which had been started by Kem's twenty-year-old daughter. Kem chose this context to mention his plans because that fight had at the time generated other fights, one of which constituted the reason why villagers no longer would cooperate in the youth group. In reaffirming his intention to go through with the conciliatory feast, Kem is requesting help. To perform the feast, various people on Kem's 'side' (that is, his kin group and the matrilineal clan of his daughter) must help him by contributing prestige food like white rice and sugar, and garden produce like bananas and yams to the prestation of food that will be delivered to the injured man. Kem cannot and should not amass all of this by himself. Here he is indicating that others should begin collecting money and thinking about the state of their gardens so that they will be able to assist him in carrying out the conciliatory feast.

This dimension of Kem's talk is what the villagers call 'hidden' (*i hait*/*ambugar*). Kem supplies no explicit information regarding his intention to sponsor the feast (except to say, obliquely, 'I'm still getting ready' [he doesn't say for what]: line 21), he gives no background information, and his referents are left unspecified (he mentions only 'this little [unnamed] problem': line 13). In order to grasp the meaning 'underneath' Kem's words, his listeners must be intimately acquainted with village affairs, and they must connect their knowledge of those affairs to Kem's one brief clue: his sudden mention of his wife's illness. By introducing the notion of sickness, of inability, into his talk, Kem blithely alerts the villagers that he is in fact unable to carry out all the preparations for the feast by himself, and that those listening should begin thinking about helping him. This is as close as Kem comes to a direct request for help. It was effective, however, because shortly after this talk, several of Kem's relatives did indeed begin making small preparations for the conciliatory feast.

The most important thing to keep in mind about Kem's speech is that the way in which he uses language to present himself and his situation is in keeping with the villagers' ideas about the expression of social sensitivity and of not 'giving *hed*'. By portraying himself as a poor man with a sick wife, Kem lays the foundation for a reaction based on sympathy. The response from Kem's listeners will not arise out of any sense of threat or force. Instead, it will be generated from within themselves. The people listening to this speech will feel moved to help him out of their own sense of social solidarity and goodwill. By correctly interpreting the hidden message in Kem's talk and by coming to his assistance, the

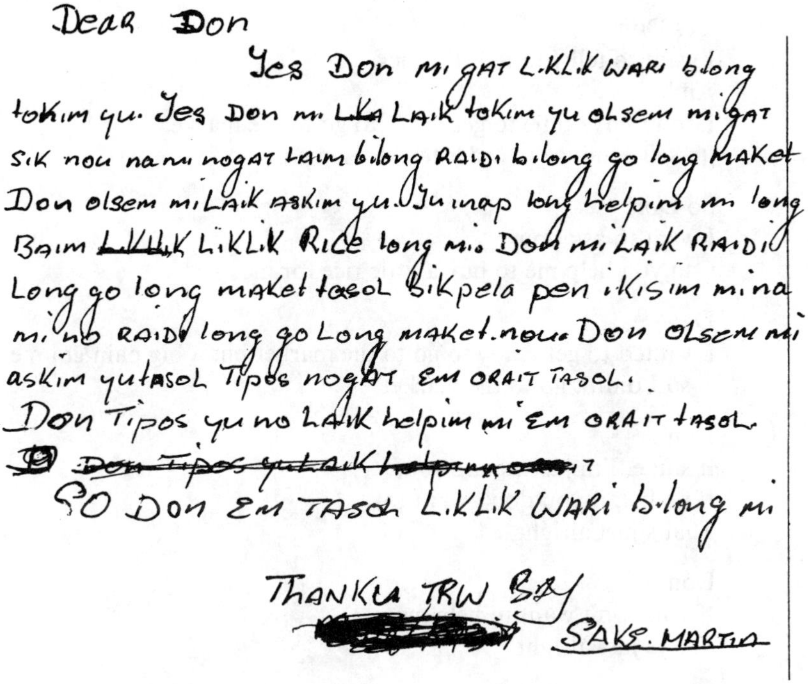

Dear Don

Yes Don mi gat L.KLiK WARi bilong tokim yu. Jes Don mi LKA LAik tokim yu olsem mi gat sik nou namu nogat taim bilong RAiDi bilong go long maket Don olsem mi LAik askim yu. Ju inap long helpim mi long Baim LiKLiK LiKLiK RiCE long mi. Don mi LAik RAiDi Long go long maket tasol sikpela pen i Kisim mina mi no RAiDi long go Long maket. nou Don olsem mi askim yu tasol Tipos nogat em ORAiT TASOL. Don Tipos yu no LAik helpim mi em ORAiT tasol. Don Tipos yu Laik helpim mi em ORAiT? SO Don Em TASOL L.KLiK WARi bilong mi

Thankiu TRW Bax SAKE. MARTin

Figure 1.3 Letter to Kulick from Allan Kasia and Sake Martin.

listeners of this speech can seize the opportunity provided by Kem to display their *save*.

From talk to text

We have dwelled on these characteristics of Kem's oratory because this particular way of using words has been carried over to the villagers' notes to one another. Notes in Gapun are oratories compressed and written down. This is exemplified by a note sent to Kulick by a village couple in their thirties. The note was delivered about a week before Kem's large conciliatory feast (the one he alludes to in his speech above) was due to be held.

Dear Don

Yes Don
I have a little worry to tell you.

Yes Don
I want to tell you that I'm sick
And
I don't have time to get ready to go to the market
[to sell produce in order to earn some money].

So Don
I want to ask you.
Can you help me to buy a little rice for me.

Don
I wanted to get ready to go to the market but a big pain got me
  so I didn't go to the market.

Don
It's like, I'm just asking you.
If no [i.e. if you don't want to]
That's just alright.

Don
If you don't want to help me,
That's just alright.

Don [crossed out]
If you want to help, alright ... [crossed out]

So Don
that's it, my little worry.

Thank You Truly
By
Allan Kasia [crossed out]
Sake Martin[6]

The parallels with Kem's speech in the men's house should be fairly
clear. The note begins with the formulaic opening phrase that villagers
with some schooling have learned to use in letters: '*Dear*'. But directly
after that comes a new opening, this time the oral marker of formal speech
'*Yes*'. This is followed by the formulaic 'I have a little worry [to tell you]'.
Just as orators use these phrases to assume the floor and announce their
intention to deliver a formal speech, so are they used in the villagers'
writing. Kulick here is not being written to so much as orated at. Note

also the frequent use of the name 'Don'. This would appear to serve the same segmenting function as 'And' in Kem's speech.

In a way markedly similar to Kem, the authors of this note first make a statement – in this case a request – only to then dissociate themselves from that statement/request and diminish its implications by in effect apologising for having made it at all. Like Kem, who spends a great deal of verbiage establishing that the villagers' work 'is good' when what he is really addressing in his talk is the fact that the 'work' has broken down completely, Sake and Allan spend more words in their note telling the recipient that he doesn't have to 'help' them than persuading him that he should help them. Like Kem's words, the overall effect of this kind of discourse is that it makes it difficult to accuse Sake and Allan of being assuming, presumptuous or pushy.

Even though this note is more direct in making a request than is Kem's speech, it still contains a great deal of indirection, and no background or contextual information is explicitly given. But in order to be able to respond to the note in an appropriate manner, the recipient must be familiar with village affairs. The note assumes that Kulick not only is aware of the impending conciliatory feast, but that he also knows how much rice Sake and Allan are expected to provide. In this case, the request for 'a little rice' is a somewhat forced diminutive, since both the sender and the receiver of the message know that for Sake and Allan to adequately fulfil their social responsibilities during the feast, at least twenty-five kilos of rice is required. Furthermore, the reader of this note is expected to be able to get 'behind' the words and understand that Sake and Allan are not requesting a contribution to help them buy rice – as they explicitly state. What they want and expect is for Kulick to buy the entire twenty-five kilos of rice for them.

The final point of similarity between Kem's talk in the men's house and this note is the amount of work done on self-effacement and the creation of a context in which the listener/recipient can demonstrate his *save*. As in Kem's talk, this is built up partly through the use of diminutives ('a little worry'; 'a little rice') and partly by the introduction of the notion of sickness, of inability. Again, the authors of the note are seeking to avoid, just as Kem did in his talk, giving the impression of forcefulness and insistence. They are not really making a request, it is implied, they are merely bringing some compelling facts about sickness to the attention of the recipient of the note, leaving him to act on those facts. How he reacts is up to him. He can respond on the basis of his *save* and display social solidarity with the afflicted person, or he may not. In any case, the decision is his. He cannot claim at some point to have been 'pushed' into doing something he didn't want to do.

Writing consensus

Just as their ideas about their place in the world in relation to God, white people and the Cargo have influenced the villagers' perceptions and uses of literacy, so have their understandings about themselves as persons played an important role in shaping how they have incorporated literacy skills into village life. Villagers' notions about the self as stubbornly autonomous and vitriolic contribute to the formation of a general social climate in which almost any type of interpersonal interaction is potentially fraught with conflict. This is especially the case with requests, since by asking another person to do something, one comes perilously close to confronting him or her – the boundary between a request and an order is as narrow as the listener's interpretation.

To lessen this potential for conflict, Gapuners have developed particular ways of making requests, involving conventions of indirection and dissociation, which greatly reduce the chance of their being interpreted as infringements or demands. Writing has presented the villagers with another powerful means of distancing themselves from their words when making requests. In notes like the one sent by Sake and Allan, the symbolic distance between a speaker and his words is multiply underscored: not only is the message delivered by a third party, but the words themselves have been fixed on paper and have physically travelled through space away from the speaker/writer. Gapuners have thus seized upon a particular dimension of writing – its potential for spatial extension – and they have elaborated that dimension in the context of their relationships to one another. Requests made in notes spare both writers and recipients the shame and embarrassment and potential for direct conflict that arise when a request is made in person. Also even the rhetorical dissociative force of direct speech is retained in most cases, because notes are structured as spoken requests embedded in discursive strategies which involve indirection and reneging.[7] In these senses, it can be said that the very structure of the villagers' writing has been shaped by local ideas concerning *save* and appropriate ways of handling social relationships.

Contextualised talk, hidden talk, and literacy

But the fact that language is so tightly linked with the expression of *save*,[8] of social sensitivity and cognisance, in Gapun has consequences beyond the structure and delivery of village notes. Because the main emphasis on speech in the community is on the expression of consensus and agreement, the point of talk becomes not so much to debate facts and express thoughts as it is to elaborate and manipulate social relationships. Kem's oratory in the previous section illustrates this. An important aspect of this speech is that it is not concerned with establishing or elaborating factual matters. Kem says nothing in his talk not already well known to each of his listeners: everybody knows that the village youth group has not performed any work for months and everybody knows why, the reason for the breakup being that the man who was president of the youth group had chased several other villagers brandishing an axe during a major fight in the village. The problem was that an impasse had been reached. Villagers would not work as part of the youth group if the president did not first compensate them for having swung an axe at them. The president, however, was a young man who clearly had no intention of doing this.

What Kem does in his oratory is attempt, in effect, to rework the factual situation at hand and lay the way open for a new interpretation of the problem. Even though Kem's role in the conflict which has resulted in the villagers refusing to work together in the youth group was extremely peripheral, he invites villagers in his speech to realign their understanding of the conflict so that he, and not the president of the youth group, becomes the focus of attention. One advantage of such a realignment is that Kem fully intends to organise (and later did organise) a conciliatory feast in order to straighten the 'problem from earlier' (that is, the fight started by his daughter, which indirectly led to the axe-swinging incident) that he refers to. The villagers, if they accept this new interpretation of who has responsibility for compensating them, will eventually receive compensation, even if it isn't from the youth group president.

This dimension of Kem's use of language reflects the fact that talk in Gapun is to a great extent concerned with establishing an intersubjectively constructed framework within which meaning can be publicly negotiated. Villagers are not really interested in the pure referential and propositional characteristics of language. They do not argue academic points nor do they dispute the absolute correctness of facts. Instead, the presentation and evaluation of utterances and actions as good or bad, true or false, and wrong or right varies with the social contexts in which they are presented and were performed. In order to be able to make such evaluations, all actions and utterances are embedded by the villagers in the context of their ongoing social relationships. Gapuners do not own radios, read newspapers or have access to other depersonalised sources of information, and so whatever they know about other people and other places, they know through their own experience or through the stories of others. In this way, knowledge about anything is ultimately anchored in the talkers and in the social contexts in and about which they speak. There is no notion of decontextualised or objective knowledge in the village. And consequently, as in the case of the fight referred to by Kem in his speech, the actual factual basis of an issue or a conflict can unproblematically be disregarded and reworked through language to better fit with current social realities (see Read 1955, articles in Watson-Gegeo and White 1990).

As far as literacy is concerned, this emphasis on contextualisation has the consequence that all written material must also become embedded through language into village relationships. In practice, this means that written messages are always accompanied by oral elaboration. Villagers reject messages sent without messengers. In one of the few cases in which this occurred during 1986–7, it involved a note sent to the villagers from the prayer leader in Bien, a village about four hours away by motor-powered canoe from Gapun. This prayer leader wrote the note asking the villagers to contribute fifty Kina to the building of a trade store in Bien whose profits would go to the local church. The letter had been given to a village man passing through Bien, and he had no clear idea of its contents.

The letter was read aloud by Gapun's prayer leader during a meeting in the men's house and was dismissed out of hand. 'If he comes and tells me, if I see his face, then I'll consider', announced one man, referring to the writer of the note. Others waved away the letter saying, 'I have some questions to ask him that he has to answer first'. So in practice, a written message without oral accompaniment is disregarded. Never do the villagers answer a *pas* (written note) with another *pas*. If they wonder about the message contained in a *pas* or have questions, they let the matter drop until it is either forgotten or somebody comes to talk to them.

The oral contextualisation of written material is a necessary component of virtually every literacy event in the village. Notes from other villagers are read aloud and explained by the messenger bearing the note, telling the time has no meaning other than self-display, lists are made not for practical use but to be announced, written-down facts have no significance unless they are orally proclaimed.

A further consequence of the fact that language is continually contextualised in village social relationships is that words, what one actually says, are considered to indicate a sensitivity (*save*) as to what one *should* say in a given context, rather than what one might like to say. That is, what one says is generally interpreted as a willingness to show *save* and be agreeable. Words are not regarded, in themselves, as revealing a speaker's intentions or inner states. To discover these things, villagers direct their attention to what might lie beyond the words themselves. They try to 'get behind' a person's words. What the speaker really thinks is thought to be 'underneath' his/her words or 'inside' them. Language is said to have 'little little corners' which a listener must manoeuvre around in order to discover the meaning of an utterance.

Meaning in Gapun is in this way the responsibility of the listener or the recipient of speech. In this sense, village communicative expectations differ importantly from those common to middle-class Euro-Americans, among whom the burden of successful communication is seen to lie with the speaker, who is expected to strain to 'get across' his or her viewpoints and thoughts to the listener.[9] While speakers in Gapun hasten to accommodate listeners in terms of language choice, opinions and topic, considerations about *save* place them under no burden to make themselves clear or facilitate listener comprehension of what they say, and ideas about provocation make it advantageous for speakers to formulate themselves as vaguely as possible.

Such an understanding of communication as something the listener or recipient must sort out and make sense of has important consequences for the way in which literacy is perceived and used. In Gapun, it has given rise to what might be called the *truth-seeking* function of literacy. We noted above that the villagers, despite their acquisition of literate skills and their application of those skills in Christian contexts, still have failed to bring forth the Cargo they expected to get through the precise manipulation of the Word. In such a context, the cultural emphasis placed on the role of the listener/receiver and of the 'hidden' meanings in words provides explanations. There is a widespread assumption among the villagers that the 'true meaning' of religious texts is escaping them, because they lack the necessary background and contextual information to perceive all the 'little little meanings' contained in the words they read. Those who possess this knowledge, the Catholic priests and certain members of the government, are 'hiding' this necessary information from them, because for a variety of reasons they do not want Papua New Guineans to obtain white skin and the Cargo. Thus, all the villagers can hope to do is read and reread the texts they possess, as several village men spend a considerable amount of time doing, hoping that someday they may stumble onto a clue that will reveal to them the 'true' meaning of the words contained in their books.[10]

Conclusion

What we hope we have shown throughout this analysis is that the villagers of Gapun, with a characteristic Melanesian eye for the novel and the useful, have been active and creative in their encounter with literacy. The matter has not so much been one of literacy 'taking hold' of Gapun, as it has been of Gapuners seizing hold of those dimensions of literacy for which they consider they have the most use. Throughout this process, the wishes and goals concerning literacy of the Church and the school have remained largely peripheral. The villagers of Gapun have their own ideas about reading and writing, generated from their own cultural concerns. It has been and continues to be these ideas, and not externally generated and culturally foreign ones which they apply to the written word in the village.

The villagers have not been 'transformed' by literacy. If anything, they themselves have 'transformed' it.

In demonstrating that point, we have been addressing ourselves to several related issues at once. First of all we have been concerned that the data presented here should have relevance for the controversy about literacy currently taking place in that part of the world from which the data were gathered, namely the Pacific. It seems to us that in this debate, neither the position of the SIL missionary linguists nor that of scholars like Peter Mühlhäusler is totally valid, because the discussion is being carried on with too little awareness of how Melanesians and Pacific islanders actually think about literacy and how they apply their literacy skills in their day to day lives. Lack of this kind of fundamental knowledge leads both positions to downplay the creativity and cultural concerns of those people being taught to read and write in this area. More research on this topic is sorely needed.

Secondly, the analysis presented here is addressing this specific lacuna in our knowledge about literacy. In a recent paper on the introduction of literacy among the Diyari of Australia, Charles Ferguson pointed out that 'although many of the recent literacy studies are ethnographic in perspective ... we still have very few descriptive studies of the introduction of literacy into particular non-literate societies' (1987: 223). We hope that this account of literacy patterns in Gapun will help to fill that gap, and will contribute to a broader understanding of the kinds of processes that are involved when a non-literate society begins to incorporate literacy skills into its communicative repertoire.

Finally, we see our discussion as fitting into the broader and increasingly more nuanced way of looking at literacy that has been emerging in recent years in the ethnographic work of scholars like Heath (1982, 1983), Scollon and Scollon (1981), Street (1984) and Duranti and Ochs (1986). Thanks to studies like these, we are beginning to fully appreciate and explore the implications of the fact that literacy, like other technologies, is culturally shaped. It is our hope that this study of the way in which villagers in a small village in Papua New Guinea have shaped their literacy will contribute, together with the ideas expressed in works like those just cited, to a more pronounced shift of emphasis away from a view of people as being passively transformed by literacy to an understanding and analysis of the active and creative role which people play in the cultural construction of literacy.

Notes

Fieldwork in Gapun was carried out for fifteen months during 1986–87 by the first author and for three months during the same period by the second author. We are deeply indebted in the villagers of Gapun for teaching us and allowing us to become part of their lives. We also gratefully acknowledge funding from the Swedish Agency for Research Cooperation with Developing Countries (SAREC) and the Swedish Council for Research in the Humanities and Social Sciences (HSFR). This paper has benefited greatly from comments on earlier drafts by Tomas Gerholm, Shirley Brice Heath, Kenneth Hyltenstam and Eija Kuyumcy, and from editorial suggestions by Brian Street.

1 Even before it was published, the main points of Mühlhäusler's (1990) paper had been disseminated and debated among SIL workers through the periodical *Intercom* (October 1986–March 1987 issues). Aspects of the relationship between the SIL and literacy in Papua New Guinea have also been discussed by Mühlhäusler 1989, Gilliam 1984 and Lynch 1979.

2 Apparently government policy has changed somewhat on this point since fieldwork was conducted, and since 1989 the official policy seems to be one of encouraging, at least, vernacular pre-school, followed by 'bridging classes' for grade one (Renck 1990: vii). Because this policy assumes the existence of vernacular-speaking teachers, it is irrelevant for Gapun, where no such teachers exist. The only consequence it could have is the increased use of Tok Pisin in the primary school that village children attend, although even this seems doubtful, since the policy seems aimed at encouraging vernacular languages, not Tok Pisin.

3 See Meggitt's 1968 discussion of the uses of literacy among the Mae Enga of Papua New Guinea.

4 Related to this is the belief that villagers have about schooling after death. A number of people explained in several different contexts that after villagers die, they first of all 'change skin' (*sensim skin*) and become white. Thereafter they materialise in Rome, where they spend their days *going to school*. Once they have *kisim save* (received/comprehended knowledge), they then go on to Heaven, where they are united with their relatives and ancestors. For a more detailed description of the villagers' ideas about school, see Kulick 1992. See also Swatridge 1985.

5 Underlined utterances were spoken in the village vernacular, Taiap. Nonunderlined utterances were spoken in Tok Pisin. For an analysis of the villagers' code-switching patterns, see Kulick and Stroud 1990b, Stroud 1992.

6 This note was written by Sake's husband Allan (Sake herself is virtually illiterate). Allan crossed out his name at the end of the note, however, in what clearly is an attempt to emphasise that Sake is the one most affected by Kulick's decision about whether or not to 'help' the couple buy the rice. In order to fully understand this gesture, it is necessary to know that Sake and Allan were Kulick's adoptive mother and father in Gapun, and they helped him and looked after him in innumerable ways. By presenting Sake as the recipient of the rice (and as the one who will be shamed should she not produce any rice during the conciliatory feast), the couple is subtly reminding Kulick of the responsibilities and feelings of helpfulness and sympathy that one should properly have towards one's mother.

7 Messages delivered on behalf of others by children or others never contain this element of rhetoric, but are usually short and formulaic, consisting of the single phrase: '*X tok long Y*' ('X wants [literally, speaks of] Y').

8 Even *kroses* (pp. 43–4) are in a significant sense ways of displaying one's *save*, even though on the surface they appear to be inflammatory and socially disruptive. Actually *kroses* are attempts at re-establishing a public consensus, since after the protagonists have satisfied their desire to publicly abuse and accuse, the matter is considered settled, or will result in some sort of settlement being arranged. It is considered far more dangerous when a person who feels wronged or offended does not 'talk out', because then the grievance will *stap sting long bel* (remain and rot in the stomach – the seat of one's emotions) and *givim tingting nogut* (give bad – that is anti-social – thoughts) to the offended person. 'Bad thoughts' are associated with dark powers outside the control of the villagers. In the case of big men, such thoughts may cause their ancestors or *tambaran* to 'give pain' to the offender or one of his or her matrilineal relatives. In other cases, 'bad thoughts' may drive a person to seek out the services of a sorcerer to kill the offender.

9 Reddy 1979 discusses in detail some of the implications of this Euro-American view of communication. For analyses of the consequences that a listener-centered view of communication has among various groups, see Clancy 1986 and Brett-Smith 1984.

10 The observation should be considered in light of Mühlhäusler's recent contention that in Papua New Guinea 'printed messages are regarded as inherently true by the first few generations of literates' (1990: 203). On the basis of our understandings of literacy in Gapun, we would dispute such a general claim. It appears that Gapun villagers do not regard written texts as any more 'inherently true' than people's words. Like spoken words, printed messages may not be 'straight'. A text may contain 'little little corners' and it may enclose its meaning in boxes, just like talk does. There are certainly truths to be found in a printed text, and this is what villagers spend time looking for. But the search for truth in texts does not differ in any substantial way from the way in which the villagers extract truths from 'inside' or 'behind' spoken words.

This whole matter of truth becomes even more subtle and contorted if recent anthropological discussions on the nature of truth and deception in Melanesian societies are considered. In light of these discussions, the question becomes whether anything at all in a large number of Melanesian societies can be said to be believed to be 'inherently true'. We find it significant, for example, that a central tenet of the ritual activities of a great many Melanesian groups appears to turn on what Barth (1987: 70) calls 'the meta-premise ... that things are not what they appear on the surface' (cf. Strathern 1987, 1988; Tuzin 1980). It seems clear to us that such a 'meta-premise' is not confined to the goings-on in the men's house, but is also involved in the Gapun villagers' view of language as 'hiding' a variety of different meanings.

References

Barth, F. 1987. *Cosmologies in the making*. Cambridge: Cambridge University Press.
Brett-Smith, S. C. 1984. 'Speech made visible: the irregular as a system of meaning', *Empirical Studies of the Arts*, 2: 127–47.

Brison, K. 1989. 'All talk and no action?: Saying and doing in Kwanga meetings', *Ethnology*, 28(2): 97–115.

Clanchy, M. 1979. *From memory to written record 1066–1307*. London: Edward Arnold.

Clancy, P. 1986. 'The acquisition of communicative style in Japanese', in B. Schieffelin and E. Ochs (eds.), *Language socialization across cultures*. Cambridge: Cambridge University Press.

Cole, M. and Scribner, S. 1981. *The psychology of literacy*. Cambridge, MA: Harvard University Press.

Cook-Gumperz, J. (ed.), 1986. *The social construction of literacy*. Cambridge: Cambridge University Press.

Duranti, A. and Ochs, E. 1986. 'Literacy instruction in a Samoan village', in B. Schieffelin and P. Gilmore (eds.), *The acquisition of literacy: ethnographic perspectives*. Norwood, NJ: Ablex.

Ferguson, C. 1987. 'Literacy in a hunting-gathering society: the case of the Diyari', *Journal of Anthropological Research*, 43: 223–37.

Finnegan, R. 1988. *Literacy and orality: studies in the technology of communication*. Oxford: Blackwell.

Franklin, K. 1975. 'Vernaculars as bridges to cross cultural understanding', in K. McElhanon (ed.), *Tok Pisin i go we*. Kivung Special Publication no. 1. Port Moresby, Papua New Guinea.

Gilliam, A. 1984. 'Language and "development" in Papua New Guinea', *Dialectical Anthropology*, 8: 303–18.

Goody, J. 1977. *Domestication of the savage mind*. Cambridge: Cambridge University Press.

1986. *The logic of writing and the organization of society*. Cambridge: Cambridge University Press.

Havelock, E. 1976. *Origins of western literacy*. Toronto: Ontario Institute for Studies in Education.

Heath, S. B. 1982. 'What no bedtime story means: narrative skills at home and school', *Language in Society*, 11: 49–76.

1983. *Ways with words*. Cambridge: Cambridge University Press.

Kulick, D. 1992. *Language shift and cultural reproduction: socialisation, self and syncretism in a Papua New Guinean village*. New York: Cambridge University Press.

Kulick, D. and Stroud, C. 1990a. 'Christianity, cargo and ideas of self: patterns of literacy in a Papua New Guinean village', *Man*, 25: 286–303.

1990b. 'Code-switching in Gapun: social and linguistic aspects of language use in a language shifting community', in J. Verhaar (ed.), *Melanesian Pidgin and Tok Pisin*. Amsterdam: John Benjamins.

in press. 'The structure of the Taiap (Gapun) language', in T. Dutton, M. Ross and D. Tryon (eds.), *The language game: papers in memory of Donald C. Laycock*. Canberra: Pacific Linguistics.

Lawrence, P. 1964. *Road Belong Cargo*. Melbourne: Melbourne University Press.

Laycock, D. and Z'graggen, J. 1975. 'The Sepik-Ramu Phylum', in S. Worm (ed.), *New Guinea area languages and language study. Vol. 1: Papuan languages and the New Guinea linguistic scene*. Canberra Linguistics C-42.

Lederman, R. 1984. 'Who speak here?: Formality and the politics of gender in Mendi, Highland Papua New Guinea', in D. Brenneis and F. Myers (eds.), *Dangerous words: language and politics in the Pacific*. New York and London: New York University Press.

Lindstrom, L. 1990. 'Straight talk on Tanna', in K. A. Watson-Gegeo and G. M. White (eds.), 1990.

Lynch, J. 1979. 'Church, state and language in Melanesia'. Inaugural lecture delivered at University of Papua New Guinea, 28 May 1979.

McKellin, W. 1984. 'Putting down roots: information in the language of Managalase exchange', in D. Brenneis and F. Myers (eds.), *Dangerous words: language and politics in the Pacific*. New York and London: New York University Press.

1990. 'Allegory and inference: intentional ambiguity in Managalase negotiations', in K. A. Watson-Gegeo and G. M. White (eds.), 1990.

Meggitt, M. 1968. 'Uses of literacy in New Guinea and Melanesia', in J. Goody, (ed.), *Literacy in traditional societies*. Cambridge: Cambridge University Press.

Morauta, L. 1974. *Beyond the village: local politics in Madang, Papua New Guinea*. University of London: The Athone Press.

Mühlhäusler, P. 1977. 'The social role of Pidgin in Papua New Guinea today', in S. Wurm (ed.), *New Guinea area languages and languages study. Vol. 3: Language, culture, society and the modern world*. Canberra: Pacific Linguistics C-40.

1989. 'On the causes of accelerated language change in the Pacific area', in L. E. Breivik and E. H. Jahr (eds.), *Language change: contributions to the study of its causes*. Berlin and New York: Mouton de Gruyter.

1990. '"Reducing" Pacific languages to writing', in T. J. Taylor (ed.), *Ideologies of language*. London: Croom Helm.

Olson, D. 1977. 'From utterance to text: the bias of language in speech and writing', *Harvard Educational Review*, 47(3): 257–81.

Ong, W. 1982. *Orality and literacy*. London: Methuen.

Read, K. 1955. 'Morality and the concept of the person among the Gahuku-Gama', *Oceania*, 25(4): 233–82.

Reddy, M. 1979. 'The conduit metaphor – a case of frame conflict in our language about language', in A. Ortony (ed.), *Metaphor and thought*. Cambridge: Cambridge University Press.

Renck, G. 1990. *Contextualization of Christianity and Christianisation of language*. Erlangen: Verlag der Ev.-Luth. Mission Erlangen.

Scollon, R. and Scollon, S. 1981. *Narrative, literacy and face in interethnic communication*. Norwood, NJ: Ablex.

Strathern, M. 1987. 'Making incomplete: a comment on female initiation in Melanesia'. MS.

1988. *The gender of the gift*. Berkeley: University of California Press.

Street, B. 1984. *Literacy in theory and practice*. Cambridge: Cambridge University Press.

Stroud, C. 1992. 'The problem of intention and meaning in code-switching', *Text* 12(1): 127–55.

Stubbs, M. 1980. *Language and literacy*. London: Routledge and Kegan Paul.

Swatridge, C. 1985. *Delivering the goods: education as cargo in Papua New Guinea.* Manchester: Manchester University Press.
Townsend, W. C. 1963. *Who brought the Word.* Wycliffe Bible Translators, Inc.
Tuzin, D. 1980. *The voice of the tambaran.* Berkeley and Los Angeles: University of California Press.
Watson-Gegeo, K. A. and White, G. M. (eds.), 1990. *Disentangling: conflict discourse in Pacific societies.* Stanford, CA: Stanford University Press.

2

LITERACY AND FEELINGS: THE ENCODING OF AFFECT IN NUKULAELAE LETTERS

NIKO BESNIER

'Papauta, Sept. 13, 1897

To Mrs. David, the lady, –

My love to you! alas my mother! The thought weeps when I think of you, together with the others, because of your kindness to me. Alas for my love! Dear, oh dear, my heart is full of love, but it is difficult because I cannot speak; but I thought I would try and send this small piece of paper to make known to you my love. Alas my mother! my love is very great, and it is difficult and hard because we shall be so soon parted. Grief continues to grow in my heart when I think of the days we were together in Funafuti. Alas! I do not forget them and you all. I feel I want to be still with you. It is hard that we have been so soon parted on shore. May you return with blessing to your home. This love of mine has nothing with which to make itself known, but I have striven to make appear before you that which was hidden, namely, my love to you. Alas, my parents, love is difficult.

This letter is hurriedly written. May Jehovah remain with us both when we are separated. Good bye.

May you live! VITOLIA.

(David 1899: 88–9)

At the end of the last century, Lady Caroline David accompanied a geological research team led by her husband to the atoll of Funaafuti, then a remote colonial outpost in the Central Pacific. After her return to Australia, she received this letter from a young Funaafuti woman who had been studying at the mission school for girls in Samoa, and subsequently quoted it in the narrative of her three-month sojourn on the atoll, a treasure of information about Victorian perceptions of Funaafuti society at the end of the nineteenth century. By the time this 'wailing letter' (David 1899: 89) was written, thirty years had elapsed since the introduction of literacy to Funaafuti. This letter, the original of which was presumably written in Samoan, thus represents one of the earliest recorded samples of writing by a Funaafuti Islander.

The historical records are too scanty to enable us to judge the extent to which Vitolia's letter represents the written output of nineteenth-century

Funaafuti Islanders; yet her letter bears a striking resemblance to the written texts that members of the same society produce today. What triggers such wailing, such outpourings of love and grief? Why does so much affect surface in a written text at such an early date after the introduction of literacy to a culture? Under what circumstances does a society exploit the written medium for such purposes?

This chapter[1] is a study of the linguistic encoding of affect in letters written by Nukulaelae Islanders, who inhabit a small isolated atoll of the Tuvalu group (formerly the Ellice Islands), 65 nautical miles to the south of Funaafuti. Taking as a point of departure a quantitative study of the distribution of affect markers across Nukulaelae spoken and written registers (Besnier 1988), this study is a qualitative analysis of how affect is encoded in letters, a register which the quantitative analysis singled out for the high incidence of grammatical affect markers. This chapter addresses two questions: What type of affect do Nukulaelae islanders express in their letters? What linguistic strategies do Nukulaelae islanders exploit to express this affect? In this study, a broad definition of 'affect' is adopted, encompassing not only the linguistic encoding of emotions, but also the expression of attitudes and points of view, stance and moods, both toward the propositional content of the discourse and toward the communicative context (Ochs and Schieffelin 1989).

While considerable progress has been made in the last few years toward an understanding of the role and nature of affective meaning in oral discourse (Haviland 1987; Irvine 1982; Labov 1984; Lutz and White 1986; Ochs and Schieffelin 1989), little attention has been paid to date to the communication of affect in writing in any speech community. The little research that has addressed the question of writing and affect has mostly focused on Western literacy genres (for example, Haviland 1984), and not on the day-to-day written output of members of speech communities. Thus, we do not have a basis on which to compare the role of affect in spoken and written communication. This paper attempts to fill this lacuna; it puts forward a number of proposals to explain the form of affective displays in writing on Nukulaelae. The extent to which these explanations hold cross-culturally remains to be tested.

Written communication and affect

Underlying the questions addressed in this paper is the need to examine more closely the role of affect in writing. Many researchers have maintained that written communication is typically less affective than oral communication (Chafe 1982; Chafe and Danielewicz 1987; DeVito 1966, 1967; Redeker 1984). These scholars maintain that, while the immediacy of an audience allows speakers to invoke more personal elements in spoken discourse, writers can afford to do so considerably less, because of the lack of a visible audience. The symptoms of this difference are the greater incidence, in spoken language, of linguistic features like personal pronouns, references to the speaker's mental processes ('I think that', and so on), expressions like 'you know', emphatic particles, hedges, and direct quotes. These features have all been characterised in research on affect as strategies with which high affect is encoded in many languages (Irvine 1982; Ochs and Schieffelin 1989).

Tannen (1982a, 1982b), Biber (1986), and Besnier (1988) all challenge the characterisation of speaking as an affectively charged communicative activity and of writing as a medium in which little affect surfaces. Tannen and Biber show that, in English, some types of writing are more affect-laden than some types of speaking, and vice-versa. While the salience of affect is an important factor in distinguishing some spoken genres from some written genres, it is not useful in explaining the differences between all spoken and written genres.

It is clear that what has led earlier researchers to conclude that written language is more 'objective' and less affective than speaking is the fact that the data that they have typically based their research on is academic writing, in which writers are expected to pose as objective and un-emotional. It is surprising that little research has focused on the structure of more run-of-the-mill written registers like personal letters as communicative events and linguistic genres (Gillogly 1984; Mikulecky 1985; Mulkay 1985; Rubinstein and Gajdušek 1970; Scribner and Cole 1981). Yet letters represent a major portion of the written output of members of numerous societies, including mainstream Western middle-class society. This paper is thus a contribution to the cross-cultural study of a little-studied written register.

To test the cross-linguistic validity of Tannen's and Biber's conclusions about spoken- and written-language relationships, I conducted a statistical analysis of the distribution of selected linguistic features across 152 texts from 7 Nukulaelae spoken and written registers, including 40 of the letters analysed for this paper (Besnier 1988). The linguistic features used in that study include, among others, morphological and syntactic markers of affect like intensifiers, pronouns, hedges, and ergative case-marking (shown in Besnier 1988 to have important affect-encoding functions). The patterns of co-occurrence of these features across texts of the corpus define a number of dimensions, along which the structural similarities and differences between text types can be measured. One of the most striking results of this analysis is the fact that letters rank higher than any other Nukulaelae spoken or written register in terms of affective-involvement markers. Letters also rank higher than four of the six registers along the dimension labelled 'affective intensity'. The general conclusion I drew from this study is that the extent to which the members of a speech community allow affect to surface in a particular register, whether spoken or written, is a function of the communicative norms at play in the society, and not an inherent consequence of orality and literacy. I suggested that, on Nukulaelae, letters are used to channel certain types of affective displays which are not judged as appropriate in face-to-face interactions. What these affective displays are and what form they take is what this paper addresses.

The speech community

Nukulaelae's population of 350 is predominantly Polynesian in origin, culture, and social organisation. Despite recent changes, the economy is essentially a subsistence economy based on fishing, the cultivation of swamp taro, and the gathering of coconuts.

Nukulaelae Islanders first came into contact with Westerners in 1821, but had few opportunities to interact with the rest of the world until the end of the century. During the 1860s, within a very short period of time, Nukulaelae islanders converted to Christianity, and, concurrently, learned how to read and write; both Christianity and literacy were introduced by missionary-pastors from neighbouring Samoa. At the same time, the Samoan pastors reorganised virtually every aspect of the social and political life of the atoll by deposing the island chiefs and establishing a near-theocracy based on their interpretation of the Scriptures. The context in which literacy was introduced was thus one of great social change (Brady 1975; Munro 1982).

Literacy activities on Nukulaelae were not conducted in Tuvaluan until recently. For many decades after the introduction of Christianity and of literacy, Samoan remained the language in which religious activities, interactions with the outside world, and reading and writing were conducted. Samoan ceased to be the official language of local government in the Ellice Islands in 1931 and that of the Church in 1958. Even though most adults understand Samoan, the use of Samoan for writing has virtually disappeared. The Tuvaluan dialect used in writing today is the Funaafuti dialect, which differs very slightly from the Nukulaelae dialect.

Until recently, the extreme isolation of the atoll and the resulting exclusion of its population from the economic life of other Pacific islands meant that there were very few opportunities and very little motivation to learn English. Today, the situation is rapidly changing, and the pressure to learn English for academic and economic success is increasing rapidly. But few individuals on Nukulaelae are proficient enough in English to write it (with some notable exceptions, which include a published writer), and English literacy conventions have had only a minor influence on the written texts produced on Nukulaelae.

Nukulaelae letters

Barely twenty years after the introduction of literacy, a visitor to the atoll commented: 'The Nukulailai [*sic*] people ... are well educated, can all read, and are most persistent letter writers. No present is more acceptable to them than a few sheets of paper and some pens ... We nearly ran out of ink before we got clear of the group' (Bridge 1886: 554). Even today, writing letters is the most salient activity in which writing skills are put into practice.

Personal letters (*tusi alofa*, literally: 'letters of empathy') are the primary link between Nukulaelae and the rest of the world. Nukulaelae residents do not usually use letters to communicate with each other within the confines of the atoll itself.[2] Letters are received about once a month when the government vessel calls at Nukulaelae, and are typically hand-carried by travellers. Some letters, particularly to and from relatives abroad, are sent through the mail, although this often poses problems because many people on Nukulaelae cannot afford stamps on a regular basis. A person planning to leave the atoll is usually the major motivation for writing letters, and the regularity of communication through letters with the outside world depends on people's movements to and from the atoll.

Every Nukulaelae adult and teenager writes letters, some much more frequently than others. But there does not appear to be a correlation between the frequency of letter-writing and age or gender. The corpus on which this study is based includes a broad range of letters; Table 2.1 summarises the composition of this corpus according to authors' gender and affiliation to emically recognised age categories.[3] The corpus comprises 145 letters, totalling 65,446 words of text (mean: 454 words per letter; standard deviation: 285). Letters are usually saved by their recipients and become part of the few personal possessions that every individual keeps in his or her trunk (*pausi*) stored in one corner of the house. This facilitated collecting these letters from their recipients.

The letters in the corpus are all addressed to close acquaintances and relatives of the writers, since Nukulaelae islanders rarely write to strangers. Some of the letters were written by Nukulaelae residents to relatives and friends on other islands, while others are letters home from Nukulaelae islanders temporarily away from the atoll: on Funaafuti, Tuvalu's capital; on Nauru, where Tuvaluans work as contract labourers for periods of two to three years; or on another island or abroad, studying or working. The text of Nukulaelae letters is sometimes paragraphed,

Table 2.1. *Composition of the corpus of letters by author*

Age and gender group	Number of writers	Number of letters
Adolescent men (*tamataene*)	14	29
Adolescent women (*tamaafine*)	20	42
Adult men (*taagata*)	7	16
Adult women (*faafine*)	14	32
Older men (*toeaina*)	5	17
Older women (*loomaattua*)	5	6
Unidentified writer	3	3
Total	68	145

particularly if the writer has had formal schooling. Older individuals tend to write their letters as continuous strings, with no paragraphing and little punctuation. As in all written texts, there are many idiosyncratic variations in the orthography used in letters, because Tuvaluan orthography is not standardised. Letters are emically recognised as a distinct communicative genre, but Nukulaelae Islanders do not distinguish between sub-categories of letters.

Affect in Nukulaelae letters

Nukulaelae letters may have a variety of social functions. Letters may also be simply motivated by the writer's need to reaffirm social bonds with particular people, and, thus, many have a phatic function. They may be tools through which economic transactions are monitored. News reporting is another possible reason for writing a letter. And a fourth common aspect of letters is admonitions from older people to younger relatives and friends. Many letters in the corpus have a multifarious function: the same letter, for example, may announce the arrival of a package, present information about current domestic events, and include a long, eloquent tirade asking the recipient to behave lovingly toward his relatives, not to drink sour toddy, and to go to church regularly.

Whatever their primary motivations may be, letters share one important characteristic: they are a medium in which affect is considerably more salient than in other Nukulaelae communicative contexts. The content of many letters, first of all, is *about* affect. Letters tell of crying, hoping, and longing; they ask for forgiveness for past and current wrongdoings; they express empathy, happiness, and love:[4]

> *A maaua i taimi katoa e maua ei nee maaua au tusi, e peelaa loa me*
> *sa aa te mea tafasili koo maua nee maaua i temaa fiaffia mo temaa*

*loto alofa kiaa koe. Teelaa laa, e faitau nee maaua au tusi kae ttagi,
ona ko te maafaufau atu moo koe.*

The two of us, every time we get a letter from you, it is like the
most joyous thing that happens to the two of us, given our love
for you in our hearts. Thus, we read them and cry, because we
keep thinking about you.   (letter 150)

[from a young woman on Niutao to her parents on Nukulaelae]
*Taapaa! [...] Kaati ko te vaaiaso teenaa ne masaki i ei a L, au i te
vaaiaso teenaa koo tagitagi faeloa kae manatu mai i te taeao kee
oko ki te afiafi. Taapaa! [...] Te maasei, au e tagi faeloa maa
kilokilo aka au ki te mataafaga. E. pelu laa naa ootou mea, ka ko
au teenei loa a tagitagi atu.*

Oh! [...] It was perhaps the week that L was sick, that week, I
kept crying and crying and thinking about you longingly from
morning till evening. Oh! [...] It is so bad, I always cry when I
look at the beach. While you are taking care of your daily
business, and I am here crying for you.   (letter 45)

[from a young woman on Nanumaga to her bond brother on
Nukulaelae]
*Ia, ee tuagaane, e peelaa loa mo tau muna teelaa ne fai mai ia taaua
koo ssai loa ttaa tuagaane. A aku koo oko loa i toku fiafia, koo see
fakattau mai loa. Aku foki koo oti ne fai ki oku maatua mo oku
tuagaane ttonu, koo oko loa i te fiaffia.*

So, my brother, regarding what you told me about our establishing an adoptive brother–sister relationship. I am absolutely
delighted about it. I also have told my parents and my blood
brothers, and they are very happy about it.   (letter 17)

[from a young man on Nukulaelae to a friend on Funaafuti]
*Ia, au e fakamolemole atu kiaa koe, kaafai seaku mea koo ssee,
fakamolemole mai.*

So, I am asking you, if I have done (or said) anything wrong, I
ask for your forgiveness.   (letter 11)

But even when affect is not the primary focus, it always lurks immediately below the surface of the discourse. It is conspicuous in discussions of
economic transactions, in news updates, and in the very fabric of the
frame of letters.

The affective displays characteristic of letters differ in nature and
intensity from affective displays found in other social contexts on
Nukulaelae. In particular, affect is expressed considerably more overtly

Table 2.2. *Distribution of selected emotion verbs*[5]

Emotion verb	Occurrence per 10,000 words in letters (N = 17200)	Occurrence per 10,000 words in conversations (N = 23809)
Alofa 'feel empathy, love, compassion, pity'	80 (n = 138)	15 (n = 36)
Fakamoemoe 'hope'	10 (n = 18)	< 1 (n = 1)
Fakatooese, fakamaagalo 'feel remorse, ask for forgiveness, excuse'	3 (n = 5)	< 1 (n = 1)
Fiafia 'happy'	15 (n = 26)	< 1 (n = 2)
Faanoanoa, see fiafia 'sad, unhappy'	6 (n = 10)	< 1 (n = 1)
Masau, masausau, manatu 'think of, long for'	20 (n = 34)	7 (n = 16)
Total	134 (n = 231)	24 (n = 57)

and intensely in letters than in face-to-face interactions. In casual conversation, for example, Nukulaelae islanders normally express affect through covert means (Besnier 1990), and affect-laden passages comparable to the above examples are very rare. In letters, in contrast, affect is overt.

Evidence of this is provided by counts of selected affect-denoting linguistic features. Emotion verbs, for example, are considerably more frequent in letters than in conversation. Table 2.2 displays the distribution of six categories of emotion verbs in a sample of forty letters from the corpus and in a corpus of twelve casual conversations (described in Besnier 1988) representing a cross-section of the types of conversational activities that take place in highly informal settings on the atoll. It is evident that emotion verbs are considerably more frequent in letters than in conversations, and hence that talk about affect is more frequent in letters.

Many of the norms that regulate the display of affect in other interpersonal contexts do not apply to letters. Letters exchanged between young male siblings display positive affect, while face-to-face interactions between young men always have a subtle undertone of negative competition that leaves little room for positive affect, particularly if the interactors are related:

> [from a male teenager to his teenage brother]
> *Mmoli atu alofaaga kia T mo te kaaiga, S mo te kaaiga, peelaa foki mo K i konaa, kae fakasilisili atu moo koe.*

> Send my love to T and his kin group, to S and his kin group, and also to K over at your end, but [my love] for you is strongest of all.　　　　　　　　　　　　　　　　　　　　　　　　(letter 20)

Letters between cousins of different sex also display as much affect as any other letter, even though avoidance taboos prevent cousins of different sex from talking to each other face-to-face, let alone exchanging any remotely affective language:[6]

> [from a man in his fifties on Nukufetau to his female cousin in her fifties on Nukulaelae]
> *Fakafetai foki moo taimi ne fakatasi ei taatou i konei, fakafetai. Koo malie katoa te loto i faifaiga ggali. Te fakamoemoe kee tuumau te loto feaalofani.*

> Thanks for the moments that we spent together here, thank you. *The heart is completely satisfied* with the beautiful actions [that took place then]. It is *hoped* that *the spirit of mutual love* will remain.   (letter 82)

The affective component of letters is thus ritualised enough to over-ride the norms of inter-personal conduct at play in other interactional contexts.

Why are letters such affect-laden events? Why is their affective content so salient? What is the nature of this affect? How is it encoded in the discourse? To answer these questions, I turn to various aspects of the form and function of letters. Taking as evidence the text of letters from the corpus, I shall demonstrate in this section that Nukulaelae writers consistently frame their letters as affect displays, and that the overtness and salience of the affect component of letters is a part of their social definition as a Nukulaelae communicative event. I shall first show that the ritualised framing devices that writers use in their letters are purely affective in nature. I shall then focus on the content of letters and argue that Nukulaelae letter writers have a strong tendency to highlight the affective component of whatever topic they address. This tendency is facilitated by the fact that affect is a pivotal element in the areas of social life that letters generally touch.

Discourse Frame

The text of Nukulaelae letters is overtly framed with the help of a number of specific framing markers, which are always present at the beginning and the end of the text.[7] Letters usually open with a greeting identical to the greeting used in face-to-face interactions (*taalofa* 'hello'). Then follow references to the health of everyone at the writer's and the recipient's ends, and a sometimes very long series of references to God's grace and kindness. While variations in the form and order of these introductory elements are found, most introductions follow a fairly set pattern:

[from a woman on Funaafuti to her mother on Nukulaelae]
*Taalofa koutou katoa! Fakafetai, e maallosi katoa loa maatou i
konei, kae koo ne maua foki nee maatou outou tusi, ne logo foki
maatou is S mo A, me e maallosi fua koutou. Ko te viikiga mo te
taavaega o ttou Tamana ki te see gata mai.*

Greetings to all of you! Thanks, we are all in good health at this
end, and we also have learnt from your letters, and have also
heard from S and A, that you are in good health. We praise and
glorify our Father for ever and ever. (letter 52)

[from a 75-year-old woman on Nukulaelae to her grand-daughter
in Australia]
*Fakafetai koo maua nee au se avanoa gali peenei o tusi atu ei nee au
te tusi teenei moo feiloai aka ei taaua. Ia, a kaafai e oko atu te tusi
teenei kae ttusa taaua i te alofa o te Atua. E avatu ei nee taaua te
fakafetai ki te Atua, auaa tena tausiiga alofa kia taaua te fakafetai
ki te Atua, auaa tena tausiiga alofa kia taaua te faanau see llei i ana
mua.*
*Ia, kae avaka nee taaua taavaega ki te see gata mai, e see gata mai
eiloa. Aamene. Ia, a maatou nei e maallosi fua. Ia, kaati laa koutou
foki i konaa, kaati e maallosi katoa.*

Thanks are due to the fact that I have this beautiful opportunity
to write you this letter so that we can both meet through it. And if
this letter reaches you, we are both equally under the protection
of God's love. We both send our thanks to God because he is
taking care of us, his sinful children before him. And we praise
him for ever and ever, for ever and ever. Amen.
So we are all in good health here. And perhaps the same applies
to all of you over there, perhaps you are all in good health.
(letter 21)

Self-deprecatory expressions are common in opening sequences. For
example, some writers state that it is their 'weak conjecture' (*fakattau
vaaivai*) or their 'silly opinion' (*manatu valea*) that the recipients are in
good health:

*E tuumau faeloa te ola mo te maalosi i luga i au i konei, mo te
<u>fakattau vaaivai</u> me e peenaa foki koulua i konaa.*

I am well and alive here [literally: life and good health are
constant upon me here], and my <u>weak conjecture</u> is that you two
are the same at your end. (letter 60)

*Au nei e maalosi fua, kae kaati e see taumate ko taaua fakatasi i te
laina e tasi. Kaafai laa e tonu te <u>manatu valea</u> teenei mai konei, [. . .]*

I am just in good health, and perhaps it is possible that both you and me are along the same line in this respect. If this <u>silly opinion</u> from this end is correct, [let us thank the Lord].   (letter 61)

These self-deprecatory statements commonly have ritualised religious connotations. Letter writers often refer to the fact that God's children are sinners by nature in opening sequences:

> *Fakafetai moo te alofa o ttou Tamana ki Tena tausiiga ki luga ia taatou, te faanau ssee mo te nofo sala i Ona mua.*

> Thanks [are due] to our Father for protecting us, <u>His wrong-doing children who stay in sin before Him.</u>   (letter 15)

Following these introductory remarks, a motivation for the letter is usually presented. Here, writers often refer to their letters as conversations (*sauttala*), in which the writer and the addressee 'meet' (*fetaui*):

> *Ia, a ko te ala o te tusi ko te fia <u>sauttala</u> atu mo koe.*

> So, the reason for the letter is that I want to <u>chat</u> with you.
>   (letter 136)

> *Fakafetai mo koo <u>fetaui</u> taatou i te lau pepa teenei. Ia, see ko mata, ka ko lau pepa.*

> Thanks for the fact that we can <u>meet</u> through this piece of paper. <u>It is not a face-to-face [encounter], but [one that takes place] through a piece of paper.</u>   (letter 42)

The same theme is sometimes referred to in the closing frame:

> *Ia, ttusi kaa fai o gata atu moo koulua, maatua pele i te loto, <u>a ko te fia sauttala atu mo koulua seki taaitai o gata</u>*

> So, the letter to you is about to end, beloved parents of my heart, <u>but the desire to chat with you is not about to end.</u>   (letter 10)

It is also in the opening sequence that writers may acknowledge having received earlier letters, which they invariably have read with great happiness (*mo te fiafia lasi*), or express their unhappiness (*faanoanoa*) about not having heard from the addressee:

> *Ia, P, fakafetai, me koo oti ne maua nee maatou au tusi kolaa ne aumai, mo tau uaeelesi foki koo oti ne maua nee au; ne faitau nee au mo te fiafia lasi.*

> So, P, thank you, because we have received the letters that you sent, along with your telegram, which we have also received; I read them <u>with great happiness.</u>   (letter 138)

Kae ko au e tai faanoanoa maalosi eiloa auaa maafai seki oko atu aku tusi i te oloatuuga a saa L. [. . .] Kae kaafai laa ne maua nee koutou, kae e aa, ko te mea loa ko au koo puli mo galo ia koutou?

As for me, I would be very sad indeed if the letters I sent along with L did not reach you. [. . .] But if you got them, so what is this, you have completely forgotten me?   (letter 27)

The closing sequence of letters always takes the form of long lists of people sending their *alofa* 'love, empathy, compassion', or to whom *alofa* is to be conveyed. Such lists commonly include the names of all members of the immediate kin group, including young children:

Koo gata i konei ttou sauttalaaga, kae fakamoemoe taatou ko te alofa o te Atua e maua ei te manuia mo te fiafia kae toe fetaui fakamuli. Alofa atu Oolepa, Vave, mo Tausegia, Saavali, Aifou, Luisa, Uiki, Vaefou, Fagaua, Alieta, kae sili ei maaua ou maatua see aogaa moo koe. Toofaa laa.

Our conversation will stop here, but let us hope that we shall obtain luck and happiness from God's love for us to meet again in the future. Oolepa, Vave, and Tausegia, Saavali, Aifou, Luisa, Uiki, Vaefou, Fagaua, Alieta all send their love, but, above all, we two, your parents who are useless to you. Good bye.
          (letter 150)

It is evident from the above illustrations that the discourse frame of letters is heavily affective. The formulas used as opening and closing sequences require the use of emotion verbs like *alofa* 'empathy, love'. Opening sequences express the writer's happiness (*fiafia*) about meeting the addressee and about having received his or her previous letter. They also express the writer's regret that the meeting takes place through the medium of a sheet of paper, and cannot take place in person. At the end of a letter, the writer must leave, but does so regretfully, because 'the desire to chat with you is not about to end' (letter 20). And letters close with a list of people to whom *alofa* is to be conveyed. Affect is thus a very salient component of the framing conventions of letters. It is of course possible, from an etic perspective, to view this affect as ritualised affect, which would not be 'meant genuinely', much like the affective connotation of the 'Dear Sir' that frames English letters addressed to complete strangers. However, it is significant that such ritualisation should have targeted this communicative event as opposed to others.[8] In what follows, I shall show that affect does permeate other aspects of the text of letters, in ways that cannot be interpreted as ritual displays.

Economic function of letters

There is a clear economic orientation in many Nukulaelae letters. Letters are used as a tool to monitor, record, and control reciprocal exchanges and gifts; as such, they have become thoroughly incorporated into the socio-economic dynamics of the community. Hand-delivered letters often accompany food baskets, packages, and money. A substantial number of letters, particularly shorter letters written in a hurry on the dock, list the content of packages:

> *E fia fakailoa atu kia koulua me koo oti ne avatu nee au te afiifii fooliki mo te toeaina ko S. Mea i loto, e tasi te t-shirt lanu moana, tasi te sulu solosolo, tasi te suipi, mo fusi ei e lua.*

> I want to let you know that I have sent along a small package with the old man S. Its contents are one blue tee-shirt, one striped loin-cloth, one deck of cards, and two belts.   (letter 42)

Many letters are written to request (*aakai*) such items as food, money, and trade goods. Nukulaelae islanders living on Funaafuti often ask for staples like caramelised coconut toddy, salt fish, coconuts, and swamp taro, because these items are in short supply on Funaafuti. More luxurious items like coconut crabs and birds are also requested. In return, Nukulaelae islanders write to their relatives on Funaafuti and abroad for money, clothes, imported food like rice and sugar, fishing gear, and, more recently, construction materials:

> [from a 40-year-old woman on Nukulaelae to her 40-year-old cousin abroad]
> *Muna a P [...] kee ttogi mai se vvele moo vvele aka tena talafa. Kiloke, a te tuaatina o S teenei e fai foki kee ttogi mai ana tteuga ki te kuata, kae kiloke, kaafai koutou e mmai, kee ttogi mai nee koe ne papa moo S. Kaati ttausaga foou koo fakaogaa nee ia a papa. Kaati laa koo too uke a mea a maatou e fai atu kiaa koe.*

> P asks [...] that you buy him a razor so he can shave his beard. Look, S's mother's brother also asks that you buy him clothes for the [forthcoming] celebrations, and look, when you come here, buy some wooden planks for S. [Because] maybe next year he will need to have wooden planks. Perhaps we keep asking for too many things from you.   (letter 49)

Gifts also need to be acknowledged, in part because baskets of food sometimes get lost, stolen, or misplaced during transportation; this is motivation for further correspondence:

[from a 60-year-old woman on Funaafuti to a 35-year-old nephew on Nukulaelae]
Ia, a ko au e fakafetai lasi atu moo pulaka a maatou ne aumai. Ne maallie maatou i te ggali o pulaka. [. . .] Ia, kae saa toe taa mai nee koe ne mea llasi iaa koe e fiittaa.

So, as for me, I want to thank you very much for the swamp taro you sent us. We were very pleased because the swamp taro was very nice. [. . .] But don't dig up any more big [swamp taro] for us, because it tires you out.   (letter 90)

As in many other Polynesian cultures, on Nukulaelae the intra- and inter-domestic economic issues are closely linked to certain key emotions. As Chambers (1975, 1983) has shown for Nanumea, another island of Tuvalu, and Brady (1970, 1974, 1976) for Tuvalu in general, *alofa*, 'empathy, love, pity, generosity' and *maa* 'shame, shyness' are the primary means through which economic reciprocity and gift-giving are socially controlled. An important component of the emic definition for *alofa*, for example, is the social action that it produces; when an individual feels *alofa* for another, the actions that the emotion triggers are giving, nurturing, and feeding. Similarly, *maa* 'shame, shyness' is what controls excessive *aakai* 'requesting', particularly among non-kin. In letters, it is these affective components of economic transactions that are the focus:

[from an adult man on Funaafuti to an older male relative on Nukulaelae]
Peelaa mo mea koo oti ne oko mai ko omotou lima, a toe ttao atu loa te fia fakafetai, ona eiloa ko tootou aallofa mai ki mea kolaa ne manako ei maatou.

As for the things that have reached our hands, I want to express again my thanks for your *alofa* toward us [expressed in the form of] the things that we have requested.   (letter 34)

[from a young woman on Nanumaga to her bond brother on Nukulaelae]
Tuagaane, kaafai e isi se mea (e) fia fai mai, fai mai. Io me ko ou kaaiga i konaa, fai mai, kee saa maagina laa, ia au nei foki maa maa iaa koe. [. . .] Kae alofa mai kia au.

Brother, if there is something you want, tell me. Or if one of your relatives over there [wants something], tell me, don't be ashamed, otherwise I am also going to be too ashamed to ask you. [. . .] And feel *alofa* towards me [and send me thing].   (letter 17)

In letters that are motivated by the writer's inability to fulfil his or her economic obligations to a relative, the affective component of economic transactions is even more salient. Such letters are written with 'a great deal of *alofa*', and the addressees are asked to 'appease their heart' and to forgive the writer for being unable to meet the addressee's requests:

> [from a teenage daughter on Funaafuti to her parents on Nuku-laelae]
> *Ia, [...] koo tusi atu ttusi mo te <u>alofa</u> lasi kia koulua maatua, auaa e seeai se mea e maua atu. Kae kiloke, matua, onosai maalie kee foki mai au i Saamoa, koo maua atu taulua sene i au io me se aa.*

> So, [...] I am writing the letter with a great deal of <u>alofa</u> toward you, my parents, because nothing is being sent to you. But look, my parents, be patient, when I return from Samoa, I shall send you some money or whatever.   (letter 87)

> [from a young man on Nauru to his parents on Nukulaelae]
> *N, kae peelaa mo te mea teelaa e manako koe moo fai tou tautino ki te aso o faafine. Kiloke, <u>malie tou loto</u>, te tusi ne maua nee au i te poo 17. Ko tena uiga, kaafai e ffao atu nee au i taku tusi, e taumuli atu. Koo oti te aso o faafine. Teelaa laa, <u>malie tou loto ki ei</u>.*

> N, regarding what you wanted for your contribution to the woman's day festivities. Look, <u>appease your hearts</u>, but I received your letter on the 17th. This means that, had I enclosed it in my letter, it would have reached you too late. <u>So, do appease your heart</u>.   (letter 36)

> [from a woman in her sixties on Nukufetau to her 40-year-old daughter on Nukulaelae]
> *S, te afiifii o A teenaa e fanatu mo K. <u>Kae faanoanoa</u> me seeai se sulu o F e maua atu. A G nei e tasi loa tena sulu mai ia T. <u>Fakamoemoe</u> ki se taimi mai mua, maafai e maua soku sulu.*

> S, K is bringing you a package for A. <u>But I feel sadness</u> about the fact that there is no loin-cloth for F. G here got only one loin-cloth from T. <u>Let us hope</u> for another time, when I get another loin-cloth.   (letter 84)

The affective component of the economic system of reciprocity is thus highly salient in letters. It surfaces in overt ways in the frequent references to emotion terms and affect-denoting expressions.

Informational function of letters

Letters are used to transmit news. It can be news about weddings, births, illnesses and deaths, or about feasts and other celebrations, games, arrivals and departures, the visit of a ship other than the usual inter-island vessel, and about atoll politics. In general, the emphasis is on news about the community or the kin group rather than the individual:

> [from a 50-year-old woman on Nukulaelae to her daughter abroad]
> *Ia, kae iloa nee koe, a te paalota teenei ne fai, koo oko loa te gali a te kaaiga o taatou. Ko M mo T koo see olo i loto i mea a te fenua. [...], konaa fale koo see olo i mea a te fenua. E iita loa ia T seki maloo i te paalota, kae iita. Koo see llei te kaaiga o taatou.*

And, you know, in the elections that took place, our kin group behaved beautifully [facetious]. M and T don't want to take part in island affairs any more. [list of names], these are the households that don't take part in island affairs any more. They are angry because T did not win the elections, and they are angry. Our kin group is in disarray.   (letter 48)

> *Kae kee fai atu taku tala kia F, teelaa ki te fekau a L. A F nei koo ita i pati a K ne fai kia F. Ana pati i te laveaaga nee ia F: 'Tapaa ee! au see taaitai loa o loto kia F'. Teelaa laa, F koo oko loa i ana kaitaua. Fai loa kia T kee naa fakafoki te fekau a L.*

And let me tell you my story about F, the one about L's marriage proposal. F is angry at K for what she told F. When she saw F, she said: 'Hey! I have absolutely no intention to [accept] F [as a father-in-law]'. So F is absolutely furious. He told T to withdraw L's marriage proposal.   (letter 65)

As with the economic component of letters, emotions and affect play an important role in the news-reporting function of letters. Nukulaelae letter writers make many overt references to the feelings of the participants in the events that they are reporting. In the above two examples, the anger and displeasure (*ita, kaitaua*) of third parties is carefully commented on as an essential element in the narrative. In the following illustration, it is *alofa* and *saalamoo* 'remorse' that are in focus:

> [from a woman in her twenties on Funaafuti to a male relative in his forties on Nukulaelae, relating her recent boat journey from Nukulaelae to Funaafuti]
> *Ia, tala o te malaga a maatou koo oko loa i te maasei. Kaati e lavea loa nee koutou te maasei o te tai. Maatou e tolu a galu ne ffati ki loto i temotou pooti. Teelaa laa, temotou pooti kaati e llave loa ia T, mooi seeai a T, kaati taku fakattau e mafuli, taku fakattau loa a aku. Teelaa laa, toku ate palele loa ne kai i toku alofa ia T. Teelaa*

*laa, toku saalamoo, ia koutou ne fai mai kee nnofo matou, a ko
matou e aummai loa.*

Now, as for the story of our journey, it was very bad. You
probably saw how bad the ocean was. We had three waves crash
inside our launch. And our launch was stable thanks to T, had it
not been for T, in my opinion, it would probably have capsized,
this is just what I think. So my liver is eaten up by my pity for T.
And I am full of remorse, because you advised us to stay, but we
left anyway.   (letter 47)

 The description of affect thus plays a major role in the informational
component of letters.

Admonitory function of letters

Letters from older people to younger relatives often include advice and
admonitions (*polopolooki*), similar to admonitions delivered orally to
young people who are about to leave the atoll or who have breached
social mores. Letter writers admonish their correspondents (usually
younger relatives) not to drink sour toddy, not to gossip in public, to
refrain from fighting, to attend church regularly, and to be generous
toward their kin:

> *Ia, N, masaua nee koe aku pati, e tapu koe i te kava. Kaafai koe e
> see fakalogo ki aku pati, ko au koo see alofa kiaa koe. I au e logo ia
> L i te inu o tamataene o taatou koo oko loa, a ko tamaliki foolliki
> eeloa. Teelaa laa, au e fai atu kiaa koe kee mmao koe mo te koga
> teenaa. Ma kaa fai nee koe, see toe avatu nee au neau mea.*

So, N, remember my words, you are forbidden from drinking. If
you do not obey my words, I will not feel empathy toward you
any more. Because I heard from L that our young men have been
drinking a lot, even little children. Thus, I am telling you that you
should stay away from this behaviour. If you engage [in this
behaviour], I will not send you any more things.   (letter 64)

> *Kae nofo fakallei koe, ttalo ki te Atua kee manuia koe (kee) toe
> feiloai taatou i se aso i tena alofa lasi, oti te inu, kae fai fakallei tou
> 21 i konaa, alofa mai laa kia A maa uke au mea e maua i konaa.*

And live properly, pray to God so that you may be lucky enough
for us to meet again one day, stop drinking, celebrate your 21st
birthday properly over there, feel empathy toward A [the
recipient's brother] here in case you get a lot of things over there.
                                                              (letter 50)

As will be evident from the above examples, the primary focus of the language of admonitions is the affective comportment of the recipient. In the following two examples, emotion verbs such as *alofa* 'love, compassion, pity' and *fakamoemoe* 'hope' play a central role in the discourse organisation of admonitory acts:

> [from a 75-year-old woman on Nukulaelae to her grand-daughter in Australia]
> *Ia, kae fai atu au kiaa koe, nofo fakallei, <u>alofa</u> ki tou maatua, mo koo seeai sou tamana, kae toe fua naa ko tou maatua. Ia, kae saga fakallei ki tau gaaluega, ko te mea kee oola llei ei koulua mo tou maatua, ia koulua koo seeai se isi tino e <u>fakamoemoe</u> koe ki ei.*

So, I am telling you, live properly, <u>be kind and generous</u> to your mother, because you do not have a father any more, only your mother is left. So pay attention to your work, so that you and your mother can live well, because you do not have any other person <u>to hope for</u>. (letter 21)

> [from a 50-year-old woman on Nukulaelae to her daughter abroad]
> *Kae nofo fakallei, <u>alofa</u> kia S mo tena aavaga, kae masaua aku pati, tausi tou foitino, kae ttalo ki te Atua kee manuia mea e <u>fakamoemoe</u> taatou ki ei.*

And live properly, <u>be kind and generous</u> to S and her husband, and remember my words, take care of your body, and pray to God so that our <u>hopes</u> may be fulfilled. (letter 48)

Even sentences that do not refer overtly to the emotional comportment of the recipient have a salient affective component. For example, the phrase *nofo fakallei* used in the imperative, which literally means 'stay in a good fashion' (translated here as 'live properly'), is an extremely common opening to admonitory sequences. As a qualitative statement about the social acceptability of the recipient's behaviour, it expresses an objective evaluation of another person's conduct, and is thus heavily affective.

Discussion and conclusion

In this chapter, I have shown that affect permeates Nukulaelae letters at several levels. First of all, letters are framed by contextualisation cues that consist of affective expressions. The opening and closing sequences of letters are indeed statements about the affective state of the writer. Secondly, the four topic areas that Nukulaelae writers address in their letters all have clear affective connotations. Discourse about economic issues, whether produced in the oral mode or the written mode, always touches on affect, because economic transactions are regulated by emotions like *alofa* and *maa*. Since letters have a clear economic function, affect surfaces frequently and saliently. Similarly, admonitions, whether oral or written, frequently focus on the affective behaviour of younger people, who are told to be kind and loving, generous and peaceful. Admonishing being one of the most important functions of the genre, it is not surprising that affect should play such an important role in the text of letters.

But even when addressing topics that are not primarily affect-oriented, such as news, letter writers bring out the emotional aspects of what they describe. In this respect, letters contrast even with the most emotionally charged oral gossip, in which affect is kept as covert as possible, as I have shown elsewhere (Besnier 1990). The salience of affect in Nukulaelae letters is thus not entirely attributable to the topics they address. In letters, there seems to be a licence to display affect that is not found in most face-to-face interactions.

Another important characteristic of affect displays in letters is that letter writers do not shy away from employing the most overt affect-communicating strategies like emotion terms and expressions, as this discussion has illustrated, in addition to more covert grammatical strategies (Besnier 1988). The result is that letters become emotional outpourings in which affect surfaces at all levels of the discourse.

Levy (1984) proposes that a culture may 'hypercognise' or 'hypocognise' particular emotions. A hypercognised emotion, for example, is a frequent topic of conversation as either socially sanctioned or socially disapproved behaviour. Furthermore, fine semantic distinctions are commonly made in the emotion lexicon to refer to hypercognised emotions, whereas no word may exist in a language to refer to hypocognised emotions. I propose that the notions of hypercognition and hypocognition can also be used to describe variations in the importance of affect across social contexts in a society. In some social events, members of a culture may deem it appropriate to express their emotions directly and overtly; affect in general, in these events, can be said to be hypercognised. In other contexts, it is appropriate to display only certain types of affect; this affect will thus be selectively hypercognised. Finally, emotional displays, of an overt kind at least, may be disapproved in a third type of context. Affect in these contexts can be said to be hypocognised. An event like Nukulaelae letters thus hypercognises affect: emotions are referred to more overtly and frequently than in other communicative events. Certain types of affect, however, appear to have a privileged position in the texts of letters: *alofa* 'empathy, love, pity' appears to be considerably more hypercognised than, say, anger. As in Tahitian (Levy 1984), many fine

distinctions are made in the Nukulaelae Tuvaluan lexicon for different
types of anger, an indication of the hypercognised status of anger in this
society. In letters, however, few references are made to anger. Anger,
thus, is a hypocognised emotion in this Nukulaelae register, in contrast to
alofa. Further research is needed to identify which affect types are hypercognised or hypocognised in particular communicative contexts.

Clearly, Nukulaelae letters are *defined* as affectively cathartic contexts
in Nukulaelae society, in which certain types of emotions may be (and
perhaps should be) hypercognised. Why should letters have come to be
defined as cathartic contexts? On Nukulaelae, letters are highly 'concentrated' communicative events: opportunities to receive and write letters
are remarkably few and far between (once a month at most), which
contrasts sharply with the constant face-to-face socialisation that life on a
tiny crowded atoll affords on a daily basis. Furthermore, Nukulaelae
islanders are highly sensitive to physical distance from loved ones, as
witnessed by the extreme emotional displays that typically characterise
farewells.[9] Longing and *alofa*, the emotions that are hypercognised when
parting or reminiscing, are also hypercognised in letters:

> *Niko, talu mai te aso ne maavvae ei taatou, i te afiafi teenaa, a*
> *maatou mo S, O, T, S, mo tamaliki katoa, koo ttagi i te masausau*
> *atu kiaa koe. I te paleleega o temotou lotu, a ko O koo fakamasau*
> *aka nee ia a tau maasani i taimi o ttou lotu afiafi, a koe e see mafai*
> *loa o fano ki se koga fakaaatea, [...] A S i te taimi teenaa koo*
> *tagi, a ko au foki koo tagi, a maatou koo ttagi katoa loa i te*
> *maafaufau atu ki ou uiga ggali mo ou faifaiga llei ne fai i loto i te*
> *kaaiga, peelaa foki ki te fenua. Koo leva kkii eiloa temotou saga-*
> *saga, takatokkato foki, kae faatoe fai temotou meakkai. Maaffaga*
> *laa o mea maasei ko te olaga nofo tasi i se maafutaga solosolo llei,*
> *kae toe maavvae i se taimi.*

Niko, on the day that we parted, that evening, all of us, S, O, T, S,
and all the children, we cried while reminiscing about you. After
our evening prayer, O started reminiscing about your habit of not
going off somewhere else during prayer, [...]. S then started
crying at that time, and I cried too, and all of us cried thinking
about your nice attitude and the nice things that you did at the
heart of the kin group, and also in the island community. We sat
or lay down for a very long time, and then finally had dinner.
<u>There is nothing more painful than living together in harmony,</u>
<u>and then another time be parted once again.</u>   (letter 156)

That letters should have come to be defined as cathartic contexts may be a
result of their association with parting and longing, which are contexts in
which such emotions are traditionally hypercognised, as witnessed again

by Lady Caroline on nineteenth-century Funaafuti, who narrates as
follows the departure from the atoll of the author of the letter quoted at
the beginning of this paper:

> But the full meaning of 'palenti too moshy cly' [i.e. 'plenty too
> much cry'] did not dawn on me until I saw [Funaafuti islanders]
> say good-bye to one of their own girls, Vitolia, who was going on
> the *John Williams* to Apia, to the High School there. All the
> village assembled on the beach. Vitolia came out with swollen
> eyes and damp countenance, in a frock just presented to her by
> another girl. When she was close up to the boat her mother clung
> round her neck, rubbed noses, and set up the most dismal howl
> that ever anyone's nerves were thrilled with. Then the mother
> stood aside, emitting fearful howls at intervals, and raining down
> a perfect tropical shower of tears; and one after another the girls
> went up to Vitolia, hung on her neck and wailed, until I feared
> the girl would be reduced to pulp with the squeezing and the teas.
> By this time the wailing had become general, and was so dismal
> and bitter I felt it was approaching the unendurable. Just then
> Vitolia was hustled into the boat and taken away. The people
> dried their eyes and left off howling to watch the boat, and in
> about half an hour were capering about all smiles and high
> spirits.   (David 1899: 277–8)

Notes

1 This chapter is based on research conducted on Nukulaelae in 1980–2 and in
  1985, with funding from the Fondation de la Vocation (Paris) and the National
  Science Foundation (Grant No. 8503061). Additional funding for the preparation of this paper was provided by the Hewlett Foundation for International
  Research and the University of Illinois Research Board. I thank the Government of Tuvalu and the Nukulaelae authorities for granting me permission to
  conduct research on the atoll, and all my friends on Nukulaelae for generously
  providing the data for this paper. Earlier drafts benefited from comments from
  Mary Hussey, Jacob Love, Naomi McPherson, Phil Morrow, and Rex
  Wockner. The usual disclaimers apply.
2 The islet on which the bulk of Nukulaelae's population resides is very small (0.5
  mile long), and messages (*fekau*) from one household to the other can easily be
  conveyed verbally, a task which usually falls on children and adolescents.
  Recently, however, Nukulaelae people have made a habit of using written
  invitations to intra-island feasts on slips of paper.
3 As in many other Polynesian societies (Shore 1982), age-group affiliation on
  Nukulaelae is not absolute but, rather, situation-dependent. The categorisation used here is based on the age group in which each individual would fall in
  most contexts. Very roughly, men and women are *tamataene* and *tamaafine*

from adolescence till marriage, at about twenty to twenty-five; from marriage till their mid-fifties or early sixties they are *taagata* and *faafine*, after which they are *toeaina* and *loomaattua* respectively.

4 In the illustrations quoted in this paper, the orthography and punctuation have been standardised to facilitate reading and comparison. Personal names have been changed to initials whenever it was deemed necessary to protect the identity of individuals. Efforts were made to keep the general 'flavour' of the original in the translations, sometimes at the expense of idiomaticity in the English translations.

5 A discussion of the referent and use of these terms is beyond the scope of this paper. For a discussion of cognate terms in two Polynesian societies, Samoa and Tahiti, see Gerber (1975) and Levy (1973). As in Ifaluk (Lutz 1982) and probably many other Oceanic languages, basic emotion terms are verbs in Nukulaelae Tuvaluan, rather than nouns.

6 Affect-denoting expressions of the type 'the heart is satisfied' (in the following example), 'my liver is eaten up by pity', and 'the desire to chat is not about to end' could be seen as attempts on the part of Nukulaelae letter writers to create more 'detached' texts, thus confirming Chafe's (1982) claim that written language is more detached than spoken language. However, this construction type is commonly used to express emotions (as well as many experiences and cognitive processes) in both spoken and written Nukulaelae Tuvaluan, so much so that they can be considered the unmarked lexicalisation pattern. This pattern appears to be true of other Oceanic languages as well, and is probably cross-linguistically common (Talmy 1985: 101 provides comparable evidence from Samoan, Yiddish, and Kaluli).

7 The notion of 'frame' is used here as in Goffman (1974). It refers to inter-actional cues that mark the boundary of a social event and that provide guidelines for the interpretation of the event.

8 Recently, much work has been devoted in anthropological circles to the cross-cultural study of emotions and affect. Central to much of this work is the warning that Western views about the relative 'genuineness' of affect displays in non-Western societies are at best suspect (Irvine 1982; Levy 1984; Rosaldo 1980, 1983, 1984). This warning is particularly relevant to Western Polynesian societies, where the boundary between emotion, affect, and social action is extremely tenuous (cf. Ochs 1986, Shore 1982 for discussions of Samoan society). In these societies, emotions are *defined* in behavioural terms.

9 The same remark applies to other Polynesian societies, as witnessed by Love's (1985) description of Samoan farewells. We may note here that, traditionally, when Polynesians set out on long-distance canoe journeys, the likelihood of their ever being seen again was very slim. Even today, Nukulaelae Islanders always express doubts as to whether visitors will ever return to the atoll in the future.

84   *Niko Besnier*

References

Besnier, N. 1986. 'Word order in Tuvaluan', in P. Geraghty, L. Carrington, and S. A. Wurm (eds.), *FOCAL 1: Papers from the 4th International Conference on Austronesian Linguistics*, pp. 245–68. Canberra: Pacific Linguistics C–98.

1988. 'The linguistic relationships of spoken and written Nukulaelae registers', *Language*, 64: 707–36.

1990. 'Conflict management, gossip, and affective meaning on Nukulaelae', in K. A. Watson-Gegeo and G. M. White (eds.), *Disentangling: conflict discourse in Pacific societies*, pp. 283–327. Stanford, CA: Stanford University Press.

Biber, E. 1986. 'Spoken and written textual dimensions in English: resolving the contradictory findings', *Language*, 62: 384–414.

Brady, I. A. 1970. 'Land tenure, kinship and community structures: strategies for living in the Ellice Islands of Western Polynesia.' Ph.D. dissertation, Department of Anthropology, University of Oregon.

1974. 'Land tenure in the Ellice Islands: a changing profile', in P. Lundsgaarde (ed.), *Land tenure in Oceania*, pp. 130–78. (Association for Social Anthropology in Oceania Monograph Series, 2.) Honolulu: University of Hawaii Press.

1975. 'Christians, pagans and government men: culture change in the Ellice Islands', in I. A. Brady and B. L. Isaacs (eds.), *A reader in culture change*, vol. 2: case studies, pp. 111–45. New York: Schenkman.

1976. 'Socio-economic mobility: adoption and land tenure in the Ellice Islands', in I. A. Brady (ed.), *Transactions in kinship: adoption and fosterage in Oceania*, pp. 120–63. (Association for Social Anthropology in Oceania Monograph Series, 4.) Honolulu: University of Hawaii Press.

Bridge, C. 1886. 'Cruises in Melanesia, Micronesia, and Western Polynesia, in 1882, 1883, and 1884, and visits to New Guinea and the Louisiades in 1884 and 1885', *Proceedings of the Royal Geographic Society and Monthly Record of Geography*, 9: 545–67.

Chafe, W. L. 1982. 'Integration and involvement in speaking, writing, and oral literature', in D. Tannen (ed.), *Spoken and written language: exploring orality and literacy*, pp. 35–53. (Advances in Discourse Processes Series, 9.) Norwood, NJ: Ablex.

Chafe, W. L. and Danielewicz, J. 1987. 'Properties of spoken and written language', in R. Horowitz and S. J. Samuels (eds.), *Comprehending oral and written language*, pp. 83–113. New York: Academic Press.

Chambers, A. F. 1975. *Nanumea report: a socio-economic study of Nanumea atoll, Tuvalu.* (Victoria University of Wellingon Rural Socio-economic Survey of the Gilbert and Ellice Islands Series.) Wellington: Department of Geography, Victoria University of Wellington.

1983. 'Exchange and social organization in Nanumea, a Polynesian atoll society.' Ph.D. dissertation, Department of Anthropology, University of California at Berkeley.

David, Mrs. E. [Lady Caroline M. David] 1899. *Funafuti, or three months on a coral island: an unscientific account of a scientific expedition.* London: John Murray.

DeVito, J. A. 1966. 'Psychogrammatical factors in oral and written discourse by skilled communicators', *Speech Monographs*, 33: 73–6.
1967. 'Levels of abstraction in spoken and written language', *Journal of Communication*, 17: 354–61.
Gerber, E. R. 1975. 'The cultural patterning of emotions in Samoa.' Ph.D. dissertation, Department of Anthropology, University of California at San Diego.
Gillogly, K. 1984. 'A comparison of letter writing in some non-Western societies.' Unpublished typescript, Department of Anthropology, University of Hawaii.
Goffman, E. 1974. *Frame analysis: an essay on the organization of experience.* New York: Harper and Row.
Haviland, J. M. 1984. 'Thinking and feeling in Woolf's writing: from childhood to adulthood', in C. E. Izard, J. Kagan and R. B. Zajonc (eds.), *Emotions, cognition, and behavior*, pp. 515–46. Cambridge: Cambridge University Press.
Haviland, J. B. 1987. 'Fighting words: evidential particles, affect and argument', in J. Aske, N. Beery, L. Michaelis and H. Filip (eds.), *Proceedings of the 13th Annual Meeting of the Berkeley Linguistics Society*, pp. 343–54. Berkeley, CA: Berkeley Linguistics Society.
Irvine, J. 1982. 'Language and affect: some cross-cultural issues', in H. Byrnes (ed.), *Contemporary perceptions of language: interdisciplinary dimensions*, pp. 31–47. (Georgetown Roundtable on Languages and Linguistics, 1982.) Washington, DC: Georgetown University Press.
Labov, W. 1984. 'Intensity', in D. Schiffrin (ed.), *Meaning, form and use in context: linguistic applications*, pp. 43–70. Washington, DC: Georgetown University Press.
Levy, R. 1973. *Tahitians: mind and experience in the Society Islands.* Chicago and London: University of Chicago Press.
1984. 'Emotion, knowing, and culture', in R. A. Shweder and R. A. LeVine (eds.), *Culture theory: essays on mind, self, and emotion*, pp. 214–37. Cambridge: Cambridge University Press.
Love, J. W. 1985. '"Oh, I never will forget you": a Samoan farewell', in A. D. Shapiro (ed.), *Music and context: essays for John Milton Ward*, pp. 453–76. Cambridge, MA: Harvard University Press.
Lutz, C. 1982. 'The domain of emotion words in Ifaluk', *American Ethnologist*, 9: 113–28.
Lutz, C. and White, G. M. 1986. 'The anthropology of emotions', *Annual Review of Anthropology*, 15: 405–36.
Mikulecky, B. 1985. 'The Paston letters: an example of literacy in the fifteenth century.' Unpublished typescript, School of Education, Boston University.
Mulkay, M. 1985. 'Agreement and disagreement in conversations and letters', *Text*, 5: 201–27.
Munro, D. 1982. 'The Lagoon Islands: a history of Tuvalu, 1820–1908.' Ph.D. dissertation, Department of History, Macquarrie University.
Ochs, E. 1986. 'From feelings to grammar: a Samoan case study', in B. B. Schieffelin and E. Ochs (eds.), *Language socialization across cultures*, pp. 251–72. (Studies in the Social Cultural Foundations of Language, 3). Cambridge: Cambridge University Press.
Ochs, E. and Schieffelin, B. B. 1989. 'Language has a heart', *Text*, 9: 7–250.

Redeker, G. 1984. 'On differences between spoken and written language', *Discourse Processes*, 7: 43–55.

Rosaldo, M. Z. 1980. *Knowledge and passion: Ilongot notions of self and social life.* (Cambridge Studies in Cultural Systems, 4.) Cambridge: Cambridge University Press.

——— 1983. 'The shame of headhunters and the autonomy of self', *Ethos*, 11: 135–51.

——— 1984. 'Towards an anthropology of self and feeling', in R. A. Shweder and R. A. LeVine (eds.), *Culture theory: essays on mind, self, and emotion*, pp. 137–57. Cambridge: Cambridge University Press.

Rubinstein, D. and Gajdušek, D. C. 1970. *A Study in nascent literacy: neo-Melanesian correspondence from a Fore, New Guinea youth.* Bethesda, MD: Section of Child Growth and Development and Disease Patterns in Primitive Cultures, National Institute of Neurological Diseases and Stroke, National Institute of Health.

Scribner, S. and Cole, M. 1981. *The psychology of literacy.* Cambridge, MA: Harvard University Press.

Shore, B. 1982. *Sala'ilua: a Samoan mystery.* New York: Columbia University Press.

Talmy, L. 1985. 'Lexicalization patterns: semantic structure in lexical forms', in T. Shopen (ed.), *Language typology and syntactic description*, vol. 3, pp. 57–149. Cambridge: Cambridge University Press.

Tannen, D. 1982a. 'The myth of orality and literacy', in W. Frawley (ed.), *Linguistics and literacy*, pp. 37–50. (Topics in Language and Linguistics Series.) New York and London: Plenum Press.

——— 1982b. 'Oral and literate strategies in spoken and written narratives', *Language*, 58: 1–21.

3

THE USES OF SCHOOLING AND LITERACY IN A ZAFIMANIRY VILLAGE[1]

MAURICE BLOCH

This chapter describes how schooling and literacy are used outside school, in one small and remote village in rural Madagascar. My example may perhaps seem untypical or even eccentric. Still, it is chosen in order to make a general point, since I do not believe that it is possible to discuss any of the effects of literacy or schooling usefully except within a specific context. Literacy can be used (or not used) in so many different ways that the technology it offers, taken on its own, probably has no implications at all (Bloch 1989). Since what goes on in schools is itself so varied, it is perhaps even more hazardous to attribute particular social, political or psychological effects to schooling.

The choice of a concrete example very remote from the sort of conditions generally described by educational experts is intended to show that many of what are normally taken to be the inevitable effects of the introduction of literacy and schooling are in fact nothing of the kind, but result from the social and cultural contexts typical of western industrialised societies. Such factors normally pass unquestioned and unexamined, since most western commentators rarely have the contrast with non-western societies forced upon them. It is from this point of view that a Malagasy village where I have twice lived comes to seem an obvious starting-point for a discussion of schooling.

In stressing the importance of looking at real contexts, I am of course merely echoing the frequent recent demands in psychology and especially in the psychology of education for 'ecological validity'. But I believe that even those who have stressed the importance of looking at education in the world rather than in the laboratory or the school have envisaged context much too narrowly; in particular they have surely ignored implicit cultural contexts of which we become aware only when working in fundamentally 'other' cultures.

I want to demonstrate the determining influence of two connected types of contexts. There has already been a good deal of discussion of the effects of my first type, the politico-social context, on schooling and literacy, and so I shall only touch on this briefly (see for example Willis 1977).

The second type of context I discuss here, by contrast, has been generally neglected. That is the significance within a specific cultural setting which is attributed to different types of non-school knowledge, and the importance of this for the way in which ordinary people evaluate and use school-knowledge. Jean Lave in her fascinating book *Cognition in practice* (1988) has shown the small use that is made of school mathematics in everyday activity, but this leads her to an over-simple contrast between practice (regarded as non-school knowledge) and abstract theory which for her is taught in school only. This may be adequate for the United States with which she is mainly concerned but, as we shall see, when dealing with Madagascar we need to distinguish more finely, between knowledge in practice and explicated knowledge, between explicated knowledge in and out of school, between meta-theories of knowledge employed in school and those employed out of school. Furthermore we shall see how actors' theories about knowledge, whether implicit or explicit, relate to their theories of person, of gender, of the body, of maturation and of birth and death.

The Zafimaniry are a small group of people living in the forest of eastern Madagascar who, until recently, relied exclusively on slash and burn agriculture. Unlike their neighbours they have never been fully integrated into state structures and for most of their history they have been concerned with avoiding such integration.[2]

The small village of Mamolena[3] in Zafimaniry country where I carried out field work in 1971 and again in 1988 and 1989 is situated in a very remote part of the country which has been relatively little affected by centralising forces in Madagascar such as government administration and large-scale trading.

Until 1947 the agents of government hardly ever appeared in the village but then, following a nationwide anti-colonial revolt, the French, represented by their army, arrived in Mamolena, killed people and burnt the place down completely. For a few years following this colonial 'reconquest' the government established fairly tight administrative control which, in milder form, lasted until about 1975. Since then, as far as the inhabitants have been concerned, the state and its institutions have gradually withered away, and, at the same time, integration into the national and international economy has diminished, so that, by now, hardly any manufactured goods are to be found in the village. The intrusive contact of radio programmes has vanished with the villagers' inability to obtain batteries, and no government representative of any kind has set foot in the place for at least the last ten years.

However, the fact that the state and its apparatuses are retreating does not mean that the inhabitants, or at least the male inhabitants, of the village are completely isolated. This is because the villagers can and do make contact with the state and the wider economic system on a largely voluntary basis by occasionally seeking it out. Firstly, a significant number of young men go on labour migration to different parts of Madagascar, often passing on their way through the national capital or other major urban centres. Secondly, villagers quite often go to the nearest administrative centre, Ambohivohitra, about two hours' walk away, either to market or for contact with government agencies.

After 1947, when the French made Ambohivohitra one of the *loci* of their repressive activities, that centre became reachable by road from the town of Ambositra for at least half the year. Since that time it has contained government offices and a fairly well-run government school where pupils were, until recently at least, taught by qualified and paid government schoolteachers. Occasionally some of the pupils at the state school of Ambohivohitra were successfully trained for the old French BEPC[4] which enabled them, in theory at least and now and then in fact, to go to the good schools available at Ambositra.

Since 1975 however the general decay of the state and its agencies has also affected Ambohivohitra. This is most obvious in the fact that the road has become impassable – or at least no transport available to the villagers can travel on it. As a result Ambositra, which used to be only three hours or so away until about 1970, is now practically two days' walk away. This has meant that the administration has become intermittent at best, since by now there is only a single administrator. This man is expected to pay frequent court to his superior in Ambositra, and has therefore to stay in that town most of the time.

The school in Ambohivohitra has suffered too. First of all educational aids such as books, paper and biros have become very scarce. More significantly, the increasing remoteness of the place has made school-teachers, who normally come from small towns in the area around Ambositra, unwilling to take up posts in the village or, if they do, stay there. Equally disruptive has been the fact that the Malagasy government insists on paying school teachers every month in person in Ambositra. This means that for at least one week of every month there is no school in the village, while the teachers collect their wages. Also the school week has recently been reduced to four days as no school is now held on market days.

Equally damaging has been the increase in the number of school-children, with no compensating increase in the number of teachers at least since 1970. The population of Mamolena is representative of the general increase in population. It has increased by 45 per cent between 1971 and 1989, but of course this means a much greater proportional increase in the numbers of children, and the population of school age has in fact more or less doubled over the period.

This has not only affected the quality of schooling in Ambohivohitra; it has also meant that the slim chance once available to Mamolena pupils of attending school in this village has vanished, since there is now literally no room for them there.

The disappearance of state administration and schooling in the last two decades has been compensated in part by the growing presence in the area of the Catholic Church, with largely foreign funding. For Ambohivohitra, and especially for Mamolena, it is the Catholic Church which has become much the more important source of contact with the outside world.

The Catholics established themselves quite securely in the Zafimaniry area during the 1930s, and in 1967 the local missionary began to build a massive, very ugly and totally inappropriate stone church in Mamolena. The money for this church and many others like it came largely from the selling of Zafimaniry carved artifacts to dealers and tourists in Antananarivo and beyond. This selling of artifacts generated large revenues for the priest, who employed the money in a programme of church building worthy of an averagely wealthy medieval cardinal.

The building programme stopped abruptly when the present incumbent replaced this priest in 1972. The new man set out to rescue the church from its building obsession and used the money for small scale development projects which, unlike most development projects undertaken in Madagascar, have actually proved on balance beneficial to the recipients.

The significance of the unfinished church in Mamolena for our concerns is that it has housed a church-run school on and off for about the last twenty years. This church school was started as a stop-gap measure by the Catholic Church until such a time as the government should decide to provide the village with its own school. This it has regularly promised to do since the 1930s but the promise has yet to materialise. In 1985, the administration told villagers that if they put up a building for a government school a fully trained school teacher would then be appointed. The school was erected at considerable expense by the villagers but it is now derelict and no teacher has ever come.

The church school has been run by a number of teachers who have always lived in Ambohivohitra and who have passed the BEPC. In most cases the teacher had benefited from at least one year's school experience in Ambositra. The school has never succeeded in training anybody to the level of the BEPC but it has, in at least three cases, trained pupils sufficiently well that they could be accepted and cope with teaching for the BEPC in Ambositra.

The school was open fairly regularly in the 1970s but during the 1980s it has had a much more troubled history and was in fact closed several times, including one long period of five years when no schooling was available.

One result of this is the variable amount of schooling received by the people of Mamolena depending on their ages. Those under twenty-five are, as a direct result of the recent troubled history of the school, relatively poorly schooled, with low levels of literacy. Those between twenty-five and forty are relatively well schooled and were probably in most cases fairly literate when they left school. Among these were at least two ex-pupils, probably more, who are fairly advanced because they benefited from further schooling in Ambohivohitra and Ambositra. However, for reasons discussed below, these stars have, without exception, left the village of Mamolena and are now living somewhere else. Finally, among the over forties the situation is very uneven. Some – those who went to school in Ambohivohitra – received fairly good education and in many cases can still read and write, though with difficulty. The majority are, however, totally unschooled since they were children at a time when there was no school in Mamolena.

What happens in school is ultimately modelled on European, mainly French, models of secular and church education. However, because the facilities available in the school are so different from what most of the readers of this chapter are used to, a short description, drawn in a modified and shortened form from my field notes for part of a fairly typical day in 1989, will evoke the reality of what is actually being discussed when we are talking of schooling.[5]

A day at school

It is ten past eight. The children are all gathered in small groups in the village under the eaves of a couple of houses waiting for the door of the church to open as a sign that the teacher has come. He appears and prepares to put a conch to his lips but before he can do this the children rush out of the village towards the school in high good humour in spite of the pouring rain.

The barefoot teacher is eighteen. This schoolteacher came close to getting his baccalaureat after two years at school in Ambositra. His salary is unclear; his predecessor got 10,000 FMG a month (approximately three pounds sterling[6]). He certainly does not get more than 20,000.

The church is much like an unfinished garage except for the fly-blown religious pictures, which are old posters of Europeans being crucified, nursing babies or growing amazing white beards. The benches on which the children sit are very rough-hewn pews, six inches off the ground. Two short rows at the front are better and attempt to be rickety desks. The only school equipment is a tiny, worn-out blackboard.

All the children are dressed in incredibly ragged, and by now mud-coloured clothes. They are clearly very cold. However, all seem to be enjoying themselves. The children in this first session are divided into two groups. On one side of the aisle there is a large group of children of approximately 7–10 year olds (about forty of them), in the other aisle a group of 10–12 year olds (about thirty).

The first part of the proceedings (15 minutes) is catechism done with great care by the school teacher who explains about the ascension of Christ. Then the secular teaching begins. The younger children basically have three items on the curriculum which take more or less equal time: reading, singing and drawing.

They are asked to draw on their slates a picture of a house, something which they are asked to do at least once a week and they do this relatively well, with great enthusiasm. The houses are entirely stereotyped but the degree of elaboration varies.

The singing consists of a total repertory of five songs, which they sing again and again throughout their school career, hardly ever learning new ones. They did the singing with great gusto and with obvious enjoyment. Among the songs, three in all this morning, are the National Anthem and a Malagasy version of *Alouette* ... It is striking how crude and simple this singing is in comparison with the subtle polyphony of the funeral wake songs which the same children will sing whenever anybody dies in the village.

Reading is the most important part of the teaching. It consists of reading a couple of simple sentences which use similar words and which are written on the blackboard. The reading is first recited in unison by the whole class with little difficulty. Then each row of children by themselves are asked to read in unison. This is more difficult. The reading in unison takes on the character of chanting. However, since the same sentences are put up on the board day after day (for several months) it is not clear how far the whole thing is an exercise in reading or memorising.

The older group of 10–12 year olds have a similar programme except that the reading exercise is slightly harder. They are also asked to write in books or on slates. Today this is exclusively copying the copperplate model of individual letters written on the board by the teacher, but on other days they copy the complete sentences which they read.

At half past nine there is a break and the children pour outside. There the children themselves organise a tug-of-war with a liana between the boys and girls, with the two sides winning about an equal number of times. At quarter to eleven the young ones leave.

My feeling about the proceedings is that in spite of the very poor content of the teaching, the atmosphere is excellent, relaxed and under control. This was in part due to the pleasant and unchallenging attitude of the children and the skill and good humour of the teacher.

The behaviour of the boys and girls is strikingly different. With the notable exception of two girls who behave exactly like the boys, the girls when interrogated are *menatra* (shy), looking away, sideways or to the ground and ultimately dissolving into embarrassed giggling, to such an extent that some have to sit down before finishing what they have to say. The boys are confident, witty, their eyes shining. They all seem to be treated in the same way by the teacher however.

After eleven the older ones (approximately 12–14) come in. They will stay until one. They are a much smaller group, thirteen in all, nine boys and four girls. It is significant that there are so few and so few girls. Marriage and economic activity soon removes the children from school. The girls however, because they marry much younger, are removed by marriage sooner than the boys.

All the children who are there can read and write to some extent. They read more complicated sentences from the board, first in unison and then individually. Then they copy them in their books. They learn a little pointless French vocabulary which is pronounced by both teachers and pupils in an unrecognisable way.

Besides this, the children do lengthy sums, such as writing every interval of 50 between 2,500 and 10,000, as well as simple problems. The answers to these sums are written in exercise books and corrected individually. On the whole, the mathematics demanded of the pupils, which they do with difficulty, is infinitely easier than mathematical sums which are being done daily by the same children in dealing with money, thereby confirming the findings reported by Lave (1988).[7]

There are also some bizarre grammatical exercises concerning stress in Malagasy. What was taught made no sense to the teacher, the pupils or me.

Sometimes, once a fortnight or so, but not on the day these notes were taken, there is a little geography – learning the names of the provinces of Madagascar and sentences concerning France, the USA, the USSR, Jerusalem, Bethlehem and Rome – and a little science in the form of reading and copying sentences like 'Water boils at 100 degrees'. (I later asked the pupils what degrees were, and found that they had no idea.)

Although the content of the teaching is not very different for the older and younger classes, what was striking was the difference in atmosphere. In the case of the older children I got the impression that the schoolteacher, although still amiable, felt that he was wasting his time and this feeling was shared by the pupils. The atmosphere of this second half was gloomy, unpleasant ... defeated. The explanation for this is all too simple: teaching at this level is meant to be directed towards passing the exam which replaces the old BEPC, but all the pupils and teachers know that there is no possibility that anybody will get through. At this stage the school represents something which is normally insignificant in the village as opposed to more 'developed' places in Madagascar: the intrusion into the village of an image of a society of which the villagers have to see themselves as the lowest echelon.

Although the older pupils may regard it as impossible for them, as villagers, to achieve academic success, they nevertheless share one thing with everybody else in Mamolena, and with everybody I know in Madagascar, educated or not; that is, they are absolutely convinced of the *value* of schooling and literacy. I find this conviction surprising and it is worth considering what might account for it, at least as far as the inhabitants of Mamolena are concerned.

The first and most obvious explanation would be that education is seen by the Zafimaniry as a potential avenue to social success and wealth. There is no doubt that much government and Church propaganda encouraged this idea and the people of Mamolena know of a few success stories from other villages to which they sometimes referred. However as far as their village is concerned clear cases of people for whom education led to good jobs are non-existent.

Education makes it possible to be elected to, largely unpaid, local administrative posts since these require at least some ability to read and write. However, whether these positions are really desired by the Zafimaniry is far from clear and it is a question to which I shall return below.

There is also an awareness that those who were successful at school have tended to leave the village and to settle in big towns such as Ambositra and the capital of Madagascar, Antananarivo. There, some of these people have been successful and others not, but this success has been unrelated to their education.

Perhaps more relevant to the valuation of school and literacy is the villagers' knowledge that the children of these more mobile village parents have been able to attend better schools in the larger centres. It is also known that in some cases at least, these children have obtained government employment – hence academic success might be said to have borne fruit at one generation's remove.

However, seen from the village, this kind of success is double-edged. Firstly, although people realise that once upon a time government urban jobs were lucrative and led to prestige and high standards of living, they also know that this is no longer the case. Villagers are continually commenting on the lack of jobs in town, the terrible living conditions of the urban poor and the fact that government employees are badly and irregularly paid at a time when the price of the foodstuffs which they must buy is rising. People know what is happening. During my recent visit, the only discussion of possible future social success through education which I heard in the village concerned a girl who was being considered for acceptance as a novice in a nunnery.

Emigration to urban centres which is made possible by education has, however, an even more profound drawback as villagers see it. People in Mamolena and other places like it have their own powerful understanding of the nature of success, and this involves having as many children, grandchildren and other descendants as possible, either in the village itself, or at least in the locality. The very children who may do well at school, leave the village and eventually produce children who can perhaps achieve some success in the outside world, become at the same time lost to their parents and grandparents, and so actually diminish their older relatives' success and prestige within the village.

The reason for the high valuation of schooling and literacy must there-fore, at least today, lie somewhere else than in the practical advantages it can confer. I would argue that this continuing valuation can only be understood when we move beyond the social-economic context discussed above, to locate what is taught in school in a different context as well, that of the organisation and valuation of knowledge in the village – that is, the way villagers think about knowledge when (as happens most of the time) they are not in, or specifically referring to, the school environment. When we put school knowledge within that context it becomes possible to understand somewhat better both why the villagers should value school-knowledge, and how they use it. The strength of the explanation depends on the fact that, as we shall see, the schooling villagers receive does not seem to affect their organisation and philosophy of knowledge; instead, school knowledge is itself interpreted within the terms of the village home culture. This finding is in accord with a number of recent studies of schooling (Willis 1977; Scribner and Cole 1981) which document the strength of home culture and the weakness of school culture.

The strength of home culture, in Mamolena at least, is not surprising to an anthropologist who has carried out field work in the traditional manner, noting daily life as it occurs, not focusing on a pre-defined 'problem', while it might escape the research approach of those who have focused on education even when thinking of themselves principally as anthropologists. This is because the home theory of knowledge and the evaluation of different types of knowledge are completely linked with the way such things as the body, gender, maturation, the nature of the living world and the understanding of productive and reproductive processes are all envisaged. In other words, it is by understanding things which at first appear totally remote from education and literacy that their meaning for the Zafimaniry can finally be grasped.

In sketching the ethnography of knowledge among the Zafimaniry I am aware that much of what I have to say also applies in lesser or greater degree to many other Malagasy. I am also aware that the discussion provided here can only be cursory and indicative. Since I am arguing that a much broader than usual cultural view is necessary in order to understand the uses of literacy and schooling, I can unfortunately present only a partial account of those factors in the limited available space.

Like most Malagasy, the Zafimaniry stress how the passage through life is one of fundamental transformation, so that little of the person is considered as fixed simply because of ancestry. For them, living human beings are best thought of in terms of what they are transforming from and into rather than as fixed entities. This transformation affects their bodies, their genders, their minds, their use of language and their appropriate spheres of action (Bloch 1986 and 1989). It is on the last three of these aspects that I shall concentrate here. The process of transformation is gradual, with no sharply marked discontinuities, but for the sake of presentation it can be divided into three principal stages.[8]

Zafimaniry concepts regarding the bodily aspect of the transformations associated with maturation are reminiscent of those of other Malagasy people (Bloch 1986; Huntingdon 1988). There is a general idea that children start life all soft and bendy but that as they mature, which occurs principally as a result of receiving the blessing of their ancestors, they straighten up both physically and morally. This transformation is not only evident in the material parts of the body but also in such less tangible aspects of the person as their style of speaking. The young speak in an unformalised tumble of words and unfinished sentences. The old often use near-formulaic expressions phrased in an archaic and fixed style. All this, as in other parts of Madagascar, is seen as part of a general process of hardening, drying, becoming more fixed, more ancestral and more moral.

In many symbolic ways, as people go through life the Zafimaniry house gradually becomes a substitute for the body. We can distinguish three stages in life; the first is when the person is not yet linked to a house and their body is likewise soft and undetermined, the second is the period when, as part of a married couple, they are developing themselves through their descendants and their house, and the third is when they start to separate themselves from normal human activity and are becoming ancestors, but for the Zafimaniry this means merging with the ancestral houses, the structure of which becomes the object of ancestor worship.

This general process of maturation has for the Zafimaniry yet a further side. It is associated with the idea that the different stages in life are also linked with appropriate spheres of activity and therefore with appropriate types of knowledge. The young, that is those who are not yet married and so are not yet associated with a house, are typically thought of as hunters and gatherers, carrying out these activities in the forest. Because young men marry later this period is longer for males. This association of the young with the forest and hunting and gathering is not merely to be understood in terms of a type of productive activity. The young are in many ways also seen as sharing the characteristics of their quarry. They are said to be like animals or even wild plants: unreliable, forming and breaking personal links promiscuously, amoral, mobile, interested in this and that.

For the Zafimaniry the typical way of doing things at this stage in life is playing, and hunting and gathering is seen by them as a type of play. Zafimaniry children play in ways which are familiar, for example imitating adult activities by making mock houses where they cook, playing at the rituals of adults, or sometimes they play more organised games such as knuckle bones or hopscotch which they score in extremely complex ways. But above all they play with wild plants and animals.

What is particularly interesting in this type of play is that it involves a combination of encyclopedic knowledge and scientific experimentation. For example, the boys in Mamolena make, apart from the ubiquitous whipping tops out of wood and liana, pop guns with bamboos and other forest plant materials. Similarly they make windmills, often with tails which direct them constantly into the wind. What is more, the brighter among the children are very happy to discuss the principles which make these toys work. Accompanying this practical and theoretical physics is a great fascination with practical and theoretical biology which involves playing with and examining animals, often in an extremely cruel way.

I was particularly struck by the scientific nature of this type of play when, as a result of a cyclone, an unknown bird, actually a sea bird never seen in those parts, was blown down near the village. It was brought triumphantly into the village by a group of children who began to examine it. They were particularly amused and interested by its beak which had two strange openings which they decided must be its nose. Then they discussed the peculiar hooked character of this beak which they felt meant that it must be a bird of prey, but they worried about what animals it could catch given its small size. Then they noted its wing span and they decided that it must 'fly high'. Finally they noted its webbed feet and decided that it must be a water bird and probably came from the sea and had been blown to the village by the high wind.

It is difficult to imagine a better organised biology lesson, but the manner of the transmission of this knowledge and the language in which it is put is totally informal, hardly ever consisting of complete sentences. In the discussion over the sea bird the children interrupted each other and pushed each other. When adults joined in, which they did with clear interest, they seemed ashamed to be participating in such frivolous activity and would move away as soon as anybody else appeared. It was obvious from their attitude that for them, as for everybody else, this was not really serious subject matter. This attitude towards knowledge about wild things is shared by everybody and is linked, not simply to the fact that this is stereotypical children's knowledge, but also to the fact that the wild things themselves are seen as of no significance to the wise since they are fluid and impermanent. This is so in spite of the fact that objectively, in terms of nutrition and other important activities, forest products are very economically significant, a fact I never found anybody willing to admit.

Activities and knowledge about wild things are thus linked to the non-house status of the young. Marriage and the beginning of the association with a house make such play inappropriate. This change occurs sooner for girls than for boys, who in the later stages of their bachelorhood develop a special version of the wild theoretical child knowledge stage associated with hunting which is linked with adventure away from the village.[9]

The married period is associated with the development, fixation and 'becoming permanent' of the house. This process in turn is associated with agriculture, which is seen as the means of sustenance of the family in the house. Because the house and marriage are viewed as a joint male-female activity this is also true of agriculture and the Zafimaniry continually comment approvingly on the mutual cooperation between husband and wife which is necessary and right for agricultural tasks.

Not surprisingly the knowledge appropriate for this period of life is, and is seen to be, governed by the principle of utility. The type of discourse in which it occurs is largely about practical matters, is perfectly shared by men and women and most typically occurs between husband and wife. As is the case for farmers everywhere, their detailed knowledge about soils, weather, plant-species and prices is awe-inspiring. However, as with the play-knowledge of the young, most of this knowledge is implicit and is therefore difficult to describe.

It would be wrong, however, to believe that this type of knowledge is never verbalised. It is manifested either in practical problem-solving or else sometimes in discussions after work. The language in which these matters is discussed also reflects the notion of utility. It is serious, calmer and more organised than the language of the young concerning wild animals and plants; conversations on these topics are often half whispered and include long pauses expressing reflection, calculation and doubt. People do not interrupt each other, they sit in proper positions. These types of dialogues usually take place at appropriate times for talk of this sort: after breakfast, after the last meal of the day or at certain stages during visits from relatives.

The practical agricultural knowledge of middle life is part and parcel of often repeated activity but it would nonetheless be misleading to think

that it cannot occasionally be used for context free or innovative specu-
lation, as has sometimes been suggested by psychologists (Perkins 1988).

For instance, because the Zafimaniry are faced by three incompatible
calendars they continually discuss ways of aligning them and for this use
mathematical principles infinitely more complex than anything taught in
school. Similarly, discussion of supply and demand and how to take
advantage of price fluctuations according to the timing of harvests
revealed rich operative ability. Again they employed good scientific hypo-
theses, the result of innovative thinking in a new situation, to explain the
spread of a pig epidemic by the fact that people did not wash their feet
properly before entering a village, by the wind, or by people buying
infected pig meat in other villages, then throwing away the bones which
were then gnawed by the pigs ...[10]

After middle age comes a stage of life which can be labelled
'elderhood'.[11] Gradually the period of life when the married pair are
primarily concerned with producing the nurturing descendants gives way
to the period when the couple become elders. As we have noted above,
this means on the one hand that they are becoming almost like ancestors
and on the other that at the same time they are becoming merged with the
fixed, hardening and beautifying house. Men slip in to the role of being an
elder more easily and more clearly than women although women may also
attain the status of elder, only more rarely and more uncertainly.

Being an elder is a status but it is also a style of behaviour which the
person adopts when he is being an elder. This is marked by posture and
linguistic code. He tends to speak very quietly, using formalised and fixed
language which is highly decorated and full of quotations and proverbs.
When an elder speaks he addresses nobody, apparently not caring if he is
heard or not, ignoring the fact that others may be speaking at the same
time since a specific linguistic exchange would negate the almost other-
worldly character of what he is saying.[12]

The wisdom of the Zafimaniry elder is much less politically relevant
than that of the Merina.[13] It is treated, rather as the person themself is
treated while they are speaking, with respect, but with a sense of being
kept at arm's length from practical life, almost of being ignored.

The discourse of elders, however, is not merely marked by form, it is
also marked by content. In other words elderhood also implies a particular form of knowledge. Elders are associated with the image of
straightness, hardness and permanence, of morality, of fixity in time and
space (marked by the holy house) but also with clarity[14] and truth. This is
because the wisdom that emerges with elderhood contrasts both with the
chaotic fluctuation of life characterised by wild things which typically
concerns the young and with the process of getting a living which is the
primary concern of the middle aged, and which is also linked with

dialectical change, although of a more orderly kind. The wisdom of elders is authoritative, it is beyond question and in a sense even beyond human life, since the elder is often represented as merely speaking the words of the ancestors who are merged with the house.

The Zafimaniry elder has become fixed and therefore like an inanimate object. What he is allowing to be expressed through himself is therefore of no practical value since it concerns things on a time scale different from human life; it is not referential but constitutive; it is worthy of being expressed and displayed for itself; it is wisdom. What is mainly spoken in such talk are blessings and special forms of thanks which are also a kind of blessing. Otherwise it tends to be *tantara*, a word which is often translated as 'history', since the contents tend to be genealogies of people and places as well as information on the geography of previous significant places and descriptions of how things should be done at rituals. *Tantara* and eldership are inseparable.[15]

Overall therefore the Zafimaniry view knowledge as one of these three kinds, each associated with different ages of life. Youth is speculatively playing with wild plants and animals. Middle age is concerned with practical knowledge and the maximisation of utility. Elderhood is concerned with history. As we pass from the knowledge of youth to the knowledge of elderhood we move along an axis of increasing fixity and of categoricality, but also of decreasing relevance for dealing with the environment.

The Zafimaniry therefore have a meta theory about different kinds of knowledge which is associated with different styles of communication and which is itself part and parcel of much more general concerns such as the maturation of the body and the person, the nature of human society and its relation to the non-human world of plants, animals and places. It is within this relatively organised system of beliefs about different types of knowledge that the Zafimaniry try to place the knowledge which is transmitted at school.

In terms of content school knowledge is seen as being of the same kind as the 'wisdom' of elders. It also comes from an absolutely authoritative beyond, which one respects but does not want to come too close to. It is therefore presumed to be categorically true but, at the same time, to be irrelevant knowledge as far as practical activities are concerned. It is not considered to be a source of information about the empirical world.

Such an association of school knowledge with wisdom explains the uncritical acceptance of everything taught at school. The Zafimaniry attitude to such knowledge is that, of course it is true and one should know it, of course it cannot be questioned since it is true, and of course it is neither fun nor relevant. The apparent anomaly which struck me so strongly in the field – that the intellectual and practical value of what was taught in the school was so poor compared with what was daily available out of school – did not matter at all to my fellow villagers. What one was taught in school emanated from such prestigious sources that it could not and should not be concerned with the practical or with the empirical world. Above all it should be, like the elders and their knowledge, beyond dialectic.

This having been said, however, school knowledge cannot in every way be that simply assimilated into the pre-existing system. This is because Zafimaniry theories of knowledge assume a homogeneity between the type of knowledge and the kind of person who professes it. If school knowledge is a form of 'wisdom' it is being transmitted by the wrong kind of people to the wrong kind of people since it is taught by the young to the very young. Furthermore, the problem is made worse by the fact that the type of communicative code that is appropriate for the transmission of 'wisdom' is inappropriate for either pupils or schoolteachers.

The problems which these anomalies pose are partly resolved and partly avoided in a number of ways. One of the ways of avoiding the problem is not giving the young a chance to display the fact that they have this 'wisdom'. So in assemblies and so on they are not given a chance to speak and pontificate and, in the village context, school knowledge is kept back by the young, until, as elders, they may finally occasionally use it as a decorative extra to *tantara*.

The problem caused by the fact that schools give 'wisdom' to the wrong persons is, however, acute when school knowledge occasionally gives authority. This occurs when it leads to the possessor of such knowledge obtaining an administrative position of some kind. This is not really a problem in Mamolena since nobody holds such a position, but in Ambohivohitra for example and in another nearby village the problem clearly exists.

In this other village there is a young man in his thirties who holds an official administrative post. He was chosen for this post mainly because of his success at school, as the job requires being able to read and write. His position is an embarrassment to every one including himself, as a short anecdote will show. Shortly before leaving the field I had said to people in Mamolena that I was interested in seeing the ancient tomb of the founder of that other village. At the market that Wednesday, after having bought three litres of rum, the elders of Mamolena suggested that we should go to that other village to ask for permission to go to the tomb, perhaps because this would offer an occasion to drink some of the rum. We first went to the elders of that village and the request proceeded with usual Zafimaniry decorum, then as we were leaving we met the young official on the path and my co-villagers decided that we should ask him also for permission.

From the first this caused problems because both the way you sit and the order in which you drink implies relative seniority and nobody could decide on precedence. This was settled in the end and things went well for a while and we addressed the young man by his administrative title of *President*. Then, thanks to the effects of the rum, a new note of irony began to creep into the way the elders addressed the official. They began to call him *Raiamandreny* (elder) and to behave towards him with increasing mock humility. The president did not know where to put himself and finally slunk away.

Schooling is therefore by and large not used out of school in Mamolena, and when it is used it quickly becomes problematic. There is one area of schooling however which does intrude and which needs to be considered separately and that is the use of literacy. Literacy is above all a communicative technique, but since communicative style, person and knowledge are totally welded together for the Zafimaniry, the use of literacy in the village presents the same problems as the use of the 'wisdom' from school.

As discussed above, the Zafimaniry associate different stages of life and different types of knowledge with different forms of communication. For them these different types of communication vary along a continuum from a point where the subject matter and the content are seen as ephemeral to one where it is seen as concerning permanent things conveyed in a language which reflects that fixity. Working with this type of notion and with a view of writing as a technology which immobilises speech, it is not surprising that they, like the Merina a century before,[16] see writing as appropriate for 'wisdom' and conversely as a sign of 'wisdom'. This categorisation therefore has a great influence on the way writing is received and used.

First of all we need to consider the reception of writing, mainly in printed form, which originates outside the village. This comes in three forms:

(1) There are the communications from the administration which are mainly read by the administrator in Ambohivohitra in the presence of the villagers from Mamolena who are summoned to listen.

(2) In many houses in the village there are old pages from French magazines which are sold in markets and are used for house decoration. For example in the house where I lived during field work there was a double page from a fifteen-year-old Express which showed advertisements for, on one page, a bra and, on the other, a credit card bearing the amazingly inappropriate message: *Maintenant avec ma carte Bleu je ne suis plus jamais pris a court*. The picture showed an elegant couple with the man being presented at the end of the

meal with a bill he clearly could not pay. As far as I could judge nobody ever made the slightest attempt to read this.

(3) Those who attend the make-do service run in the church on Sunday are read to by the catechist from the Bible. There are two striking aspect of these readings. First of all, as the relatively young man painfully and sullenly reads the same texts, week after week, the elders stand all together in a row at the back of the church, doing something like presiding, and in this way removing whatever authority the catechist might gain from his profession of 'wisdom'. Secondly, it is clear that what is read on such occasions is almost totally meaningless to the hearers and they never show the least interest in its content. This is perhaps because the language is very difficult to understand as a result of the total disregard for punctuation which characterises the catechist's way of reading. It is also because of the strangeness of the content. For example, a text which came up again and again was the Bible story of the miraculous fishing expedition which involves the casting of nets on either side of the boat, but the Zafimaniry have no experience of fishing from boats with nets. To make matters worse, the translation renders such words as boat by the totally inappropriate Malagasy *sambo kely* which means 'little ocean liner' or 'tanker'.

In fact none of this matters much and the content of these different written messages is all treated in much the same way, a way which is totally consistent with its being assimilated to the 'wisdom' of the elders. All these messages, whether government communications, bra ads, or scripture, are all presumed to come from an immensely powerful beyond and because of this they are taken to be true without question, but also because of this, these messages are not, nor expected to be, informative in a practical way or expected to be immediately relevant to anything in one's life or one's environment. Any attempt to try to analyse what the stuff might mean by ordinary people would be both subversive and imprudent.

Written material produced outside the village does not, therefore, pose a problem for the village theory of the distribution of knowledge. Written material produced inside the village, however, does potentially pose such a problem in much the same way as the use of school knowledge by the young administrator does. This is because those who can write tend to be the fairly young and therefore not appropriate exponents of 'wisdom'. By and large, however, the problem is solved by making the actual writers appear to be scribes for the wisdom of the elders.

There are two kinds of writing which normally emanate from the village. Firstly, there are the messages, four or five lines long, that are sent to neighbouring villages inviting the villagers to rituals or announcing death. Although these are often written by the young, because their form is completely fixed they are seen as emanating from a kind of village 'collective will' of which the elders are the epitome.[17]

Secondly, apart from these totally standard letters there are other, rare, but very important letters which are occasionally sent to, or received, from distant kin and which give important news. One very interesting aspect of these letters is their form which itself suggests the oratory of elders since it is totally modelled on the oratorical exchanges which characterise the special forms of greetings which a returning relative should address to the elders of his family.

On such occasions the returnee, after a lengthy and totally fixed section of the 'how are you' kind of exchange, gives a standardised account of what she has done during her absence. The response is as follows: first a standardised greeting section again, then thanks for the information which should repeat as exactly as possible what has been said by the returned person, then a brief standardised account about what is new in the village. This speech is answered by the returnee in a similar manner. She will thank the elder for the news and then will repeat it.

The general effect of this procedure is that it transforms the fluid events recounted into fixed *Tantara* spoken and endorsed by the elder. In this way knowledge which bore some of the characteristics of that appropriate to middle age is converted into the wisdom of the old in that the speech of the young has somehow been 'taken over'.

Letters follow this pattern too in that they consist of the same kind of greetings, then replicate the previous letter, if there has been one, then they give new news (three or four lines at most), then they sign off with other conventional phrases.

Writing a letter again puts the facts beyond doubt and makes it part of the domain of the absolute truth, like the received writing from the church, the government or the old magazines. Here however there is a difficulty. Such information should emanate and be received by the elders but on the whole the elders are rarely competent readers and writers. The problem is however not great. The action is represented as the junior person writing under the dictation of the elder and reading the letter to the elder who thus becomes the true recipient. This is somewhat of an ideal scenario since what tends in fact to happen is that everyone gets into a huddle trying to make as much sense as they can of the paper . . . but this is what the Zafimaniry say should happen.

This way of representing writing so that it appears to emanate from those in authority negates any of the cognitive and revolutionary potential writing has sometimes been said to have (Goody 1968, 1977). This is because the basic rules concerning knowledge out of school have somehow reorganised the school knowledge to their logic. This might however be considered to be due to the institutionalised nature of letter writing. However, even in cases of innovative uses of writing in the village the control of literacy by the young does not seem to have any significant effect. This is what appears in the following example which is particularly interesting in that it involves precisely the situation which Goody suggested would have fundamental sociological implications since it concerns the writing-based criticism by the literate young of the oral record professed by those in authority.

When I had returned to Mamolena in 1989 after an absence of seventeen years this caused such surprise and interest that I found people falling over themselves trying to be helpful. By then they had decided that what I had been trying to do during my earlier period in the village was to learn *Tantara* since this was the only possible explanation for what I had been doing from within their theory of knowledge. As a result, when the villagers realised that I had come to do the same thing again we began to talk about the history of the village. Then, very soon into this discussion, a middle-aged man whom I had known as a child produced a school note book of sixteen pages filled with neatly written material which turned out to be a history of the village consisting largely of genealogies and I was told that all I needed was in there. I thought the Goody 'great divide' had occurred while I had been away.

In fact I soon realised that my past presence in the village was not unrelated to the existence of this document. What had happened was that I had spent a lot of time talking with a highly respected blind elder, sometimes recording what he said, but most of the time taking notes which I would write up in the evening. This clearly was *Tantara* and the villagers had decided that they too wanted a permanent record of this *tantara* for themselves since they rightly knew that the elder would not live long. They therefore approached a young man and asked him to do what I was presumed to have done, that is to write at the elder's dictation the history of the village.

This was the document which was produced. In a sense exactly the scenario predicted by Goody occurred. As the book was brought in, two elders in a spirit of subdued competition were telling me their version of the *tantara* of the village. Although they were disagreeing on some points, this disagreement was quickly hidden through use of the normal Zafimaniry displays of politeness appropriate among elders. This was not so easy for the written record. The man who had brought in the book began to check the oral against the written and from time to time he pointed out that what was being said did not match up with what was written there. This caused temporary discomfort but in fact it was quickly dealt with. These impertinent interruptions were sometimes listened to in puzzlement but soon they were simply ignored. The fact that it was a young man who was using writing in this way meant that he could not really intervene in the exposition of 'wisdom' by elders. This however did not mean that the book itself was treated with disrespect. The very opposite was the case. The book was clearly a most treasured possession and when it was put away it was given a small offering of rum.

Again the social and cultural framework had subdued the implications of schooling and literacy to its rationale and had meant that, whatever intrusive potential such elements might have, they were rapidly tamed. Thus neither writing nor schooling have made any significant difference to the basic organising principles governing the evaluation of knowledge, rather literacy and schooling have been put to use to reinforce previously existing patterns. Although this is so in Mamolena, it would be dangerous to assume that this is so in other parts of Madagascar and that it would be so in different circumstances. For example, even in Zafimaniry villages peopled by descendants of slaves the situation is not quite the same and schooling does have more significant social implications. Several factors seem to have come together in Mamolena to create this state of affairs. These include the poor economic situation of the country, which has led to the weakness of the educational institutions and the lack of jobs for those with education, and the peculiar suspicion of state authority characteristic of the Zafimaniry and which is probably due to their specific history. Nevertheless, a crucial factor is, I believe, the significance of the way the Zafimaniry view different types of knowledge, which, as we saw, is inseparable from their beliefs about bodily maturation, the person, the nature of society and the plants and animals which inhabit the natural world.

It is consideration of this latter type of context which seems to me to be lacking from most discussions of schooling and literacy. The traditional problematic of the social and psychological sciences has tended to define in advance what is relevant to such research. What the Zafimaniry case shows, is that the empirical enquirer cannot afford to do less than try to observe life in almost any and every aspect.

Notes

The research on which this work is based was financed by the Spencer Foundation of Chicago. I would like to thank Fenella Cannell for assistance in preparing this chapter.
 1 Like the recent article by Street (1987) which takes a similar line, the title of this paper is intended as an indirect tribute to Hoggart's famous book *The uses of literacy* (1957).
 2 For further ethnography on the Zafimaniry, see Vérin 1964, Coulaud 1973, Bloch 1975b.

3 The names of villages in this paper have all been changed to maintain confidentiality.

4 This exam, which in French schools was a low level qualification, was very significant in Madagascar until the level of higher qualification, the Baccalaureat, was lowered.

5 From my earlier field work there and from the recollections of older villagers, I believe that such a day is basically similar to any schoolday in the past in Mamolena and not all that different to what went on in similar schools in the area for the last fifty years, apart from the fact that no serious attempt is now made to teach any French.

6 1989 exchange rate.

7 This is in part due to a special difficulty most Malagasy have with Arabic numerals. In most dialects of Malagasy, including Zafimaniry, numbers are spoken the opposite way to the way they are written. This obviously causes problems in the learning and teaching of arithmetic. Official Malagasy, a language which the government has attempted to introduce to overcome dialectical variation, puts the digits in the European order and in school there are occasional attempts to teach this way. Clearly, however, neither the teacher nor the pupils can actually use this way of talking about numbers in their sums or in ordinary speech and the attempts to introduce 'official Malagasy' seem only to create further confusion.

8 In fact the intermediary stages between these main stages are also very interesting but cannot be discussed here.

9 This includes looking for valuable trees deep in the forest as well as going on wage work.

10 Here are a few further examples:

(i) It was explained to me that Taro does not grow so well now that the forest has retreated. This was attributed by a Zafimaniry to the fact that by now the *decayed vegetable matter* of the forest does not wash down into the swiddens so well any more.

(ii) Winnowing from a basket on the head as opposed to winnowing with a tray, requires a really scientific approach since the height of the basket is calculated in terms of the strength of the wind so that the rice lands fairly separate from the chaff. The weaker the wind the higher the basket. The process produces three piles in a continuum: one rice, one chaff, one mixed, and so on. The interaction of height and wind speed was perfectly explained to me by a woman who noticed me watching her winnowing.

(iii) When filling up his granary with the rice from his harvest, a young married man is measuring it out in numbers of baskets by putting one grain of maize for each *daba* in a small box as a mnemonic. He further informs me that he will not touch the rice before September, when the price rises. Until then he will buy some if he has to. For this he will go to a market in the wet rice-growing area where it will be cheap and where later he hopes to sell dear.

11 The Malagasy term is *Raiamandreny*. It does not denote an absolutely fixed status and can indeed, in some contexts, simply mean parents. It can be applied to both women and men but is more often applied to men.

12 Actually one can distinguish two forms of elder speech. One is of the extreme formalised kind and is used for blessings and thanks: the other, a little more assertive, is used for *Tantara*. This will be expanded elsewhere.
13 For the characteristics of the oratory of Merina elders see Bloch 1975a, pp. 5–12.
14 See Bloch (forthcoming, a and b).
15 The Zafimaniry make a very sharp distinction between *tantara* and *Anganon*, normally translated as 'tales', and they explain the difference by saying that one is true while the other is not. (Not that *Anganon* are necessarily untrue but that they lack the categorical truthfulness of *tantara*. What 'true' in this case means, is to be believed 'beyond question'. It can also be qualified as clear, *mazava*, which again implies that it cannot be doubted (see Bloch, forthcoming, b).
16 See Bloch 1989.
17 In fact, often the letters do not exist as such but people will say that a 'letter' *Taratsy* (lit. 'paper') has been sent or received to say that an invitation or notification has been formally done.

References

Bloch, M. 1975a. *Oratory and political language in traditional society*. London: Academic Press.
1975b. 'Property and the end of affinity', in M. Bloch (ed.), *Marxist analyses and social anthropology*. London: Malaby Press.
1986. *From blessing to violence: history and ideology in the circumcision ritual of the Merina of Madagascar*. Cambridge: Cambridge University Press.
1989. 'Literacy and enlightenment', in K. Schousboe and M. Trolle Larsen (eds.), *Literacy and society*. Copenhagen: Akademisk Forlag.
forthcoming, a. 'The resurrection of the house', in J. Carsten and S. Hugh-Jones (eds.), *About the house: buildings, groups and categories in holistic perspective*. Cambridge: Cambridge University Press.
forthcoming, b. 'People into places: Zafimaniry concepts of clarity', in A. Gell and E. Hirsch (eds.), *The anthropology of landscape*. Oxford: Oxford University Press.
Coulaud, D. 1973. *Les Zafimaniry: un groupe ethnique de Madagascar à la poursuite de la fôret*. Antanarivo: F. B. M.
Goody, J. (ed.), 1968. *Literacy in traditional societies*. Cambridge: Cambridge University Press.
1977. *The domestication of the savage mind*. Cambridge: Cambridge University Press.
Hoggart, R. 1957. *The uses of literacy*. Harmondsworth: Penguin.
Huntingdon, R. 1988. *Gender and social structure in Madagascar*. Bloomington, IN: Indiana University Press.
Lave, J. 1988. *Cognition in practice*. Cambridge: Cambridge University Press.
Perkins, D. N. 1988. 'Creativity and the quest for mechanism', in R. J. Sternberg and E. E. Smith (eds.), *The psychology of thought*. Cambridge: Cambridge University Press.

Scribner, S. and Cole, M. 1981. *The psychology of literacy*. Cambridge, MA: Harvard University Press.
Street, B. V. 1987. 'The uses of literacy and anthropology in Iran', in A. Al-Shahi (ed.), *The diversity of the Muslim community*. London: Ithaca Press.
Vérin, P. 1964. 'Les Zafimaniry et leur art. Un groupe continuateur d'une tradition esthétique Malgache méconnue', *Revue de Madagascar*, 27: 1–76.
Willis, P. 1977. *Learning to labour*. Farnborough: Saxon House.

4

ARABIC LITERACY AND SECRECY AMONG THE MENDE OF SIERRE LEONE

CAROLINE H. BLEDSOE and KENNETH M. ROBEY

Introduction: the sociology of literacy[1]

By all accounts, the invention and spread of writing mark a great advance in human history. Nations struggle to raise their literacy rate, believing that reading and writing are essential for full popular participation in social and economic development. However, efforts to increase literacy have been poorly matched by the efforts of social scientists to understand it. We do not yet fully understand how the introduction of writing into a non-literate society necessarily changes communication or the nature of social interaction. Nor do we sufficiently understand the sociological factors behind why some people, and not others, invest considerable resources to achieve literacy, or why many put high priority on literacy in a foreign language.

Almost every serious thinker on the topic of literacy straddles the dilemma between the *technical potential* of literacy – how it logically could be used – versus how its *social functions* adapt it to the local culture. Simmel (1950) sees the issue as a contrast between the ability of a written message to tangibly fix the content of the information it transcribes (facilitating communication), versus the potential manipulation of that content in social context. Lévi-Strauss (Charbonnier 1969: 26) states that on the one hand, writing has facilitated information accumulation, 'the pre-condition of ... the source of our civilization.' On the other, he insists that writing only appeared in human history when societies became stratified into masters and slaves: 'it [writing] was connected first and foremost with power' (p. 30).

The most widely accepted approach to the sociology of literacy has focused on the technical potentials of literacy, considering writing as a superior mode of communication, in contrast to traditional oral modes (for example, Goody and Watt 1962; Goody 1968a, 1968b, 1971, 1977; Goody et al. 1977). This school holds that literacy extends communication beyond face-to-face interaction and reduces dependency on memory for storing and retrieving information:

The importance of writing lies in its creating a new medium of communication between men. Its essential service is to objectify speech, to provide language with a material correlative, a set of visible signs. In this material form speech can be transmitted over space and preserved over time; what people say and think can be rescued from the transitoriness of oral communication.

(Goody 1968a: 1; see also Olson 1977: 268)

The inherent pragmatic value of writing for transmitting ideas across space and time is said to ensure its spread – except when 'factors that prevent the realization of the full potentialities of literacy' interfere (for example, technological constraints; the 'tendency to secrecy'; the '*guru* tradition', wherein the teacher becomes the broker of knowledge; (Goody, 1968a: 11–13)). Hence, 'restricted literacy' is aberrant, while the full use of literacy is taken for granted as a logical consequence of the medium itself.

Goody must be credited with expanding the scope of literacy study to a wide cross-cultural level and, through it, developing innovative ideas for examining literacy in particular settings. He has also creatively lent his strong social anthropological background to a field much in need of social structural perspective. However, the tenet that literacy possesses qualities that surpass those of orality in communication neglects the equally logical potentials of writing for obfuscation and lying. These potentials are multiplied by using a non-indigenous language, when skills in the language are not widely distributed, and when writing and comprehension are taught separately. Moreover, 'restricted literacy' cannot be dismissed as aberrant. People in all societies 'restrict literacy' in one way or another (Street 1984). To assume certain properties of writing *a priori* as a clear positivist construct reduces literacy and 'restricted literacy' to tautologies.

Street (1984: 5) challenges what he calls the 'autonomous model' of literacy: the view that literacy acts independently to enhance communication because of the inherent clarity, endurance, and precision of the written word. Drawing on other studies (especially Clancy 1979; Graff 1979; Finnegan 1973; Heath 1982; and Parry 1982) as well as his own, he develops an 'ideological model' of literacy. This model

treats sceptically claims by western liberal educators for the 'openness', 'rationality' and critical awareness of what they teach, and investigates the role of such teaching in social control and the hegemony of a ruling class. It concentrates on the overlap and interaction of oral and literate modes rather than stressing a 'great divide'. (Street 1984, 2–3)

Like Street, we ask how literacy has been incorporated into indigenous patterns of knowledge management, rather than assuming its wholesale adoption with all its alleged technical potentials. Instead of asking why literacy is restricted in particular societies, it makes more sense to ask how societies utilise and even reinterpret various aspects of literacy into their own cultural systems. As Kulick and Stroud (1990: 287) argue, 'far from being passively transformed by literacy, [individuals] instead actively and creatively apply literate skills to suit their own purposes and needs' (see also Reder and Green 1983). The Mende of Sierra Leone view literacy less as a mnemonic device than a resource to bolster the legitimacy of claims and provide (or preclude) access to secret domains of knowledge whose meanings are dangerous to those without legitimate social and ritual qualifications. This means that writing skills can be withheld or divulged strategically to gain power and dependants. Thus, although the Mende of Sierra Leone use literacy in some contexts to enhance communication and social integration, the more interesting issue is how they use it for secrecy and separation. Literacy becomes a potential *resource* to achieve goals that do not necessarily correspond to those posited by the 'autonomous' model of literacy.

Because Mende society has several spoken languages and codes of writing that are used by overlapping subgroups in a post-colonial setting of rapid change, it provides an excellent arena for asking how literacy in non-native languages has been incorporated into a local context that emphasises secrecy. Although our primary focus will be local uses of Arabic, we will first describe the uses of writing in general for secrecy, then turn to specific uses of Arabic writing. Finally, we contrast this with recent trends in both English and Arabic, to highlight how different social situations of learning modify the way a written language is perceived and used.

Though we do not explicitly compare speech and writing, much of our argument applies equally to oral competence. Indeed, we view the two modes as more similar than different in sociological impact since both provide ample opportunity for ambiguity and secrecy. In fact, any mode of communication can be used to conceal secrets and emphasise boundaries between the knowledgeable and the ignorant. For example, West African secret societies employ special sign languages, songs, and dances with hidden meanings (Harley 1941). And masked spirits speak 'a secret language of restructured Mende' (Hommel 1974) that require special interpretation for the public.

The Mende people live primarily in the eastern and south-eastern hinterland of Sierra Leone, a region of historically mobile populations and ethnic intermingling. They are a Mande-speaking group numbering almost a third of the country's population of four million. They traditionally grew upland rice, supplemented by swamp rice farms. Polygyny is allowed, though gerontocracy prevents most men from acquiring more than one wife at a time until middle age. Mende families are ideally patrilineal, but households frequently include siblings of the spouses, foster children, elderly widows, clients, and so on. In this Central West Atlantic Region of Africa, defined by d'Azevedo (1962b), a critical social feature is the presence of secret associations such as the Poro and Sande societies that initiate practically all boys and girls, respectively, into their membership. These societies manage power through ritual authority based ideologically on hidden and allegedly dangerous knowledge that is inaccessible to non-initiates and low ranked members (see Murphy 1980, 1981; Bledsoe 1984).

Literacy and secrecy

The secrecy inherent in these institutions and the social control it facilitates suffuse social life. A classical sociological approach to secrecy and restricted knowledge is that of George Simmel (1950: 332), who observed that secrecy and how one uses it are independent of the content it guards. Bellman (1984: 16–17) restates this for a neighbouring group in Liberia, the Kpelle: 'the contents of the secrets are not as significant as are the *doing* of secrecy'. Access to secrets can be the basis of differentiation between the privileged who share it and those from whom it is hidden (Simmel 1950: 345). It can also determine the success or failure of individuals in advancing politically (see, for example, d'Azevedo (1962a: 29) and Murphy (1980: 193, 199) on groups in Liberia).

Simmel notes that written expressions, like all forms of communication, contain a mixture of clarity and ambiguity and that secrecy plays on this. Like Simmel, we stress that writing can function as any other medium in concealing information, rather than making it more accessible. This phenomenon is so easily documented that one might argue, in fact, that the tangible qualities of writing in contrast to speech offer special opportunities to manipulate and conceal meaning.

People can teach literacy only to a select few and control the rate and quality of instruction. They also send written messages to prevent nonliterates, including the bearer, from discovering the content. Written messages can even be used to exclude other literates from secrets. The contents of a message can be written in code or in a foreign language, then sealing the paper in an envelope for delivery. And possessors of a written document can alter it, or refer to it but prevent others from reading it.

The Mende, like other groups, make wide use as well of multi-lingual literacy to exclude certain audiences. Muslim leaders usually correspond about religious matters in Arabic, thereby excluding nonbelievers as well as the less literate from their affairs, and many Muslim traders keep their business records in Arabic to thwart tax collectors. However, multi-lingual literacy is only one tool of semantic exclusion. Distinctive writing styles or vocabularies can keep ignorant various subgroups within the literate population. Government agencies in Sierre Leone, control knowledge of their affairs and preserve monopolies of desired resources by writing in bureaucratic English.

Written words themselves can have multiple underlying meanings with pragmatic utility when the aim is to deceive. Writers can craft ambiguities into the text by using cryptic allusions, as in 'love business'. To prevent apprehension by irate spouses, lovers often correspond through written notes that are signed 'the person with whom you are familiar', 'you know who', or a pseudonym. Places of rendezvous can be cloaked in metaphor. In 'love business' correspondence, as in other arenas, the sender and receiver need not be literate themselves in order to exploit the secrecy potentials of writing. They may ask older schoolchildren to write and translate for them.

Just as writers can purposefully make a text ambiguous, readers can put a certain slant on a document's interpretation. Hence, the literal meanings of the words, if indeed these can be translated or ascertained, may be less important than negotiated claims about their meanings. (This assertion is supported by 'reading theory' in literary criticism, according to which the way a text is interpreted depends less on the meaning intended by the writer than by the historical and cultural context of the reader; for example, Cohen 1974.)

Concerning the factual content of written texts, no matter how 'fixed' the medium or how clear its original intent, people recognise that a document's meaning, like that of oral communication, is always open to reinterpretation, revision, or denial. Even a stone gravemarker that is inscribed with relatives' claims that the deceased held particular offices (largely to legitimate the political statuses of descendants) can be erased, altered, challenged, or simply ignored.

A possessor of a written document can also reveal or reinterpret it at strategic times. A chief's brother may keep written records of the movement and conduct of each of the chief's wives. Since the brother and his descendants are potential rivals to the chief's descendants, his primary purpose is not to assist his memory; it is to create a future resource, should he try to unseat his brother's children by disputing their paternity. Similarly, bureaucratic officials can use alleged literacy incompetence to trap those who fail to provide adequate bribes: they may deny promotions or services or levy fines, basing their actions on the supplicant's failure to fill out forms correctly. This, then, is not simply the passive consequence of bureaucratisation but a deliberate use of writing codes to 'find fault', a common Mende expression.

Finally, writing can facilitate outright falsification. One school principal reported that students commonly forged his name on notes to their illiterate caretakers, requesting money for fictitious school fees, which the students embezzled. On the other hand, written messages – even forged ones – can help confirm a truth rather than falsify. When school exams and report cards were delayed one term, a boy feared that his parents would not believe him if he merely told them. To convince them, he composed a note explaining the matter and signed it 'from the acting principal'.

Writing, of course, has other uses besides those pertaining to secrecy practices. It can communicate meanings beyond those literally transcribed on the paper. Writing enhances the importance of the message and shows respect for the receiver. People frequently approach someone of high status for a favour by handing him a written message. Whereas writing might communicate the literal message less expeditiously than saying it, this circumvents face-to-face 'shame' for the supplicant, even if he delivers his own message in person, as he often does. Similarly, the use of calling cards among urban professionals, elegant paper and letterheads, typewritten script, and a clean, multicolored airmail envelope all signify respect for the person addressed as well as the importance of the message and its sender. Conversely, a writer wishing to insult the recipient might write the message in red ink or on a crumpled, casually ripped piece of paper.[2]

The Mende and literacy

Although lacking an indigenous script, the Mende today have several available codes of writing. Arabic was introduced in the eighteenth and nineteenth centuries by Mandingo and Fula traders and other propagators of Islam from the north. English arrived from the coast with British colonists, traders, and Christian missionaries. Missionaries also employed the international phonetic script for transcribing religious texts into Mende. They taught Mende literacy in their schools for a time, as did schools under the newly independent country, but its use is declining. Another Mende script, invented in 1921 by a local Mandingo man (see Dalby 1967), gained some popularity in the 1920s and 1930s but has virtually disappeared today. Krio, an English-based creole language, originated among the ex-slaves who resettled in Sierra Leone from the Americas or were freed from slaving vessels and relocated by the British. Krio is the unofficial national spoken language, though standard English overshadows it in written documents.

Learning Arabic and English both entail learning a new language and a relationship between the language's spoken words and its written characters. However, literacy in the two is taught by a different process and entails a different teacher/student relationship. Arabic traditionally is studied from the Qur'ān (alternatively: Koran) under a *karamoko*[3] (Arabic teacher, Islamic scholar) who demands stringent discipline, laborious work, and long-term commitments from his students. English is taught in Western-style schools where the obligatory nature of the teacher/student bond is less intense. In recent times, Muslim sects such as the Ahmaddiyah established schools on the Western model that offer classes in Arabic.

Just as they disseminate knowledge selectively in secret associations, the Mende have incorporated Islamic and European knowledge into their social hierarchies. Much of it is concentrated in written texts such as the Qur'ān, the Bible, or government documents that are directly accessible only to the literate. A person who can read and write has potentially exploitable access to powerful ritual texts, private records of debts and agreements, and special knowledge of laws and bureaucratic regulations.

The Mende view Arabic and English as languages of important, outside civilisations that have powerful knowledge for ordinary local people. Literacy can enhance access to these realms. But because the two realms are quite distinct, the modes of writing that provide access to them are also viewed distinctly – not uniformly as simply two manifestations of one literacy phenomenon. Hence, each literacy implies unique advantages for pursuing certain goals. English is the official idiom of government schools, the national bureaucracy, and Christian churches; Arabic is the language of Islam and has special ritual application in charms for healing and protection by a *Moriman* (a Krio term for a specialist in Muslim magic). Both languages are used in personal correspondence and record-keeping. But because most Mende who learn Arabic are trained only in its religious aspects, and because English as the official national language is taught in schools, they tend to use English for more mundane purposes.

Arabic literacy among the Mende

The first writing to reach most Mende areas was Arabic in the eighteenth century. Arabic literacy spread through West Africa with the propagation of Islam by trade, invasion, migration, and missionisation. Other factors such as competition for clients and students seem to have encouraged geographic mobility among Arabic scholars. People associate knowledge with distance and mobility: one must travel in order to gain more knowledge. Foreign study and religious pilgrimages increase a scholar's prestige.

Famous *morimen* and *karamokos* regularly embark on long journeys to market their magic and recruit new students. The supposed origin of certain charms and magical books in faraway places like Egypt or India adds to their aura.

West Africans associated Arabic writing not only with religious matters but also with correspondence and record-keeping in government and commerce. When indigenous people in Sierre Leone began converting to Islam, a few learned Arabic, and even non-Muslim political leaders came to employ Muslim traders and missionaries for letter writing and translation (Skinner 1973). Initially, however, few West Africans achieved any degree of literacy in Arabic, and sometimes the only book they read was the Qur'ān.

Southern Mende were less influenced by Islam than their northerly neighbours, who experienced more influence from Islamised trading and conquering groups from overland. Working inland from the coast, Christian missionaries sought to counter the spread of Islam, making greater efforts to convert and 'civilise' the Mende. Consequently, Western-style schools that teach English are more common in Mende areas than in areas dominated by other ethnic groups. After initial resistance, people became eager to learn English and other secrets of the white man (see Gittins 1977 for an insightful account of the relationship between the Mende and Catholic missionaries).

Today even non-Muslim Mende have frequent contact with Muslims – Mende as well as people of other ethnicity such as Fula and Mandingo – especially in business concession areas that attract outside workers. Most Mende villages have at least a few residents who are literate in Arabic. The people whom this study concerns live primarily in the north-eastern part of Mendeland that has a higher percentage of Muslims, approximately 75 per cent, than the south.

Those who first brought Arabic writing to Mendeland, mostly Fula and Mandingo, enjoyed an initial monopoly that they used to advantage. Foreigners are believed to carry powerful outside knowledge, which can entail considerable prestige and, on the other hand, suspicion. Literate immigrants convinced local people that Arabic writing, and those who understood it, held special powers (see also A. K. Turay, in Skinner 1978: 58). Although other groups such as the Mandingo and Fula still claim greater religious knowledge than the Mende, many Mende compete with them in exploiting this knowledge. Local ritual specialists now often substitute Muslim magic based on written charms for indigenous magic and sorcery, and Muslim ritual specialists enhance their reputations as purveyors of powerful 'outside' knowledge by studying in Guinea or by acquiring scholarships to study in the Middle East.

Morimen and mori magic

Two kinds of specialists, *morimen* and *karamokos*, use powers explicitly derived from their knowledge of Arabic writing to earn income, gain prestige, and recruit apprentice learners. *Morimen* use Arabic texts with alleged ritual efficacy to help clients in a multitude of concerns: to pursue love affairs, cure barrenness, gain employment, win court cases, harm enemies, pass school exams, defeat witches, or drive away demons of madness. They do so by predicting and controlling the future. *Morimen* also provide protective magic for founding a town, erecting a house, naming a child, and other ritual occasions. Certain verses in the Qur'ān and other sacred texts are believed effective in these matters, for they are directives that God will obey.

A *moriman* uses his command over Arabic writing, which is widely regarded as the literal word of God, to obtain God's assistance. He evokes a verse's power by writing it on paper, rolled into a tight wad and tied with string or inserted in a small amulet pouch. He may also write the verse on a special length of board with a piece of burnt wood from the *luba* tree and wash off the words with water to make a black potion, *nesi* ('holy water'). The *moriman* blesses the amulet or liquid and instructs the client on its use. The client may wear the amulet or bury it, or he may drink the *nesi* or rub it on himself. Sewing up the Arabic writing in a leather pouch or dissolving it in water lends an air of secrecy to the event. To further hide their knowledge, *karamokos* are said to avoid teaching during midday hours, and *morimen* work their most powerful magic at night in dim candlelight and prefer black ink for writing charms and making *nesi*, which then appears as a black liquid. Trimingham (1959: 114) noted that a bottle of *mansai* (the equivalent of Mende *nesi*) should not sit in the sunlight, lest it lose power.

The actual writing, the physically drawn words, is the centre of *mori* magic. Simply thinking, reading, or speaking the words are rarely effective. Even when a non-Muslim Mende wishes to use *mori* rituals to cause or prevent a certain event, he will seek assistance from someone skilled in Arabic writing, rather than simply Arabic recitation – and, of course, someone who knows *mori* magic. When the *moriman* works in the presence of his clients, therefore, he makes certain that they are aware that he is employing literacy skills. He may display openly his books containing the sacred texts, and does not conceal his writing. However, his clients are unlikely to copy his actions to attempt the same deeds on their own. Even if they see the verses he is using, they do not know specifically why those have been chosen; in most cases, the specific potential of the words cannot be discerned from a literal understanding of the meaning. Learning which verses have what magical qualities appears to be a task separate from the initial literacy skills. Moreover, simply writing or reciting the appropriate words or even understanding their meaning or their deepest ritual powers meaning is considered insufficient for most magic to work. The *moriman* must also bless the amulet or *nesi* and thereby indirectly bless the recipient. To do so, he himself must have been blessed by special people and deities.

The idea of 'blessings' pervades Mende society. Both Muslim and Christian elders bless younger kin, parents bless children, masters bless apprentices, teachers bless students, and so on, ritually calling for their ancestors to ask God (*Ngewo*) for the good fortune and success of the subordinates who have served them well or people who have done good deeds for them. For a *moriman* to control powerful magic and prosper, he must have worked hard for, and demonstrated unquestioning fealty to, his own teacher who taught him secret knowledge of the craft. (See Skinner's discussion (1978: 44) of the Islamic concept of *barakah*, spiritual blessedness passed down from the Prophet or a Sufi saint by links of master to disciple.) If he has received these blessings, his own work will be efficacious. Without them, he will be ineffective, and he can go crazy or die if he attempts to use the secret skills he has learned. A *moriman* who receives the requisite blessings can pass them on, without diminishing his own accumulation, in each magical item he manufactures. One earns blessings from benefactors and ancestors through obedience, suffering, and hard work; but blessings transferred from *moriman* to client are more readily available like commodities, through purchase.

Besides obtaining their magical skills through training and blessings from their teachers and parents, *morimen* can make contact through dreams and visions with *jinai* who befriend and aid them. *Jinai* are powerful spirits that can make special demands of God. Although God, like earthly patrons, will only comply with properly channelled requests from humans that come through his highest ranking clients (in this case, the ancestors of the supplicants), the *jinai* can pressure the ancestors, their fellow spirits, to bring these requests to God, even if the ancestors do not want an undeserving descendant of theirs to succeed. (They capitulate, however, partly because they fear the *jinai* may harm the descendant they do wish to succeed.) Although the resultant successes may be short-lived, in contrast to achievements obtained through legitimate merit from elders and ancestors, *morimen*'s clients are anxious for immediate results.

Some *jinai* are good, some are bad; but, like the Mende, all are obsessed with secret knowledge. *Jinai*, in fact, have their own secret society, much as humans do. Therefore, although *jinai* are indigenous spirits, they are attracted to, and willing to assist, good Muslims who are higly learned in the Qur'ān and do not reveal secrets of questionable ritual transactions, in which people or body parts may be sacrificed symbolically as payments. A *moriman* who learns the necessary texts and acquires blessings from his own teachers and assistance from a *jinai* can act as a broker in this chain of supernatural solicitation to gain considerable wealth and power. Some *morimen* become full-time magical specialists and well-paid advisers to chiefs and high officials in the national government. Abraham (1978: 160) reports that some observers attributed partial blame for the Mende hut tax resistance of 1898 to *morimen* agitators who made magic for local resistance efforts.

Karamokos and Arabic education

Among the most important ways of benefiting from Arabic literacy is to teach it. *Karamoko* means literally 'one who can read' (Arabic: *qura'ra* – 'to read', 'to recite from the Qur'ān'). A *karamoko* may be a scholar, teacher, proselytiser, healer, or diviner. (In some contexts, *karamoko* and *moriman* are interchangeable, but we follow the general Mende use of *karamoko* for a teacher–scholar versus *moriman* for someone whose reputation rests mainly on his business in Islamic magic.) A *karamoko* teaches 'Arabic learners', usually young children from the ages of five and up, in exchange for their labour and gifts from their parents or sponsors at various stages in the learning process. Parents of the students may also give girls to the *karamokos* (as do many clients of a successful *moriman*), who will become his wives eventually. Some study Arabic with him, but others are sent purely as wives. Arabic literacy is primarily a male prerogative. Girls who study with a *karamoko* generally do not board in his household unless they are to marry him later, because parents fear sexual tampering. People also say that the hardship of Arabic learning is too severe for girls, and that in any case women cannot keep secrets. Hence, those women who do become literate in Arabic and read the Qur'ān are usually wives or close relatives of *karamokos*. Few women achieve fame through Islamic magic, though the wife of one famous *karamoko* argues religious points with him and assists with teaching.

Students generally live in the *karamoko*'s household and work on his farm under strict discipline for years, making it advantageous for the *karamoko* to draw out the learning process as long as possible. A poorly behaved, disrespectful student cannot hope to gain the more important knowledge held by the *karamoko*, although gifts from parents or sponsors can strongly influence him. As with *mori* magic, the idea of 'blessings' reinforces the *karamoko*'s monopoly. Without blessings one cannot succeed. Consequently, the *karamoko* only bestows blessings upon respectful, obedient, and hardworking students who have demonstrated their merit over many years.

Arabic learners 'buy blessings' not simply for good scholarship but more particularly for working on the *karamoko*'s farm and enduring severe discipline. They generally work longer hours at domestic chores or in the fields than they spend studying Arabic. Instruction takes place in the early morning and late afternoon or evening; the middle of the day is for the learners' work tasks. Even the youngest students must perform house chores, deliver messages, or scare birds away from crops. Many students are fed so poorly that they must beg or work for food in the village. Many people admire the children for what they are doing and feed them readily, but others look down on them, for most are ragged and dirty. The learners also endure severe beatings for intransigence or failure to learn. Reported one *karamoko*:

> The native men believe that the Holy Alquaran came down from God with a cane to beat the learners. [However,] they also believe that God the Almighty gives Arabic learners their payment, so they may inherit heaven when they die ... So whether or not the Arabic learners eat to their satisfaction, they learn Arabic whole-heartedly, because they believe that their payment will be to inherit heaven when they die. The Arabic learners have a strong belief that when they are severely punished or starved, this is a way of gaining more blessings from their *karamokos*. So for that reason, even if they are maltreated and they happen to report matters to their parents, the parents will simply tell them to return to their *karamokos* and bear up with conditions to gain more blessings, so they will get good reward by inheriting heaven and live after death.

Suffering and hardship are not simply unavoidable accompaniments of learning. *Gbale* ('hurting, suffering') is seen as essential to gain the knowledge one seeks. The Mende believe strongly that a spoiled child with an easy life can never achieve desired goals (see also Bledsoe and Isiugo-Abanihe 1989), especially those involving secret powers. A Mende proverb states: 'When the child is well fed and happens to come across a grave, he will see that it is just a sort of heap, an ordinary heap'. That is, the child does not realise that there is something decaying, powerful, and dangerous under the mound of earth. To perceive and to be able to control secret powers, one must pay the cost by suffering and hard work. If one is too comfortable and well fed, one will be lazy and will not be motivated to learn. The philosophy, 'No success without struggle', an often-stated adage in Sierra Leone, is carried to an extreme for Arabic learners who are seen as being given a chance to master the powers of Arabic literacy. Consequently, a father is more likely to remove his child from a *karamoko*'s household if the child is not learning enough than if the conditions are harsh.

The philosophy that rationalises the living conditions students are expected to tolerate also shapes how and what they learn. In Arabic literacy instruction, the skills of speaking, reading, writing, and understanding a new language can be imparted separately and sparingly, thus extending the master's profit-making potential almost indefinitely. Learners learn mainly by rote memorisation. They start with the alphabet and then memorise portions of the Qur'ān. The *karamoko* or an advanced student recites a verse, and the learners practise until they can repeat the lines perfectly on their own. Then they go on to the next verse. They learn writing by repeatedly copying on wooden slates (*walas*) what the teacher writes. Many *karamokos* forbid students to see the actual Qur'ān or to write on paper until they have first memorised several *surahs* (sections of the Qur'ān). Students learn to treat written Arabic words with great respect. During instruction they practise all Arabic writing on the *wala* and then erase it. One man explained, 'It is important to use the *wala* in teaching the Qur'ān because [if they wrote on paper] they might treat the words of the Qur'ān lightly and scatter them around.' If a student, for example, were to casually practise writing Arabic characters on a wall of a house, he could be punished. 'It is an insult to the Muslim people,' commented another man. 'They really think the Arabic very high, so they don't like to see that.'

Students also learn that Arabic writing can be dangerous. A paper found bearing Arabic writing would be a fearful object because it might be intended to harm the finder. This would be suspected especially if the meaning of the words were obscure, though a reader who understood their literal meaning still would fear they harboured a ritually dangerous meaning. Scarce and expensive though paper is, people hawking small food items such as peanuts in the market never use pieces of paper they find that contain Arabic script to wrap wares for customers. People particularly fear pieces of what is known locally as 'writing pad' paper, which is sold in stores but is known to be used by *morimen* to work their rituals because it is easy to fold into an amulet pouch. Above all, people would fear for such a piece of paper if it contained Arabic script written in the tell-tale dark brown ink, *nesi*, which must be used in Arabic rituals.

The fact that beginning students (and often non-Muslims) are not allowed to see the Qur'ān or scatter its words casually is paralleled by efforts to hide its meaning. Unlike the Bible, there are no Mende translations of the Qur'ān, a fact related more to secrecy practices than to fiscal problems. The few English translations of the Qur'ān that exist are treated furtively. When the investigator expressed interest in seeing one, a Muslim friend produced it, but made her promise to tell no one she had it and to return it soon.

Understanding the meaning of the words, then, is another skill that is carved into highly discrete spheres of achievement. Initially the *karamoko* only teaches the pronunciation and graphic representation of Arabic words, withholding their meaning until the student has memorised the entire Qur'ān. For students who complete the initial phase of scholarship, learning the meaning of the Qur'ān requires starting from a new state of ignorance, learning the meaning of texts that until now they are only supposed to know how to write and pronounce. To further draw out his process, the *karamoko*, if he is Mandingo, as many claim to be, the translations likely will be in Mandingo, which his Mende students must learn also.

Learning the ritual magical potentials of certain passages of the Qur'ān comprises yet another realm of endeavour. Students must learn new, 'deeper' meanings of the same texts whose literal meaning they learned before. Despite textual allusions to possible ritual uses, full knowledge of these uses depends on how specialists have construed the verses' meanings and powers. The whole process may take years and many students drop out, having gained only enough knowledge to allow them to participate in prayers in the local mosque. (Some Arabic teachers never teach meaning because they can only decode at the phonetic or surface semantic level. Others who are pressured to explain certain passages may secretly pay a more advanced *karamoko* to explain the meaning to them. Still others try to bluff, construing their knowledge as more profound than its actual content would suggest.)

Only the most advanced and trusted students learn what are allegedly the important secret meanings behind the most sacred Qur'ānic verses and other texts (*Hadith, Kitaba,* and so on). Eventually a few may earn the privilege of copying the *karamoko*'s most secret and powerful texts that he received from his own teacher. Copies of the Qur'ān and other Arabic texts used by *morimen* and *karamokos* are generally handwritten, having been passed along or copied in a long chain of teacher/student exchanges. The student who behaves properly and learns assiduously will be allowed to copy his master's book. Although Qur'āns are ultimately linked to the Prophet's initial written record of God's word, the Mende hold that a book's power rests in part on the reputation of its forebearers. A hand-copied book thus comprises a material link to the accumulated blessings of one's scholarly ancestors.

A student's hard work and assiduous learning, together with his master's blessings and copies of his master's books, help him to establish himself eventually, if he desires, as a *moriman* or a *karamoko*. As one *moriman* explained, 'For all these [hidden areas in the Qur'ān] I owed great obligation to my late *karamoko* who helped me to know all what I am able to get [for] my living today.'

Just as writing itself is critical to a *moriman*'s command of magic, writing is also critical to a *karamoko*'s control over students. When a child first goes for instruction, the *karamoko* writes a Qur'ānic passage on the learner's hand with black ink (*lubei*). He puts salt on the hand and the learner licks it off, swearing obedience to his new master. A *karamoko* may also 'swear' students upon a specific verse in an open Qur'ān not to seduce his wives or to leave before he is satisfied with their performance. Although students who seek better understanding and 'cleverness' for their learning sometimes make a ritual potion with written words and wash their faces with it, they must exercise extreme caution; the *karamoko* warns them that if they try to employ texts for *mori* magic without his permission, the words will turn against them and make them go crazy.

All this suggests that the Mende culturally dichotomise literacy skills much more than if they were simply different modes of communication in the same language.[4] The social effect of slicing up these cognitive skills and imparting them for good behaviour is to place enormous control in the hands of those who are seen as legitimate practitioners (see also Bloch 1968). The more general process of Arabic learning also teaches students that the social structure of the Islamic as well as lay learned, like the process of Arabic learning, is heavily stratified and secretive, and that entrance into its upper ranks is attained only by scrupulous obedience to leaders.

Arabic literacy and 'wealth-in-people'

Although a *karamoko* gains blessings from God for teaching others, he obviously gains practical benefits. Within the West African context, Arabic instruction under a *karamoko* becomes a variation within the widespread system of 'rights in persons' (Kopytoff and Miers 1977) or 'wealth in people' (Bledsoe 1980), in which wealth derives less from creating bonds of duty and obligation with *people* than from ownership of land or material possessions. Other such relationships include patronage, marriage, and child fosterage.

In the past, tutelage under a *karamoko* was compared explicitly to slavery. Indeed after the French abolished slavery in Senegambia, the Jakhanke made 'wider use of Qur'ān school students who were now relied upon to provide services previously rendered by slaves' (Senneh 1979: 137; see also Park 1870 (1799): 261). In some cases, ex-slaves were recruited to remain in Jakhanke households, ostensibly as students. Even today, many Sierra Leoneans compare *karamokos'* treatment of Arabic students to slavery which is enforced by the strategic control of meaning and literacy. Explained one local *karamoko*:

> Alphas [*karamokos*] who know [the meaning of the texts] but don't teach with meaning ... don't want to teach the children quickly so that they will learn and understand quickly. If they do

teach the meaning, they [the students] will leave their *karamokos* without working for them for many years. The *karamokos* feel the Arabic learners are their slaves, so if they should teach them with meaning and dispatch them, they will no longer have people to perform their domestic work.

Phrasing his explanation in a key contemporary idiom, the same man offered a perceptive explanation of why *karamokos* control meaning: 'The reason why they [*karamokos*] teach without meaning is that the Alphas are not paid monthly.' That is, because *karamokos* do not receive regular salaries from outside sources, they depend on students for labour and on the students' parents for fees and other assistance. However, the debt is construed conversely: the knowledge the *karamokos* impart is infinitely more valuable than mundane physical labour. Indeed, even the hardest working, most loyal students cannot repay such a debt, making the *karamoko*'s good will and blessings essential.

The alleged need for students to suffer and 'buy blessings' increases the incentive for a *karamoko* to reveal privileged knowledge judiciously. The longer he can delay giving up secrets, the more he benefits. Although he does impart some important secrets, he may withhold his most powerful ones to maintain a competitive advantage over former students. The fact that some students continue their Arabic education in Egypt, Kuwait, Saudi Arabia, or other Islamic countries may threaten his monopoly. However, when they return, he may demand that they share valuable knowledge learned abroad, because they are still under obligation for past teachings and will suffer if their former master curses them.

Students can never be certain what knowledge is left to gain. With famous *karamokos*, older students hoping for yet more valuable secrets may even marry (assisted by their *karamoko*) and build households nearby, but continue working part-time for their master. Although some *karamokos* attract few students and are relatively poor, a famous Mende *karamoko* in Pujehun District had forty-five young Arabic learners in his household at the time of the research, and thirty married ones living nearby who were working on his farm or teaching his younger students. The oldest was thirty and had been with his master for twenty-four years. This *karamoko*, however, reported that his own teacher had had over one hundred students at a time. Another *karamoko* with twenty-six resident learners said that his own teacher had had over two hundred students. Moreover, accepting each new student widens the network of families from whom a *karamoko* may acquire new learners as well as wives from grateful clients. Former students also may send their own children to their old teacher.

In this system of more traditional Arabic education, then, the literate few use their knowledge to control the labour and loyalty of the less literate. Many people specifically compare this practice of converting claimed Arabic knowledge into wealth in people to the Poro and Sande societies, wherein elders manage monopolies of knowledge that is cast as secret and dangerous in order to acquire youthful labour and payments from parents during initiations (Bledsoe 1980: 46–80; 1984; Murphy 1980). (These institutions do not compete directly, however. A *karamoko* may even sponsor some of his students for Poro initiation with the parents' permission.)

English literacy and pumoi education

The ways in which the Mende have incorporated Arabic literacy become clearer when contrasted to Mende perceptions of English literacy. Although people use English literacy as a resource for obtaining wealth and power, they associate it less directly with secret knowledge and supernatural power. They tend to value Western knowledge for its application to everyday technologies like transportation and manufacturing and to mobility within the modern business and government hierarchy. In contrast, they value Arabic knowledge for its direct connection to supernatural *jinai*, ancestors, and God.

The Mende label the white man's material and conceptual imports *pumoi* things. People associate the word *pu* with 'modern', but some suggest that it also connotes 'adding on' (*pu* – 'to add' or 'to put on'); thus, getting new material possessions. Hence, a *pumoi* (*moi* – 'person') is a 'modern, civilised' person, black or white, who has continual access to more and newer clothes, food, furniture, wage jobs, and so forth. *Pumoi* also implies an easy life without hard work. The Mende say that European outsiders were able to dominate Africans during colonialism because of their powerful knowledge of Western civilisation, especially its technology. A person who desires a *pumoi* style of life today must learn this special knowledge. The key to this goal is English literacy.

Although Westerners perceive schools and literacy as freely spreading information, Mende teachers and bureaucracies manage modern knowledge much the same as knowledge in secret societies is managed (see also Murphy 1981: 679 on the Kpelle of Liberia). Teachers sometimes use their positions to obtain labour and money from students and parents. They do this most effectively with schoolchildren who live with them during the school term. But school teachers, like Arabic teachers, attempt to use the idiom of 'blessings' to reinforce hierarchical relationships with all their students. Stressing the virtues of obedience, teachers may demand student labour in their households and on their farms, allowing the students to earn the blessings that are considered necessary for future career success.

Yet there are some important differences in how English and Arabic literacy have been incorporated locally. School children are occasionally beaten by teachers and are sometimes hungry when they come to school. But hunger is not usually tied to misbehaviour in school and students receive milder treatment from their teachers than Arabic learners do. Because they are cast as *pumois* in the making, schoolchildren are usually clean and adequately clothed, compared to their Arabic counterparts. Many school-children can avoid farmwork altogether, because *pumois* do not do this. A *karamoko* explained that *pumoi* education, in fact, encourages privileged treatment for children because it prepares them for an easy *pumoi* life without visible hardship. If you are a *pumoi*, he explained, 'everything comes to you'.

There are also differences in the degree to which *pumoi* and Arabic knowledge are said to be secretive and, therefore, susceptible to manipulation. Arabic education focuses on writing, on the text itself, and on secret meanings that can only be discerned after years of study and obedience to the master. Although a schoolteacher, like a *karamoko* or a secret society leader, may try to control privileged knowledge and bestow blessings, the fact that English is used widely makes this more difficult, though by no means impossible. Moreover, students sometimes challenge teachers' attempts to withhold knowledge and blessings. They argue that teachers already receive salaries to impart knowledge and thus have no right to demand non-school work or power to dispense blessings. Such students insist that if they have the blessings of their families or caretakers, to whom they are primarily indebted, they can succeed very well without teachers' blessings. For such reasons, teachers do not control student labour as effectively as *karamokos*.

To be sure, Christianity is thought to possess magical powers that parallel *mori* magic. Jehovah's Witnesses, for example, because they make proclamations about the future, have been incorporated into Mende thought as the Christian equivalents of *morimen*, and can thus intervene with God by striking bargains with *jinai*, who can also foretell the future. But although many people contend that *pumois*, like *karamokos*, have secret magic that is not revealed by missionaries or in schools, their interpretation of this fact reveals important differences. Many people believe that certain Biblical passages, like those in the Qur'ān – especially the Old Testament's alleged sixth and seventh books of Moses – are God's actual words, and have the power to direct either *jinai* or God himself. The problem is that Christian and Judaic leaders, anxious to preserve knowledge monopolies, strategically omitted certain sections of the Bible as it was passed on to them to copy – sections that originally represented the word of God. (Similarly, Fisher (1963: 142) reported that the Ahmaddiyah sect in Sierra Leone claims that Christians also tampered with the New Testament to create loopholes permitting alcohol consumption, wearing shoes in church, and so on.) According to one man, a Christian:

> With the Qur'ān, all books the prophets wrote are in them. With the Bible, though, certain books have been extracted, because they are so powerful that the religious men, the clergymen, said if they were in use or exposed to the public, then Christians would be involved in those things [potentially bad activities]. The sixth and seventh books of Moses are two of these. You have passages in them that you can use by giving certain instructions and they occur.

Like Arabic texts, these so-called missing books from the Bible are held in awe and fear. Few people are skilled in their use, and unassisted laymen who manage to find out how to order them from abroad, and do so at great expense, are said to die or go crazy if they try to use them or even read them without careful guidance. These Christian texts with alleged ritual efficacy, however, are not part of the standard canon that religious devotees learn, and they are little known. Thus, unlike Arabic texts, these magical *pumoi* texts are not important to most Mende.

On the whole, however, the knowledge dispensed in *pumoi* education and sacred texts lacks the aura of secrecy, mystery and danger that enshrouds Arabic. Whereas people avoid using bits of paper containing Arabic writing, particularly if the meaning were obscure, they readily use papers containing the most esoteric, incomprehensible English writing. In Freetown, a woman hawking fried plantation chips next to the US Agency for International Development office was selling her wares in pieces of paper that had been discarded by the Agency. Although the meaning of the bureaucratic prose was incomprehensible even to the most literate native English speakers, the woman and her customers evidenced no concern about possible harm.

People symbolise this contrast between Arabic and *pumoi* knowledge by associating *morimen* with blackness, darkness, corners, and concealed places[5] and *pumoi* knowledge with light and open spaces. As a man explained:

> The Muslims you go to in the night and go into the corners [to consult them], unlike the Christian teachers who do things in the open air. They have that free mind of exposing their secrets. The Muslims, though, are trained to keep secrets intact.

The Mende generally agree that the white man has fewer deep secrets and is less interested in secrecy than they. On the whole, *pumoi* knowledge is more open to inspection, less carved into the levels of highly discrete achievement, and more freely given than more traditional secrets. One man observed that although *pumois* do write secrets on paper and seal them in envelopes, most *pumoi* knowledge is not necessarily embedded in writing nor hidden in secret texts. Indeed, the ready availability of most *pumoi* knowledge can threaten monopolies on traditional secrets, as in the case of English translations of the Qur'ān. Another case in point is that most elders violently disapprove of schoolchildren, even girls, reading biology textbooks about reproduction because of Sande society prohibitions.

To the extent that modern schoolteachers can exploit their positions in the *pumoi* system, they depend less on writing and literacy per se. Their dominance over students largely rests on controlling school admissions, scholarships, exams, promotions, and contacts with the wider bureaucracy. They also can judiciously instruct certain students on how to behave and dress at interviews for college or white collar jobs, gain powerful bureaucratic patrons, pressure subordinates, neutralise rivals, and so on. Success in the *pumoi* system also includes displaying impressive books in one's office, getting letters of recommendation, and filling out bureaucratic forms. Ironically, then, *pumoi* success does not depend so directly upon literacy per se as it does for *morimen* and *karamokos*. Some might argue, in fact, that mobility in the modern world depends more on the use of a *moriman* and his command of Arabic literacy to make charms for success, than on English literacy.

In the past, the Mende may have identified *pumoi* knowledge more directly with English literacy, believing, perhaps, that English writing contained power similar to that of Arabic texts. But as *pumoi* curricula expanded and schools taught more than reading, writing and Christianity, the Mende realised that learning English was only preliminary to learning other knowledge, which was available outside of the Bible. Finally, the fact that written *pumoi* knowledge was so eagerly taught by *pumoi* teachers may itself have dismissed its mystical aura.

Modern Arabic education: traditional and pumoi knowledge

In recent years, several Muslim associations such as the Ahmaddiyah and the Muslim Brotherhood have set up schools modelled on *pumoi* schools (see, for example, Anderson 1970). These Muslim schools, often in urban settings have regular classrooms, textbooks, exams, and formal administration, and they teach *pumoi* subjects like science and social studies. This format is necessary to qualify for Sierra Leone government aid to run the schools, but it is also motivated by Muslim parents' desires to prepare their children for success in the *pumoi* world without giving up their religion. These parents fear that children instructed by non-Muslims may become less respectful and obedient to elders and authorities – and less able to keep secrets – than children reared under traditional Muslim discipline. But although teachers in Muslim schools flog their students more frequently than teachers in other schools, they still do not instil discipline as well as *karamokos* are reputed to do. Consequently, many parents still send their sons to *karamokos*, at least for the early years when it is felt that training in obedience, respect, and secrecy is most critical.

By contrast to *karamoko* instruction, these schools are far less concerned with teaching the Arabic language. Arabic is one subject among many. Some schools such as the Ahmaddiyah even conduct religious studies principally in English. Consequently, most Mende respect the Ahmaddiyah schools more for having good laboratory facilities in science than for teaching the word of God. Another key departure from *karamoko* instruction is the degree to which the meaning of the Arabic words and writing is imparted. Arabic instructors in modern schools generally teach meaning much earlier than do *karamokos*, and the Ahmaddiyah sect actually publishes an English translation of the Qur'ān, which it may make available to students.

Although these schools do not teach secret meanings with magical power, *karamokos* resent them for taking away their students and for revealing the meaning of Arabic. Still, because the deeper ritual meanings of the texts are not taught, *karamokos* claim that their most important secrets remain intact. The head of a Muslim Brotherhood school stressed that his school did not replace private lessons, and many of his students boarded and studied with *karamokos* on the side. Hence, the older system of Arabic instruction and its efforts to control powerful secrets are not entirely supplanted.

On the whole, then, English literacy has not replaced Arabic literacy, and modern arenas for learning Arabic have not replaced more traditional ones. Indeed, sending one or two sons to a *karamoko* is a wise investment for parents, provided others can pursue *pumoi* tracks. Since the Mende value many domains of knowledge, even someone who is firmly set on a *pumoi* career is advised not to neglect other realms of knowledge. And assistance gained through Arabic ritual specialists continues to provide security for the risky world of *pumoi* achievement. Schoolchildren drink magical *nesi* to pass exams, and civil servants in the national bureaucracy contract services from *morimen* to ensure promotions or to undercut rivals.

Conclusions

The sociology of literacy must analyse writing both as a mode of communication and as a potential resource in social relationships. This paper has examined the complexities entailed by cultural uses of reading and writing in the Mende context of secrecy, ritual, and social stratification. We have focused on the uses of Arabic writing, uses that depart considerably from Middle Eastern societies in which knowledge of Arabic is the language of everyday correspondence and verbal discourse (though the use of sacred lettering around mosques suggests that it retains a sacred aura if marked contextually).

Why did Arabic literacy successfully penetrate and achieve importance within the traditional Mende system of secrecy and power? Goody et al. (1977) might suggest that its superiority as a mode of communication across space and time, in contrast to oral communication, is a factor. Yet we would argue that writing is equally suited to maintain secrets as to facilitate communication. Instead of replacing the oral idiom, it comprises one component of the total pool of potential knowledge resources that the Mende strive to attain and manipulate in competition with others. In fact, the Mende seem to value literacy not *in spite* of the difficulty of attaining it, but *because* of it.

Taken to their logical conclusion, the subtle manipulations and plays on ambiguity that we have described for the Mende must also figure as a 'potential' of literacy. Can it be, then, that societies which have *not* developed these potentials for secrecy and ambiguity in writing to so fine an art must have 'restricted literacy'? This possibility is far removed from the thrust of Goody's argument. However, it suggests that the distinction between 'full potential' versus 'restricted literacy' is ultimately based on definitions that presuppose its conclusion.

Notes

This paper is based on fieldwork by Bledsoe among the Mende of Sierra Leone carried out in 1981–2. We are grateful to C. Magbaily Fyle and the Institute for African Studies at the University of Sierra Leone for assistance during the course of the project. Financial support for the research was provided by the National Science Foundations and the Ford-Rockefeller Foundations. Support for the analysis was provided by the Population Council and the Rockefeller Foundation. We are grateful to William Murphy, Ray McDermott, Brian Street, Dan Wagner, David Smith, and Vera John Steiner for comments and suggestions.

1 This study uses 'literate' in the broad sense of having knowledge of writing. This ranges from those who speak, read, and write fluently, to those who can recognise a few passages in a book like the Qur'ān, and cannot interpret other texts.
2 Such facts counter arguments that emphasise the 'great divide' between speech and writing. Tannen (1981), for example, argues that whereas in speech, paralinguistic devices can imply meanings that may differ from the content of the words, in writing, these different meanings must be coded lexically. Such arguments, while more subtle and intended to demonstrate a distinction between literacy and orality in 'cohesion', and not in their ability to decontextualise, actually reinforce the logic of the position they attempt to question. Our

observations make it clear that writing, too, involves paralinguistic means of encoding meaning, a fact paralleled by similar uses of writing and writing materials in our own society (see also Street 1987.) They also undermine the view that writing creates detachment and is not context-dependent.

3 The phonetic transcriptions for Mende and Krio words had to be simplified in some cases for facility in publication.

4 Reading and writing are considerably dissociated in some cultures. For example, in seventeenth century France, Furet and Ozouf (1982: 76) state that reading was an instrument of salvation and gave access to God's word and the moral domain, whereas writing belonged more to the 'civil' domain of utility and commerce. Similar cultural dichotomies can be articulated by separate languages. So-called 'dead' languages of religious and classical scholarship (now mostly read and in very limited contexts) endure because they continue to 'communicate' about – not with – the past. In keeping with our position, the modern 'interpreters' of these texts often disagree about their meaning.

5 Islam generally associates the colour black with power. A black flag precedes the armies of Islam into battle, and the most sacred Muslim pilgrimage is to the black stone *Ka'bah* at Mecca. Black is also linked with malevolent potential in Mende magic and witchcraft. In some parts of West Africa *Zawiyah*, a Muslim school or place of prayer, literally means 'corner' in Arabic. It can also be a tomb of a Muslim holy man (Skinner 1976: 510). In Krio, 'corner-corner' (*kona kona*) business refers to secret encounters, usually of a sexual nature.

References

Abraham, A. 1978. *Government and politics under colonial rule.* Freetown: Sierra Leone University Press.

Anderson, E. C. 1970. 'Early Muslim schools and British policy in Sierra Leone', *West African Journal of Education,* 14: 177–9.

Bledsoe, C. H. 1980. *Women and marriage in Kpelle society.* Stanford: Stanford University Press.

1984. 'The political use of Sande ideology and symbolism', *American Ethnologist,* 11 (3): 455–72.

Bledsoe, C. and Isiugo-Abanihe, U. 1989. 'Strategies of child fosterage among Mende "grannies" in Sierra Leone', in R. Lesthaeghe (ed.), *African reproduction and social organization.* Berkeley: University of California Press.

Bloch, M. 1968. 'Astrology and writing in Madagascar', in J. Goody (ed.), *Literacy in traditional societies.* Cambridge: Cambridge University Press.

Charbonnier, G. 1969. *Conversations with Claude Lévi-Strauss.* London: Jonathan Cape. Translated by J. and D. Weightman from *Entretiens avec Claude Lévi-Strauss.* 1959. Paris: Union Générale d'Edition.

Clanchy, M. 1979. *From memory to written record: England 1066–1307.* London: E. Arnold.

Cohen, R. 1974. *New directions in literary history.* Baltimore: The Johns Hopkins University Press.

Dalby, D. 1967. 'A survey of the indigenous scripts of Liberia and Sierra Leone: Vai, Mende, Loma, Kpelle and Bassa', *African Language Studies,* 8: 1–51.

d'Azevedo, W. L. 1962a. 'Uses of the past in Gola discourse', *Journal of African History*, 3: 11–34.

1962b. 'Some historical problems in the delineation a Central West Atlantic region', *Annals of the New York Academy of Sciences*, 96: 513–38.

Finnegan, R. 1973. 'Literacy versus non-literacy: the "great divide"', in R. Horton and R. Finnegan (eds.), *Modes of thought*. London: Faber.

Fisher, H. J. 1963. *Ahmadiyyah: a study in contemporary Islam on the West African coast*. London: Oxford University Press (published for the Nigerian Institute of Social and Economic Research).

Furet, F. and Ozouf, J. 1982. *Reading and writing: literacy in France from Calvin to Jules Ferry*. Cambridge: Cambridge University Press. Originally published in French (1977) as *Lire et écrire: l'alphabétisation des français de Calvin à Jules Ferry*. Paris: Editions de Minuit.

Goody, J. 1968a. 'Introduction', in J. Goody (ed.), *Literacy in traditional societies*. Cambridge: Cambridge University Press.

1968b. 'Restricted literacy in Northern Ghana', in J. Goody (ed.), *Literacy in traditional societies*. Cambridge: Cambridge University Press.

1971. 'The impact of Islamic writing on the oral cultures of West Africa', *Cahiers d'Etudes Africaines*, 11: 455–66.

1977. *The domestication of the savage mind*. Cambridge: Cambridge University Press.

Goody, J. and Watt, I. 1962. 'The consequences of literacy', *Comparative Studies in Society and History*, 5: 304–45. Reprinted in J. Goody (ed.), 1968. *Literacy in traditional societies*. Cambridge: Cambridge University Press.

Goody, J., Cole, M. and Scribner, S. 1977. 'Writing and formal operations: a case study among the Vai', *Africa*, 47: 289–304.

Graff, H. J. 1979. *The literacy myth: literacy and social structure in the nineteenth-century city*. New York: Academic Press.

Harley, G. W. 1941. 'Notes on the Poro in Liberia'. Cambridge, MA: *Papers of the Peabody Museum*.

Heath, S. B. 1982. 'What no bedtime story means: narrative skills at home and school', *Language and Society*, 11: 49–76.

Hommel, W. L. 1974. *Art of the Mende*. College Park: University of Maryland Art Gallery.

Kopytoff, I. and Miers, S. 1977. 'African "slavery" as an institution of marginality', in S. Miers and I. Kopytoff (eds.), *Slavery in Africa*. Madison: University of Wisconsin.

Kulick, D. and Stroud, C. 1990. 'Christianity, cargo and ideas of self: patterns of literacy in a Papua New Guinean village', *Man*, n.s., 25: 286–304.

Murphy, W. P. 1980. 'Secret knowledge as property and power in Kpelle society: elders versus youth', *Africa*, 50: 193–207.

1981. 'The rhetorical management of dangerous knowledge in Kpelle brokerage', *American Ethnologist*, 8: 667–85.

Olson, D. 1977. 'From utterance to text: the bias of language in speech and writing', *Harvard Educational Review*, 47: 257–81.

Park, M. 1870 (1799). *Life and travels of Mungo Park*. Edinburgh: William P. Nimmo.

Parry, J. 1982. 'Popular attitudes towards Hindu religious texts'. Unpublished MS.

Reder, S. and Green, K. R. 1983. 'Contrasting patterns of literacy in an Alaskan fishing village', *International Journal of the Sociology of Language*, 4: 9–39.

Senneh, L. O. 1979. *The Jakhanke*. London: International African Institute.

Simmel, G. 1950. *The sociology of Georg Simmel*, edited and translated by Kurt H. Wolff. Glencoe, IL: Free Press.

Skinner, D. E. 1973. 'The Arabic letter books as a source for Sierra Leone history', *African Research Bulletin*, 3(4): 41–50.

1976. 'Islam and education in the colony and hinterland of Sierra Leone (1750–1914)', *Journal of African Studies*, 10: 499–520.

1978. 'Mende settlement and the development of Islamic institutions in Sierre Leone', *International Journal of African Historical Studies*, 11: 32–62.

Street, B. 1984. *Literacy in theory and practice*. Cambridge: Cambridge University Press.

1987. 'Literacy and orality as ideological constructions: some problems in cross-cultural studies', in *Culture and History* 2. Copenhagen: Museum Tusculanum Press.

Tannen, D. 1981. 'The myth of orality and literacy', in W. Frawley (ed.), *Linguistics and literacy*. New York: Plenum.

Trimingham, J. S. 1959. *Islam in West Africa*. Oxford: Oxford University Press.

PART 2

Local literacies and national politics: ethnicity, gender and religion

If literacy practices are frequently linked with concepts of self and the construction of identity, as a number of ethnographers are suggesting, then the ways in which literacy is used within the communicative repertoire may have implications for the relationship between such foci of identity as ethnicity, gender and religion on the one hand and forms of state organisation and national politics on the other. Literacy, like language, register and dialect, may become a focus for drawing boundaries against outsiders and for struggles between minority and dominant power. The papers in this section examine different ways in which literacy practices play a role in such processes, focusing upon the association of forms of literacy with ethnic identity in the Horn of Africa (Lewis), with gender relations in the southern US (Rockhill) and with religious difference and identity in Alaska (Reder and Reed Wikelund) and in Nigeria (Probst).

Writers within the autonomous model of literacy, such as Ong, Gellner and Goody, have variously suggested a strong and predictable link between literacy and the development of nationalism. Gellner, for instance, suggests that literacy is an indispensable qualification for the development of effective national identity, an argument linked perhaps to Ong's assertion that writing 'heightens consciousness'. Ioan Lewis makes use of some detailed ethnography on literacies in the Horn of Africa to challenge these simplistic assumptions and to contend that the relationship between literacy and nationalism is more complex and less predictable. The differences in the uses and meanings of literacy in an area 'where three great literate traditions have contended and interpenetrated for over a thousand years' provide a case study that may be of relevance to other parts of the world. He examines the recent introduction of widespread mother-tongue literacy among the previously oral Somali and shows how the strength of oral tradition and the conventions associated with it persist through a period of increasing spread of literacy. Whilst acquainted with Arabic through their adoption of Islam, Somalis never indigenised the script to transcribe the vigorous, dominant medium – oral Somali. Oral language served communicative needs adequately; complicated messages, for instance, were regularly encoded in poetic form or accurately memorised and the movement of nomad groups facilitated quick dispersal: 'in this populist oral culture, poetry in many different genres, and oratory, occupied the centre of the stage'. Reputations, particularly positions in the political hierarchy, depended on skills in language arts. As in the New Guinea case, indigenous concepts of language were crucial to the attitudes taken towards literacy: in this instance, words were viewed not as 'magical' things as many writers on oral language have assumed, but as instruments, capable of inflicting deadly wounds as well as of healing. Within this strongly oral tradition, different literate traditions began to emerge during this century so that by the time of independence Somalia had three written languages: Arabic, English and Italian. Lewis describes how a new roman script for the national language was used to spread literacy as part of a much-publicised campaign in the 1970s, linked to common development assumptions about the role of literacy and also to Somali concepts of national identity. This would appear to fit with the standard views on the relationship between nationalism and literacy expressed by Gellner and others. However, events in the Ogaden at the end of the 1970s, as Ethiopia conquered areas previously under Somali control, led to shifts in this pattern that should make us adopt a more cautious view of the likely relationship. The 'literacy miracle' appears to have been short lived and the larger political events in the region were followed by a return to oral tradition as a means of asserting political position and nationalist sentiment. The literacy campaigns 'did not produce a radical sustained transformation of nationalism into a modernist mode of the type associated with literacy by Gellner and others'. Instead traditional oral forms, such as praise poems and oratory became the focus of political activity: radios and tape recorders became widespread and provided the medium for political discourse: 'in this surge of electronic rhetoric, Somali politics retains its overwhelmingly oral character, bypassing the written word'. Whilst in Ethiopia literacy had become a central element in national consciousness, across the border in Somalia it remained peripheral. Such variation is to be explained with reference to differences in local conditions and in the communicative repertoires in different cultural traditions. Adaptations of new forms of communications to these local repertoires is associated by Lewis with differences in larger level political and nationalist movements. This perspective enables him to bring out some of the complexities in the relationship between literacy and nationalism that have been understated in standard approaches and suggests rich arenas for further research.

   Kate Rockill, a sociologist interested in public and state discourses upon literacy as well as in local lived experiences, attempts to link macro and micro levels through an analysis of literacy as power. In a surprisingly rare attempt to focus upon issues of gender and literacy, she contrasts state and male discourses on literacy and illiteracy in the United States with the experience of women's lived literacy practices. The purpose of the paper is to bring these representations into the same space and to explore why they are so different. To do so, she has to re-conceptualise dominant social science notions of politics, education and literacy – in keeping with the move towards an ideological model of literacy – and to likewise revise common assumptions about gender by demonstrating its integral relation to race, class and ethnicity. As in many of the other papers in this volume, an understanding of literacy practices requires exploration of wider contextual issues not at first sight associated with them: in this case women's dreams of salvation, male violence and machismo and dominant ideologies of liberty and equality in contemporary America. Against the dominant rhetoric that evokes literacy as integral to Liberal Democracy, Rockhill focuses upon actual literacy practices in the lives of Hispanic women in Los Angeles to show 'how power is lived through the everyday practices, social regulations and images of desire which govern their sexuality and use of language'. Whilst dominant images of 'illiteracy' associate it with individual inadequacy, lack of intelligence or an unwillingness to learn, the women whom Rockhill interviewed expressed deep longing and desire for literacy as the key to the American dream but were for the most part constrained from achieving it by their situation, by the violence of their men and by the way public institutions and funding operate.

In practice, women conducted most of the literacy work of the household, and that associated with the purchase of goods, interface with public services and their children's schooling. But the specific skills they thereby acquired remained 'invisible', in contrast with the men's uses of spoken English in the public arena. When the women attempted to break out of this domestic prison and enter the public domain, the men resisted, often violently: if women were naturally associated with illiteracy, stupidity and confined domestic chores, then their passage towards literacy, public work and intelligence represented a threat to the man's position and an undermining of the gendered family structures on which they depended. The complexities of this situation for Hispanic women probably reflects that of many women: on the one hand they represented literacy as crucial to their dream of 'becoming somebody', a 'lady' as depicted in dominant images in magazines, films and so on; and on the other they explained that literacy was unnecessary for their lives; on the one hand literacy was a means of empowerment, on the other a means of being assimilated to dominant middle class America, its myths and fantasies. The sociological reality was that women were more likely to develop the English literacy crucial for such a shift if they divorced or separated: married women tended to see 'success' through their husbands or sons, and the only way they could acquire the kind of literacy they desired for themselves was through sustained schooling – which their husbands and sons denied them. This picture of yearning and loss, desire and threat contrasts strikingly with dominant discourses on literacy and illiteracy that accuse the illiterate of lack of will and of undermining public ideals of Liberty. Part of the explanation for this contrast is that social science accounts of literacy have tended to decontextualise it from lived experience, to represent it as a fixed, unified commodity, a technical skill to be acquired by willing individuals. Once the social science discourse shifts, to expose the socially constructed nature of literacy, its insertion in 'social and political relations, ideological practices and symbolic meaning structures', then we will be in a position to see through and to challenge the dominant distortions and myths of literacy that rule the public domain in contemporary society.

Whereas in the case of contemporary America, public discourses upon language and literacy are articulated within largely secular state institutions, in many of the cases discussed in this volume religious institutions play a dominant role, through both religions 'of the book' and local religions with their own texts and discourses. Reder and Reed Wikelund provide a particularly thorough account of one such complex of relations in Alaska, from the introduction of literacy associated with the Russian colonists at the turn of the century through to the recent introduction of American-influenced schooled literacy. Initially a Russian colony, Seal Bay was exposed to specialised literacies in the Cyrillic alphabet by two powerful institutions: the Russian Orthodox Church and the Russian American Company that controlled the sale and distribution of products from native hunting. Although the script was the same, the literacy practices of church and company were distinct, a patterning of literacy into separate domains of activity and influence that became a pervasive feature of the organisation of literacy practices over the whole period. When Alaska was purchased by the United States in 1867 a new writing system based on Latin script was introduced, but by then the Russian-based literacy practices in Cyrillic script were so well established as to represent the 'local' literacy against this 'outside' form. The new literacy was associated with different institutions – the government school and the new public sector. Competition between the different literacy practices associated with these different historical developments and institutions was a central feature not only of literacy but of the social structure in general. Interactions between literacy and ethnicity have persisted along these lines even after the struggles over the scripts themselves ended. Crucially two systems of social 'meaning' have been bound up with literacy development – the notion of 'village' and of 'outside'. These categories remain even as their content changes, so that what may once have been 'outside' – American schooled literacy; Russian religious literacy – may come to be viewed at another time as integral to 'village' life. Again Reder and Reed Wikelund find it unhelpful to use traditional concepts of a single autonomous literacy to analyse this situation and suggest instead that 'the role of literacy in the development of this community ... seems intimately tied to the social meanings which its various practices have assumed'. These meanings include both local identities and ethnicity and relations with larger political and religious institutions, whether the Russian Orthodox Church, the American Education System or the Government.

Peter Probst also deals with the relationship of literacies to political and religious identity, in this case with reference to an indigenous religious movement in Nigeria that emerged out of and in protest against aspects of missionary Christianity in the 1920s. Josiah Oshitelu, the prophet of the Aladura movement, recognised the significance of the written word and its potential whilst studying at mission schools. When he was expelled from the Church Missionary Society for preaching his own messianic message, he carefully recorded the visions and messages that formed the basis of his alternative sect in six massive journals. These became an alternative 'book', written in his own invented script and marked by a series of seals that Probst interprets as giving the prophet a symbolic privilege, removing him and his followers from the rest of society. The book and seals represent a mark of authenticity to the new prophet, the signatures of religious authority and the independence of the new movement from the missionaries' source of power. Probst invokes Derrida's claim that in written society truth is established in different ways than in oral: 'whereas in traditional oral society the definition of truth is established in a more socratic or dialectical manner, the extension of the spatial and temporal boundaries provided by writing and print changes the cultural instruments of the knowledge of reality'. Truth has now to be established by use of written documents (what Clanchy calls 'a literate mentality'). However, this re-presentation of the 'great divide' between oral and literate cultures, with literacy in Derrida's version being the less subject to critique and challenge, is not borne out by the ethnographic data. The new prophet frees himself of the violent control of the colonist's book by asserting his own alternative scriptural text: the written word is a basis for both fixity and challenge. Oshitelu, having developed his own alternative bible, then confronts the same questions that led him to challenge the religion of the book in the first place: is the book freely available to all members of the church to make their own interpretation, or is interpretation a matter for the leaders?

Probst quotes Goody as suggesting that the development of written texts in religions leads towards the latter outcome, to a routinisation, such that open interpretation by all gives way to standard pronouncements on the meanings of the scriptures by an elite. Probst, however, finds some evidence that the process is not quite as predictable as this: 'the increase of the use of writing within the congregations did not lead to the disappearance of the prophets as the arguments provided by Goody seem to imply. Rather, writing and print have become incorporated into the indigenous forms of religious experience'. As in the Papua New Guinean villages described by Kulick and Stroud, indigenous ideas about the power and use of words persist in the uses of literate media, they are not simply superseded by literacy. In the Aladura case the traditional belief that words are thought to have an inherent power of their own, which can be made available to attract God's help and protection through prayer, persists to enable the Aladura movement to maintain the role of prophets as grass roots interpreters of the Scripture: the uses of literacy by the movement do not necessarily entail the abandonment of these indigenous 'socratic' principles, literacy in itself does not necessarily mean the routinisation of religious beliefs. The claims made by Goody and Derrida have to be contextualised: the 'consequences' 'depend on the social institutions in which they are embedded and the manners in which writing and print are exploited in different cultural contexts'.

5

LITERACY AND CULTURAL IDENTITY IN THE HORN OF AFRICA: THE SOMALI CASE

I. M. LEWIS

Literacy and nationalism

Languages, Samuel Johnson remarked, are the 'pedigrees of nations'. This view of the political significance of language is endorsed by those modern political scientists who define a nation as those people 'who speak the same language' (Minogue 1967: 154). Other students of nationalism go further and add literacy as an indispensable qualification for the development of effective national identity (Gellner 1983). This of course is in line with Professor Ong's bold claim, that writing 'heightens consciousness' (Ong 1982).

The validity of this thesis would seem, at first sight, to be demonstrated all too graphically by the case of the Horn of Africa, where three of the world's great literate traditions have contended and interpenetrated for over a thousand years, producing extreme nationalist conflicts. I would like to suggest however, by considering the very recent introduction of widespread mother tongue literacy among the previously oral Somali, that the relationship between nationalism and literacy is rather more equivocal. Even in the case of core Christian nationalism, which since the conversion of their rulers in the fourth century has constituted the central dynamic of the Ethiopian state, elite court and restricted religious literacy has arguably been more an expression and instrument of national consciousness than its source.

Horn of Africa culture history

The three great traditions represented in the Horn of Africa are of course Judaism, Christianity and Islam. Although the first is most directly associated with the so-called 'black Jews' – the indigenous Falashas – the Judaic tradition also strongly colours the politically dominant Christian tradition of the Semitic-speaking Tigreans and Amharas who have controlled Ethiopia since its foundation at Axum (see Ullendorff 1968; Jones and Monroe 1935). Commanding the Ethiopian highlands where they live as settled farmers, these two ethnic groups are traditionally hierarchically organised into a ruling military stratum, clergy and lay peasantry. Christianity has been firmly appropriated and indigenised in this dominant,

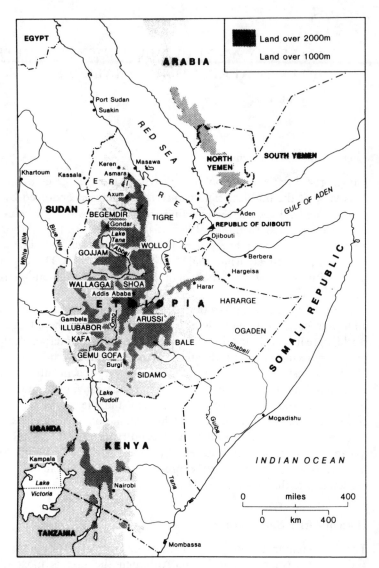

Figure 5.1 The eastern Horn of Africa.

local, *literate* tradition: first in the liturgical language Ge'ez, and later in the related Tigrinya and Amharic languages. Since the Amharas succeeded in installing themselves as the ruling ethnic group in this expanding Christian conquest-state some 500 years ago, Amharic has been known officially as 'the language of the king', and was the medium in which the extremely important Minister of the Pen recorded royal decisions and

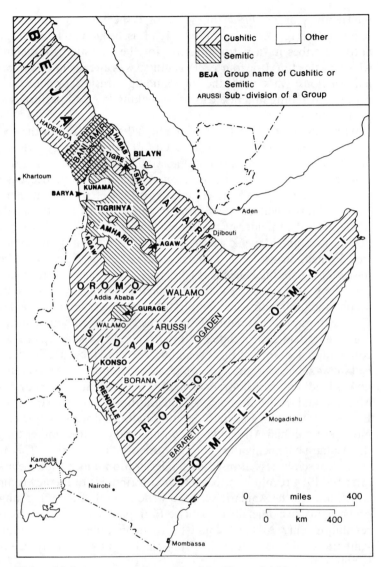

Figure 5.2 Languages and peoples of the Horn of Africa.

court history. The historic mandate of the Amhara ethnic elite to conquer and convert neighbouring peoples in the name of the Lion of Juda was conveyed and enshrined in the famous national epic *The Glory of Kings* (or 'the pride of kings'), written if not composed in the fourteenth century. This unique charter, which traces the origins of Ethiopian kingship to Menelik I, issue of Solomon and Sheba, like the *Old Testament* for the Hebrews, or the *Qur'ān* for the Arabs, is the repository of national and religious feelings (Ullendorff 1960: 144). It is, as Donald Levine (1974: 92) aptly describes it, 'a national script' for the Christian Ethiopian state, which by this time (the fourteenth century) was already locked in protracted religious wars with the surrounding Muslim principalities and peoples, including illiterate Cushitic-speaking lowland pastoralists, such as the Somali.

Although the oral tradition of the Somalis lays claim to the sixteenth century Muslim conqueror Ahmed Gran (1506–43), under whose fierce attacks the Amhara Kingdom almost collapsed, there was little direct contact between the two ethnic groups until the closing decades of the nineteenth century and the colonial partition of the Somali nation, in which Ethiopia, with its new European guns and rifles, participated under Menelik II, the founder of the modern empire-state. In this scramble for new possessions Menelik was as emphatic as his European competitors (the French, British and Italians) in stressing his God-given civilising mission to share the benefits of Christianity with new 'heathen' subjects. This long history of isolation,[1] religious animosity and sometimes accommodation with Islam, and in the modern era military conflict with European powers, has naturally sharpened Ethiopian nationalism.

Just as it had appropriated and indigenised Christianity, the Amhara core national culture of this expanding African Habsburg empire absorbed new subject groups, offering the possibility of assimilation and upward mobility with conversion and Amharic-isation – the key, for both Menelik and Haile Selassie, to integrating Ethiopia's ethnic mosaic. Ethiopia thus pioneered the 'nation-building' process characteristic of most post-colonial African states, with literacy in the mother tongue of the Amhara elite being the final signature of full citizenship. The surge of ethnic consciousness aroused by modernisation under Haile Selassie led after the 1974 revolution (to which it contributed) to literacy campaigns which utilised the Amharic script to write several of the other languages of the eighty-five officially recognised Ethiopian 'nationalities'. Before the revolution only Amharic could be written;[2] after the revolution only Amharic could be written in. Ethiopia had now, literally, a national script.

Language and religion among the Somali

Despite their early conversion to Islam, reflecting their proximity to Arabia and peripheral involvement in the ephemeral Islamic states which encircled Ethiopia in the Middle Ages, the Somalis, so far as we know, had not previously translated their strong sense of *cultural* nationalism into political terms. They had never constituted a state. It was characteristic also of their mixed Islamic literary and Somali oral heritage that although this first manifestation of nationalism, coinciding with Ethiopian, British and Italian colonial penetration, was couched in the classic Muslim form of a *jihad*, led by a sophisticated Somali sheikh well-versed in Arabic literacy, the success of the 'holy war' depended crucially on this man's power of oratory and genius – still widely recognised – as a major *oral* poet. I refer, of course, to the fiery Somali crusader Sayyid Mohamed Abdille Hassan, whose guerrilla forces defied the Christian colonisers of his people from 1900 to 1920. His banner was the banner of Islam, his book the Holy Qur'ān; but his battle cry was delivered in oral Somali, not written Arabic. (His oral legacy has provided, retrospectively, an oral charter for modern Somali nationalism, including literacy in the mother-tongue.)

Arabic is the language of the Qur'ān, which must be transmitted in Arabic. From the time of their adoption of the faith, centuries ago, the Somalis have had access to Arabic, the language of Islam. But despite a vernacular tradition of Arabic instruction going back to the twelfth century (see Lewis 1969: 75–82), Arabic has remained the prisoner of its exalted status as the Word of God, the magical language of religion, known, orally and to some extent written, only by religious specialists and a few merchants and sailors. Indeed the distinction between these religious specialists and the warrior laity, who form the majority, constitutes the most pervasive division (after that of gender) in the strongly egalitarian social system of the Somalis. The two roles are complimentary, since the warriors need holy mediators to regulate their internal problems and to negotiate on their behalf with God. Thus, traditionally, these exponents of Islam, with limited literacy in Arabic, teach the Qur'ān in itinerant religious schools; solemnise marriage, divorce and death; assess damages in disputes; mediate and dispense blessings and therapeutic potions. The subordination of their restricted literacy tradition to the priorities of this primary oral culture is epitomised by the regular oral treatment which they provided for illness. This involved the digestion of holy writ through drinking a decoction made by washing into a cup powerful passages transcribed onto a piece of paper from the Qur'ān.

Despite (and because of) its unique religious significance, Arabic remained marginal, restricted to ritual contexts and external trade. It was not indigenised and the Arabic script was similarly little used to transcribe the vigorous, dominant medium – oral Somali (for which it is in any case not linguistically a perfect vehicle). The men of God who controlled this prestigious, if minority, literate tradition clearly had vested interests in maintaining its exclusiveness, and they were not necessarily anxious to extend its use to promote written Somali. Equally, some Somalis have suggested that, as a people proudly tracing their origins (through painstakingly constructed *written* genealogies) to the family of the Prophet Muhammad, they were reluctant to advertise to the literate Arab world that Arabic was not actually their mother tongue.

Undersigned or underwritten in this fashion by Arabic, the language of the faith, oral Somali well served the needs of a highly articulate and linguistically self-conscious people. Language was primarily for communication and complicated messages were regularly encoded in poetic form for rapid word-of-mouth transmission among the nomads, in what B. W. Andrzejewski (1982: 75) has called 'the oral postal service'. In this populist oral culture, oratory, and poetry in many different genres, occupied the centre of the stage. Opinion within one's own clan and outside it was influenced and formed by poems and oratory which captured the imagination of the listener. Reputations depended crucially on skill in these arts, which also entailed possessing a good command of the seemingly endless store of Somali proverbs. As the Somali historian Said Samatar (1982: 75) points out, the Somali term for an orator means, literally, 'capable of speech', implying that those who lack oratorical skill are, virtually, incapable of speech, dumb. Without going into details, let me simply say here that thousands of oral poems, going back well over a hundred years, survive into the present, remembered for their artistic perfection and eloquence, a heritage endlessly replenished by new compositions (Andrzejewski and Lewis 1964: 130). Seldom exceeding one hundred lines, and frequently containing archaic expressions, poems were composed and recited verbatim either by their authors or by those who had learnt the poems, aided by the alliteration and scansion principles of the different genres. Modern poets and poetry reciters regularly possess a memorised repertoire extending up to fifteen hours of 'playback' time.

In this highly articulate oral culture, words are viewed as things – not in the magical vein associated with orality by Professor Ong, but rather as instruments, capable of inflicting deadly wounds which entail claims for compensation for defamation (*haal*), paralleling those applicable in cases of physical assault (*haq*). As a line from a famous poem by Salan 'Arrabey (d. 1940) on ingratitude puts it, 'The tongue is like a sword cutting off life'. The two systems of aggression, 'speech feud' and 'blood feud', are apt to intersect and reinforce one another. As a traditional Somali elder reflects:

> Camels are looted and men killed because of poetry. The more camels a clan owns, the greater their resources. Camels bring men together. If a clan loots camels and kills men from another clan, the injured clan may bide their time and not rise in immediate revenge. But if the victorious clan attempt, as they often do, to immortalise their victory in verse, then the looted clan feels

humiliated and immediately seeks to remedy their honour and avenge their wrongs. Thus revenge follows revenge, and feud, feud.   (Samatar 1982: 27)

Towards Somali literacy

The first significant initiative towards literacy arose out of this oral culture itself, when in the wake of the expansion of colonial rule following the defeat of Sayyid Mohamed in 1920, a prominent elder of one of the major north-eastern clans (then under Italian jurisdiction) invented the first phonetically perfect script for Somali. The Osmaniya script, as it became known after its inventor's name, is written from left to right, unlike Arabic, and some of its characters are reminiscent of Amharic. When, twenty years later, the first modern Somali nationalist organisation was launched in what was then British-occupied (Italian) Somalia, this 'Somali writing' acquired a new and wider impetus as a vehicle for nationalism. This was in line with the motives which had inspired the script's inventor, who felt that national pride required his mother-tongue to become a written language. This would also facilitate communication between widely separated cells of the new nationalist organisation in a script which would be indecipherable by European and Ethiopian administrative officials.

By 1947, when the Somali Youth League had become firmly established as the main nationalist party, the promotion of this script was one of its four major policy aims. However, changes in the leadership of the League soon led to a fierce debate between Osmaniya supporters and advocates of Arabic – viewed as the natural medium for a Muslim nation. The possibility of using Latin characters to write Somali also began to be examined by some nationalists. In 1957, three years before Somalia attained independence, the Somali Youth League government printed a page of the official newspaper in Somali transcribed into roman characters. This bold experiment produced such violent reaction, particularly on the part of traditional religious leaders, that it was not repeated. The pro-Arabic lobby denounced the use of the Latin script with the derogatory, punning slogan, '*Laatiin waa laa diin*' ('Latin is irreligion').

At independence in 1960, the Somali Republic (comprising the former British and Italian Somalilands) thus found itself with three written languages, Arabic, English and Italian. This confusing situation made it all the more urgent to solve the problem of finding an acceptable script for Somali. In 1966 a distinguished UNESCO Commission of Linguists, led by B. W. Andrzejewski, added its weight to the choice of Latin. But public opinion remained divided and volatile and the Somali government hesitated.

Written Somali

It was left to the military who seized power in 1969 to resolve the issue. In 1972, following what had for some years been the informal practice in the police and the army, General Siyad's regime adopted a very practical roman script for the national language.[3] What has been hailed as the 'Somali miracle of instant literacy' was initiated with the launching in 1973 of a concerted urban literacy campaign. Government officials were enlisted in 'crash courses' in the new script, with the prospect of losing their positions if they failed to master it. Adult literacy classes drew large and enthusiastic attendances from the most educationally deprived sectors of the urban population, including women. The next step in this 'cultural revolution', as it was proclaimed by the then Minister of Information and National Guidance, General Ismail Ali Abokor (later imprisoned), was to extend literacy to the neglected nomads who form the majority of the population. Accordingly, in the late summer of 1974 a task force of 30,000 secondary school students and teachers was dispatched in truckloads to the interior, to teach the nomads to read and write and to impart the basic principles of 'scientific socialism', now the official policy of the state. These privileged urban students were thus to share the fruits of the 'Glorious Revolution', as the *coup* was retrospectively named, with their nomadic 'comrades'. The guiding slogan, provided by President Siyad himself, was: 'If you know, teach. If you don't, learn.' As the general explained, in a major public speech:

> The key ... is to give everybody the opportunity to learn reading and writing ... It is imperative that we give our people modern, revolutionary education ... to restructure their social existence ... This will be the weapon to eradicate social balkanisation and fragmentation into tribes and sects. It will bring about an absolute unity and there will be no room for any negative foreign cultural influences.

The goals of modernisation, nationalism and independence are all fused here: a modern, integrated nation, consisting of those who not only 'speak the same language', but who also read and write it. (All this, of course, is very much in the spirit of Professor Ernest Gellner's theories of nationalism, although I have no reason to think that General Siyad's ideas emanated from this source.)

As it happened I was in Somalia in the summer of 1974 and saw the beginnings of the acute drought which was to cause the 'Rural Prosperity Campaign', as the programme was originally called, to be turned into a humane and well-organised famine relief operation. The emphasis of the campaign quickly shifted to an endeavour to meet the survival needs of the drought-stricken nomads – who, once grouped in relief camps, became enthusiastic recruits to the literacy classes.

Since 1974 however, with a substantial drift back to the nomadic economy, after several years of good rains, it has obviously been difficult, despite considerable effort, to sustain high levels of rural literacy. It is officially claimed that over 1.5 million people participated in the two literacy campaigns and that, by 1982, 400,000 of the urban population were literate, in addition to the half million children enrolled in schools, where written Somali had also been established. These generous figures may also include some of the refugees who poured into Somalia after the Somali–Ethiopian conflict of 1977–8. More accessible statistics of Somali literacy can be gleaned from the records kept at the BBC Somali pro-gramme of listeners' letters received from the Horn of Africa. These increased from a figure of 2,500 in 1973 to over 6,500 in 1983, the proportion of letters written in Somali in the same period rising from 12 per cent to 90 per cent.[4] However, difficult as it is to gauge the true numerical strength of the new literacy, there is no gainsaying its popular-ity or its genuine populist character. Many people, with no experience of 'modern education', have achieved a greater mastery of the Somali ver-nacular, their own mother tongue, than those brought up in towns and given literacy training in foreign languages such as Arabic, Italian and English, which previously favoured the educated elite. The new mother-tongue literacy also corrects the sex bias of previous forms of formal education, such as Arabic, which gave men a great advantage over women. It is not surprising that this genuinely populist measure should be widely acknowledged as the most popular of all those introduced by the General Siyad government.

The revolution in Somali literacy has created, nationally, corresponding demands for reading material and for stimulating new forms of literary production. In addition to the news stories and other material published in the daily *October Star*, the ideological bureau of the Somali Socialist Revolutionary party has produced a flood of propagandist pamphlets and manuals, as well as its monthly organ *Halgan* ('Struggle'). Hundreds of school textbooks as well as primers for adult literacy have been prepared by the curriculum department of the Ministry of Education. Over six million copies of books had been printed on the national press by the later 1970s, including the first Somali novels and written plays, scholarly dictionaries, collections of poetry and traditional folklore, and history books edited by the Somali Academy of Science and Culture. There were also translations of works by foreign authors as diverse as Brecht and G. A. Henty, as well as less celebrated writers (as I discovered when, purely by chance, I stumbled upon a group of keen translators, busily rendering some of my own accounts of Somali history into Somali). More novel, in a culture which, unlike Christian Ethiopia, has no tradition of visual art, are the propagandist posters, and shop and office signs, which literacy has encouraged. During the era of 'scientific socialism' these included posters at Orientation Centres displaying the revolutionary trinity of *Jaalle* (Comrade) Markis (Marx), *Jaalle* Lenin and *Jaalle* Siyad. At a less elevated level one notices various new names for restaurants and shops – including, in Mogadishu, a shop (*daas*) called '*Daaski Dallas*'!

This remarkable development in mother-tongue literacy, producing a unique 'orally written literature' (Andrzejewski 1984: 227–9), has with little doubt been the most popular and effective of a package of modernising measures that included, in the lofty name of Scientific Socialism, the official abolition of the clan loyalties which had traditionally divided the nation, and the replacement of kinship by 'comradeship' (see Lewis 1988: 209–25). These secular innovations once again brought to the fore the complex issue of Somalis' Islamic identity. To reassure the local guardians of the faith, and for other strategic reasons, Somalia prudently joined the Arab League in 1974.

The consequences of literacy

In the historical context we have briefly sketched, it is clear, I think, that having experienced for centuries the rivalry between the Amharic Christian and Arabic Muslim literate traditions, swelling sentiments of national pride fired the Somali quest for a national script. But has literacy actually increased national consciousness, as would be argued by Ong and other students of literacy? This, as we have seen, was according to President Siyad one of the major objectives in introducing Somali writing. That it has been achieved is the conclusion of H. M. Adam, the Somali political scientist who has made the closest study of the problems of writing his native tongue. 'The writing ... of the language,' he says, 'has facilitated national integration and ... strengthened Somali identity' (1983: 41). Although I cannot cite other than random personal impressions, in the wake of the national literacy campaigns, at least in urban centres in Somalia, there did seem to me to be a discernible increase in Somali linguistic self-consciousness and national pride. Certainly such nationalist sentiment found enthusiastic expression in 1977 in the campaign, initially intoxicatingly successful but ultimately disastrous, to liberate the Ogaden region of eastern Ethiopia (ethnically western Somalia). By this time, following the Ethiopian revolution of September 1974 and the ensuing power struggle in Addis Ababa, Ethiopia had become extremely vulnerable and the Western Somali Liberation Front guerrilla forces were able to drive out the Ethiopian garrisons with remarkable ease. As they liberated each settlement the WSLF proudly replaced all the Amharic signs and notices with announcements in the new Somali script, and opened schools to teach Somali writing. To the bitter dismay of Somali ambitions, however, all this was quickly swept away when, a few months later, after the superpower somersault which brought the Soviet Union to Ethiopia's side, Russian- and Cuban-supported Ethiopian forces reconquered the Ogaden. If they wished to write in their own language, those Somalis who remained in the region had now to do so in Amharic characters. This restoration of linguistic hegemony has encouraged other ethnic nationalist movements, such as that of the vast Oromo nation, to follow the Somali initiative in using Latin characters to write their own national language.

Literacy and secondary orality

Events in the bitter years since the Ogaden debacle indicate that while the 'instant literacy' we have examined may have fuelled nationalistic feeling inside the Somali Republic, and in the adjacent Ogaden prior to the 1977–8 Somalia–Ethiopia conflict, it did not produce a radical and sustained transformation of nationalism into a modernist mode of the type associated with literacy by Gellner and others. In defeat, patriotism has been replaced by rancorous clan strife, which, far from being eradicated by the regime of 'scientific socialism', in fact became the latter's primary recipe for survival.

The resurgence of this powerful oral political tradition at the disposition of those who control state literacy may seem a little paradoxical. But written or unwritten language is after all a means of expression and not an end in itself. And it is not only written Somali that is involved here. We have in fact so far quite ignored, and now touch on in conclusion, what in the short term seems much more significant in its general social and political implications than Somali writing, impressive though that is. I refer, of course, to what Ong has called 'secondary orality'. By the time literacy had made its dramatic entry onto the Somali stage, the transistor revolution was already firmly entrenched, reinforcing, extending and amplifying Somali oral culture. The highly articulate Somalis, as might be anticipated, took to radio, telephone, loud-speaker and tape-recorder with marked enthusiasm. When cheap transistor radios and cassette recorders became readily available in the late 1960s and early 1970s, they were immediately extremely popular, sweeping Somali culture into the exciting world of secondary orality. Today it would scarcely be an exaggeration to say that every nomadic family has a radio, and from being a nation of bards the Somalis have rapidly also become a nation of radio buffs, listening avidly to Somali broadcasts from local stations and from places as distant as London, Moscow and Peking. As they produce new works, poets now frequently use tape-recorders to supplement their memories. New 'pop' radio songs (*heello*) with musical accompaniments (Johnson 1974) relentlessly beat out the party line. Equally, opponents of the regime both inside and outside the country compose stinging attacks on its leaders, sometimes in the form of opaque love songs. As in traditional Somali politics, the president's poets exchange vitriolic verse with his opponents outside Somalia. These vigorous poetical polemics constitute oral chain letters, stored in cassettes which circulate round Somali communities scattered all over the world. In this surge of electronic rhetoric Somali politics retains its overwhelmingly oral character, bypassing the written word. Somali writing, though indispensable in certain contexts, falls into second place, as an ancillary medium for communication – a written extension of an oral culture with its tendency towards fixed forms. Thus literacy, which symbolically as well as literally is so central to the Ethiopian (Amhara) national consciousness, remains, I believe, peripheral to Somali identity. Yet across the border, within the Ethiopian pluralist mosaic, the extension of literacy in Amharic characters inflames reactive sentiments of ethnic nationalism amongst those subject peoples who, like the Somalis, would write their language in their own way. In this case, by a kind of poetic justice, the rejection of unacceptable literacy heightens national consciousness.

Notes

1 Familiar from Gibbon's famous orotund reference: 'Encompassed on all sides by the enemies of their religion, the Æthiopians slept near a thousand years, forgetful of this world, by whom they were forgotten (1957, v: 69).
2 In Eritrea, more currency was allowed to Tigrinya, and of course Ge'ez remained as a specialised archaic religious medium. Arabic was also used as a written medium by literate Muslims.
3 This had been developed by one of the first presidents of the Somali National Academy of Culture, Shirre Jama Ahmad, founder of the first Somali literary magazine *The Light of Knowledge and Education*.
4 Figures kindly supplied by the BBC Somali Programme, London.

References

Adam, H. M. 1983. 'Language, national self-consciousness and identity – the Somali experience', in I. M. Lewis (ed.), *Nationalism and self-determination in the Horn of Africa*, pp. 31–42. London: Ithaca Press.
Andrzejewski, B. W. 1982. 'Alliteration and scansion in Somali oral poetry and their cultural correlates', in V. Görög-Karady (ed.), *Genres, forms, meanings: essays in African oral literature*, pp. 68–83. Oxford: Journal of the Anthropological Society of Oxford.

1984. 'Somali literature', in L. S. Klein (ed.), *Encyclopaedia of world literature in the twentieth century*, IV, pp. 277–9. New York: Frederick Ungar.

Andrzejewski, B. W. and Lewis, I. M. 1964. *Somali poetry*. Oxford: Clarendon Press.

Gellner, E. 1983. *Nations and nationalism*. Oxford: Basil Blackwell.

Gibbon, E. 1957 (1788). *The decline and fall of the Roman Empire*, 6 vols., Everyman edition. London: Dent.

Johnson, J. W. 1974. *Heellooy, heelleellooy: the development of the genre heello in modern Somali poetry*. Bloomington, IN: Indiana University Press.

Jones, A. H. M. and Monroe, E. 1935. *A history of Ethiopia*. Oxford: Clarendon Press.

Laitin, D. 1977. *Politics, language and thought: the Somali experience*. Chicago: Chicago University Press.

Levine, D. 1974. *Greater Ethiopia*. Chicago: Chicago University Press.

Lewis, I. M. 1969. 'Sharif Yusuf Barkhadle: the blessed saint of Somaliland', in *Proceedings of the Third International Congress of Ethiopian Studies*, 75–82. Addis Ababa.

1988. *A modern history of Somalia*. Boulder and London: Westview Press.

1990. 'The Ogaden and the fragility of Somali segmentary nationalism', *Horn of Africa*, 13 (1 & 2): 55–61.

Minogue, K. 1967. *Nationalism*. London: Batsford.

Ong, W. J. 1982. *Orality and literacy: the technologizing of the word*. London: Methuen.

Samatar, S. S. 1982. *Oral poetry and Somali nationalism*. Cambridge: Cambridge University Press.

Ullendorff, E. 1960. *The Ethiopians*. London: Oxford University Press.

1968. *Ethiopia and the Bible*. London: Oxford University Press.

6

GENDER, LANGUAGE AND THE POLITICS OF LITERACY

KATHLEEN ROCKHILL

In this paper, the ways in which literacy has been conceptualised as power in discourses of power are critiqued and contrasted with the experience of Hispanic immigrant women in the United States. The politics of language are seen as central to the politics of literacy; both of these are looked at from the standpoint of how women live them in their everyday lives. Because it is caught up in the power dynamic between men and women, literacy is lived as women's work but not as women's right; women yearn to become literate, to go to school, but are confined to the home.

> I don't want to be a housekeeper all my life. I would like to be somebody, you know ... I would like to go out to talk to people, to work, to do something interesting, to help somebody. It's terrible, because they say, 'You are the woman. You have to stay in the home, you have to do dinner. You have to do *everything*'.

Maria feels confined to her home all day by a husband who refuses her permission to leave the house. Isolated, alone, she despairs that she is 'no one'. Her husband stopped her from attending English classes because, she says, he was jealous that she was going to meet someone else. She tries to talk to her mother and sisters but they tell her she must do as her husband says. She dreams of running away with her young child, escaping to Mexico where she would be able to work as a beautician. Maria passionately echoes the voices of many other Hispanic immigrant women who we interviewed in Los Angeles. True, there are variations, but the theme of longing, cross-cut by confinement, runs throughout.

Maria's yearning stands in stark contrast to the professional discourse of adult education which points to a 'lack of motivation' as a major explanation for adult non-participation in literacy programmes. As Gillette and Ryan observe:

> Certainly, we know far more today than we did two decades ago about the organisation of literacy activities. But *the most fundamental requirement is still the desire of the participant to learn* and, second only to that, the will of the instructor to teach.
>
> (Quoted in Fordham 1985: 17, emphasis added)

If the distance between Maria's urgent desire and their dispassioned analysis is enormous, even greater is the chasm between her experience and the mounting panic in the United States about the threat posed by the swelling number of illiterates. Typical in tone is the position expressed by the director of the Mayor's Committee on Literacy in Philadelphia warning that the millions of illiterate Americans are 'hostages to a problem of frightening dimensions':

> Frightening because adult illiteracy costs billions of dollars each year ... Frightening because it is embedded in the social land-scape of crime, drug abuse and hopelessness in a land of plenty. Frightening because of the tremendous human cost ... for the parent who cannot read to her [sic] child and the senior citizen who cannot read the Bible.
> But frightening, too, because of the debilitating effect of illiteracy on our ideals of citizenship and liberty. Is it any wonder that with one of five adults unable to fully read a newspaper that voter turnout has steadily fallen to record lows?
>
> (*New York Times*, 13 September 1986, p. 17)

From positions of male power, voices resonate around the world, warning us that illiteracy is dangerous, a threat to liberty, to economic and technological development and to the moral well-being of society. Who hears the cries of longing, sealed within the confines of four walls, exhausted by overwork and worry, spoken in a language ruled 'illegal', by women with no right to speak in public, let alone in their own homes?

The purpose of this paper is to bring these voices into the same space and to explore why, apart from the obviously concealed fact that their languages are different, they don't speak the same language. More precisely, this article considers how literacy has been constructed as power in discourses of power (that is, professional, social science, government) and contrasts those frames with the ways in which women who cannot read and write English well, live literacy and power in their everyday lives. An underlying theme is that politics, education and literacy must be reconceptualised if women's experience, as well as the experience of adult second language learners, are to be taken into account.

While the focus is upon gender, the work shows that the way women live sexual oppression is integrally connected to the ways they live race, class and ethnicity. The point is that these are not experienced as a series of 'commatised' background variables but they are lived together in the mosaic of people's lives.

It is difficult to find studies that consider the simultaneity of gender, race, ethnicity and class as lived. In their review of four leading journals of educational research in the United States, Grant and Sluter (1986) conclude that most studies treat these as separate factors. I agree that 'integrationist' research is needed. However, if we are to accomplish this, we must cease thinking about race, gender, and so on as discrete categories of individual attributes which in some (mysterious) way signal social context, and instead think about them in terms of power relations which are lived through the construction of our subjectivities. As the work of Foucault suggests, this means thinking differently about power as 'coextensive and continuous with life ... [as] linked with a production of truth – the truth of the individual himself [sic]' (1982: 783). In the words of Biddy Martin:

> Power comes from below; it is induced in the body and produced in every social interaction. It is not exercised negatively from the outside, though negation and repression may be one of its effects. *Power in the modern world is the relation between pleasures, knowledge and power as they are produced and disciplined.*
>
> (Martin 1982: 6, emphasis added)

To study how power operates to maintain domination, we must take into consideration the concrete, everyday material practices and social relations which regulate our subjectivities, as well as the symbolic and ideological meaning structures through which we interpret our experience. A full range of feminist inquiry is pointing us in these directions. Noteworthy are studies of how class and gender are lived (for example, MacKinnon 1981; McRobbie 1982; Radway 1984; Smith 1977; Steedman 1986; Walkerdine 1984). While studies that include race and ethnicity are rarer, the work of Davis (1983), Ng (1988), Silvera (1983) and Westwood (1984) is highly suggestive.[1] Some of this work is beginning to signal ways in which sexuality, especially the dream of salvation through romance, is fundamental to how women live 'class' materially, as well as psychologically and culturally.

The focus upon literacy in the lives of Hispanic women in Los Angeles provides a dynamic arena for seeing how power is lived through the everyday practices, social regulations and images of desire which govern their sexuality and use of language. It is noteworthy that Hispanic women in general, and Mexicans in particular, have completed fewer years of formal schooling than any other group singled out in official United States statistics (Hunter and Harman: 1979).[2] Through contrasting the experiences of these women with a range of public and social science discourses about literacy, the importance of language and literacy in power relations, whether at the national, state, local, familial or intimate male/female level of interaction, is revealed.

This article is based upon research into literacy which I initially began in 1972 when I received funding from the U.S. Office of Education to study the phenomenon of school drop-out. In 1979, what was to become a very significant shift in my work occurred when the National Institute of Education funded my continuing study of illiteracy, with the proviso that I concentrate upon non-English-speaking adults. At the time, I welcomed the shift, for the years of prior work had shown me how many of those targeted by current literacy policies were limited-English-speaking adults. This was even more dramatically the case in Los Angeles, the city to which I had recently moved.

In this paper, I draw upon life history interviews conducted by me and my co-workers with approximately fifty 'working-class', Spanish-speaking adults who had settled on the west side of Los Angeles. The interviews included a detailed inventory of situations in which the person was confronted with the English language and a description of how these situations were handled. Augmentation by a community ethnography, including systematic interviews of social and health service personnel, has allowed me to situate the person's experience and better understand how knowing/not knowing English structures daily interactions, practices and choices. The simultaneous attention paid to professional, social science, policy and media discourses about language and literacy has provided yet another view on how adults who are not fluent in English have been constructed as illiterate.

The Santa Monica–Venice–West Los Angeles area was selected because of extensive community contacts and because of the increasing numbers of Spanish-speaking people settling in a vicinity where English is the dominant language. Numbers are difficult to pin down, for so much of the recent Hispanic incoming population is undocumented – 'illegal aliens' in the view of most of the English-speaking public. In 1980, the official census figures for Los Angeles put the number of Hispanics as 27 per cent of the population, as non-Hispanic whites declined to 48 per cent of the total (*New York Times*, 24 August 1986, p. E5). With estimates of illegal immigration ranging from 2 to 12 million, and dramatically increasing since the economic crisis of Mexico in 1982, one can be assured that the numbers are much higher than actually recorded. In one of the rare studies of Hispanics who have moved to the west side of Los Angeles, we found that almost without exception, anyone who had entered the country since 1975 is undocumented (Rockhill: 1982).

With this background, I now want to turn to the various ways in which literacy has been practised and interpreted as power.

Literacy as power

Literacy is power. While most would agree that this equation is too simplistic, it is still the assumption that dominates most discourses about literacy. The power of literacy has been framed primarily in terms of economic development, equality of opportunity and the possibilities of liberty and democracy.

Whereas once literacy was pluralistic in conception, and there were a multiplicity of literacies associated with specific skills, during the processes of state formation, industrialisation and the movement toward mass schooling in nineteenth-century North America, literacy began to take on symbolic and ideological dimensions that went far beyond being able to read and write (Graff 1981; Soltow and Stevens 1981). As literacy became associated with liberty, 'illiterates' carried the burden of society's evils. In the process, literacy, schooling, education and intelligence also became inextricably linked to a morality of individual responsibility for economic well-being (Cook-Gumperz 1986). As such, literacy is an excellent example of the individualising and totalising power of the modern state described by Foucault (1982). This shift from 'literacies' to 'literacy' as ideology is integral to its use as a means of governance. Whereas once the state feared the development of literacy among the working class, by the mid-nineteenth century, literacy was being mandated as a means of social and moral regulation in industrialised countries (for example, see Corrigan and Gillespie 1978).

In a major extension of the use of literacy to regulate people, since the 1960s the state's differentiation between literates and illiterates has been the means by which adult educational services have been organised for poor people. In the United States, literacy is provided through adult basic education (ABE), a federal programme that developed as part of the 'War on Poverty'. Since the early 1970s, a central aspect of adult education's campaign for federal funds has involved demonstrating the high rate of illiteracy in the country. This has been accomplished by radically redefining literacy in terms of the 'functional' tasks that must be performed in order to function effectively in life. Pragmatically, this has meant measuring performance on a range of documentary-related tasks that involve complex reading skills. In the first study of its kind, the Adult Performance Level Study found 23 million functional illiterates, 56 per cent of whom were Spanish surnamed (Adult Performance Level 1975). Today's estimates are higher, ranging from 23 to 27 million adults, with another 20 millions categorised as borderline.

As functional literacy definitions become more enmeshed in highly questionable ideological uses of social science to justify particular forms of governance, they feed into the moralistic and jingoistic politics which underlie proclamations about the high rate of illiteracy in the United States. This is epitomised in the current national crusade against illiteracy which has involved the unprecedented use of the media. So ABC–TV launches its 'battle cry' against illiteracy with host Peter Jennings standing in the Library of Congress, telling viewers that illiteracy threatens both our national security and our ideals: 'Literacy and liberty . . . the two are inextricably linked'. He recites the 'appalling' statistics: '20 million adult Americans are illiterate; 20 million more read at or below the eighth-grade level' (*New York Times*, 30 September 1986, p. 25). The connections to morality are nowhere clearer than in Education Secretary William J. Bennett's drive to establish 'moral literacy' as a fundamental teaching of schools and colleges (*New York Times*, 10 October 1986, p. 1; 31 October 1986, p. 18).

Although the panic about immigration is not mentioned in the moral panic about literacy, the two come together in the latest laws that affect the foreign born. The most dramatic of these is the California law which declares English to be the official language. The law is aimed at making government funding of bilingual services illegal (*New York Times*, 26 November 1986, p. 12). Since these services are crucial to limited English-speakers, overnight, by executive fiat, another several million will, operationally, become 'functionally illiterate'. This racist mandate reflects the general national hysteria about the erosion of America's standards, and the swelling numbers of 'illegal aliens' who are seen as a drain on an already troubled economy. (The reported poverty rate among Hispanics – those counted! – has risen to 29 per cent, *New York Times*, 4 September 1986, p. 11). The angry charge of white Americans is that recent immigrants have been unwilling to learn English. This is not true. Everyone we interviewed talked of repeated efforts to learn English, with virtually everyone having attended classes soon after arrival. But, sustained attendance is extremely difficult and complex, especially for women, as shall be seen below.

Only a few days before the California referendum on language was passed by a two-thirds majority, President Reagan signed a new national policy on immigration. The 'Alien Law' grants legal status to those who can prove continuous *illegal* residence in the country for five years prior to 1982. So people who have had to continuously prove that they were *not* present, now have to prove their illegality to the government. In addition to the risk of deportation if they are found to be ineligible for legal status, they are subject to taxation for all non-reported income (pay stubs are the primary way of proving continuous residency), *and* required to demonstrate proficiency in English (*New York Times*, 26 October 1986, p. 1; 7 November 1986, p. 8). The meaning of the latter has not yet been made clear, but the provision of more English classes is seen to be essential (*New York Times*, 26 November 1986, p. Y12).

The provision of opportunities to overcome 'illiteracy' is seen as central to the liberty of the individual, as well as the nation. Focusing attention upon 'illiterates' is a strategy used by educators of conservative as well as progressive political persuasions in order to fight for the economic support necessary to expand programmes. Expansion is legitimised as essential to 'equality of opportunity'. The equality argument complements the social control/moral regulation position in that both speak to the necessity of enhancing individual freedom through regulation (for 'his' own good!). The complementarity of the positions depends upon theoretical and ideological dichotomies between self and society, agency and structure. Thus, as the argument goes, freedom is increased through the social provision of more educational opportunities from among which the individual, as agent, is morally obligated to choose. The adult educator's responsibility is clear – to fight for the provision of more education – and once this is accomplished, to mobilise and motivate adults to participate in the 'opportunities' so provided (Bhola 1985; Dave 1976; Jarvis 1986). Lodged firmly in liberal conceptions of the rational individual and benevolent state, it is argued that the way through structural inequities is to bring 'marginal' adults into the mainstream. (For a critique of how this ideology was used to obliterate working-class education in the US, see Rockhill 1985). With the provision of 'opportunities', success is dependent only upon individual capacity and motivation. This is the litany that pervades the literature of adult education. Literacy becomes a basic prerequisite to equality, to individual success. As such, it becomes a commodity, an object, an 'it' to be acquired.

Theories of inequality decontextualise and split apart the learner from what is to be learned, as well as from the forms and structures through which 'it' is provided. In the process of establishing literacy as a universalistic formula through which equality can be realised, literacy is treated as though it occurs in a vacuum. Thus, all learners are treated as the same, but symbolically are dichotomised as literate or illiterate – that is, learners or non-learners – and literacy is established as an isolatable, measureable, uniform 'thing', a skill or commodity that can be acquired if one only has the necessary motivation to participate in learning opportunities or literacy programmes. That is, literacy is treated as though it is outside the social and political relations, ideological practices, and symbolic meaning structures in which it is embedded.

Inequality theories do not take difference into account in a way that can get at how inequality is constructed and domination is reproduced and lived in the power relations of everyday life. Instead, quite the opposite occurs, as lived differences and the practices that give rise to them are concealed and sealed behind conceptions that mask, categorise and mark. This is vividly exemplified in the labelling of one in five adults as functionally illiterate. In establishing literacy as a uniform, clearly discernible 'fact', the related 'facts', that a large proportion of the adults classified as illiterate are not fluent in English – and that more than half of these are women – are ignored. So we fail to see how literacy is integral to gender, cultural and language politics, for literacy means, at the very least, reading and writing in the *dominant* language. Concealed by the banner of liberty and equality is the ethnocentrism, racism, and sexism inherent in literacy policies.

More radical conceptions of literacy as power argue that literacy can empower, through collective action and the enhancement of individual capacity. There have been numerous international declarations on the right to learn, the right to read, the right to literacy (for example, UNESCO 1985). Yet, as Limage (1980) argues, 'literacy has never been formally enshrined as a basic human right'. In his stirring call, Kozol (1985) urges 'illiterate' adults to get angry, to lobby, to organise, to demand they receive the education to which they are entitled.

Those who argue for literacy in terms of empowerment do not challenge the dominant ideology which constructs vast numbers of people as illiterate, thereby rendering them powerless. Like liberals who argue in terms of equality of opportunity, more radical voices are also lodged within the unifying ideology that sees illiteracy as the characteristic that keeps people powerless. So Kozol reasons: 'When illiterate people are powerless, when they see their children rendered powerless, when they recognize that one essential aspect of that impotence is inability to read and write, to understand, *to know*. . .' (p. 92). Although Kozol goes on to attribute this condition to social injustice rather than ignorance, he does not disagree with the ideology of mass adult illiteracy and its equation with powerlessness and ignorance.

Theories of resistance have romanticised 'the culture of the poor' without considering how it, too, is pervaded by dominant ideology, as well as differences and contradictions (Walker 1986). Power is undifferentiatedly connected to structure and conceptualised as out there, not lived in our subjectivities and the concrete relations of everyday life. In contrast, empowerment is connected to agency and resistance. If we accept that power is multiple and pervades our subjectivities, which are also multiple, then we must ask: resistance to what? in what form? The people we interviewed asserted that learning to read and write English was crucial to getting ahead, *and* they said that it was unnecessary, for one could get by all right without it, *and* one could never learn enough for it to make a real difference in their lives. Yet, the women especially yearn to learn the language. 'God willing, I will learn one day', runs like a refrain throughout their interviews. Is their goal to become empowered? to act in accord with their rights? to resist? If so, who, what and how do they resist? Conceptions of empowerment, resistance and rights do not capture the way the women we interviewed talk about their longing for literacy, how they think about their lives, what is meaningful to them, or the conflicts they live. These conceptions do not reveal how power is lived in the concrete material practices, relationships, or dreams of women. Empowerment arguments are directed at participation in the public spheres of national, economic, political and, so some extent, cultural activities (Fordham 1985; Kozol 1985). Totally absent from consideration is empowerment in the so-called private sphere of the home, including religious, family, sexual and male/female relations.

Literacy as communicative form and practice

An important bridge in the agency/structure, empowerment/power dichotomies is the idea that literacy is socially constructed in the practices of everyday interaction. In this view, literacy is seen in terms of cultural and communicative practices and patterns, which take place in face-to-face interactions and are situated in different types of communicative settings (Cook-Gumperz 1986; Heath 1983; Sola and Bennett 1985). Key to this developing body of research is the idea that literacy is multiple and that it involves different forms of communication. While the effects of moral regulation, social control and universally prescribed, functional standards for performance are recognised as central to the social construction of literacy requirements, the shift in focus to what actually happens as people do the work of literacy production and performance gives rise to questions that signal how literacy is actually lived in concrete practices and daily interactions. Rather than measure people's deficiency with respect to an abstract performance standard, this work relies upon ethnographies of community and classroom interaction to see how it is that people *do* communicate and accomplish 'communicative competence'. While this approach addresses questions of language difference, the concentration has been upon differences in dialects within the same language. The distinction is not always clear-cut, however, as the approach emphasises that dialects are embedded in a range of communicative patterns that signal different cultural meanings, as well as different language structures.

The significance of this research is that it recognises a multiplicity of literacies, which makes it possible to ask questions about the nature of power relationships among them. Thus far, inquiry into relations of power has been limited to showing that the literacy requirements of schooling and mainstream culture differ from and are invested with more power than those of life in the community and home. The work of Bennett (1983) and Sola and Bennett (1985) is exceptional in that they begin to probe into 'the relationships of power, communicative practice and consciousness'. In their studies of Hispanic students learning English, they conclude that, 'the struggle for voice ... is an important piece of a larger struggle between a majority community and the classes that rest on the labour of the community. This is the struggle for hegemony over the productive processes of consciousness formation' (Sola and Bennett 1985: 109). Hence, they argue that literacy practices are riddled by power relations which reflect broader struggles for domination, struggles (re)enacted in face-to-face interactions.

While Sola and Bennett do not address the question of functional literacy, the implications are major. Most obvious is the question of how, from among a range of skills, certain ones become privileged as functional requirements and how these conform to particular cultural, gender and ideological prescriptions. A related point is that the latest emphasis upon functional literacy privileges documentary reading over any other practice, in the process creating a passive stance (Levine 1982), as well as a tacit acceptance of the governance procedures through which lives are socially regulated. Furthermore, a successful decoding of the forms requires a comprehensive understanding of how the American system works, as well as an astute knowledge of how to safely replicate experience in acceptable documentary form. The series of interactions that immigrant women in particular have with bureaucracies is much more complex than 'filling in the blanks' on an information sheet. In an account of immigrants working their way through the health care system, I trace the multiplicity of interlocking, ambiguous, bureaucratic regulations with which they must be familiar in order to know and collect the benefits for which they are eligible. These were bizarre to immigrants who had come from cultures where help is exchanged through relationships of reciprocity rather than doled out through bureaucracies, and where the condition of establishing eligibility is mutual trust and caring, not proving that one is not ineligible (Rockhill 1984).

The significance of the dimensions of meaning, cultural form and the power relations in which they are embedded is crucial to understanding the experience of language difference, where one's world is necessarily structured by possibilities of communication. The primary way of getting by is to restrict one's range of activities to the Spanish-speaking community. That this is not solely a function of language furthers the argument that language means more than words. These words must be situated in terms of the regulatory processes of society, especially those that affect legal status, health, housing and work possibilities. Then, too, there is the desire to live among those with whom one can communicate, who share similar values and provide an informal network of support.

Literacy as gendered

The vividness with which language and gender structure the possibility of literacy is nowhere clearer than in the situation of women who speak little

English, especially since access to schooling is highly problematic. Because there are two primary ways of learning a second language – through informal interactions mixed language settings *or* through formal study in school situations – adults who cannot readily participate in formal schooling situations have to depend upon informal contact with spoken and written English to acquire the language. Where access to schooling is restricted, access to various public domains where the second language is spoken becomes crucial to the eventual acquisition of literacy, and vice versa – that is, where access to the public is restricted, schooling is more crucial. Because women are restricted in both cases, literacy becomes highly problematic for them.

In my research, I've come to see that the situation of women with respect to literacy is defined by a pervasive male/female power dynamic, cross-cut by differing constructions of masculinity and femininity, that are not considered in the literature. In fact, with rare exceptions, discourses about literacy, whether about power, skills or social relations, are strangely silent on the questions of gender or of women – especially strange since women are the primary participants in literacy programmes. This may be shifting with UNESCO's (1985) signalling women as a primary 'target population'.

A developing feminist critique is beginning to raise questions about the traditional occupations and roles for which women are being prepared through functionally-defined literacy programmes (Bhasin 1984; Ellis 1984; Horsman 1988; Ramdas 1985; Riria 1983). To make the obvious point, literacy is much more than a set of reading and writing skills – literacy is always about something and it is a language. It cannot be separated from the content or the linguisitic forms of the texts read, or the social and pedagogic politics of their production and reading. Perhaps the most vulnerable to feminist critique are the life skills components of basic literacy and job preparedness programmes through which women are taught how to dress and perform properly (Morton 1985). The extent to which women's literacy practices, including participation in schooling, are ruled by the men in their lives, is yet to be systematically documented, although examples are a taken-for-granted part of our popular culture (for example, the film, *Educating Rita*). As Ramdas (1985) argues, 'there must be a clear recognition of the role played by men in preventing women from going out of their homes . . .' (p. 103).

The study we conducted in Los Angeles points to gender differences in everyday literacy practices, as well as the integral relationship between the sexual oppression of women and literacy. The most striking pattern is that the women we interviewed tend to use and to depend more upon the written word, whereas men acquire and use more spoken English. This has a great deal to do with the silencing of women, their confinement to the domestic sphere, and the structure of work available to people who speak little English. Women talk of being afraid to speak, ashamed of not knowing English. Men stress the importance of talking, of making themselves understood by whatever means necessary.

The men we interviewed feel at ease in the public in a way that women do not. The public takes on a special meaning – it is either a male ethnic grouping, or the public world where English is spoken, a world that women venture into only if they must in order to go to church, to work or to attend to the family's needs. Although restricted by racism, in comparison to the Hispanic women interviewed, the men owned the public by defining 'their' woman's participation in that sphere. Women do not go out of the house without their approval, and if they do go out, there is no public place for them to congregate, unless it is at work – or at school. This is part of the threat that school poses to the gendered traditions of the people – for it is a public place where women can potentially meet other people, be exposed to other ways of thinking, of being, or living.

Women rarely go out alone; whenever possible they go with a child, relative or friend. Even if they are going to school, they will not go unless they have someone to go with. Confinement to the home is reinforced by the vulnerability they feel due to not knowing English well enough to defend themselves, especially true in the high-crime districts in which they live. Having few options to pick up spoken English, the cycle of vulnerability spirals.

Women do most of the literacy work of the household. In addition to the uses of literacy involved in housework, they attend to the purchase of goods, as well as transactions around social services, public utilities, health care and the schooling of children. In our detailed inventory of English-language situations in everyday life, women report handling almost all of those which involve the use of the written word. Through detailed repetition, some acquire sets of literacy skills. Where community workers provide help to those who seek it, the woman acts as the mediator. It was very difficult to get accounts of the literacy work that women do in maintaining their homes and families. They don't notice it; literacy is another piece of the invisibility of women's work.

When women enter the public domain where the English language is spoken, they do so in ways that involve specific transactions in a variety of situations which do not occur on a regular basis. They do not experience frequent, repeated contact in linguistically similar situations, so they cannot learn to speak English through this work. Whenever possible, they go with someone who can help them with English, as well as with the bureaucratic regulations they will encounter.

The work available to women is an extension of their work at home and does not provide them with the opportunity to learn English in the same way that men can. The men who learn more English work in situations where they have contact with the English-speaking public. Examples are work in construction, gardening, small restaurants and stores. After working for a while with friends or relatives, who help them learn the ropes and the language, men can sometimes manage to get together enough capital to strike out on their own. The range of work options open to women is much more limited, including their access to any form of capital. The choices narrow down to domestic or factory work. The latter usually means working in a Spanish-speaking job ghetto at tasks that require minimal interaction. Unless a domestic worker happens upon a very unusual employer who helps her to learn English, she is confined to the home where she works and often lives in isolation, learning only the few English words that are specific to housework, or to serving the family.

As the confinement of women to the home suggests, the gendered politics of literacy is about more than male/female differences in everyday communicative practices. These differences are constructed culturally and socially, through the delegation of women to the private sphere. Literacy is integral to the power dynamic between men and women, to material differences in the options available to them, and to man's domination of woman through her sexuality.

Violence was common in the lives of many of the women we interviewed. Where present, expressions of male violence typically included the charges that the women were 'stupid', 'illiterate', 'whores'. I believe that the linkage of these words is symbolically significant, signifying that to be a woman and illiterate is to be a stupid whore, whereas to be literate is to be a 'lady'. Men feel legitimated in dominating whores in a way that they do not with ladies: to control their woman they keep her illiterate, and accuse her of being a whore if she goes out of the home, leaving her no exit. The converse is the fear that if she does go to school she will become a 'lady' and leave her man.[3]

Several women related stories of being physically beaten. Some flee their homes, some call the police and a few turn to the priest, but most remain silent, too ashamed and afraid to give any more than a fleeting glimpse of the violence they live – a violence enshrined as normal by the family, church and other social institutions. Over the course of months, Modesta talked of plans she and her husband had to attend English classes – plans which never materialised. Then one night, she broke down and sobbed, offering a hushed explanation: 'He drinks a lot. He is very much like a man. Right now, things aren't going very well for us. He loves his children very much but he treats me badly. Very badly.'

In my original work, I did not connect this and other stories of violence with the question of literacy or of learning English. Now I see it as central. Over the years, I have been stuck by a multiplicity of anecdotes about women whose husbands would not allow them to go to school. We need to know more about what it means to live in the face of male rage and violence. In my case, when I lived daily in the face of threat, never knowing what act would be interpreted as a transgression, an attack upon MALE RIGHT or power, I did all I could not to set off that rage and withdrew into the safety of a kind of death. While not all of the women talked of violence, several of those to whom I became closer over the course of my research talked, painfully, angrily, of similar experiences of violence, sometimes explicitly directed against their going to school. Their situations differ from mine in that they have fewer options. In addition, the fear of their husbands seems lodged in the worry that their wives will be influenced by contact with 'gringos' – both men and women – and thus challenge their family traditions. Men who have better education and/or are in more daily contact with the English-speaking world tend to be more supportive of their wives learning English.

In varying degrees, women resist complete male power over their lives, turning to education as a form of resistance, with some small successes in overcoming the pressures under which they live. Women express a strong desire to take classes in order to learn English. They do go, but, except for the young and highly educated, they stop attending. The typical pattern is one of several attempts. They explain stopping in terms of the enormous pressures of their daily lives, including resistance at home. They talk about worry, anxiety, too much on their minds and feeling too old to concentrate upon the difficult and time-consuming endeavour of learning the language. The hope that one day conditions will be right lingers on: 'I am thinking of going to school within the next year. I went a few years ago, but I didn't continue . . . you always regret it for not going to school, and for not learning . . .'

Gladys frames learning English in terms of going to school and learning. There is a point at which taking classes is no longer a question of learning English but of going to school. Initial efforts to learn the language are framed in terms of self-defence, or survival. This shifts to a frame of advancement, of getting ahead. It is important to understand this distinction in order to understand how it is that literacy can be both the taken-for-granted work of women and a threat. As long as the reading and writing of spoken English which are learned are seen as the rudiments of survival, there is less threat. Learning and education are a different matter; they carry a symbolic dimension of movement into a better, more powerful class and culture – another world, another life, which is both desired and feared. As has been noted, the symbolic significance of literacy is connected with its attachment to schooling. For the women we interviewed, schooling brings with it the possibility of becoming a 'lady' – somebody.

Once literacy carries with it the symbolic power of education, it poses a threat to the power relations in the family. When men feel a need to be in control, they not only want power over their wives, but to control what they think and do. This is especially so when the man feels little or no power at work, or is not the family's primary breadwinner. Furthermore, immigrant men are denied alternative forms of social status and are confronted by the chauvinism of an alien culture. The shock of immigration, in and of itself, can be demasculinising. If 'machismo' reigns, the man is easily threatened by any sign of the woman's independence. The words of Maria echo the feelings of many: 'I don't want a macho. I want a man'. Part of her desire to be 'somebody' is to think for herself, to advance herself through the world of work; this is precisely the meaning of literacy as 'empowerment' that can be threatening for women in traditional family relations.

Women are more likely to develop their English literacy skills once they are separated or divorced. Several of the women we interviewed had left their husbands because of violence. They talk hopefully of changing their lives through education, especially those who are younger and know enough English so that they can see the possibility of finding a different kind of work.

The women we interviewed do not frame their experience in terms of rights. When they tell their stories, they tell about their children and their husbands. In the trauma of immigration, they recede into the background; fighting for survival, they turn toward their children for hope, and measure progress in terms of the family's acquisition of material goods. As the husband struggles to hold on to signs of power and social status in a demasculinising situation, the woman painfully learns to put her dreams aside and do what she must to supplement the family's income. So Elena tells us:

> I consider myself to be a successful woman because I went to the school and they told me that my son was the best and that he likes to study. That is a triumph for me. And then, my husband says to me, 'My work is going better and better.' This is also a success for me.

When women do talk about going to school, they frame it in terms of desire, not rights. Women in their late teens and early twenties and/or women who are living alone, have the desire to learn enough English to go to school and find office work. The dream is to be a secretary or a receptionist, but it is more than this – it is to enter the world of middle-class America, to wear dresses and high heels, to look and be the female image they see smiling back at them in magazines, on their TV screens and billboards. That these jobs are highly literacy dependent is part of the dream – and the reality that they live. For women, there is no middle level work, where speaking, reading and writing skills are used but do not have to be highly developed. The women we interviewed cannot learn enough English to move into the next strata of jobs open to them. There are few ways out of domestic or factory work – except through sustained schooling, and they cannot do this unless they are supported, in some way, to participate. As we have seen, quite the opposite is true (Rockhill 1987).

Conclusion

The politics of literacy are integral to the cultural genocide of a people, as well as the gendering of society. The construction of literacy is embedded in the discursive practices and power relationships of everyday life: it is socially constructed, materially produced, morally regulated, and carries a symbolic significance which cannot be captured by its reduction to any one of these. Literacy is caught up in the material, racial and sexual oppression of women, *and* it embodies their hope for escape. For women, it is experienced as *both*, a threat and a desire: to learn English means to go to school, to enter a world that holds the promise of change and, because of this, threatens all that they know.

Literacy is women's work, but not women's right. The women we interviewed do the work of literacy in the privacy of their homes, but most do not have the right to change – to be 'somebody' – their husbands object, sometimes forcefully. They live in a very ambiguous situation: they cannot do what they are socially mandated to do – and want to do – to learn English, to go to school.

The dependence of women upon schooling to learn English is related to their exclusion from forms of work or other forms of activity where they might learn the language informally. The question that literacy poses for Hispanic women cannot be separated from the ways in which language structures their worlds, the symbolic significance of schooling, and the ways that both of these are defined by culturally prescribed practices of sexism. Because the professional and social science discourses about literacy have decontextualised it from lived experience, none of the foregoing has been evident. To frame literacy in terms of equality of opportunity, rights, or empowerment is absurd in the face of a fist – or, less dramatically, in a gendered society where the conception of rights is alien to women who have been told all their lives that they must obey and care for others.

This account began by posing the question of what might happen if the voices of Hispanic immigrant women, educational professionals and public policy makers, each of whom is speaking to the question of literacy from very different perspectives, were brought into the same space. In doing so, we've seen how alien the view of those in positions of power is to the experiences of the Hispanic women interviewed. To portray illiterates as a threat to the American tradition of liberty, as unmotivated to learn, unwilling to participate in educational opportunities which would provide the conditions necessary to promote equality and/or as not seeing how literacy can empower them, is never to have heard the urgent plea of Maria and others. Their cries of yearning have been systematically excluded. Despite the 'fact' that Hispanic women probably have the highest rate of 'illiteracy' of any group in the USA, they are not the illiterates imaged by those who have turned their attention to this issue. The rhetoric suggests that the unarticulated image is that of a male – be he black, white or an 'illegal alien'.

In order to see women, and to understand their experiences with literacy, we need to look at how language in general, as well as the particularities of reading and writing English, enter into their everyday lives. It is also important to look at schooling, both in terms of its symbolic meaning and the material realities in women's lives. To seriously act upon the principle of literacy or learning as a right – or even a possibility – for women, it is necessary to reconceptualise how 'the political' and 'the educational' are constituted so that the primary sites of oppression in their lives are not systematically excluded from our politics or our classrooms. Our work suffers from a splitting between the public and the private which reinforces precisely the same gendered practices through which women are oppressed in their everyday lives. The gendered politics of literacy reflect these practices. If we open the doors of our minds to the power of the fist, the power of the sexual, the power of the family, church and other cultural forms, perhaps we can begin to find ways to address the contradictory constructions of women's subjectivities with respect to literacy/learning/education. They are in a double bind: to act upon their desire for change requires a choice that few feel they can make – a choice between love, family and home, or violent upheaval. However violent the love they live may be, for most, the unknown of the latter is the more threatening.

Notes

1 Since the original publication of this article the connection among gender, race, class, ethnicity and sexuality has become the central debate amongst feminists, generally posed as a conflict between identity and difference.
2 The term 'Hispanic' is used in this article because it was the preferred term of community activists during the time we were doing our research; for example we joined other community workers organising a 'Hispanic Resource Organisation'.

3 The concept of literacy as threat/desire is more fully developed in Rockhill (1987). I continue to be uneasy about the possibility that my interpretation of the connections between literacy acquisition and violence against women will be taken to mean that this is a problem specific to Hispanic immigrants. While I do see a particular colouration to the ways in which those connections are lived by the women interviewed in my study, I stress that the general connection between violence against women and education goes far beyond Hispanic, immigrant, or even literacy populations. Since publishing this work, I have been greeted by women of differing classes, educational levels, and ethnic backgrounds, who tell me that they have experienced a similar dynamic; as I indicate in the article, the connection has been a phenomenon in my own life. We have well documented the pervasive violence against women and children; we need much more work to see the various ways in which it affects educational experience and attainment for women. We also need further work to identify the various culturally specific ways in which these connections are lived, and their implications for educational practice.

References

Adult Performance Level Project 1975. *Adult functional competency: a summary.* Austin: University of Texas.
Bennett, A. T. 1983. 'Discourses of power, the dialectics of understanding, the power of literacy', *Journal of Education*, 165: 63–74.
Bhasin, K. 1984. 'The why and how of literacy for women: some thoughts in the Indian context', *Convergence*, 17 (4): 34–43.
Bhola, H. S. 1985. 'A policy analysis of adult literacy promotion in the Third World: an accounting of promises made and promises fulfilled'. Unpublished manuscript.
Cook-Gumperz, J. 1986. 'Literacy and schooling: an unchanging equation?', in J. Cook-Gumperz (ed.), *The social construction of literacy*. Cambridge: Cambridge University Press.
Corrigan, P. and Gillespie, V. 1978. *Class struggle, social literacy and idle time: the provision of public libraries in England as a case study in 'the organisation of leisure with indirect results'.* Brighton: Moyes Labour History Monographs.
Dave, R. H. 1976. 'Foundations of lifelong education: some methodological aspects', in R. H. Dave (ed.), *Foundations of lifelong education*. Oxford: Pergamon Press.
Davis, A. Y. 1983. *Women, race and class.* New York: Vintage Books.
Ellis, P. 1984. 'Women, adult education and literacy: A Caribbean perspective', *Convergence*, 17 (4): 44–53.
Fordham, P. (ed.), 1985. *One billion illiterates, one billion reasons for action: report on the international seminar 'Co-operating for Literacy'.* West Berlin, October 1983. Bonn, International Council for Adult Education and Deutsche Stiftung für internationale Entwicklung.
Foucault, M. 1982. 'The subject and power', *Critical Inquiry*, 8: 777–95.
Graff, H. J. 1981. 'Literacy, jobs, and industrialization: the nineteenth century', in

H. J. Graff (ed.), *Literacy and social development in the West: a reader*, pp. 232–60. Cambridge: Cambridge University Press.

Grant, C. A. and Sleeter, C. E. 1986. 'Race, class and gender in education research: an argument for integrative analysis', *Review of Education Research*, 56: 195–211.

Heath, S. B. 1983. *Ways with words: language, life and work in communities and classrooms*. Cambridge: Cambridge University Press.

Horsman, J. 1988. 'Something in my mind beside the everyday: (il)literacy in women's lives in a Nova Scotian county'. Ed.D. thesis, Ontario Institute for Studies in Education.

Hunter, C. St. J. and Harman, D. 1979. *Adult illiteracy in the United States*. New York: McGraw-Hill.

Jarvis, P. 1986. *Sociological perspectives on lifelong education and lifelong learning*. Athens: University of Georgia.

Kozol, J. 1985. *Illiterate America*. New York: New American Library.

Levine, K. 1982. 'Functional literacy: fond illusions and false economies', *Harvard Educational Review*, 52: 249–66.

Limage, L. J. 1980. 'Illiteracy in industrialized countries: a sociological commentary', *Prospects*, 10: 151–5.

MacKinnon, C. A. 1981. 'Feminism, marxism, method and the state: an agenda for theory', in N. O. Keohane and B. C. Gelpi (eds.), *Feminist theory: a critique of ideology*, pp. 1–30. Chicago: University of Chicago Press.

Martin, B. 1982. 'Feminism, criticism and Foucault', *New German Critique*, 27: 3–30.

McRobbie, A. 1982. 'The politics of feminist research: between talk, text and action', *Feminist Review*, 12: 46–57.

Morton, J. 1985. 'Assessing vocational readiness in low-income women: an exploration into the construction and use of ideology'. MA thesis, Ontario Institute for Studies in Education.

Ng, R. 1988. 'The documentary construction of "immigrant women" in Canada', *Working Papers on Women in International Development Series*, no. 160. Michigan State University, March 1988.

Radway, J. 1984. *Reading the romance: women, patriarchy and popular culture*. Chapel Hill: University of North Carolina.

Ramdas, L. 1985. 'Illiteracy, women and development', *Adult Education and Development*, German Adult Education Association, no. 24, pp. 95–105.

Riria, J. 1983. 'Cooperating for literacy – the perspective of women'. Paper presented at the Berlin Conference, Co-operating for Literacy.

Rockhill, K. 1982. 'Language learning by Latino immigrant workers: the socio-cultural context'. Washington, DC: unpublished report to National Institute of Education.

  1984. 'Health crises in the lives of non-English-speaking Latino immigrants: language, legalities and trusted advocates'. Unpublished manuscript.

  1985. 'The liberal perspective and the symbolic legitimation of university adult education in the USA', in R. Taylor, K. Rockhill and R. Fieldhouse. *University adult education in England and the USA*, pp. 123–74. London: Croom Helm.

1987. 'Literacy as threat/desire: longing to be SOMEBODY', in J. Gaskell and A. McLaren (eds.), *Women and education: a Canadian perspective*, pp. 315–31. Calgary: Detselig.

Silvera, M. 1983. *Silenced*. Toronto: Williams-Wallace.

Smith, D. E. 1977. *Feminism and Marxism: a place to begin, a way to go*. Vancouver: New Star Books.

Sola, M. and Bennett, A. T. 1985. 'The struggle for voice: narrative literacy and consciousness in an east Harlem school', *Journal of Education*, 167: 88–110.

Soltow, L. and Stevens, E. 1981. *The rise of literacy and the common school in the United States*. Chicago: University of Chicago Press.

Steedman, C. 1986. *Landscape for a good woman: a story of two lives*. London: Virago.

UNESCO, 1985. *Final Report*. Fourth International Conference on Adult Education, Paris, 19–29 March 1985. Paris: UNESCO.

Walker, J. C. 1986. 'Romanticising resistance, romanticising culture: problems in Willis's theory of cultural production', *British Journal of Sociology of Education*, 7: 59–80.

Walkerdine, V. 1984. 'Some day my prince will come ... young girls and the preparation for adolescent sexuality', in A. McRobbie and M. Neva (eds.), *Gender and Generation*. New York: Macmillan.

Westwood, S. 1984. *All day, every day: factory and family in the making of women's lives*. London: Pluto Press.

7

LITERACY DEVELOPMENT AND ETHNICITY: AN ALASKAN EXAMPLE

STEPHEN REDER and KAREN REED WIKELUND

Introduction

When Vitus Bering left St Petersburg in 1725, he embarked upon one of history's great explorations. After a year of demanding overland travel across Siberia, Bering reached the coast of Kamchatka on what is now called the North Pacific. There he made ready to set sail on the most challenging part of his expedition. Catherine the Great had sent him to discover if the land masses separated by the great ocean were in fact joined in the far north. This question, which had puzzled the Russians for over a century, was not completely resolved until Bering's second voyage in 1741, when the water passage that now bears his name was finally crossed and contact was made with the mainland of North America. The discovery of the Bering Strait and America was, however, one of the least remarkable eventualities of Bering's expeditions.

The intensive Russian penetration and colonisation of the Western Pacific rim which followed Bering's seminal expeditions had a most profound impact on the subsequent history of the indigenous peoples of the area. The early Russian presence brought many changes to the native Aleut and Eskimo cultures. All spheres of existence were affected and numerous innovations brought lasting change to the indigenous ways of life. Smallpox epidemics, alcoholism and other devastating diseases decimated the native population. New tools and technologies were imported and applied to traditional hunting and fishing activities. The Russian-American Company also introduced some radical new economic concepts – those of money, paid labour and credit – which had a profound impact on the social and economic organisation of the existing cultures. With the Russians came their Orthodox Church, through which the colonists and traders endeavoured to evangelise the indigenous people.

All of these innovations – material and conceptual – have had a lasting impact on the area. But there is one innovation, in particular, that will be examined closely here – the use of writing. The impact and development of literacy among the indigenous population is well illustrated by the case of the Seal Bay community on Kodiak Island in south central Alaska.[1]

Brief sketch of Seal Bay

Seal Bay is a small Koniag Eskimo fishing village which has felt the influx of Russian, Scandinavian and white American settlers. It was the largest community on the southern end of Kodiak Island in the late 1800s, but appears to have enjoyed relative isolation until well into the twentieth century. As commercial fishing developed on Kodiak Island, a few Scandinavian fishermen married into the community, which has experienced steady growth since the 1920s. About that time the isolation of the village was broken by the establishment of a government school. Gradually, contact with the outside world increased. In the late 1930s the first post office was established. Commercial fishing contacts continued to develop, as villagers fished for canneries owned and operated by outsiders. Over the years, villagers gained knowledge of government programmes and 'benefits' (that is, public assistance); by the 1950s and early 1960s, Seal Bay was actively participating in government subsidy programmes (Befu 1970).

This gradual development was abruptly accelerated by a series of tidal waves which nearly destroyed the entire village in 1964. Seal Bay immediately came into continuous contact with numerous government agencies and services, resulting in rapid changes in attitudes and ties with the outside world (Davis 1971). This had a particularly striking impact on the need for certain literacy skills among the adult population. Then, nativistic movements, culminating within less than a decade in the passage of the Alaska Native Claims Settlement Act of 1971, increased even further the need for native villagers to take on increasing responsibility in the complex legal and bureaucratic dealings of the world beyond the village.[2] Along with these developments, transportation and communication facilities improved at a rapid rate. By the late 1970s, the once isolated Seal Bay found itself linked to the outside world by twice daily aeroplane passenger service, daily mail deliveries and telephone and television direct via satellite.

Literacy in Seal Bay

In the early days of the Russian colony, specialised literacies in the Cyrillic alphabet were introduced by powerful institutions, the Russian Orthodox Church and the Russian-American Company. Although they shared a common script, the literacy practices of Church and Company were distinct and each had its characteristic domain of influence on local affairs. This early patterning of literacy into domains of activity and influence became a pervasive feature of the development and organisation of literacy over the next two centuries. The purchase of Alaska by the

United States in 1867 set the stage for the subsequent introduction of a new writing system, English, into the Eskimo community of Seal Bay. By the time this new literacy entered the village in the 1920s, Russian-introduced literacy practices in Cyrillic script were well established in village life. The new English literacy, like its Russian predecessor, was introduced by an external society whose language and customs were alien to villagers. A new institutional base was also associated with the new writing – the United States government school, which eventually expanded into another domain, the Public Sector. As this paper illustrates, competition between the literacy practices of the Russian-rooted institutions – Church and Company – and United States-rooted institutions – School and Public Sector – was a central feature not only of literacy development in the community, but also of the evolving social structure of the modern village. The resulting pattern of interactions between villagers' literacy and ethnicity has persisted long after the technological distinction between the two literacies – their different scripts – ended.

Research methods

Ethnohistorical, documentary and ethnographic research methods were used to study literacy development in Seal Bay. Preliminary historical research and literature reviews were followed by several brief trips to the site to arrange logistical matters during the fall of 1978. Intensive fieldwork was conducted continuously from January to June 1979. The two authors lived in the village during alternate, partially overlapping stays of five to six weeks each throughout the fieldwork period.

The fieldwork involved observation of and participation in the everyday life of the community as fully as possible. Extensive field notes were kept of these activities. One author (Wikelund) became particularly involved with women's activities and social groups (for example, a group of women who regularly take *banyas* or steambaths together; and the Church Sisterhood – sewing, baking, fund-raising) whereas the other (Reder) participated in men's activities (for example, fishing; small engine repair and maintenance; a men's *banya* group). Taking lessons in speaking Alutiiq,[3] the aboriginal language of the Island, helped build initial rapport with older villagers and facilitated collecting historical material orally. More structured research activities were also used. For example, a questionnaire-based survey was conducted. The survey consisted of in-depth interviews with heads (or their spouses) of twenty-nine of the approximately eighty households; information was gathered about each family's background, language abilities, education, work experience and literacy activities – such as reading habits, record keeping, use of written materials in various tasks, and so on.

To place this contemporary data in historical perspective, extensive documentary information was also collected on the history of Kodiak Island and particularly Seal Bay – including data from diverse local, state and federal government agencies, church archives, postal, telephone and air transportation records, previous field studies (Befu 1961, 1970; Maruyama 1964; Davis 1971) and other bibliographic sources. A two-week follow-up trip to Seal Bay was conducted in February 1980, to collect information needed to fill in 'holes' in the research data which had been identified by preliminary analysis of the field data.

Characterising literacy

Synthesising these data, the description of literacy development in Seal Bay draws on Scribner and Cole's (1978, 1981) view of literacy as a set of socially organised practices. Considered as a set of practices, literacy is not conceived as the individual's knowledge of how to read and write in a given script, but as socially organised activities in which that knowledge is applied for particular purposes in specific contexts of use. The present work characterises literacy practices in terms of three interrelated attributes: their *technology*, their *function* and their *social meaning*. The technology of a literacy practice refers to the system of graphic signs used for encoding messages as well as the material means used for producing, storing and distributing those messages. The function of a literacy practice is the social purpose for which the activity or activities are conducted. The term 'social meaning', first applied to literacy by Szwed (1981), is not completely adequate for present purposes, but it does refer to a critical aspect of literacy development. Lacking a more suitable term, 'social meaning' is used here to refer to the complex of beliefs, attitudes and values associated with the activities in question. For example, beliefs about who should engage in a particular literacy practice, in what situations and under what circumstances – that is, the propriety of participation – as well as the social distinctions marked by use of literacy in a particular context are often aspects of the social meaning of a literacy practice.

These three attributes have been described in detail elsewhere (Reder 1987, 1990, in press; Reder and Green 1981). Here the chief concern is with one of them – the social meaning of literacy. Social meaning will emerge as a critical concept for understanding the development of literacy in Seal Bay; intimately tied to the ethnicity of villagers, it is a key element in the socialisation of knowledge about the technological and functional characteristics of literacy.

The development of literacy in Seal Bay

The diagram in figure 7.1 will serve as a model of the historical development of literacy in Seal Bay and as an outline for discussing interactions among literacy practices in different domains of village life. The major domains considered here are represented by the four corner boxes of the diagram and the dotted central box in the middle.[4] The pair of vertical lines down the middle of the diagram separates the two historically distinct strands of literacy development, the Russian on the right and the American on the left. These lines also symbolise a major emic distinction made by villagers between two kinds of activities and values: 'Village' and 'Outside'.

The arrows connecting the vertically adjacent corners, Church–Company and School–Public Sector, represent long-standing and well-established relationships between these pairs of domains. These affinities stand in contrast to equally well-established tensions between the horizontally adjacent domains: School versus Church and Public Sector versus Company. This pattern of affinities and oppositions operates homeostatically in Seal Bay; this small village thrives by keeping overt conflict to a minimum. The equilibrating role of the Village Governance domain[5] in the village is suggested by its central position in the diagram. The dotted lines are meant to suggest the dynamic nature of its role in village affairs and values.

The development of the distinct concepts of 'Village' and 'Outside' literacy practices has been described in greater detail elsewhere (Reder and Green 1983). However, brief definitions of these two concepts are presented here to ensure clarity in the ensuing discussion of conflicts between domains of activity and the critical role of social meanings attached to different literacy practices.

The literacy practices associated with the Orthodox Church and the 'Company', which developed during the Russian period in Alaska and evolved as the salmon industry grew, are designated as 'Village' literacy here since the inhabitants of Seal Bay think of them that way. These practices are very much a part of native identity today, despite the fact that they were originally introduced through contact with an outside culture and despite the use of English literacy in each of these domains today.

In contrast, 'Outside' literacy practices introduced in English through the American school and later expanded through contact with outside government agencies continue to be representative of the white 'Outside'. Even though native adults recently have begun serving on the village and island-wide school boards, and some are now employed as teacher aides, the school remains socially and ideologically apart from the rest of the community. Similarly, despite the incorporation of specialised literacy

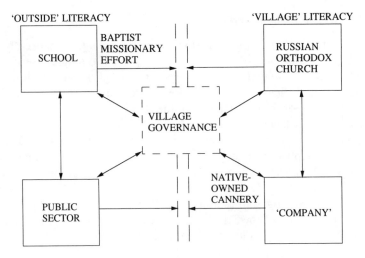

Figure 7.1 Model of historical development of literacy in Seal Bay.

roles (and related jobs) into village life as contacts with outside agencies expanded, the social meanings attached to these relatively new literacy practices, although always evolving, have been more resistant to change than has the technological and functional knowledge villagers have acquired to fill these roles.

Conflicting social meanings in literacy development: 'Village' versus 'Outside' literacy

Examining the ways in which value systems have shaped and been shaped by changes in literacy practices provides perhaps the best perspective on the significance of social meanings in literacy development. The distinct social meanings that have developed as integral components of Village and Outside literacies in Seal Bay are not static features of the literacy practices. Rather, they are dynamic, reflecting the changing social contexts in which writing is used. The historical development of literacy in this Alaskan village offers several examples: (1) a critical decade followed the entry into the village of Baptist missionaries who tried to introduce Outside literacy practices into the Village domain of the Church – these events stimulated strong factional forces in the village which helped to keep Church and School literacy practices quite separate; (2) a decade later, changes introduced in Orthodox Church literacy had far-reaching consequences for village life; and (3) the diverging social values implicit in Company and Public Sector activities have served to keep Village and Outside literacy practices apart.

The School–Church conflict

The arrival of a Baptist missionary in the village in the early 1950s brought the use of spoken and written English into religious services long before the Russian Church incorporated English into its liturgy and hymns[6]; and the use of English literacy continued to have considerable significance for the maintenance of the Baptist faith long after its disciples had left the village.

The intense encounter which developed between Russian Orthodoxy and the Baptists can be analysed on different levels. At one level, of course, this clash can be seen as an interdenominational quarrel, an ideological battle. However, it was also a factional dispute within the village between the well-established Village domain of the Church and the Outside domain of the School, each spearheaded by a distinctive literacy having its own technology, functions, and social meaning.

Ideological conflict

Although the Russian Orthodox religion and its associated literacy practices had originally been introduced through foreign influences, by the time the Baptists entered the village the religion had been sufficiently internalised that it had become an integral part of the villagers' ethnic identity; Russian Orthodoxy was synonymous with being a native villager. Relatively few individuals converted to the Baptist faith during the decade missionaries resided there. Nevertheless, missionary efforts in the village raised considerable controversy and factional strife. Even today villagers emotionally recount tales of one missionary's years in the village. During the 1950s, missionary efforts met strong opposition from adults, although children apparently enjoyed Baptist social activities and even adults attended special parties (Befu 1970: 39). Missionary efforts served many different needs, through such secular activities as writing letters for illiterate people, providing radio contact with the outside world, teaching agricultural techniques, and so on. The missionaries were also teachers at the village school.

The influence of a Baptist missionary woman who spent many years in Seal Bay continues to be felt today. A lay reader had stopped attending Orthodox Church services, but resumed responsibilities for reading after the older reader died in 1965. However, in 1969 he left the village with his family to reside in Anchorage and converted to the Baptist faith. Seal Bay was left without a strong lay reader. One of the missionary's strongest converts – the daughter of an active Orthodox couple and wife of the oldest son of an influential Orthodox family – has remained in the village, firmly maintaining her Baptist faith despite heavy family and social pressure, and she has resolutely persevered in sending her children away to a Baptist high school and a Bible college. The religious controversy in the village appears far from over, since this woman's daughter planned to return from college to do missionary work in the village.

Village–Outside conflict

The confrontation between Russian Orthodoxy and the Baptists must be seen as more than an interdenominational dispute. The missionaries entered the village as white outsiders and challenged a vital element of traditional life, seeking to replace it with traditions and practices from the Outside. By establishing permanent residence in Seal Bay, these religious missionaries followed a pattern well cut before them by previous 'cultural missionaries', the school teachers, who also entered and established residence as outsiders, rejected and at times actively suppressed native ways and sought to replace them with Outside ways. The fact that the missionaries also served as teachers in the village school must only have strengthened their identification with the Outside.

Although this was a very divisive clash between School and Church domains, it was likely not the first. Black (1977a: 105) notes that school teachers during the period when schools were run by the Bureau of Indian Affairs in the Aleutian Chain were generally hostile to the Church, recognising its role in maintaining native identity and solidarity. We have no specific records of previous tensions between the school and the Church in Seal Bay, but it is likely that school teachers there were similarly oriented. Nor was the missionary crisis the last factional crisis between Church and School domains in Seal Bay. Recurrent tensions and numerous disputes between Church and School leaders were evident during the fieldwork in 1979. Although some of the tension resulted from personal conflict between the priest and head teacher, this appeared only to ignite already well established factional strife between allegiances to these two institutions.

Literacies in conflict

Conflict between literacy traditions also played an active role in the missionary clash. The missionaries tried to replace the well-established oral use of Slavonic and Alutiiq in church services with the use of English in the Baptist services. Furthermore, the sacred Slavonic writings, too, were to be replaced by materials written in English. The attempt to introduce the School-based literacy into the domain of the Church threatened the existing social order of the village. The missionaries' dual status as school teachers only intensified the difficulties.

The literacies in conflict in these events differed in many interrelated ways. The Baptists' use of literacy differed considerably from its use in the Orthodox Church with regard to the three characteristics of literacy practices identified earlier. The technology of the Baptists' literacy was English-based and used the Roman alphabet, whereas the Orthodox literacy used Cyrillic script in Slavonic and Alutiiq. Few if any Orthodox parishioners understood the Slavonic services they attended; participation was by rote, and comprehension of the oral language was limited. The Baptists, on the other hand, offered services based on English literacy practices and pressed the point that individuals should be able to read and understand the written Word. In the Orthodox Church, literacy expertise was concentrated among village specialists, rather than widely distributed among individuals. Finally, Orthodox literacy was taught by community members, whereas English literacy was taught by school teachers.

These contrasts between the literacy practices as they applied to the two religions were clear to villagers. Davis (1971: 190) reports that during the height of the controversy, villagers attending the Baptist services criticised the failure of the Russian Church to 'read the Bible', that is, the failure of individuals to understand what was read (since it was in Russian). Converts today still repeat that criticism. Another of Davis' observations points to the conflict among literacy practices underlying the schism. The missionary woman frequently handed out papers to the children, often containing religious writing and pictures. The children occasionally let these papers fall and remain on the ground outside, which offended the Orthodox believers to whom this was sacrilege; they held the very graphic aspect of such pictures and Scripture to be sacred, much as the icons in the Church.

The conflict between the literacy practices of Orthodoxy, which required interpretation of written materials by a literacy specialist, and those of the would-be-reformers, which emphasised direct lay understanding of the Word, has ample precedent, of course. Luther's Reformation pivoted on the same contrast between the literacy practices of that era's orthodoxy and reformers. Olson describes the new 'orientation to text' heralded by Luther: 'The meaning of Scripture depends not upon the doctrines of the Church but on a deeper reading of the text' (1977: 72–3).

The significance of School-based literacy in the Seal Bay religious confrontation is evidenced by the well-developed English literacy skills of the Baptist converts at that time as well as today. Although not everyone who converted has highly developed English literacy skills, the number who do suggests that the use of English in the practice of the faith played a role in attracting them away from the more traditional Russian Church, which at that time continued to use Slavonic in its services. For example, the Baptist convert mentioned earlier has been a 'literacy specialist' in the village. She has filled the important role of local postmistress for more than a decade. In 1979 she also served on the Village Health Committee and was an active member of the Advisory School Board. The overall membership of Seal Bay's Advisory School Board in 1979 seemed to reflect this opposition between the School and Church domains. Although the vast majority of Seal Bayites are Orthodox, only one of the five members was an active Orthodox parishioner, one participated only marginally, and three were non-Orthodox.[7]

The penetration of English literacy into the Church

We have seen that the confrontation in Seal Bay between Russian Orthodoxy and the Baptists included a clash between different traditions of literacy practice. Conflict between the social meanings villagers attached to Slavonic and English writing was an important element in the dispute. Although the missionaries' forced departure from Seal Bay, after tidal waves virtually destroyed the village in 1964, eased the factional tension, the subsequent Church-initiated transition from Slavonic to English services during the last decade provides further evidence of the impact of Outside literacy on traditional Village activities.

One measure of how fully the Slavonic literacy practices had been incorporated into village life comes from the significance of the lay reader – the literacy specialist of the Church domain. Such specialists had played a key role in the maintenance of the faith over the years. Their traditional expertise had been passed on for generations through established patterns of socialisation within the Village domain, quite independent of the Outside domain. In addition to other conflicts stimulated by the missionaries' challenge, their School-based literacy threatened the social order within the parish itself because it would replace traditional expertise and social roles with those derived from School learning.

During the last ten years, resident non-native priests and seminarians have gradually introduced the use of oral and written English into the church liturgy. This recent incorporation of English into church practices has been more widely accepted – perhaps because it did not embody the radical ideological challenge of the missionaries' efforts, perhaps because the parishioners themselves had recognised a lack of religious leadership and requested a resident priest. Nevertheless, there are indications of major social change taking place within the village parish in response to the replacement of traditional patterns of literacy specialisation with those derived from School-based specialisation of English literacy.

The introduction of English in the last decade has had a significant impact on literacy practices in church activities. Not only do many more individuals understand the language of the service, they also follow oral readings with their own materials and read additional religious materials outside the setting of the services. The change in language has also brought changes in the leadership roles available to lay persons. The position of lay reader traditionally has been a man's role. Among the Aleuts of the Aleutian Chain, literacy in Aleut and in Slavonic was passed down from father to son or uncle to nephew, though women were not prohibited from learning it (Ransom 1945: 334–5). There is little documentation of this in the Kodiak area. In Seal Bay, women as well as men remember being taught by the lay reader, but the major readers within the current community's memory were men. In the last ten to fifteen years, however, young women have been assuming this role. There may be many reasons for this shift in leadership and authority in the Church. A likely one is that the gradual changeover to use of English in church services, while expanding access to the role of reader, has reduced the prestige which traditionally accompanied the position.

In Seal Bay, the introduction of English literacy in the Church has led to a reversal in the traditional relationship between age and participation in prestigious roles. Older people who traditionally commanded respect because of their accumulated knowledge of Church ritual and Scriptures in Slavonic now find they must listen for a younger person's lead in the English version. If they wish to follow the priest's suggestions, they also must request a younger person's aid in reading the Scriptures at home. Furthermore, the socialisation of Church literacy practices, once transmitted almost entirely within the Village domain, has been to a considerable extent supplanted by literacy training in the Outside domain of the School. The role of the resident priest in providing additional religious training and literacy instruction is noteworthy in this regard; a highly educated non-native who speaks the native language, the priest wishes to maintain the language and native culture and thus represents a curious mixture of outsider and stalwart of the Village domain.

Thus, the introduction of English in Russian Orthodoxy, originally intended to increase access to and understanding of church teachings, has generated an undercurrent of discomfort. People have been reluctant to give up their emotional ties to the Slavonic liturgy and some have difficulty openly embracing the use of English in the service, perhaps since English is so heavily, if subconsciously, associated with outsiders who have long threatened native culture and language maintenance, whether through the school or through another religious group (the Baptists). For the present, an outsider fills the most prestigious leadership position in the Church – the role of priest – and in 1979 two visiting seminarians did much of the Scripture reading during services, although some choir members read short passages.

Company versus Public Sector

The opposition between Village and Outside in the context of Church–School interaction has been considered. This section briefly sketches a few manifestations of that opposition in the context of interactions between Company and Public Sector in Seal Bay. The data are limited here, and so the formulation must be considered tentative.

The basic opposition between Company and Public Sector in Seal Bay derives from the contrasting economic systems they represent. The Company, beginning with the Russian-American Company and continuing through contemporary firms, has offered villagers an economic base, a credit system for economic security and a reward structure for individual productivity. The Company system, although introduced by foreigners, like the Church has become well accepted as part of village life. The long and continuing history of the Company's close relationship with the Church in Seal Bay helps maintain its 'Village' status in the face of increasing bureaucratic penetration and outside regulation of the fishing industry. A variety of relationships exists between individual fishermen and the Company, many of which are based on a shared interest in minimising outside regulation of fishing.

In contrast, the Public Sector of Seal Bay offers a different economic system to villagers. Gradually introduced through the school and outside agencies, both direct government subsidies and publicly supported jobs in the village offer economic opportunities which engender dependence on an economic system which some perceive as threatening to village life. The most outspoken opponents of the Public Sector (especially the welfare component) in Seal Bay tend to be 'Company men'. Although few if any people feel that individuals 'who really need it' should forego direct government assistance, some villagers still consider the traditional patterns of subsistence, individual enterprise and communal sharing of necessities during shortages to be a better way of doing things. Although Public Sector employment (which includes jobs such as telephone clerk, City Council secretary, City clerk-treasurer, and so on) is certainly not tantamount to drawing welfare in villagers' eyes, the two share a common Outside origin and continued economic dependence on outside agencies. Villagers attach different social meanings to participation in the Company and the Public Sector, parallel with opposition between the Church and the School.

The contrast between the Public Sector and Company systems in part derives from the different senses of economic security and dependence involved in each. In the Company domain, the practice of extending credit against future earnings to fishermen during hard times or poor seasons is well established, although this has tended to indenture their labour exclusively to the Company. Hence a certain measure of economic security has been traded for a certain dependence on the Company. The Public Sector, on the other hand, provides some economic security in return for engagement with outside agencies and procedures which are still looked upon with considerable mistrust and suspicion by many villagers. It has offered money, not so much in return for native initiative and efforts, but more in relation to native conformity, acculturation and acceptance of Outside values, procedures and regulations.

Bureaucratic literacy tasks – dealing with a plethora of forms and regulations – are involved in gaining access to government 'benefits'. They are also a major part of the publicly funded jobs in the village – for example, clerical tasks involving the manipulation of files and forms. Although literacy is clearly perceived as a necessary part of the activities which bring this 'outside' money into the village, the activities themselves ('indoors work' and 'getting benefits') are negatively valued by most villagers for reasons discussed above. The social meanings attached to the use of writing in these domains are similarly coloured in a negative way. These negative social meanings, rooted in the history of Outside intrusion into village life, persist no matter how skilfully an individual may handle the literacy tasks involved. Literacy cannot help free the individual from dependence on the Outside.

Literacy applied to the Company domain, however, is perceived as a helpful part of a fisherman's life and business relationship with the commercial fishing industry. Even without sophisticated technological literacy skills, mastery of how to use others' literacy skills can serve to minimise one's dependence on the Company and has enabled some Seal Bayites to achieve economic independence from the Company and others to operate collaboratively with Company practices.

In the fishing grounds, literacy seems to have been increasingly incorporated into established patterns of activity and interpersonal relations with little conflict in values. This also is the case for many other activities Seal Bayites view as an integral part of village life: men with little education or interest in most written materials regularly pore over complex repair manuals to maintain small engines for their boats or three-wheelers. The same applies for various construction projects individuals undertake. Young boys, in playing 'fix-the-motor' or fishing games, will 'consult' manuals and charts much as their older brothers and fathers do. Where the application of literacy is experienced as a tool, useful for conducting 'village' tasks, the social meanings of literacy expertise are positive.

Thus, the distinct social meanings of literacy in the Company and Public Sector seem closely tied to the different socioeconomic contexts in which villagers perceive writing being used. Writing applied in positively valued contexts draws on social meanings characteristic of Village values, in contrast with the Outside values attached to use of writing in activities perceived as being distant from or intruding into village life.

On the whole, literacy seems to draw upon the social meanings already evolved for the activities in question. In the episodes of contact between Church and School domains, however, literacy was seen to play a much more active role in maintaining the dual system of social meanings. The Orthodox Church's subsequent change from Slavonic to English literacy practices also effected major social change in the village. This social change seems to be the product of overlaying the traditional roles and socialisation processes associated with Village literacy practices with those established for Outside literacy practices. Different social meanings accompany the 'new' technology and conflict with those still prevailing in the Church domain. Indeed, considerable opposition among Village and Outside literacy practices continues to be evident in contemporary Seal Bay.

Village Governance

The final 'box' of the model in figure 7.1 represents the last domain to be considered here – Village Governance. Its central position in the diagram reflects the vital role which internal government has played in recent Seal Bay affairs. The broken lines convey two points about its function: (1) the village government mediates relations between Seal Bay and outside agencies; and (2) it serves as a homeostatic mechanism in the village social order, easing tensions from factional disputes. Unique literacy practices have evolved in recent years within the Governance domain, whose characteristics have served to balance the conflicting social meanings of Village and Outside literacy.

Development of Village Governance

A brief overview of the history and development of leadership in Seal Bay will help illustrate these functions of Village Governance. The Russian-American Company apparently recognised and utilised existing native leadership patterns. Although there is little information about pre-contact Koniag culture and society, early Russian descriptions provide a few clues about native leadership styles. The chiefs were family men, with very little power over their neighbours and no power to punish crimes. They maintained order without force by showing concern and caring for the well-being of others through favours and other political means. There seemed to be no central authority and only a limited government or means of enforcing regulations (Black 1977b: 84). The Russian-American Company selected native individuals, whom they called *toions*, to serve as intermediaries between the Company and natives in obtaining compliance with Company requirements and hunting quotas.

Native respect for individuality and only a small need for formal political structure within the community appear to have continued into the twentieth century. The introduction of American schools, following the sale of Alaska to the United States in 1867, increased the need for an intermediary with the outside world, but the teachers themselves originally filled that role. The position of chief continued to be significant and may have served as the community's link to the teachers.

As contact with the outside world slowly increased, factionalism apparently rose within the community. Davis (1971: 181–3) reports that attempts to form a village council in the early 1960s were ineffective due to a lack of consensus and continual quarrelling. In 1963–4 there was an increase in political activity in Seal Bay. Under the leadership of two native men, both of whom had come from other Kodiak villages, a stronger formal council was established and the first village-wide rules were put into effect. These were *written* rules. It is unclear what prompted this increase in governance activity, but it is important to note that the chief and second chief had gained experience living elsewhere and had supplementary cash incomes; both characteristics may have given them sufficient independence from existing patterns of factionalism and economic ties to be politically effective. At this time the council members also stood out from the community: they were relatively literate in English; they included three of the four owners of small village businesses; and (recalling that, at this time, the Orthodox versus Baptist confrontation was very active) they included two non-Orthodox individuals. Thus, from its inception the council represented a variety of the community's factions.

Role of Village Governance in dealing with outside agencies

The disaster of the tidal waves of 1964 played a critical role in forming the present leadership of Seal Bay. The ensuing evacuation, temporary residence in Anchorage and resettlement of the community, brought many outside service agencies to the village scene and created an unprecedented demand for village leadership capable of representing villagers' interests in dealings with these outsiders. The expertise gained through the months of interaction and negotiations with the outside agencies provided a valuable education for a new chief, who has been a community leader since that time and who today fills the position of mayor with considerable political ability.

After the village was reconstructed, village leaders continued to gain experience in dealing with outside institutions. Council activities were expanded to include many new functions and literacy activities: operating the village power plant and billing residents for its service, maintaining the airstrip, writing ordinances regarding land distribution and the setting of rents, filling out applications to agencies for funding village improvements, and meeting and corresponding with native leaders from other villages and with outsiders. As the complexity of these functions and contacts increased, so too did the political sophistication of village leaders. Village leadership was further strengthened by the rising nativistic movements throughout Alaska in the late 1960s and 1970s. The political and economic gains won by native interests, through the Alaska Native Claims Settlement Act of 1971, further increased native participation in the complex outside world of paperwork and formal legal and administrative procedures.

Demands on community leaders to represent the village to the outside world continue to become increasingly complex. Considerable political expertise is necessary, in addition to a firm understanding of sophisticated legal and bureaucratic proceedings. For example, village representatives frequently travel to regional, state and national meetings dealing with issues of housing, health, local governance, education, fishing, economic development, native culture and so forth, where discussions are held about regulations directly affecting village populations. Regional and statewide native corporation meetings consider complex land and resource issues. Although village representatives do not have legal training, they are able to interact on both the local and outside levels and shrewdly negotiate the interests of the community.

To manage relationships with outside agencies effectively, village leaders have had to learn to deploy literacy for their own ends. Davis (1971) reports several incidents during the evacuation and resettlement of Seal Bay which indicate a growing awareness on the part of village leaders of the importance of using writing in dealing with outside agencies. The incidents range from learning to 'get promises in writing' to using regional newspapers to influence outside attitudes and actions towards the village. These lessons were well mastered by village leaders; skill in deploying writing for their political purposes has kept up with the demands for literacy in the increasingly complex relations between the village and the outside. Although a few leaders have well-developed English literacy skills, one of the most significant components of the village's bureaucratic literacy is the leadership's grasp of the significance of writing for effecting political ends and their use of literacy specialists as technicians in bureaucratic matters. Some leaders, for example, have others write or edit letters, the substance of which they specify (not unlike the contemporary business person). Specialists (for example, from the regional Native Corporation office) describe written regulations orally to the leaders or occasionally to the public at meetings in the village. Or an outside specialist, such as a lawyer, will assist and work with village leadership. Outside literacy specialists are used to the extent that previous contacts justify the requisite trust; a young white lawyer, who had spent a year with Volunteers in Service to America (VISTA) in Seal Bay before attending law school and who habitually fishes in the summer on Seal Bay boats, is the regular attorney of the village.

Duality of function: balancing Village and Outside relationships

Village Governance has increasingly assumed two functions in village affairs: negotiating village interests with the outside world and mediating intra-village factionalism, which arises (in part) because of villagers' conflicting orientations to the outside world. To handle both functions effectively, Village Governance must maintain a precarious balance. To deal effectively with outside agencies, village leadership must engage in bureaucratic relationships and follow externally defined legal and administrative procedures. At the same time, the leadership must avoid alienating factions within Seal Bay opposed to further acculturation and engagement with the outside. A critical means of maintaining unity in the face of factionalism has been to include representatives of the competing factions on the council and other governing bodies. For example, though their numbers are few, non-Orthodox families have been well-represented, as have non-Company fishermen.

The necessary balance of intra-village and village-agency relationships has been achieved largely through the creation of a new form of political leadership within Seal Bay, which incorporates characteristics of both Village and Outside domains. As described above, village leaders have mastered control over bureaucratic literacy by developing effective knowledge of the many functions of writing in Village–Outside affairs and of how to deploy literacy specialists for their own ends. In so doing, they have not fully accepted the social meanings and values which are attached to bureaucratic literacy use in the outside. This is an important distinction. By accepting bureaucratic literacy as a necessary technology for mediating Village–Outside relationships, villagers have *not* accepted it as a norm for mediating internal activities. The viability of the leadership in the community appears to depend to a considerable extent on their attachment of dual social meanings to their use of writing: one meaning perceived by outsiders and another by villagers. The physical setting of the city office provides an interesting indication of this. The city office is the (English) literacy hub of the village. It is there that Outside visitors report when they enter Seal Bay. The walls are literally covered with signs, letters, official certifications, and other written materials. The village 'library' is there; all official records are kept there; all but the largest meetings are held there; individuals go there to meet with the clerk about welfare matters; and so forth. The mayor's desk in the city office is located in the middle of the large central room into which one enters, rather than in one of the small adjoining rooms in which the secretary and the clerk work. Instead of having what might seem to outsiders a more prestigious office that can be reached only after running a gauntlet of secretaries, the mayor sits in the public room – one of the key gathering spots in Seal Bay. It is here that all visitors are sent. Villagers must come here to use the only telephone in the village. Villagers congregate here informally on a regular basis. Thus, the mayor is accessible to anyone who enters the building and is able to observe everything going on in that community centre. Above all, in the midst of a highly literate setting, he emphasises direct personal interaction and maintains close ties with the community.

Davis (n.d.) has noted that, in general, the leadership qualities valued by outsiders are distinct from those valued by the villagers themselves. Here these dual social meanings of bureaucratic literacy are an integral part of this distinction, part of a broader, more comprehensive system of dual behaviour for keeping Village–Outside relations distinct from intra-village relations. Other uses of literacy also reflect this duality to a certain extent. Signs posted in the village, for example, do not assist villagers to find things. But they do help outside visitors locate the city office, the Post Office, a store (but, interestingly, not the 'Company' store). Many letters and notices posted in the city office are for visitors to read. Some notices are posted by the council as formalities to which no one (not even council members) conforms.

None of this is meant to suggest that use of writing in Seal Bay is not being incorporated into Village activities and values; as compulsory schooling continues, the educational attainment of the community rises, and as the village continues to acculturate, writing continues its penetration of village life. But the factionalism rooted in Village and Outside literacies prevails, and Village Governance, an innovative product of diverse literacy demands, continues to be shaped by literacies having distinctive social meanings.

Conclusion

Literacy has developed in Seal Bay in two distinct historical strands, each introduced by an external society, having a characteristic script, domains of application and social roles for literacy experts. Over the years, against a changing historical backdrop, these developmental lines have converged and come into conflict at times in Seal Bay. The many initial distinctions between the literacies have progressively dissolved as use of Cyrillic script has gradually been supplanted by English literacy. Despite the levelling of many differences between the literacies, however, some vital differences remain. Most persistent are the two systems of social meaning which have been so intimately bound up with literacy development in Seal Bay: Village and Outside.

The development of literacy in its various domains in Seal Bay displays a long history of oppositions between the categories of Village and Outside. It is critical to note that these are *emic* categories, terms with which Seal Bayites view and discuss events in their lives. They are not fixed categories such that a given activity is always in a particular category; the classifications are contextually-bound. What may once have been viewed as external to village life, part of the Outside realm, may later be (in villagers' eyes) incorporated into Seal Bay life and accepted as part of the Village realm. Literacy practices offer many examples of how contextually bound such perceptions are. For example, Russian-innovated practices, presumably once alien to the community, later became an integral part of native identity.

Literacy in Seal Bay has done more than merely reflect the existing social values and distinctions in daily life. In many contexts, literacy has played a leading role in the overall development of the community, as, for example, in sharpening contrasts between Village and Outside in confrontation between Church and School, or in developing innovative new leadership roles in Village Governance. In the former example, literacy served to define and reinforce contrasts between social meanings, whereas in the latter it served to harmonise tensions between them.

The role of literacy in the development of this community thus seems intimately tied to the social meanings which its various practices have assumed. The stability of the distinction between Village and Outside literacies despite the convergence of their originally distinct writing systems is of considerable theoretical interest. The technology of writing has long been recognised for having expanded the domains of space and time over which information can be communicated. In this sense, writing has broadened the horizons of *textual* messages. In Seal Bay, the stability of the social meanings of writing suggests that literacy also broadens the horizons of the *contextual* messages associated with writing. It is these contextual messages, rooted in the historical contexts in which the various Village and Outside literacy practices have evolved, which form the essences of 'social meaning'.

Although the roots of these social meanings lie deep in the history of Seal Bay, they are continually regenerated in the contemporary activity of the village. The participant structure of groups formed to perform a literacy practice – as well as the physical context in which a group performs its work – regenerates the characteristic Village and Outside social meanings for use of writing.[8] Differences in the social roles of literacy experts and modes of socialising technological and functional knowledge of writing are distinctive features of these Village and Outside literacy practices.

As the outside world continues to penetrate the once isolated village of Seal Bay, contrasts between Village and Outside values can be expected to remain clear in villagers' minds, even if the boundaries between the two continually shift over time. The enduring role of literacy as a vehicle for extending the vital contrast between these social meanings over time and material changes in village life is intimately linked to the maintenance of ethnic identity in Seal Bay.

Notes

This paper is condensed from an article entitled 'Contrasting patterns of literacy in an Alaska fishing village', published previously by Stephen Reder and Karen Reed Green in the *International Journal of the Sociology of Language*, 42 (1983), 9–39. The work was originally reported at the 1979 Annual Meeting of the American Anthropological Association.

The fieldwork was conducted under a grant from the National Institute of Education (Grant no. 400–80–0105). The authors would like to thank Lydia Black, Nancy Yaw Davis, Shirley Brice Heath, Margaret Lantis and Sylvia Scribner for their thoughtful comments on an earlier draft. Special gratitude is due the villagers of Seal Bay for accepting the authors into their homes and their lives. The authors assume sole responsibility for the interpretations and conclusions presented here.

1 The six major villages on Kodiak Island at the time of this study ranged from 90 to 350 inhabitants; Seal Bay (a pseudonym) is one of the larger villages.
2 Similar to Native American and Chicano populations in other parts of the United States, during the 1960s native populations in Alaska experienced a political awakening and began to demand their political and economic rights. Taking pride in their ethnicity, natives in increasing numbers assumed leadership roles in their communities and in statewide native concerns.
3 This is the Kodiak Islanders' name for their native language. Linguists have also referred to this language as Sugpiaq, Sugcestun, Suk Eskimo, Chugach Eskimo, and Pacific Gulf Yupik (See Leer 1978: 4). Natives recognise the link between their language and other Eskimo languages, but prefer to be called Aleuts rather than Eskimos and refer to their language as Aleut when speaking English.
4 Three of the four domains are emic components of village life. 'Church', 'Company' and 'School' are institutions and activities so labelled by village residents in everyday (English) conversation. 'Public Sector' is the authors' term; reasons for using it here will become clear. The development of literacy in each of these domains is discussed in detail in Reder and Green (1983).

5 An emic domain of activity, called 'city office' or 'office' by Seal Bay residents.
6 The extent of use of English in lay sermons is unclear.
7 On a two-week return visit in February 1980, a striking change was observed in the relations between the Orthodox Church and the school in Seal Bay. The head teacher had been transferred and a teacher who had taught in Seal Bay a year before returned to the village to take his place. The composition of the School Board had shifted dramatically. The couple, who had been closely aligned with the head teacher who was transferred, left the village to study, and most of the other School Board members had been loyal to that teacher also and felt unable to remain on the Board with the new head teacher (with whom some had disagreed during his previous teaching stay in the village). Thus, it was an entirely new Board – on which all members were Orthodox; in fact, both the priest and his wife were on the Board. In addition, the priest and the new head teacher were consciously cooperating, carefully notifying each other of scheduled events. (During this visit, the formerly rigid church schedule was even modified to accommodate an unexpected School Board meeting hosting the Village Schools Principal from Kodiak.)
8 In their work with the oral traditions of Northern Athabascans, Scollon and Scollon (1980, 1981) have speculated on the relevance of participant groups in structuring literacy practices.

References

Befu, H. 1961. *Ethnographic sketch of an Eskimo village at Old Harbor, Kodiak.* Unpublished manuscript.

    1970. 'An ethnographic sketch of Old Harbor, Kodiak: an Eskimo village', *Arctic Anthropology*, 6 (2): 29–42.

Black, L. T. 1977a. 'Ivan Pan'Kov – an architect of Aleut literacy', *Arctic Anthropology*, 14 (1): 94–107.

    1977b. 'The Konyag (the inhabitants of the Island of Kodiak) by Iosaf [Bolotov] (1794–1799) and by Gideon (1804–1807)', *Arctic Anthropology*, 14 (2): 79–108.

Cipolla, C. M. 1969. *Literacy and development in the west.* London: Penguin Books.

Davis, N. Y. n.d. *A village view of agencies.* Unpublished manuscript.

    1971. *The effects of the 1964 Alaska earthquake, tsunami, and resettlement on two Koniag Eskimo villages.* Ph.D. dissertation, University of Washington. Ann Arbor, MI: University Microfilms International, no. 71–24, 028.

Gibson, J. R. 1976. *Imperial Russia in frontier America: the changing geography of supply of Russian America, 1784–1867.* New York: Oxford University Press.

Heath, S. B. 1980. 'The functions and uses of literacy', *Journal of Communication*, 123–33.

Leer, J. 1978. *A conversational dictionary of Kodiak Alutiiq.* Fairbanks: Alaska Native Language Center, University of Alaska.

Maruyama, M. 1964. *The village of Old Harbor, Kodiak Island, Alaska.* Unpublished manuscript.

Olson, D. R. 1977. 'The languages of instruction: the literate bias of schooling', in

R. C. Anderson, R. J. Spiro and W. E. Montague (eds.), *Schooling and the acquisition of knowledge*. Hillsdale, NJ: Lawrence Erlbaum Associates.

Ransom, J. E. 1945. 'Writing as a medium of acculturation among the Aleut', *Southwestern Journal of Anthropology*, 1 (3): 333–44.

Reder, S. 1987. 'Comparative aspects of functional literacy development: three ethnic American communities', in D. A. Wagner (ed.), *The future of literacy in a changing world*. Oxford: Pergamon Press.

1990. 'Getting the message across: cultural factors in the intergenerational transfer of cognitive skills', in T. Sticht, B. McDonald and M. Beeler (eds.), *The intergenerational transfer of cognitive skills*. Newark, DE: Ablex.

(in press). 'Practice engagement theory: a sociocultural approach to literacy across languages and cultures', in R. M. Weber and B. Ferdman (eds.), *Literacy across languages and cultures*. Albany, NY: State University of New York Press.

Reder, S. and Green, K. R. 1981. 'Comparative aspects of the community structure of literacy.' Annual report of the Functional Literacy Project. Portland, OR: Northwest Regional Educational Laboratory.

1983. 'Contrasting patterns of literacy in an Alaska fishing village', *International Journal of the Sociology of Language*, 42: 9–39.

Scollon, R. and Scollon, S. B. K. 1980. 'Literacy as focused interaction', *The Quarterly Newsletter of the Laboratory of Comparative Human Cognition*, 2 (2): 26–9.

1981. *Narrative, literacy and face in interethnic communication*. Norwood, NJ: Ablex.

Scribner, S. and Cole, M. 1978. 'Literacy without schooling: testing for intellectual effects', *Harvard Educational Review*, 48 (4): 448–61.

1981. 'Unpackaging literacy', in M. F. Whiteman (ed.), *Variation in writing: functional and linguistic-cultural differences*. Hillsdale, NJ: Lawrence Erlbaum Associates.

Szwed, J. 1981. 'The ethnography of literacy' (paper presented at the National Institute of Education Conference on Writing, Long Beach, California, Summer 1977), in M. F. Whiteman (ed.), *Functional and linguistic-cultural differences*. Hillsdale, NJ: Lawrence Erlbaum Associates.

8

THE LETTER AND THE SPIRIT: LITERACY AND RELIGIOUS AUTHORITY IN THE HISTORY OF THE ALADURA MOVEMENT IN WESTERN NIGERIA

PETER PROBST

Introduction

The Yoruba word *aladura*, meaning 'one who prays', generally refers to a set of churches which formed a powerful religious movement among the Yoruba in western Nigeria during the first decades of this century. To date, there have been three main lines of interpretation which received general recognition: first, in form of a theological analysis (Turner 1967); second, in a discussion of social protest (Mitchell 1970); and finally, through the sociology of religion (Peel 1968). In this article I propose to introduce another aspect of interpretation. Following the many passing remarks made by the authors with respect to the use of writing within the Aladura churches, I will read their accounts in terms of how people perceived and experienced the written word in the specific context of the Christian-colonial order and consider whether and how this experience has influenced people's actions and religious behaviour.[1] In doing so, I am going to take up a theme which has become widely popular in the anthropological field under the heading 'the consequences of literacy'.

The best-known as well as the most critical arguments of this discussion stem from the work of Jack Goody (1968, 1977, 1986, 1987). Over the last twenty years he has repeated his ideas on the 'logic of writing and the organisation of society' (Goody 1986) with an astonishing steadfastness. This has, perhaps, something to do with the totality of his engagement. In what way, he asks, do simple societies differ from complex ones and what is the process of transition from one to the other? For Goody, the first question provides the answer for the second. Since it is the possession of writing that constitutes the difference, it is also the implications of writing through which the modes of transition in the history of human society can be observed.

With respect to the realm of religion, this line of thought works with the following, admittedly curtailed, arguments. In non-literate societies there is no concept of one religion valid through space and time. Rather, what one finds is a multitude of different beliefs and practices, eclectic in the way they incorporate new elements and gain adherents, and particularistic in the way they are territorially and socially confined to certain places and ethnic groups. Furthermore, they are contextualised in the sense that the local belief system is embedded in the general social structure, thereby understood only when this structure is taken into account. All this experiences a drastic change when literacy enters the scene. With literacy, adherents of a certain belief system are now no longer defined by birth and the practice of certain rituals and prayers but first and foremost by their attachment to a sacred text, a holy book, in which the doctrine is written down. As a result of the canonisation of this text, eclecticism, flexibility and diversity evolve into exclusiveness, rigidity and orthodoxy; contextuality turns into autonomy since the independence of writing from the constraints of time and space makes the norms and values of literate belief systems valid everywhere regardless of specific actions and localised circumstances. All men are now supposed to be treated according to the same universal standards as laid down in the scriptures. As a result, literate religions also cover a wider societal scope than non-literate belief systems; the organisation of their worshippers transcends the spatial boundaries of the clan, tribe or nation. Within this wider scope, literate specialists take control of professionalising religious activities and rationalising religious discourse. The tensions which arise from this pattern lead to those differentiations we are familiar with from the history of Christianity, Islam or Hinduism, all representatives of great, complex societies.

I do not want to dwell here on the causal importance Goody attributes to the role of writing in human history. A lot has been written about the uni-dimensional (Street 1984), deterministic (Parry 1986), and ethnocentric (Bloch 1989) picture he draws of this development. Rather, what interests me is the new perspective one gets when looking at historically and culturally different modes of living through the eyes of literacy. Here, I think, lies the essential merit of Goody's work in the sense that he has opened up a new and, in my view, extremely fruitful field of research.[2] What I set out to do below is, then, an attempt to interpret the material written about the Aladura churches with the help of some of Goody's ideas. In contrast to him, however, I am not primarily concerned with demonstrating any particular 'consequences'; instead, the material in question turns our attention to the specific social institutions in which these 'consequences' are embedded and the manners in which writing and print are exploited in a different cultural context.[3]

Focusing mainly on the Church of the Lord, one of three main churches of the Aladura movement, I will try to show that many of the conflicts within the movement centred around the specific features of writing and print. Not only was it a problem between the independent churches and the Western mission organisations from which they broke away, but the question of the significance of literacy caused constant friction also among the members of the indigenous congregations themselves. In particular, it was the issue of the Bible as a fixed text which resulted in the provision of an instrument for defining, allotting and controlling religious authority in a changing social environment. It was a conflict that can be understood as the opposition between the 'letter' and the 'spirit', symbolising the two distinct religious concepts which came into collision under the conditions imposed by the Christian-colonial order. The development and result of this conflict are the central issues I address below.

The background: literacy and the rise of the movement

In southern Nigeria the establishment of colonial rule came in the last decade of the nineteenth century. It marked the emergence of a new cultural climate which became known in Yoruba society as *aiye Oyinbo*, 'the world, or the age, of the European',[4] of which Christianity was an integral part. The first white missionaries had arrived in 1841. From Abeokuta, mission stations were opened up in Ibadan and Ijaye and by 1863 another four stations had been established further in the interior. Besides their own evangelisation interest, the missionaries produced extensive and valuable first-hand information on the country which was used by the British to plan their colonial policy in the area. The authors of this information were mainly Creoles who played a crucial role in the early phase of Christianisation.[5] As freed slaves, who had grown up in the Victorian-Protestant milieu of Sierra Leone, they returned to their native homes with a thorough confidence in the persuasive power of the scriptures. In Nigeria they began to work as catechists and missionaries for the British and American mission societies which had recruited them. From their pens stem the first ethnographic and linguistic accounts of Yoruba society, texts dealing with indigenous cosmology, oral history, Yoruba grammars, and dictionaries. The close relationship they established with native society made them valuable transmitters of the Christian Gospel for the missions, which planned to create a self-supporting and self-propagating Church under local leadership. The effects of this policy bore fruit in the steady increase of converts, many of whom began to see the literate black missionary as a symbol of the dawning of the modern African career under the rising conditions of a new cultural order.

At that time, the system of education was still controlled mainly by European and American mission organisations, whose leaders were quite aware of the general social atmosphere described by the Nigerian historian J. F. Ade Ajayi, as follows:

> The most promising routes to success, wealth and distinction lay through the teaching and service in the church, commerce or professional training in bookkeeping, medicine and so on. And

the key to these was grammar school education. Carpenters, masons, sawyers, coopers, blacksmiths, tailors, bakers, printers, mechanics and other artisans were needed and were encouraged, but they were almost always servants of the successful clergyman, merchant, doctor or lawyer. Industrial education taught skills. Literary education taught knowledge and knowledge was power. Literary education was therefore superior.   (Ajayi 1963: 522)

It is thus not surprising to learn that the majority of the conversions to the Christian faith literally proceeded *through the book*. Many of the converts did not go to school but learned to read and write by themselves or were taught by literate clerks. The indigenous view of Christianity, concentrated not so much on the religious superiority as on the recognition of the 'cultural capacity' (Peel 1983) of the new faith, measured in the numbers, status and connections of the new Christian leaders and their adherents that gave rise to that recognition.[6] Their high reputation in the eyes of the public reflected the high degree of their participation in the new cultural technique of reading and writing. In fact, the acquisition of basic literacy through *Iwe ABD*, the Yoruba primer, was so closely linked with conversion to Christianity that Peel, in his study of the Ijesha-kingdom, doubts if it is possible to determine which occurred first:

The great bulk of early converts, those who got the tide running in Christianity's favour, did not go to school and here it was Christianity's link with literacy through Iwe ABD rather than with formal education and qualification which mattered. The reciprocity between them was so constant that a priority of motive is impossible to determine, as in the remark of that respondent who said to his father: '[he became Christian] after buying a book called ABD and studying it. The end of it was his conversion'.   (Peel 1983: 168)

According to the statistics the number of baptised Christians grew from 7,500 to 60,000 between 1895 and 1920 whilst the number of catechumens increased from 1,200 to 17,000 (Mitchell 1970: 494). Even if one assumes that only half of these converts had a rudimentary knowledge of reading and writing, the question arises as to the effects this Christian mass-alphabetisation had. What happened to these literate converts all over the country? How did they use their newly acquired skill? Where did they go to?

Most of them returned to their earlier professions as farmers and traders. Those however, who had already made up their minds to follow the signs of the time, became absorbed in the new literate environment. They remained in the mission churches and worked there as catechists and teachers in newly established schools, or joined the colonial administration in the urban centres of Lagos, Ibadan or Abeokuta. Traditional Yoruba life had always been localised in the big cities so that rural migration and social mobility was nothing new (Bascom 1960). But under colonial role the British administration not only profited from this feature, it also accelerated its pattern considerably. From roughly 1900 onwards, the administration, the government agencies in the form of the Nigerian railways and the Nigerian Post and Telephones Company required large numbers of clerks. Many of them came from the rural hinterland. They had left their small villages and now flooded into the big cities. Here, they knew themselves to be the new men in a changing society. In fact, the demand for literate clerks was immense. In the first two decades of this century they were even more in demand than literate carpenters, masons, and printers. As Ajayi writes:

> It was the age of clerks. Clerks and interpreters were needed for the new government offices, the native courts, the expanding import and export trade. There was such a shortage of clerks locally that the government was recruiting them on the Gold Coast and the West Indies. There was such a demand for clerks that parents frequently removed children from school to seek employment before they were properly trained.
>
> (Ajayi 1963: 527)

Within the social strata of the Christian-colonial order, these masses of clerks constituted a kind of 'lumpen literati', a semi-educated proletariat, disliked by the Europeans because of their self-confident opposition and arrogance. Among the white community, complaints concentrated more and more on the 'so-called clerks' who were seen to compose 'a formidable array of useless drones', only surpassed by the Lagos schoolboys, who were described by a Catholic missionary as walking: 'arrogantly about the streets . . . a packet of books in their hands, believing themselves to be doctors before they are scholars; such that later when they are employed they become unbearable both to those who have to command them and those who have to obey them' (quoted in Ajayi 1963: 520).

In other words, a new social category of *évoluées* had emerged. Through the Book, they saw themselves as sharing in the power of the white missionaries and colonial administrators. In this situation they became important middlemen between the strange mysterious world of the Whites and the non-literate pagan majority of Africans. Among the latter they were often seen as the new 'wizards', whose literacy was believed to provide magical access to supernatural power.[7] They were in the possession of literacy and certainly appreciated this privilege and the authority it gave them in their non-literate social environment. However, they not only had to cope with the resentments they were subject to, they also discovered that their power and expectations *vis-à-vis* the White Man were extremely limited. Often, frustration and anger were the result.

At this time of need and deprivation the scriptures were offered as a mere abstract intellectual comfort in view of a divine life after death. Protestantism, as the dominant form of Christianity in Yorubaland, was in many points incompatible with the traditional Yoruba world-view and the pressing needs of African life. It aimed at an abstract principle of morality and ethics, which greatly differed from the African perception of evil conceptualised in terms of real powers, such as witches and spirits. Its absolute requirements including monogamous marriage, male domi-nance, and the emphasis on the exclusiveness of denomination were in contrast with the Yoruba practice of multiple cult memberships, poly-gyny, and the acceptance of certain women as religious leaders. As long as the masses of Christian converts were able to live with the hope that they would eventually become fully accepted and integrated into the new social and economic environment of the Christian-colonial order and had the confidence that they would soon be granted equal access to education, political responsibilities, and adequate salaries, these incompatibilities remained of no actual significance. But when the historical process reached a stage where these hopes and expectations could no longer be satisfied, the tide was turned. The inflammatory spark came with the events of the early 1920s when, after several decades of missionary activities, the traditional religions had begun to wane. Christianity was still steadily growing but the missionaries' resources to cope with this growth were extremely limited and loud complaints about the low spiritual state and the need for a spiritual revival of the Christian faith began to be heard. The situation became even more precarious when a series of plagues and famines coupled with a collapse of the new cash crop economy struck the Yoruba towns and their hinterland. It was in these conditions that the Aladura movement originated.

Among the movement's most prominent leaders was Josiah Oshitelu. His prophetic career clearly demonstrates the form of protest many African Christians articulated at that time. For Oshitelu this protest was not limited to the establishment of independent churches alone. Sig-nificant for the politico-religious implications of writing in these days, independence meant for him also independence from the Holy Book of the White as a means of political and religious domination.

Oshitelu's scriptural visions

Josiah Oshitelu belonged to the generation of young Yorubas who grew up in the spirit of the *aiye Oyinbo*, the world of the European. Educated in

Anglican mission schools in the early 1920s, he saw the rapid growth of a monetary economy, the disastrous effects of a series of plagues and famines, and the impressive dominance of colonial district administrators and Christian missionaries. He lived and preached mainly in the Ijebu area near the coast where he was born in 1902 in the small town of Ogere. Initially, his parents resisted his desire to go to school and tried to keep him at home. Frightened by a mysterious divination of an Ifa priest they finally agreed, however, and in 1913 Oshitelu entered the mission school in Ijebu Ode where he stayed for the next six years. After finishing elementary school he went to Erukute near his home town north of Lagos. There he served for six years as a teacher catechist in the Church Missionary School. Under the supervision of the missionary in charge of that district, he acted further as secretary of the local church committee so that he seemed well on his way towards a decent career in the service of the Anglican Church, when in 1925 he suddenly experienced a series of terrifying visions. Greatly troubled, he was granted a year's leave to find a cure. Frightened by the images he had seen, which he believed were caused by witches, he first tried the traditional remedies he knew from his youth. Finding no relief, he finally followed the advice he was given by his neighbours to consult Shomoye, a Christian elder, who had the reputation of being a man of the spirit. Shomoye told him that he was not bewitched but being called and 'tested' by God for an important mission. He should throw away his traditional charms and medicines, put his faith in God, and fast. He was indeed afflicted by evil powers but they could be overcome by using certain psalms and constant prayer. Shomoye's advice turned out to be effective. In his dreams, Oshitelu saw his tormentors reduced to harmless animals. Audible voices assured him that an important task lay ahead. Convinced of his prophetic authority, he postulated fasting, praying, and firm faith in God as solutions to the evils of the world.

Oshitelu did not hide his visions and devotional techniques. As a prophet he was in possession of special powers and knowledge of God's secret names. In the tradition of Elijah and John the Baptist, he declared himself chosen by God for a messianic mission which he perceived in revelations such as:

> Gradually the seals of power will come to you. Your good time draws on apace ...
> I will build a new Jerusalem in you. You are the one whom Jesus Christ has sent like the last Elijah to repair the Lord's road and make his way straight ...
> I will give you the key to power like Moses and will bless you like Job ... I am the God of Kah ... the God of Jah.
>
> (Turner 1967, I: 40)

It was not long before Oshitelu was dismissed from the Church Missionary Society for 'erroneous beliefs and teachings'. Significantly, this expulsion from the mission church came at a time when a severe outbreak of the plague had disastrous effects in the Ijebu area followed by a serious economic depression and famine. From Ogere, Oshitelu's hometown, an eyewitness wrote in the *Nigerian Spectator* of 11 April 1925: 'I was stricken with awe when I was walking through the narrow streets of Ogere, for there are no voices in many parts to be heard, save the deep moaning of the bereaved' (Mitchell 1970: 478).

Prior to his expulsion, Oshitelu and the other Aladura preachers explained the catastrophic events as signs of God's anger about the pagan practices of his people and the false and deceptive government. Only faith in God, the power of prayer, and the abandonment of paganism could overcome them. The result was a marked increase in witch-hunting and vehement attacks against the present political conditions expressed in apocalyptic visions which prophesied the early uprooting of the government and the coming of the millennium.

Yet despite this messianic character of its early phase, the movement remained under a largely unbroken Anglican influence. Its leaders resented any radical gnostic beliefs and only six months after the outbreak Oshitelu was expelled from the movement. He managed, however, to establish a foothold in a few major towns and gathered a considerable number of followers and assistants around him. On this rather slender basis Oshitelu's Church of the Lord gradually expanded into the northern and eastern regions of Yorubaland and from there all over the country. In the early 1960s the congregation had established over seventy branches throughout Nigeria and when its founder died in 1966 the Church of the Lord had developed into an international religious organisation which extended through four West African countries and even had a small branch in London.

Like many other Yoruba prophets in the first decades of this century, Oshitelu made great use of his literacy. In this he was not exceptional since reading and writing were in the air anyway. As we have seen, they were activities closely connected with the specific cultural atmosphere at that time and thus quickly picked up and used for a large variety of social purposes. This phenomenon is impressively reflected in the development of printing. Printing had been introduced in Yorubaland in the second half of the nineteenth century.[8] It had existed in Lagos from the late 1860s and several newspapers were being printed locally by the 1890s. But the use of this new technology was still restricted. The actual change came with the firm establishment of colonial rule from the first decade of the twentieth century onwards when printing spread now almost exponentially all over the country. Soon, it became a feature of a wide range of social activities and all kinds of social functions became increasingly accompanied by it. In such an atmosphere, the religious domain did not remain unaffected. One of the most momentous results was the mass circulation of pamphlets virtually everywhere, thus reaching far into the rural areas away from the main cities. The actual impact of printing is perhaps best expressed in the case of an illiterate prophet who was told in a vision: 'Print it in books, effect complete circulation, and I will make you a holy Apostle for the whole world' (Peel 1968: 115).

Oshitelu realised the significance of the written word and its potential during his early years in school. From the very beginning of his prophetic career in 1925 he, therefore, carefully recorded all his visions and messages in an exercise book, which was later incorporated into the first volume of six massive journals containing all his revelatory experiences for the next years – nearly 10,000 entries, all made with great neatness and systematically ordered. The bulk of his writings dates from 1925 to 1934, the year he ended his apprenticeship under Shomoye.

On 4 April 1926, only two months after his dismissal from mission service, the journal of Oshitelu's visions states that he saw 'a book open, written in strange arabic language' (Turner 1967, I: 41). Entries like this continued showing other elementary forms of written characters. Turner, who studied these journals, remarks that it seems as if Oshitelu was 'experimenting' towards a more fully elaborated Holy Script. This finally appeared a year later and was written, like Arabic and Hebrew, from right to left. In the course of his entries Oshitelu often used it to subtitle a series of sixty numbered seals that he recorded in a supplementary journal also containing a great variety of drawings. One of them shows the 'Key of the Holy Writing' with several lines of the Holy Script. Unfortunately, there is no clue to the 'key' as such, and the Yoruba text merely says: 'preserve this for the glory of my majesty' (Turner 1967, I: 44).

Turner's material on Oshitelu's writings during that time is rather scanty; however, his brief information about Oshitelu's scriptural visions does enable the extraction of some important aspects. First, mention should be made of Oshitelu's revelatory experience of Christianity and Islam as book religions in a traditional oral society. One impressive feature was the perception of the concept of writing as a new technology of communication which can contact and manipulate supernatural powers, a task which seemed much more efficient with the help of the book than by previous means.[9] Against a background of the experience of the political and economical superiority of Islam and Christianity represented by the missionaries and mallams, the Yoruba, particularly those in close contact with the representatives of the dominant written culture, quickly realised that power was available through the scriptures, so that the scriptures themselves became recognised as a power or force whose

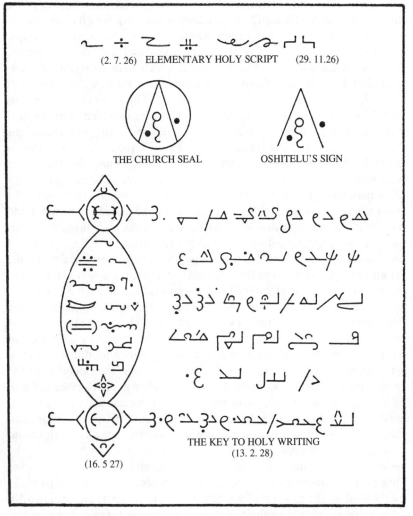

Figure 8.1 Examples of Oshitelu's scriptural visions.

use had to be learned. In this context, Oshitelu's Holy Script is first of all a reflection of the literate religious system in which he was educated and which he greatly appreciated. But why, then, was it a script he alone could understand?

Oshitelu declared himself a prophet chosen by God to announce the coming of the millennium. Like the old Biblical Apostles he was endowed with a divine quality of communication to interpret the holy power of God (Schütz 1975). His vision texts, in which the sacred *logos* broke through into the Holy Script, were signs of his special gift, a kind of *divine literacy*, which clearly fulfilled the necessary criteria for charisma in the Weberian sense. It broke with the traditional order by the use of unique and 'extraordinary' letters of the Holy Script and it evidenced definite relations to the sacred and supernatural which were so vividly demonstrated in the prominent figure of communication referring to a source of authority higher and greater than anything that is established in this world. Seen in this perspective, the seals Oshitelu recorded in his journal were not only a symbolic privilege serving to remove the prophet and his followers from the rest of society and to integrate them into a *communitas* strengthened by an identity of electedness since they knew that these seals were revealed only to them. In fact, these seals have to be seen as a mark of authenticity of the prophet's real religious calling. They were the signature of the very religious authority who had called the prophet and demonstrated the rightness of Oshitelu's directives and, thus, the rightness of his communication. Therefore, the group privilege to be in possession of the sacred seals and the Holy Script was a sign of the group's independence from the missionaries' source of power expressed in the uniqueness of the Holy Script's letters as revealed to the prophet.

More important, they were also a response to what Derrida has called 'the violence of the letter' (Derrida 1976).[10] The application of this concept within anthropology refers to the subtle cultural dimensions of writing. Whereas in a traditional oral society the definition of truth is established in a more socratic or dialectical manner, the extension of the spatial and temporal boundaries by writing and print changes the cultural instruments of the knowledge of reality. Given the necessary institutional conditions for the maintenance of this achievement, the art of oratory and rhetoric (by which it was formerly possible to agree on what is right and wrong) becomes confronted with another form of truth. With the encroachment of literacy, truth, whether of land boundaries, of genealogies or – as in our case – of access to the sacred, is now at least partially established by the priority of written documents and the cultural institutions to which they owe their existence. The *violent* implications of this process in the realm of social consciousness correlates with the experience of the violent forms of colonial domination which accompanies this development. It was this experience, I suggest, that was at the background of Oshitelu's scriptural visions.[11] With the proclamation of a new Holy Script, Oshitelu made himself not only spiritually independent from the missionaries' faith but also *immune* to the violent potential of their book by claiming the authority of writing for his own ideas.

But there are still other, more concrete factors, which might have led to Oshitelu's writings. First of all, there was, of course, the influence of Islam. Its history in Yoruba society probably goes back to the seventeenth century. Its most rapid expansion, however, was at the beginning of the twentieth century.[12] Considering this period, it seems very likely that Oshitelu was deeply impressed by the use of the Qur'ān in Islamic ritual and Muslim literature on the magic use of words and letters will have been among the material in circulation at the time of Oshitelu's invention. The social upheaval during the 1920s in Yorubaland was accompanied by great religious turmoil. Adherents of Rosicrucianism, members of Freemasonry lodges, honourable Muslim mallams, and young Christian converts from traditional Yoruba religion with its complex cosmology and sophisticated system of divination formed a highly syncretistic atmosphere, one which created a real boom in new medicines, healing techniques, and occult literature. In Lagos the newspapers in the 1920s carried advertisements for 'a quite extraordinary range of potions, medications, charms and other nostrums for all kind of sickness of varied origins and reputability' (Peel 1968: 128). In the streets 'manuals stemming from Muslim or western esoteric sources' (Peel 1968: 170) were available for dream interpretation and the catalogues of diverse 'healing homes' offered, next to charms and potions, a long list of books of secret lore as well. Among this sort of literature the most popular and most widespread article was *The Sixth and Seventh Book of Moses*, commonly known as Moses' Book. According to Margaret Field, who came across one copy during her fieldwork in Ghana in the late 1950s: 'It claims to be a collection of translations of ancient and medieval treatises originally in Hebrew, concerning "Moses' Magical Spirit Art!" It is profusely illustrated with black-and-white representations of "Seals", "Tables", "Magic Circles", "Schemhamforas", "Semiphoras" and so on' (Field 1960: 41).

These seals and tables are accompanied by specific 'conjurations' and 'procedures' that enable the reader to fulfil his wishes and to acquire certain preferable virtues.[13] Apparently, the book refers, though in a rather platitudinous mode, to ancient Jewish cabalistic writings. Rediscovered and popularised at the time of the Renaissance – a period which, by the way, also brought the invention of printing – this mystical system enabled the elect to ascertain the secrets of the Bible as to the meaning and plan of creation. As such it was taken up by a number of sects like the Rosicrucians and Freemasons, through whom it became known to a wider audience. Considering the background, it seems likely that Oshitelu knew of Moses' Book and assimilated it accordingly in the elaboration of his own Holy Script. In particular, the cabalistic idea must have been especially appealing to him, since the Hebrew letters in which the sacred texts are written down are not just ordinary signs invented by man to synthesise and render meaningful events but, rather, reservoirs of divine power, symbols behind which the biblical secrets are hidden. Evidence for this argument is a remark Oshitelu himself once made in connection with his later publication of *The book of prayer with uses and power of psalms*. He said, 'Some will say this is Moses' Book therefore it is bad' (Turner 1967, II: 74), and thus acknowledged explicitly an otherwise only implicit source.

The use of such occult literature has been popular up to now in the Church of the Lord and many of its members possess books of this genre (Turner 1979: 179). This is due to the very nature of the Aladura churches in which the concept of power that can be made available through prayer is the main characteristic feature. But despite this gnostic touch, the official religious outlook of the church is rational, with the Scriptures as its sole basis. In the eyes of Turner, who has written a detailed theological analysis of the congregation: 'The church desires to be a biblical church and holds the bible in great reverence. This is partly a cultural reaction on the part of a people whose pagan background is devoid of literature and who desire to assure themselves and the world that they have passed fully into the new way of life based on writing and the book' (Turner 1967, II: 83).

The unwritten words of God

When Turner began his theological analysis of the Church of the Lord he had to look through a vast array of letters, reports, programmes, minutes, records, booklets, and pamphlets which contained an extended statement of the congregation's religious outlook and the Christian life required of its members. The texts he examined regulate the internal structure of the church, especially in matters like the ordination to the ministry and the election of new members; they give instructions on how to commence the rites of infant and adult baptism; they govern the way a marriage should be held; and they inform the readers about the proper ways to bury the dead. They tell how to pray, fast, love and how to read the Bible, and they explain the six main prohibitions concerning magic, idolatry, sex, food, alcohol, tobacco, and litigation. Furthermore, they narrate the early beginnings of the church, pass on the 'Wise Words' of its important leaders and give accounts of the life history of its founder. In short, these texts serve as constant reminders and reinforcement of a correct Christian way of living by guiding and structuring the members' religious behaviour and experience. Or, as the members themselves say, they 'keep a Christian's lamp always burning bright' and enable him to 'practise all the good ways, wishes and works of Jesus' (Turner 1967, II: 69).

It is important to keep in mind that this marked dominance of the written texts within the congregation was due not so much to an external missionary imposition but rather the cumulative result of the Church's positive response to literacy starting with Oshitelu's journals in the 1920s.

The church encouraged its members to become literate and use the technology of communication in order, as it is said, 'to develop fully' (Turner 1967, II: 120). This means to learn to understand and exhaust the power of God with the best means available. Religious maturity in terms of religious experience, knowledge and respect is the aim, and for this the key role of literacy was clearly recognised. As Turner remarked, such knowledge was proudly shown in the regular competitions the community organised. He reports the eagerness with which people participated in the weekly bible classes and 'Quarterly Bible Tests': 'There are constant exhortations to bring one's own copy to service; many do so and are then able to share in the competition to be the first to stand and read the texts referred to by the preachers as the sermon proceeds' (Turner 1967, II: 83).

This strong reliance upon the scriptures and the will to fulfil the literate standards of 'proper' Christian faith, seen as a necessary adjustment to contemporary modern society, led the Church, however, into an increasing conflict with its own tradition. The importance of visions, as taught by its founder and the official recognition of the concept of spiritual power in the context of healing, constituted the very identity of the Church. But, as Peel has pointed out, it also invited the proclamation of novel revelations and dissident views which disrupted the institutional order of the Church and diverged from its large body of fixed doctrine drawn up and compiled since the works of Oshitelu and subsequent church leaders.

In general terms, what had happened was an institutionalisation of the movement and a certain 'canonisation' of its religious content.[14] The personal charisma of the numerous prophets as the basis of their authority had become, partially at least, replaced by drawing up a written canon of the 'true' interpretation of the Bible.

One can see here that the incorporation of literacy, against whose implications Oshitelu once rebelled, had led the Church of the Lord into the same structural dilemma that had trapped the mission church from which Oshitelu had originally broken away. It is a dilemma that is framed in Christian history as the old opposition between orthodoxy and gnosticism. The Aladura churches were caused difficulty by their interpretation of spiritual power based upon the orthodox Christian position of the openness of the Christian gospel, which makes it potentially accessible to everybody. This became manifest in the missionaries' proclamation that God has offered a way to salvation for all, that the divine message is written down in the Bible which contains the truth – final, complete and available to everybody. But such a position also entails a democratising element that inevitably challenges any clerical meritocracy that tries to establish itself as the custodian of the truth and supervise a correct interpretation of the scripture. Postulating free access to the Bible, whether it be for the spread of God's rule or for the exhaustion of 'spiritual power', necessarily implies encouraging literacy in order to read the Holy Words for oneself. The result is the increase in individual religious knowledge which invariably leads to a threat to the church authorities. As the church members begin to feel that it is possible to be as qualified in religious matters as their leaders, they realise they can study the Bible without the guidance of the priests. Once there is dissatisfaction with the Church's answers to burning questions the way is opened for the formation of heretical and gnostic beliefs. In Western history this development is accompanied by the vigorous persecution of such beliefs, some of which bear a remarkable resemblance to African beliefs in the 'unwritten words of God'. A prominent example in this context is the movement of the so-called 'Spiritualists'. Though it goes back to the first century, it is primarily connected with the name of St Francis who, significantly, lived and preached in a period which saw the emergence of written culture in the Middle Ages (Stock 1983). For St Francis and his followers the remark of St Paul in his second epistle to the Corinthians 'written not with ink, but with the spirit of the living God ... for the letter killeth but the spirit giveth life' was the scriptural justification of their revolt against a Christian faith represented by the Church which seemed to them reduced to spiritually empty book learning. It is a gnostic criticism, which not only brings to memory the concept of the *violence of the letter* but fits stunningly into the Aladura material. Thus Peel, for instance, writes about the 'popular level' of the movement: '... from the less well educated prophets, one hears more of spiritual illuminism and the view that it is not book learning but the simple faith and spiritual gifts of ordinary men which are preached in the Gospel' (Peel 1968: 236).

This view was a response to the 'elitist' tendency which started off under the conditions of increasing literacy in many Aladura churches. In the eyes of their pastors, illiterate prophets were often seen as an embarrassing sign of the religious backwardness of their congregations. However, prophets belong to the very identity of the Aladura movement and traditionally had a great pull among the people. So the problem here was how to accommodate them in the Church. Attempts were made to set up new criteria of religious authority in order to restrict their influence. In this context, literacy became a crucial issue. For those whose Christian life was based upon the literate study of the Bible and who spent their spare time interpreting the events it narrates, the attitude towards visions and the concept of spiritual power was certainly different from that of the uneducated mass. It is against this background one has to assess such informal comments as 'The Holy Spirit is for those who have been purified by the word of God and not for every Dick and Harry' (Peel 1968: 141) or the scathing label of 'bushman' for illiterate prophets (Peel 1968: 76).

Against the constant warning of the pastors that the 'Gift of the Spirit' would lead to error if not legitimated by the Bible, the prophets replied that the scriptures were not the only path to truth because otherwise there would be only *alufa* (pastors). Rather, there were prophets who were able to interpret the 'unwritten words of God' which were revealed to them in visions. The Biblical rule, they said, is for prophets to be judged by superior prophets, and pastors only by pastors; pastors were essentially 'teachers' and had no power to override prophets. If they nevertheless tried to do so, they were deserting the precedents of Apostolic times. They opposed the idea that only a handful of men sitting in a 'committee' should decide on matters which concern the community as a whole and they mourned the disappearance of the 'deep love' they remembered of the early generation. They saw themselves as the one 'whom God has sent' and regretted that 'common sense' would now dominate the Church instead of 'spiritual revelation' and 'power' (Peel 1968: 238ff).

The future: The letter or the spirit? Routinisation or ritualisation?

In Weberian terms, the prophets' complaints were articulations of their experience of the increasing routinisation and institutionalisation of the Aladura movement in which they were granted a central role in the initial stages.[15] These complaints were responses to a process which Weber saw as inevitable in any historical transition from an original charismatic authority towards a more permanent and formally accepted legal constitution of authority (Weber 1964). In his grand vision, the material I have presented here constitutes just one example of the continuing secularisation and rationalisation of social institutions, a process he believed is the historical fate of Western culture. This prospect might affect African societies as well, considering the constitutive role of literacy in the emergence of bureaucratic structures and taking into account that much that has been written on this subject emphasised the cognitive potentials of this specific 'technology of the intellect' (Goody 1977, 1987). Referring to Goody's argument that writing fosters criticism and leads to previously inconceivable questions resulting in a massive exfoliation of knowledge, Maxwell, for example, writes about the impact of literacy on the religion of the Bemba in Zambia:

> Where Bemba religion tended to mystify cosmic origins and physical occurrences, Christianity proclaimed that, the more people knew about the cosmos as scientific fact the more they knew about God who created it. In brief, while Christianity had already made its peace with the literate sciences, oral religion, relying solely on the resources of its symbol system, could not

cope with the rising new consciousness of Bemba literates ... As a people becomes reflective and introspective under the impact of their literate skills, they begin to resent and then doubt any symbol system which inhibits their interior growth and their external quest for greater knowledge. Within the oral disposition, if they intend to take symbols seriously, they have no recourse other than to interpret them 'literally'.   (Maxwell 1983: 162–3)

Peel's description of the sceptical attitude of the literate Aladura pastors towards the gnostic faith in the 'unwritten words of God' could be interpreted in a similar vein. On the other hand, one should recall Turner's observation that there is persistent recourse to certain visionary and occult texts such as Oshitelu's early writings, or *The Sixth and Seventh Book of Moses* which has been popular up to now. In fact, both phenomena exist simultaneously, a situation which not only mirrors the indigenous ability to cushion and modify the demands of the surrounding literate culture of the Nigerian state in a way that translates and incorporates the alien elements of the outside world into the familiar order of the traditional environment. It also shows that local literacies may be flexible and resistant to central authority at the same time as asserting their own authority over internal resistance. This particular capacity of African society to resist the pressing demands of the 'world system' in which it is embedded has been demonstrated in many anthropological studies and it is also evident in the material I have discussed in this paper.[16]

The last and perhaps best example in this context comes from Parrinder. In the early 1950s he visited several gatherings of the Church of the Lord in Ibadan. In his *Religion in an African City* he writes:

A particular feature of this sect is the use of 'seal' words. These are long, indecipherable inventions, printed in their hymnbooks and pamphlets, and which are taken as revelations of the Lord. Some appear to be variations on well reported exclamations such as 'Hallelujah' which gives the long seal word 'Ollahhallahhajieu-haahhieohuhuhllalti'. Others are developing repetitions: 'Gieobiee Gieobieerar', 'Arieubb-Arieuullate-Arieubbllattakukllal'. These have no Yoruba or English translation. The 'seal' words are given in ecstasy, when speaking in tongues.

(Parrinder 1953: 123)

Parrinder's account points to the indigenous capacity to establish literacy within the religious discourse of the church members without changing the underlying pattern of a traditional belief-system on which this discourse rests. Certainly, the constant reminder Peel reported of the pastors on the warning of valuing visions above Scripture can still be heard being preached today. It is thus a reflection of the 'literate mentality'[17] created by the gradual incorporation of the Aladura movement into the politico-economic order of the colonial and post-colonial structures which gave literacy an eminent place in the symbolic environment of the Yoruba. But despite this process, the increase of the use of writing within the congregations did not lead to the disappearance of the prophets as the arguments provided by Goody seem to imply. Rather, writing and print have become incorporated into the indigenous forms of religious experience, where they now form new media for the expression of the distinctive Christian life style of the church members. As Eades (1980) reports, the Aladura prophets still play an important part in contemporary Yoruba society. They do so due to the unbroken symbolic basis of the Aladura religious practice, that is the traditional belief that words are thought to have an inherent power of their own, which can be made available to attract God's help and protection through prayer. Thus, the recitation of certain 'holy names' or passages from the psalms as magical formulas are still just as common as the preparation of charms using written verses from the Bible. It is this particular ability of the Aladura churches to synthesise traditional forms and values with new modes of life and organisation which also grants the coexistence of the letter *and* the spirit in the future.

Notes

1 I should like to thank J. D. Y. Peel in this context. His detailed comments have been a great help.
2 See, for example, the stimulating articles in Graff (1981) and Trolle-Larsen and Schousboe (1989).
3 Against this background, Brian Street (1984) has recently put forward an 'ideological approach' which he characterises as follows: 'Literacy can only be known to us in forms, which already have political and ideological significance and it cannot, therefore, be helpfully separated from that significance and treated as if it were an "autonomous" thing' (Street 1984: 8). As important as Street's criticism is, there remains a want of clarity with respect to the actual nature of literacy, significantly revealed by the difficulties he has in his attempt to tackle the problem. In his view literacy is: '. . . more than the "technology" in which it is manifest. No one material feature serves to define literacy itself. It is a social process, in which particular socially constructed technologies are used within particular institutional frameworks for specific social purposes' (Street 1984: 95). Unfortunately, Street does not elaborate this point in his argument further. He does not make clear what the specific relationship between literacy as a 'social process' and the 'technology in which it is manifest' is. Instead, he leaves this link open to a vague terminology and a general cultural relativism.
4 Written communication by J. D. Y. Peel.

5 A more complete picture of this group is given by Herskovits (1972).
6 This is certainly not a unique situation. Similar descriptions can also be found for East Africa. Here, the name for early Christian converts was often identical with that of literates. In Uganda, for example, they were called *abosomi*, that is people who can read the book (Sundkler 1976: 548). Among the Kikuyu, conversion to literacy was referred to as *guthoma*, or to become literate. To backslide was called *guthmoka* as reverting to illiteracy. The converts to Christianity were named *athomi*, literates, whereas the rest were *agikuyu*, the people who remained in the Kikuyu culture (Kichibo 1978: 384). These instances correlate with Peel's observation: 'It appears that the first name spontaneously given by locals to the Christians was *onibuku*, "book people", and not *onigbagbo*, "believers", which was the name the Christians themselves used' (Peel: personal communication).
  With respect to the process of conversion, this picture conforms to Horton's model (Horton 1971). Relying primarily upon the work of Peel, Horton saw conversion to either Christianity or Islam as basically a cognitive and explanatory response to the experience of a complex situation of change. The intellectual nature of this model is so closely linked with the issue of literacy that Fernandez is able to argue: 'Literacy generally moves people toward more abstract lineal syntactic thought. The intellectualism that Peel reports and Horton focuses upon in his argument may thus be a consequence of literacy and not an African thought revolution' (Fernandez 1978: 221).
7 Aluko's novel, *One man, one wife*, gives evidence of the special Yoruba climate in these years. In the eyes of the rural villagers Royasin, a teacher and catechist, is rated an important man. Aluko describes him as 'the wizard, who knows the White Man's secret, the wizard, who reads telegrams and writes letters, the wizard, who understands and speaks the White Man's strange tongue' (Aluko 1959: 38). For other aspects of the same phenomenon see Ayandele (1966: 289).
8 For the following information I am indebted to J. D. Y. Peel.
9 For the ritual use of white technology as significant objects in a context of political power see also the Heavenly Telephone, an exclusive hotline to the throne of heaven which the Zulu prophet Khambule was reported to have (Sundkler 1976: 119) or the *kalite mazulu*, the 'passports of heaven' of the Kimbanguists during the 1920s (Anderson 1958: 161).
10 To understand this concept in reference to anthropology I am indebted to an unpublished paper by Janzen (1972). See also Janzen and MacGaffey (1974).
11 See also Harbsmeier (1988) in this context.
12 See Trimingham (1959) and Gbadamosi (1978) for a detailed account of this issue.
13 It is perhaps worth mentioning that I found the *Sixth and Seventh*, as the book is also known, still widely used in much the same way during my own fieldwork in the Cameroon grasslands in 1985–6 (Probst 1990; Probst and Bühler 1990). This is merely in keeping with the book's unbroken popularity in the West (see Sebald 1988).
14 On the process of canonisation see Janzen (1985: 226).

15 A similar position can be found in Pagels (1982) who argues that the issue of orthodoxy and gnosticism in the history of the early Christian Church articulated 'very different kinds of experience' (Pagels 1982: 148). Her suspicion that they appealed 'to different types of persons' could be interpreted in terms of the different levels of literacy among the people in question.

16 See also Parrinder (1953), who quotes from a book entitled *Orunmalaism, the Basis of Jesuism* published in 1943 by a Yoruba journalist: 'We shall begin on the hypothesis that the Bible is an Ifa Book ... Like the Bible, Ifa tells us of the existence of Witches, and Sorcerers ... In the Gospels the Jews thought Jesus was either Elias or one of the prophets reincarnated ... Divination is not a foreign teaching in the Christian Bible, there are Urim and Thummim, Joseph's Divination Cup, the Ephod ... We read of Jesus practising Geomancy by writing with his finger on the ground and divining thereafter ... I should like to see the Bible rewritten with a view to introducing Yoruba Philosophic and Theosophic terminologies therein' (Parrinder 1953: 127).

17 This term is taken from Clanchy (1979) who uses it to describe the social transformations which took place in England during the middle ages.

References

Ajayi, J. F. A. 1963. 'The development of secondary grammar school education in Nigeria', *Journal of the Historical Society of Nigeria*, 2: 517–35.

Aluko, T. M. 1959. *One man, one wife*. London: Heinemann.

Anderson, E. 1958. *Messianic popular movements in the Lower Congo*. Uppsala: Almquist and Wiksell.

Anene, J. C. 1966. *Southern Nigeria in transition 1885–1906*. Cambridge: Cambridge University Press.

Ayandele, E. A. 1966. *The missionary impact on modern Nigeria 1894–1914*. London: Longman.

Atanda, J. A. 1973. *The new Oyo Empire: indirect rule and change in western Nigeria 1894–1934*. London: Longman.

Barber, K. 1981. 'How man makes God in West Africa. Yoruba attitudes towards the Orisha', *Africa*, 21: 202–24.

Bascom, W. R. 1960. 'Urbanisation among the Yoruba', in S. and P. Ottenberg (eds.), *Cultures and societies of Africa*, pp. 147–59. New York: Random House.

Bloch, M. 1989. 'Literacy and enlightenment', in M. Trolle-Larsen and K. Schousboe (eds.), *Literacy and society*, pp. 15–38. Copenhagen: Akademisk Forlag.

Clanchy, T. M. 1979. *From memory to written record: England 1066–1307*. London: Arnold.

Derrida, J. 1976. *Of grammatology*. Baltimore and London: Johns Hopkins University Press.

Eades, J. S. 1980. *The Yoruba today*. Cambridge: Cambridge University Press.

Fernandez, J. 1978. 'African religious movements', *Annual Review of Anthropology*, 7: 195–234.

Field, M. 1960. *In search for security*. London: Faber and Faber.

Gbadamosi, T. G. O. 1978. *The growth of Islam among the Yoruba*. London: Longman.

Goody, J. 1968. 'Introduction', in J. Goody (ed.), *Literacy in traditional societies*, pp. 1–26. Cambridge: Cambridge University Press.

1977. *The domestication of the savage mind*. Cambridge: Cambridge University Press.

1986. *The logic of writing and the organization of society*. Cambridge: Cambridge University Press.

1987. *The interface between the written and the oral*. Cambridge: Cambridge University Press.

Graff, H. J. 1981. 'Introduction', in H. J. Graff (ed.), *Literacy and social development in the West*, pp. 1–13. Cambridge: Cambridge University Press.

Harbsmeier, M. 1988. 'Inventions of writing', in J. Gledhill, B. Bender and M. Trolle-Larsen (eds.), *The emergence and the development of social hierarchy and political centralization*, pp. 169–85. London: Unwin Hyman.

Herskovits, J. 1972. 'The Sierra Leoneans of Yorubaland', in P. Curtin (ed.), *Africa and the West: intellectual responses to European culture*, pp. 75–98. Madison, WI: University of Wisconsin Press.

Horton, R. 1971. 'African conversion', *Africa*, 41: 85–108.

Janzen, J. M. 1972. *Literacy and culture among the BaKongo*. Waterloo. Unpublished manuscript.

1985. 'The consequences of literacy in African Religion: the Kongo case', in W. van Binsbergen and M. Schoffeleers (eds.), *Theoretical explorations in African religion*, pp. 225–52. London: Routledge and Kegan Paul.

Janzen, J. M. and MacGaffey, W. 1974. 'Literacy and truth', in J. M. Janzen and W. MacGaffey (eds.), *An anthology of Kongo religion*, pp. 1–27. Lawrence: University of Kansas Publication in Anthropology, no. 5.

Kichibo, S. G. 1978. 'The continuity of the African conception of God into and through Christianity', in E. Fashole-Luke et. al. (eds.), *Christianity in independent Africa*, pp. 370–88. London: Collins.

Maxwell, K. B. 1983. *Bemba myth and ritual. The impact of literacy on an oral culture*. New York: Lang.

Mitchell, R. C. 1970. 'Religious protest and social change', in R. J. Rotberg and A. A. Mazrui (eds.), *Protest and power in Black Africa*, pp. 458–96. New York: Oxford University Press.

Pagels, E. 1982. *The gnostic gospels*. Harmondsworth: Penguin.

Parrinder, E. G. 1953. *Religion in an African city*. Oxford: Oxford University Press.

Parry, J. 1986. 'The Brahmanical tradition and the technology of the intellect', in J. Overing (ed.), *Reason and morality*, pp. 200–25. London and New York: Tavistock.

Peel, J. D. Y. 1967. 'Religious change in Yorubaland', *Africa*, 37: 292–310.

1968. *Aladura: a religious movement among the Yoruba*. Oxford: Oxford University Press.

1977. 'Conversion and tradition in two African societies: Ijebu and Buganda', *Past and Present*, 77: 108–41.

1983. *Ijeshas and Nigerians. The incorporation of a Yoruba kingdom 1890s–1970s*. Cambridge: Cambridge University Press.

Probst, P. 1990. '*Text im Kontext. Eine Untersuchung zum politischen Verhältnis von Schrift und Gesellschaft bei den Wimbum im Grasland von Kamerun.*' Unpublished Ph.D. dissertation, Freie Universität Berlin.

Probst, P. and Bühler, B. 1990. Patterns of control. On medicine, politics and social change among the Wimbum, Cameroon grassfields', *Anthropos*, 85: 375–86.

Schütz, J. H. 1975. *Paul and the anatomy of apostolic authority.* Cambridge: Cambridge University Press.

Sebald, H. 1988. 'The 6th and 7th Books of Moses. The historical and sociological vagaries of a grimoire', *Ethnologia Europaea*, 18: 53–8.

Stock, B. 1983. *The implications of literacy. Written language and models of interpretation in the eleventh and twelfth century.* Princeton: Princeton University Press.

Street, B. 1984. *Literacy in theory and practice.* Cambridge: Cambridge University Press.

Sundkler, B. G. M. 1976. *Zulu Zion and Swazi Zionists.* Oxford: Oxford University Press.

Trimingham, J. S. 1959. *Islam in West Africa.* Oxford: Clarendon Press.

Trolle-Larsen, M. and Schousboe, K. (eds.), 1989. *Literacy and society.* Copenhagen: Akademisk Forlag.

Turner, H. W. 1967. *History of an African independent church*, 2 vols. Oxford: Clarendon Press.

1979. *Religious innovation in Africa.* Boston: G. K. Hall and Co.

Weber, M. 1964. *Wirtschaft und Gesellschaft. Grundriss der verstehenden Soziologie.* Tübingen: J. C. B. Mohr.

PART 3

Literacy variation in urban settings

Throughout this volume a number of authors have made use of the concept of 'vernacular literacy'. Camitta, for instance, defines the kinds of texts produced by adolescents outside of school in urban Philadelphia, by drawing a contrast with schooled texts: 'the kinds of written texts I wish to study are not essays, the officially designated discourse genre of academia, but rather those adolescents choose to write within the framework of adolescent culture and social organisation. These texts I shall call 'vernacular' in the sense that they are most closely associated with culture which is neither elite nor institutional. By vernacular writing I mean writing which is traditional and indigenous to the diverse cultural processes of communities as distinguished from the uniform, inflexible standards of institutions'. She refers to a variety of disciplines for support, citing work in linguistics, cultural studies, literary criticism and so on, in which the common feature of vernacular discourse is its derivation from folk or popular traditions and a lack of conformity to the standard. In the school context, however, such discourses have been treated mainly in moral and disciplinary terms, as rebellious, as inadequate attempts at proper literacy, along with graffiti and other literate forms that differ from the essay text model (see Hodges 1988 on graffiti). In the context of development programmes too, local literacies have been treated as inadequate to the needs of the 'modern' world, signs of underdevelopment and backwardness, to be supplanted by a standard (frequently English).

Anthropologists and sociologists, as we have seen, have begun to study these local or vernacular literacies in various parts of the world, but only very recently has similar attention been given to literacy variation in the metropolitan cultures (but see Fingeret 1983; Heath 1983a; Levine 1980). The papers included here represent some of the first distinctive attempts to take seriously the literate sub-culture of urban society in the United States and the United Kingdom. They derive from the same theoretical and methodological roots as the papers in the other sections of this volume but are especially concerned to challenge previous approaches to the study of literacy in contemporary urban settings, which have marginalised their particular subjects and understated the rich complexity of local and vernacular literacies to be found there.

Camitta spent three years with adolescents at a Community High School in Philadelphia, talking about their writing and sharing the intimacies this involved. The experience forced her to revise assumptions and beliefs about writing that she had held as a teacher at the school and which she suggests are dominant in educational circles in the United States. She gradually became aware of the texts and contexts for unofficial or self-sponsored writing practised by adolescents: writing, she discovered, was an important and varied activity and identified major areas that 'organised' adolescent culture. The written material included rap verses and rehearsal notes, letters, entries in journals, diaries, poems, rhymes and parodies and texts copied into notebooks. Moreover, the interest generated in writing when it was free of school constraints led to much oral sharing amongst students, including a great deal of verbal interaction around the texts: they might read texts aloud to each other, offer feedback or take it in turns reading texts silently and then commenting on them. Camitta concludes that 'collaboration, both oral and written, as it takes place in the printing process, is a kind of performance in which an audience for the text is actualised, as opposed to fictionalised'. Further, 'we saw writing take place in what has traditionally been characterised as a condition of oral literature and performance, that is, in the context of face-to-face communication'. Thirdly she noted the recursive nature of this kind of writing: 'performance of texts took place at any point in the drafting process and revision, as a result of audience feedback, was during not after drafting. This aspect of composition can be compared with the improvisation that takes place during oral performance of traditional texts'. These findings have considerable implications for the analysis of oral and literate practices, in modern and traditional settings, and for folklore as much as for anthropology.

Amy Shuman worked with adolescents at an inner-city Junior High School in the eastern United States. Whilst her interest, like Camitta's, was in oral and written narratives, her particular focus was on storytelling rights: in standard written form these involve questions of legal copyright; in the context of vernacular literacies rights are embedded in everyday social relationships and interactions. These Shuman investigated through a variety of methods: she lived among groups of adolescents at the school for three years, tape-recorded many conversations especially naturally occurring narrative performance, conducted interviews and designed a questionnaire with the help of the students themselves. She also obtained copies of written material, often on lined notepaper, she photocopied diaries and kept a 'Daily Diary' herself and allowed students access to the parts that concerned them.

Again, the relationship of written to oral conventions is crucial: 'oral storytelling rights differ among cultures and groups, and therefore are subject to constant misunderstanding among people who operate according to different systems'. Rights in written stories amongst urban adolescents are equally complex, conventionalised and subject to misconception. Indeed, the stories Shuman examines are themselves about rights: she describes them as 'junior high school fight stories, that is narrative accounts of quarrels about who has the right to say what to whom. In the communities from which these adolescents come, it is they rather than the older or younger people who are assigned the task of managing written documents: they mediate the community to the state through documentation, filling in forms, writing letters and so on. They also, however, keep their own narratives and diaries that record fight stories and provide discourses on storytelling rights within their community. And they use both speaking and writing to categorise their experience. As other authors in this volume have pointed out, general theory regarding the respective roles and associations of written and oral communication do not hold in such contexts: 'in contrast to conventional models that assume the use of speaking for face-to-face communication and writing for absent-author communication, the adolescents often used oral narratives to convey messages to absent third parties (through he-said-she-said rumours) and used writing as part of face-to-face exchanges in which documents were collaboratively produced and read aloud or as solitary communication with oneself in diaries'. The difference between proximity and distance, and the standardisation frequently created by distance, was more consequential than writing itself. This, then, underlines the point that not all writing belongs to the genre of the essay and not only literacy but also genre can be an important way of distributing knowledge and attitudes towards texts in a community.

Shuman does not evaluate the students' texts by standard school criteria of competence, but rather as part of a single community's repertoire: from this perspective they represent choices among channels and genres of communication, rather than examples of greater or lesser deficiency, as the current debate in the United States about 'standards' would appear to require. The practices described by Shuman do not represent anomalies, rather they demonstrate 'a need to re-evaluate the current models used for categorising writing and speaking'. Communicative competence, then, is relative to the speech community and its norms. Labov and others have demonstrated that there is much more of interest in the language practices of the inner city than is elicited by the standard tests and popular judgements: the work of Shuman, Camitta and others is now revealing the rich repertoire of written as well as oral practices to be found there.

Gail Weinstein-Shr lived and worked with Hmong refugees in Philadelphia and brings to attention aspects of the linguistic repertoire of such new immigrant groups that have likewise gone unrecognised in much previous literature. The shift in focus in literacy studies led her to ask new questions: 'how does life in a literate environment affect or change social relationships?', 'how do social relationships influence the way that literacy is acquired and used?'. Literacy is a relatively recent innovation for the Hmong, so it is possible to observe rapid changes as it is introduced 'into their repertoire of communicative resources'. Over a period of six years Weinstein-Shr conducted household surveys and developed several in-depth 'portraits' of Hmong adults in the city as well as meeting a number of them in the English language classes that she ran. She examines the ways in which kinship and literacy existed for the Hmong historically and how they now operate in their new lives in urban Philadelphia. She describes two men's lives in detail and brings out contrasts in their ways of using literacy and their ways of making/maintaining relationships, in the context of Philadelphia's wider community and a general discussion of literacy and social process. Whilst one man, Chou Chang, uses the standard literacy learnt in classes to mediate between his community and the agencies of the state, another, Pao Youa, seems to 'fail' in the formal classes and yet uses literacy with considerable skill to reinforce aspects of traditional Hmong culture and his own authority in relation to it. Chou spends a great deal of time writing letters to welfare offices: Pao keeps cuttings from newspapers in scrapbooks, collects reference materials and maintains personal journals that together take on the authority of chronicles, making him the history and news keeper for his community. Like Shuman and Camitta's adolescents, he extends the range of literacy practices well beyond the narrow definitions of the school and the classroom. Both men have adapted the new literacy to current needs, one via new relationships with the host authorities, one through building on traditional forms of authority. Both are active and creative mediators of this addition to their community's communicative repertoire, not simply passive recipients of a new technology. Weinstein-Shr concludes that the study of the functions and uses of literacy in specific people's lives can provide general insights into human organisation and social process. She also suggests ways in which anthropological insights can contribute to informing literacy instruction and educational practice as urban society becomes increasingly culturally diverse.

Mike Baynham adopts a similar perspective in studying aspects of the linguistic repertoire among the Moroccan community in London. He focuses on the notion 'mediators of literacy' as a communicative practice and compares it to the involvement of interpreters, formal and informal. He suggests that there are interesting comparisons and overlaps between mediated literacy events and communicative events in which interpreters are involved. Both communicative events, mediated literacy events and events involving interpreting are common in the setting from which the data are drawn – the Moroccan community settled in the Ladbroke Grove area of West London. Community members who regularly function as mediators of literacy on a semi-formal basis, such as volunteers in a community organisation, are often drawn into interpreting as well. The two event types contrast in that mediated literacy events typically are a mix of oral and literate modes around some kind of 'work on text' – the 'mode-switching' of his title, on analogy with the sociolinguist's 'code-switching' – while the interpreting event favours the oral mode, though not of course excluding the literate. He compares the events described here with the framework for mediators of literacy proposed in Wagner's work on literacy in Morocco (Wagner et al 1986), proposing certain adaptations for the London context. The paper extends the work on emergent sociolinguistic repertoires of second generation community members with specific reference to literacy practices.

9

VERNACULAR WRITING: VARIETIES OF LITERACY AMONG PHILADELPHIA HIGH SCHOOL STUDENTS

MIRIAM CAMITTA

It makes you feel good knowing you have a friend who will accept your writing. It makes you feel good to feel that safe.

Conversation, eighteen year old female.

LET ME BE ME

Let Me Be Me
Let Me Dream til I can fulfill Dreams.
Let Me follow Dreams, so that I May see where they May lead me,
Let Me write til my hands are to fall,
Let me spread all the Joy
Which I have received,
Let Me be Me, For there's
No One Like Me.

Poem, seventeen year old female.

The two teenage writers whose oral and written commentary about writing are quoted above, consider writing to be at the heart of their quests for meaning and identity. At eighteen, each had, for several years, kept diaries, maintained intensive correspondence with friends and relations, and composed poetry. Each believe that writing is central to transacting social relationships, to making meaning out of their lives, and that the act of writing signals that the truth is being told about them. Although much of what they wrote was private, an important component of their writing was its social aspect – its place in the web of activities that structured their intimate relationships.

Both of these writers were participants in a three-year study that I conducted of the writing of adolescents living in Philadelphia, a large urban centre in the north-eastern section of the United States. For each, as for many of the others with whom I worked, writing was a familiar, everyday activity. Used in a number of conventional ways, writing offered them options for expression as did dance, instrumental music, drawing and song.

This kind of writing is vernacular, that which is closely associated with culture which is neither elite nor institutional, which is traditional and indigenous to the diverse cultural processes of communities as distin-

228

guished from the uniform, inflexible standards of institutions. As such, the texts represented in this study are not essays, the officially designated discourse genre of academia, but rather are those that adolescents choose to write within the framework of adolescent culture and social organisation, those that have come to be called 'unofficial'. Taken as a whole, they are the discourse of social life.

Perhaps because traditional definitions of the vernacular associate it with political or social subordination, vernacular discourse is often eschewed in institutions of education as deviant or non-standard. Nonetheless, a major goal of my study was to present a rationale for looking at vernacular writing as a range of significant and meaningful literate skills and resources that are artificially disconnected from the process of literacy education as it is officially conducted.

I was particularly interested in looking at adolescent vernacular writing as a set of texts and practices that comprise conventionalized written expressive behaviours that are formulated within the adolescent community, and which are employed for culture-specific purposes. In this sense, I construed vernacular writing to be varieties of literacy shaped by expressive conventions directly influenced by the social and cultural configurations of adolescent life. I saw vernacular writing as literate behaviour that conformed, not to the norms of educational institutions, but to those of social life and culture. In this way, I envisioned literacy much in the way that processual anthropologists and performance-centred folklorists now look at culture – as social discourse comprised of meanings and expressions of experience that are negotiated in the context of social interaction or 'performance'.

Recent folklore scholarship suggests that tradition, which once was linked exclusively to the canon associated with oral tradition, is located not within the genre but in its performance. Following this line of thought, meaning is not a function of form, but of process.

Although the scope of the study did not encompass writing as it is practised as a consequence of the educational curriculum, the study was initiated at City High School (a fictional name for a public high school in a north-eastern city of the United States) because it was there, in my capacity of teacher, that I was able to locate individuals who would participate in the work.

The students with whom I worked lived in the greater Philadelphia area, and attended the one of four sites of City High School which shall be referred to as colony 'A'. They were white, black, hispanic, male and female. They ranged in age from fourteen to eighteen. The actual participants in the study were my students; however, they were able to tell me a great deal about the writing practices of their friends and relations whose texts were included in their 'writing collections'.

An alternative to the 'regular' high public school, City High School began in the late 1960s as an experiment in humanistic learning and teaching, modelled in part on the British Summerhill project. Today, City High School, although much changed in format over the twenty years of its existence, still strives to create a familiar, informal, personal and humane environment in which learning takes place. To accomplish this, it is composed of decentralised smaller colonies of students and teachers; keeps students and teachers on a first-name basis; and makes one-on-one counselling and advising an integral part of teacher-student interaction during an extension of the home-room structure called 'family group'.

Background

My work in adolescent writing among the students at City High School and their associates was preceded by a literacy research project in which I initially collaborated as an on-site teacher, and to which I later consulted as a folklorist. The findings of the project, based upon the researchers' ethnography of adolescent culture, established that writing was an important and valued activity among adolescents and identified major areas that 'organized' adolescent culture – music, fashion and sports.

The results of the literacy project both documented the existence of texts and contexts for adolescent writing in the community and strongly suggested the existence of conventions surrounding its production that were in opposition to the linear method of composition – planning, drafting, revision, publication – advocated in traditional classrooms. These results corroborated the findings of Emig, Perl and Elbow, who noted the interplay of collaboration, performance and recursiveness in their studies of the writing process in 'naturalistic' settings (Emig 1971, 1977, 1981; Perl 1979, 1980; Elbow 1973).

The project researchers took the position that writing would improve if motivation were increased. Thus, they sought to implement the findings of their community ethnography by making adjustments to the standard language arts curriculum. In so doing, they hoped to bridge the 'discontinuity' between the culture of school and that of community, thereby providing students with a greater motivation to write.

The project researchers found evidence in their ethnography of the adolescent community that writing took place outside of the classroom, in the form of lists, notes, diaries, journals, and poems. This evidence they sought to couple with their findings that music, fashion and sports were the major social and cultural preoccupations of adolescents, in making innovations to the standard curriculum that reflected the major interests of adolescents. Accordingly, my colleagues and I who were involved with this project developed a curriculum organised around the themes of music, fashion and sports. We also reorganised the classroom structure into small-group clusters, and provided peer-consultation time during writing activities. Additionally, we met weekly with the researchers to discuss the progress of the project, and collaborated in the school ethnography.

The implementation phase of the literacy project yielded important observations about writing, which, taken together with the ethnographic findings, implied several things about the relationship between writing and culture. One of our most significant observations had to do with the vernacular writing process, which has been characterised elsewhere as 'collaborative', 'recursive' and 'performative'.[1] We noticed, in particular, that when students were allowed to write about topics that were important to them and part of their own experience, namely those aspects of their culture identified by the researchers as major domains of social organisation, their enthusiasm for those topics generated talk about their writing. As we listened to students talk to each other about their writing, we realised that students solicited advice about mechanical, thematic, lexical and organisational issues. Students naturally shared their writing, we found, with each other, either orally, in which case they took turns reading their texts aloud to each other and offering feedback, or silently, in which case they took turns reading each other's texts and commenting on them.[2]

This observation led us to believe that collaboration, both oral and written, as it takes place in the writing process, is a kind of performance in which an audience for the text is actualised, as opposed to fictionalised (see Sutton-Smith 1970). We saw writing take place in what has been traditionally characterised as a condition of oral literature and performance, that is, in the context of face-to-face communication.

A third observation we were able to make about writing had to do with its recursivity. Performance of texts, we saw, took place at any point in the drafting process, and revision, as a result of audience feedback, occurred during, not after drafting.

Our observations of students writing in non-directed situations, then, led us to speculate that recursiveness, performance and collaboration were three components of a 'vernacular' or 'natural' writing process when we observed students composing outside of the classroom setting as well.

Had we discovered a vernacular writing process that had its origin in adolescent culture? If so, what meaning did it have with regard to adolescent culture? Although we had left the writing process up to the students, by stepping out of its direction, we had nonetheless specified the forms that their writing should take. What were the texts of vernacular writing? What relationship did they have to adolescent experience? My

own study of adolescent vernacular writing sought to answer these questions, through ethnography and the methods of literary exegesis.

Methodology

My research occurred at a time when anthropological approaches to the
study of literacy emphasised 'naturalistic' studies of writing, often
employing such anthropological techniques as ethnography, taking life
histories, and participant observation. This shift in methodology essentially implied an interest in the diversification of written literacy in specific
cultural settings as opposed to descriptions of pedagogy in classroom
situations (Basso 1974; Brodkey 1986; Gilmore and Smith 1982; Heath
1978, 1982; Hymes 1982; Szwed 1981). These studies have in effect relocated the gaze of the researcher from classroom application of ideal
standards of written literacy to everyday, ordinary contexts of use.
Further, these studies document a tradition of writing that exists outside
of the academy, is culturally significant, and will continue to exist influenced by, but not dependent upon, the conventions and practice of the
academy.

Ethnographic studies of writing contextualise its practice in communities, and conceptualise it as both channel and text of cultural expression.
Ethnographies of writing, therefore, document not only institutional
practices, but extra-institutional practices as well. It is the focus of
ethnography that makes its application to the study of writing and
literacy exceptional – that is, upon writing as cultural behaviour.

It is within this scholastic framework that I conducted my study of
adolescent vernacular writing. My primary concern was to articulate the
use and meaning of specific texts, and the conventions which informed
their construction, within the context of adolescent culture.

The setting for vernacular writing

My study of adolescent writing looked at writing in three kinds of
settings: in the environs of the school proper, before and after the official
school day, and during non-assigned student time; in my classroom; and
in the homes of several of the participants. However, through interviews
with the adolescents who participated in my study, and through reading
the contents of written artifacts, it became clear to me that almost any
time or place can be an opportunity for writing. Adolescents write when
they are alone, with friends, amongst their classmates, and in large groups
of strangers. The scenes of adolescent vernacular writing are the school
classroom, when they are supposed to be following the lesson; the hallways and entranceways of the school building; the bus or subway stop;

the bus or subway; the bedroom, in the middle of the night; the attic, during the day or early evening when the rest of their family is around the house; the basement, with friends, where they rehearse raps, graduation speeches and routines for talent shows.

The activities of about 170 students at colony A of City High School were observed both in and outside of classes. During non-assigned school time, students could be found clustered about in small groups, seated around the many long cafeteria-style tables in the hall, in the vestibules or landings, propped on the old, deep window sills at either end of the hallways, or sprawled over the four, large marble steps leading up to the front door. These spaces were the settings for conversation, 'hanging out', and also for writing: inscribing slam books, autograph and year books; composing group and individual letters, flyers announcing school-related events and out-of-school social events; copying chain letters; composing raps and practising them; writing in journals and notebooks; sharing writing; composing flyers announcing 'jams', school dances and bake sales; and reading letters and notes from other students. I was sometimes drawn into these writing activities as a consultant, although most often, I was a casual observer.

Much of the writing that adolescents do is a form of social activity. For example, some types of writing that took place during free time, such as letter-writing, students told me, were meant to be exchanged during class, or in-between class periods. Some students used lockers as places to exchange letters. One student used a classroom desk that she shared with another student who had the same teacher at a different time period as a place to drop off letters that she had composed either during free time, at home, or in class.

In the classroom, vernacular writing flourishes on a surreptitious basis. Here, students write during times when they have finished the assigned work, and sometimes, instead of doing it. Among the one hundred students whom I met daily in my classes, I observed, as in non-assigned student time, that students were writing in their diaries, composing letters, and copying song lyrics into their notebooks. However, writing in class, although similar in form to non-assigned writing outside of class, must be conducted surreptitiously, and practices and texts are subject to the constraints of the setting. Thus, private and personal writing, such as diary and letter-writing, can be carried out at the same time as teacher-assigned writing is supposed to be taking place, because superficially it looks the same to the teacher. More public forms of writing, those that engage other students, such as inscribing slam books or yearbooks, also take place in class, but to a lesser extent than they do outside of it, because it is more difficult to circulate a book than it is to pretend to be writing for an assignment. More easily circulated than the slam book because of their size and shape, although not without the danger of detection and the resulting negative sanction imposed by the teacher, are notes, letters, and what some students call 'funny things', or humorous texts. An example of the latter follows below:

GREETINGS EARTHLINGS

I am an Alien from another world. I just transformed myself into this piece of paper. Right now I am having sex with your fingers. I can tell you are enjoying it because you are smiling.

Please pass me to someone else's fingers because I'm a horny little baster. (sic)[3]

Another form of writing, adapted specifically to the classroom, or any context where oral conversation is difficult, or proscribed, is the 'dialogue note', so-called because it is comprised of short queries or statements requiring an answer. The dialogue note, a 'quick communication fix', as one individual described it, is passed between two individuals, who take turns writing and answering, as can be seen below:

trouble –
Are you going to the fair or theater tomorrow with [teacher's name]?

Love,
Reds

Reds,
    I said I was. but ...
Trouble,
    But what ...
I don't want to go to Jersey that late ...
Just go with [teacher's name]

Love,
Trouble[4]

Several adolescents who participated in the study had dialogue notes in their writing collections that had been written on a bus, when the correspondents were prevented from conversing orally because they were not seated next to one another. One individual showed me a dialogue note, written on a bus, that had been passed to a young man who interested her and her friend, becoming a sort of letter of introduction.

The third setting in which I was able to study adolescent writing was in the homes of those students who agreed to work with me more intensively, about ten in all. These individuals were essentially my key informants, who not only shared their extensive writing collections with me, but devoted many hours to interviews and conversations about their lives, adolescent life in general, and about writing as they experienced it and as they believed others did. Although I was able to discuss writing with many students at colony A, only these ten became regular informants, and only five of those were key. Through these students, I became privy to letters, diaries, poetry, and their large collections of writing. While many of these texts were composed in other settings, they were archived at home in larger collections of writing, and among personal possessions and memorabilia.

Conducting fieldwork in respondents' homes seemed to elicit detailed descriptions of how they lived on a daily basis, the kinds of relationships they had with their friends and relations, their complaints and their problems. Topics we discussed, when I did not direct the conversation, mainly were about the relationships respondents had with friends, relations, and lovers.

Many of the texts that I read in the setting of my students' homes paralleled the intimate and personal content of the conversations we were having. Letters, diaries, journals and poems were filled with the uncensored expression of feelings and details about their experiences. Often, the conversation amplified the content of the texts, or texts were used to exemplify a topic of conversation. For example, Shelly, in discussing the conflicted but intense relationships she had with her best friend and her boyfriend, showed me letters and poems she had written which touched upon various aspects of the conflict. At times we discussed her dissatisfaction with her appearance. Then she brought out photographs of herself taken at a time when she liked the way she looked, and showed me current journal entries which consisted of lists of foods and their calorific values that she had consumed on the day of the entry, a description of her exercise regime, and letters to friends in which she was critical about her appearance.

My fieldwork experience with Shelly was repeated often with other informants. Monique showed me a narrative she had written about her father and then talked about him, and about what she had written about him in her bedroom, where she constantly feared he would explosively intrude, although it was the one place in her home where she believed she had privacy. Seated on the sofa in her living room, Angela showed me letters and poems that friends and relations had written to her by way of explaining the web of personal relationships which were most important to her, as her brother, sister and cousin crowded around us, leaning familiarly on our shoulders, and sitting comfortably on the floor at our feet. In what he described as his inner sanctum in a house too crowded for privacy – an attic too hot during the summer for anyone else in his family and therefore his by default – John showed me the parodies and poems he had written in order to better explain to me that there was a sensitive and vulnerable underside to his public clowning at school.

Writing roles/literate behaviour

The individuals who contributed most intensively to my research – my key informants – were essentially writers or authors. They practised writing routinely and regularly. However, many students at City High School, although not exactly authors, were conversant with a variety of written genres and could assume a number of roles in a writing event. It is thus possible to argue that adolescents form a literate community within which various forms of literacy are practised.[5] In addition to being authors, they were the editors and the critical audience for those who were authors; the publishers and the consumers of adolescent literature; the readers of poetry and the recipients of notes. They acted as consultants and as ghost writers. They were experts of a sort, familiar with the forms of taste and style, but not regular producers of texts.

Individuals acting in extra-authorial roles collaborated with authors in the production of texts. They read and responded to the written form. They helped writers with lexical and metrical choices, as well as with content decisions. They often collaborated in the editing stage of the composing process. They were the scribes, working either in manuscript, typescript, dot matrix, or photocopy. Their role in the literate community was to participate in the reproduction and transmission of written texts. These individuals often disseminated copies of written texts among other adolescents. They were motivated by taste, that is, they sought to reproduce and disseminate texts that appealed to them, that were interesting or amusing.

Finally, being part of the literate adolescent community meant being a reader/editor of adolescent literature, those who determined which texts were circulated and which were not. Often self-appointed, reader/editors gained standing as arbiters of taste if the texts reproduced met with widespread enthusiastic reception.

Sylvia, a fan of Vicki's poetry, typed and reproduced Vicki's poem on the office copier, then distributed it among several students who were known by her to be poetry aficionados. Lonnie's raps circulated among rap enthusiasts, promoted by his collaborator, Anthony. Nikia acted as rap adviser and consultant to Lonnie, although she herself did not compose raps. Monique, Theresa and Jan circulated their books of poems among friends, who borrowed them for up to a week at a time. John's biting letters that satirised a teacher and a student enjoyed a wide circulation among City High School students. They were so popular that several students came forward and claimed authorship.

In addition to direct and indirect involvement with writing and the production, publication and dissemination of written texts, adolescents collected, archived and artifacted writing and written texts. Adolescents collected their own texts and those of other adolescents. They also collected texts from magazines, newspapers, greeting cards, textbooks and anthologies, and from other sources as well. These collections were archived, with no regard for provenance or authorship, in books, folders, envelopes, boxes and drawers. Certain texts were artifacts, such as greeting cards and books; others were artifacted, that is, made into books or greeting cards, appended to greeting cards, or transformed into plaques. These collections were very important to adolescents, counted among their most important possessions. Christa willed her collection to Monique, her best friend. When Janet assembled her collection of current writing, she asked her best friend to keep it 'safe' for her. Vicki's self-made book of original poetry circulated among her friends and admirers of her writing.

Vernacular writing process

As suggested by the findings of the literacy project, aspects of cultural process attributed to folk or vernacular culture, such as performance and collaboration, are central to the processes of vernacular writing, where the text is the vehicle for accomplishing culture. Bauman and Bruner have each suggested that performance necessarily entails collaboration by involving the audience directly or indirectly in the construction of the text (Bauman 1987; Bruner 1986). The act of sharing a text with a reader or listener is a kind of performance that makes writing a collaborative venture between author and an audience composed of readers or listeners. The response of this audience to the text often inspires the author to change the text, which then reflects both the contributions of the audience as well as the author.

Performance may occur during drafting, as it does in the construction of personal letters. Partially or wholly composed letters are frequently read aloud to an audience of at least one listener, or given to a reader, who offers advice about rhetorical strategies that is often considered crucial to the effect of the letter upon its intended receiver.

Letter-writing among students at City High School is frequently a collaborative activity, often involving a sharing event that functions as performance. Several of these students read drafts of letters aloud to friends prior to sending them, at which time they receive advice about phrasing, tone and content. Shelly and her friends confer over the composition of 'Dear John' letters, offering advice in the form of comments such as 'No, don't say it like that', or 'Don't write that', because 'it sounds like you want him back'. Christa, whose main mode of communicating with her estranged father is through letter-writing, plans and revises her letters with exacting care, often soliciting advice on wording, spelling and diction. For Christa, each letter is seen as a way to improve their communication, through accurate portrayal of her feelings.

Performance may occur after drafting, as it often does in rap composition, when written rap texts are performed in a rehearsal-like setting. The audience, in this case, often acts in the role of consultant, offering advice about rhyme, diction, and meter, that is later incorporated into the next draft of the rap text. Participants in rap composition recognise that this kind of collaboration will result in a more professional and polished product.

Rap is original verse, composed in rhymed couplets. Although it is intended to be orally performed to the beat of popular music, it is often composed in writing. Adolescent 'rappers' and erstwhile 'rappers' often carry notebooks in which are inscribed their own raps, and in which they record the raps of other amateurs and professionals. A major component of rap composition is the 'rehearsal' performance, in which the rapper tries out his rap orally in front of a small audience of friends.

At rap rehearsals at City High School during free time, students often solicited and received advice from a small audience of editors and 'consultants'. The rap consultant and editor listens to the rapper perform the rap orally, then offers advice about metrical construction and performance, diction, and rhyming. Sometimes, the editor or consultant reads the rap and 'corrects' it, that is, substitutes words that don't sound right, because they aren't in the particular slang vocabulary of the moment, or because they don't rhyme or conform to the meter.

In this way, raps are revised as a result of the feedback rappers receive in these rehearsal/performances. Rap consultants or experts who are often a part of the rehearsal/performance audience, and act as editors of rap texts, enter into collaborative composition with rap composers. The rap rehearsal is more extensive outside of school, however, taking place in informal spaces in students' homes, places where they can have the privacy to rehearse, such as recreation rooms and basements. What takes place in school is only one of many rehearsals, in front of a variety of audiences and 'experts', for the rap is subject to countless revisions and rehearsals until the rapper gets it just right, that is, ready to perform at a party.

The performance of a rap or of a letter is a collaborative venture, engaging audience and author in a critical dialogue. Through that dialogue, the experience of the individual is brought into focus with that of the group, through the interplay between author and audience which reshapes experience for each via the text. Thus, a text is subject not only to the conventional rhetorical strategies that reflect the collectivity of cultural expression, but is often collectively shaped during its actual composition.

This collaboration between author and audience that takes place during the creation of a text points to the role that writing has *vis-à-vis* culture. Sharing texts is an event that is the locus of the experience of the individual author with that of the audience. Sharing or performing texts brings the experience of the individual into focus with the group. The performance of the text and the response of the reader/listener/audience to the text of individual experience has the effect of reshaping experience for both the author and the audience.

Vernacular texts

The vernacular writing of adolescents constitutes a non-canonical literature marked by both its play with the conventions of folk as well as formal literature. The style, structure, and content of this literature frequently result in innovations to the traditional genres. It is a body of literature composed of cultural material that is appropriated and reassembled in vernacular and often creolised formats.

Two vernacular formats are the result of 'patchwork' and 'mosaic', composing techniques employed by adolescent writers which date to the middle ages (Bakhtin 1986). In the case of both patchwork and mosaic, texts are constructed through the appropriation of words and phrases from oral tradition, popular culture or literary texts. The mosaic technique is differentiated from patchwork in that mosaic texts are constructed entirely from materials appropriated from various cultural sources, while patchwork texts are original to the author with occasional insertions of appropriated material.

Mosaic

Help! I need somebody! Help! Not just anybody! Help! I need somebody now. Lady love never smiles so lend your love to me a while, do with me what you will, break the spell and take your fill. On and on we rode the storm the flame's back and the fire's gone, on this empty bed is a night alone, I realized that long ago. Is anybody out there? Is anybody there? does anybody wonder? Does anybody care?[6]

Patchwork

Dad's Obstacle Course

Why do you confuse me so?
So many questions unanswered, untold
Should I stay or should I go?
Which way is up?
(I think you went down.)
Where's the door 'gotta get out of here.[7]

In each of these examples, borrowed lyrics, phrases and words refer to their sources implicitly, combining in a way that is both original to the writer and derivative of others. Patchwork and mosaic are examples of vernacular authoring techniques by which culture is reorganised by the individual through the appropriation of its materials.[8]

Another composing technique that resulted in the creation of vernacular formats is merging two or more genres or by embedding one genre into another. An example of the former is the poem/letter, in which the poem is framed by the letter format, and poetic diction substitutes for conversational prose narrative. An example of the latter is the embedding of a poem, popular song lyrics or a rap into a letter.

Functions of vernacular writing

Adolescents act on experience by writing it. They control, shape, and manipulate its properties – time, space, and inhabitants – through texts and their use.

Adolescents actively seek to change experience through writing, to act upon it by creating alternative realms through their texts. For example, Angela and Jeanette write when they are bored or don't 'go out'. Kathy, who is often banished to her room in the evenings as a punishment and is denied use of the telephone, amuses herself by writing. Shelly, who writes when she has 'nothing to do', claims, 'Writing is something to do to fill up your time'. This use of writing transforms experience from empty to full, from isolated to peopled, from inactive to active.

Writing can change the quality of experience by transforming it into something else. Joke and play texts such as the 'Greetings Earthling' letter transform the experience of the classroom into play; short notes, such as 'Dear Reds', provide a structure for conversation when it is disallowed.

Writing can also change the temporal dimension of experience by bringing the past into the present, the writer moving from the immediate world to the world of the text. For example, Laurie and her cousin amuse themselves during boring summer evenings, by composing a list of 'funny things' that happened to them or to other people, or funny things they said or heard. Through the process of compiling the list, the two retrieve the funny experience from the past, and evoke its amusing qualities. Making diary or journal entries during times of boredom, as many adolescent writers do, recalls the events of the day, bringing the more exciting elements of the near past into the present.

Writing can also change the shape of social relationships, especially by encouraging intimacy. One way this can be accomplished is by using writing to open the way towards intimate conversation. Angela writes to a troubled friend, offering support in hopes that her friend will then speak to her about her problems. Jim, Christa's erstwhile suitor, courted her with letters in which he would try to express confusing ideas and feelings. The letter established topics about which they would later talk at length.

Writing also evokes intimacy through the realm of the text. When Danny's relationship with Angela had cooled off, he tried to re-establish his relationship with her by resurrecting the feelings via a letter:

> I know these past couple of months, we really haven't spoken to each other. But I wanna refresh your memory and say, 'I still love you'. Sometimes I get so depressed, just thinking about how much fun we had together, and wishing those years would come back again. You're just, my heart. I know I haven't written in a long time. I guess because I didn't know what to write. Then I said to myself, just write how you feel. And this is how I feel, You are my Shining Star, I'm sure of that.[9]

Shelly hoped to recapture the first fresh feelings of a new relationship by recreating them in a poem/letter she sent to her boyfriend:

> Let's go back in time,
> Let's do it all again.
> Give life a second chance because
> everyone needs a break.
>   Last year we were young,
> We laughed at love and lovers.
> They were so blind. But we
> Soon began to walk hand
> in hand and we slowly began
> to feel what they felt. Our hearts
> grew, for no reason, we would
> cry. For no reason we felt the feelings
> that for so long we only
> laughed about. Now our hearts
> are broken and a part of
> us has died. We are still young
> but no longer children. Now
> We are the ones being laughed
> at. But we know what they
> don't know. Let's go back and
> start again. Love will fool us again.[10]

Writing is both act and text. As an expression of religious feeling, it is both an act and article of faith. In the following letter, Vicki describes her spiritual experiences at a revival meeting at her church. In so doing, she is both 'testifying' (reporting on the experience of faith) and witnessing (experiencing faith).

> Salvation was sought after by the old and the young. Little girls and boys walked down the aisle with tears in their eyes, looking for Jesus and they found him. He was definitely there. His presence could be found all over.[11]

Meaning

Writing is perceived by adolescents to be powerful, in that it can alter experience in a variety of ways. They also believe that writing, when it comes from 'within', is 'telling the truth'. Because adolescents believe that in writing they express their 'true' inner selves, that texts are the renderings of the 'true' person, they often see texts as talismans of the self. Christa, for example, describes written texts as a 'piece of oneself'. This attitude about writing is reflected in the importance of the practice of keeping texts in collections, of giving them as gifts, and even of willing them to best friends. Vicki gave the following poem to a friend as a gift, because, as she explains, 'it comes from within', where love resides, and is therefore a 'gift of love'.

> ### Gift of Love
>
> I didn't have the money
> To buy you a real gift
> But I had the thought
> It took to write you this . . .
>
> A gift that's bought with money
> Isn't at all the best
> And a gift that comes from within
> Is much better than the rest
>
> The best gift of all
> That I'll ever have to give
> Is my gift of love
> And to you this gift I give.[12]

More importantly, adolescents believe that writing is a way to find meaning, or truth, through the act of writing itself. Jill describes what it feels to find meaning when she is writing poetry, as 'feeling inspired', having newly discovered the words to better understand a thought or a feeling. For Christa, writing can lead her out of confusion into understanding: 'Writing helps you figure things out'.

Writing is not only a vehicle for finding meaning, it creates meaning out of the existential void, as Laurie suggests in this excerpt from a letter:

> Don't ask me why I'm writing because I don't even know. It seems I don't know anything anymore. There's so much confusion in my head and I don't even know what I'm confused about. So here I am at 3:00 in the morning just listening to the radio and smoking cigarette after cigarette. Something inside of me is yearning to come out and I don't know what it is.[13]

Conclusion

In conversations with adolescents about their writing, and through reading their texts, I came to understand better the ways in which writing figures in adolescent social life – as a part of conversation, a mode of self-disclosure, a personal statement and monument to the individual. I saw that personal and creative writing is a motion towards intimacy, and that its exchange weaves the strands of friendship and understanding.

For adolescents, writing, thinking, talking and feeling are interconnected activities, multiple channels and levels of discourse upon a topic. Talking with me about their personal lives when we were supposed to be talking about writing was not a divergence from the task, but in fact, exemplified the way that writing was connected to the rest of their lives.

Adolescents express their inner life through writing, believing that in the act of writing they are telling the truth about themselves. Writing invents and authenticates the individual through the process of discovery, inscribing the experience of the individual in time, and becoming a souvenir of that experience.

The vernacular writing of adolescents is cultural dialogue, a discourse that shifts back and forth among ideas and texts, fashioning experience discursively. For Edward Bruner, culture, or society, is constituted by the public performance (through texts) of the individual apprehension of experience (1986). The text, according to Bruner, stands in a dialogic relationship to the individual and society: it is constructed by the individual, who, through the public performance of the text, constructs society, which, in turn, influences the construction of the text on the individual level.

For adolescents, writing is personal and social, an act of invention in which everyday actions are shaped and influenced by the content and by the symbolic value of written texts. Adolescents appropriate cultural materials and incorporate and transform them into their own written texts. They collaborate with other individuals in the construction of those texts. And they work out their identities against the experience of others through performance or publication of their texts.

Adolescent writing acts upon and shapes experience through public performance, or publication. Adolescents know that writing is transformative, and that their writing practices, both social and artistic, are influenced by that knowledge. This knowledge is a mutually-shared frame of reference which informs the traditions which surround the production and practice of writing.

Notes

1 For Edward Bruner (1986), culture, or society, is negotiated through the public performance of texts which represent the individual apprehension of experience. The text represents at least one version of experience to society created by the individual, who, through the public performance of the text, constructs society, which, in turn, influences the construction of the text on the individual level.

2 Bruner (1986) suggests that the term 'experience' represents the individual's apprehension of reality; that 'expression' represents the 'framing' and 'articulation' of individual experience into texts and that the enactments or performances of texts (expressions) accomplish culture.

3 Intercepted in class during the early stages of my fieldwork.

4 Classroom correspondence, from writing collection, 1984.

5 Kenneth Goldstein (1972) develops the concept of repertory using the example of song texts and demonstrates the ways a text can figure in the repertory of a singer. Some of those ways are as traditions remembered but not performed, known but not every one having been performed, relearned for current performance, and currently performed. Goldstein discusses the disappearance of certain texts from performance traditions that are nonetheless available for performance should the situation merit it. This idea is particularly useful in understanding that literacy and the texts of literacy are subject to circumstance and setting in the same way that song texts are in Goldstein's example. Moreover, I make the suggestion that performance entails not just the duplication of a text, but additionally, knowledge about its form, style and content.

6 Student's writing collection, 1982.

7 Student's writing collection, 1982.

8 For a discussion of the disappearance or death of the author, see Foucault 1977: 113–38, 'What is an author', and Barthes 1977: 142–8, 'The death of the author'.

9 Angela's writing collection, 1983.

10 Shelly's writing collection, 1982.

11 Vicki's notebook, 1983.

12 Vicki's writing collection, 1981.

13 Letter to the researcher, 1983.

References

Bakhtin, M. M. 1986. *The dialogic imagination: four essays*, ed. M. Holquist. Trans. C. Emerson and M. Holquist. Austin: University of Texas Press. (First published 1981).

Barthes, R. 1977. *Image, music, text*. Trans. S. Heath. New York: Hill and Wang.
Basso, K. 1974. 'The ethnography of writing', in R. Bauman and J. Scherzer (eds.), *Explorations in the ethnography of speaking*. New York: Cambridge University Press.
Bauman, R. 1987. *Text, story and event*. Cambridge: Cambridge University Press.
Brodkey, L. 1986. 'Tropics of literacy', *Journal of Education*, 68 (2): 47–54.
Bruner, E. M. 1986. 'Experience and its expressions', in V. W. Turner and E. M. Bruner (eds.), *The anthropology of experience*, pp. 3–32. Chicago: University of Illinois Press.
Camitta, M. P. 1987. *Invented lives: adolescent vernacular writing and the construction of experience*. Philadelphia, PA: University of Pennsylvania.
Cook-Gumperz, J. and Gumperz, J. J. 1981. 'From oral to written culture: the transition of literacy', *Writing: the nature, development and teaching of written communication*, vol. 3 of *Variation in writing: functional and linguistic cultural differences*, pp. 80–109. Baltimore, MD: Lawrence Erlbaum.
Eco, U. 1979. *The role of the reader: explorations in the semiotics of texts*. Bloomington, IA: Indiana University Press.
Elbow, P. 1973. *Writing without teachers*. Oxford: Oxford University Press.
Emig, J. 1971. *The composing process of twelfth graders*. Urbana: Research Report no. 13, NCTE.
    1977. 'Writing as a mode of learning', in *College composition and communication*. Hillsdale, NJ: Lawrence Erlbaum.
    1981. 'Non-magical thinking', in *Writing: process, development and communication*. NCTE 28, no. 3.
Foucault, M. 1977. *Language, counter-memory and practice: selected essays and interviews*. Trans. D. F. Bouchard. New York: Cornell University Press.
Gilmore, P. and Smith, D. 1982. 'A retrospective discussion of the state of the art in ethnography and education', in *Children in and out of school: ethnography and education*. Washington, DC: Center for Applied Linguistics.
Goldstein, K. 1972. 'On the application of the concepts of active and inactive traditions to the study of repertory', in A. Paredes and R. Bauman (eds.), *Towards new perspectives in folklore*. Austin: University of Texas Press.
Heath, S. B. 1978. 'Outline guide for the ethnographic study of literacy and oral language from schools to communities', *Working Papers in Language and Education*, no. 2. Philadelphia: Graduate School of Education, University of Pennsylvania.
    1982. 'Ethnography in education: defining the essentials', in *Children in and out of school: ethnography and education*. Washington, DC: Center for Applied Linguistics.
Hymes, D. 1982. 'What is ethnography?', in P. Gilmore and A. A. Glatthorn (eds.), *Children in and out of school*. Washington, DC: Center for Applied Linguistics.
Scollon, R. and Scollon, S. B. K. 1981. 'The modern consciousness and literacy', *Narrative, literacy and face in interethnic Communication*. Norwood, NJ: Ablex.
Scribner, S. and Cole, M. 1981. 'Unpacking literacy', in M. F. Whiteman (ed.),

Writing: the nature, development and teaching of written communication, vol. 3 of *Variation in writing: functional and linguistic cultural differences*. Baltimore, MD: Lawrence Erlbaum.

1981. *The psychology of literacy*. Cambridge, MA: Harvard University Press.

Smith, B. H. 1983. 'Contingencies of values', *Critical Inquiry*, 10: 1–35.

Sutton-Smith, B. 1970. 'Psychology of children's folklore: the triviality barrier', *Western Folklore*, 29: 1–8.

Szwed, J. F. 1981. 'The ethnography of literacy', in *Writing: the nature, development, and teaching of written communication*, vol. 3 of *Variation in writing: functional and lingustic cultural differences*. Baltimore, MD: Lawrence Erlbaum.

10

COLLABORATIVE WRITING: APPROPRIATING
POWER OR REPRODUCING AUTHORITY?

AMY SHUMAN

Literacy has become a name for many issues, including the invention of modernity, the invention of history or technology, the representative of education in general, or a name for a privileged domain of culture. In previous work, I have tried to undermine the force of this all-encompassing term; specifically I have tried to redescribe literacy as a problem of standardization, entitlement to rights, and appropriations of power. I have argued that it was not writing at all that transformed the world both cognitively and socially, but standardization.

I have taken as the focus for my discussion collaborative writing, both because some scholars have suggested that collaborative writing offers an alternative to the configuration of authority found in single-authored texts and because the collaborative writings I collected involved explicit contests about reputation. Many scholars contend that literacy is best investigated within the context of discourse systems as a whole (Gee 1988: 37). Along these lines, collaborative writing provides one opportunity for investigating literacy within the context of the social relationships that provide the context for interpreting any text.

In *Storytelling Rights*, I describe the uses of writing and speaking in the everyday lives of urban adolescents. By the 'everyday' here, I refer to non-standard uses of both writing and speaking.[1] Among the adolescents, what I found was that the differences between writing and speaking were a matter of use rather than style or form. Writing was used to appeal to an authoritative voice (in the use of fill-in forms, especially, or in petitions) and to say things that could not be said face-to-face. The adolescent uses of speaking and writing challenged the idea that writing is used to create authoritative distance and speaking is a face-to-face or proximate activity. I found that the adolescents used both writing and speaking for both distance and proximity. I then argued that the kind of writing that often stands for literacy is only one kind of writing, a privileged form, and that the real issue in discussions of literacy is not how writing creates the possibility for a kind of cognitive distance (which I showed was equally available to speakers), but how particular forms of writing have been designated as privileged. Thus the questions of rights, or entitlements, are implicit in any discussion of literacy. In my larger study of writing and speaking in the everyday life of adolescents, collaboratively produced writings provided an example of how writing can be part of face-to-face communication (Shuman 1986). From 1979–81, I 'attended' a Philadelphia junior high school and collected writings produced by the students as part of their everyday interactions.[2] (I also recorded daily talk and storytelling, not discussed here.) Almost all of their writing was collaborative; some of these collaborations brought students together to contest, negotiate, or manipulate adult authority, and other collaborations reproduced or played with adult authoritative discourse.

Collaborative written play

In my larger work, I distinguished between writing interactions in terms of the kinds of authoritative relationships involved.[3] For example, I characterised the students' forged notes to school authorities as deceptive writing in which both students and teachers were complicit participants in an implicitly understood system. As long as students complied with the formal expectations of the genre of notes (excuse plus signature), the authenticity of the signature was not challenged. Authenticity was not challenged as long as authoritative relationships were maintained, both through the respectful interactions in which students presented notes to authorities as a means to legitimise their (the students') actions and through adherence to the formal conventions of the note.

Writing forged notes often involved collaboration. Forgery required the ability to copy, both the mechanical copying of a signature and the appropriate copying of the type of message an adult might write. This effort often required collaboration, as it was safer to ask a friend to imitate the adult's handwriting since the adolescents understood the first premise of successful forged notes to be that they were not to have been written in one's own hand. The main goal was to avoid the charge that 'you wrote this yourself'.

The adolescents also appropriated adult forms in their collaborative playful writing with each other. As in the forged notes to adults, in this type of exchange the form itself retained authority; adherence to the requirements of the genre was the only necessary guarantee of authenticity.[4]

The adolescents' playful writing characteristically involved face-to-face exchanges in which they read aloud, filled in forms, and made handwritten copies of texts. If, instead of assuming the categories of speaking and writing, we describe a continuum between proximate and distant communication, playful collaborative writing could be described as proximate and as adhering to the same social conventions as proximate (face-to-face) oral exchanges. Typically, the girls sat together in the school lunchroom and produced written texts. For example, they brought question-

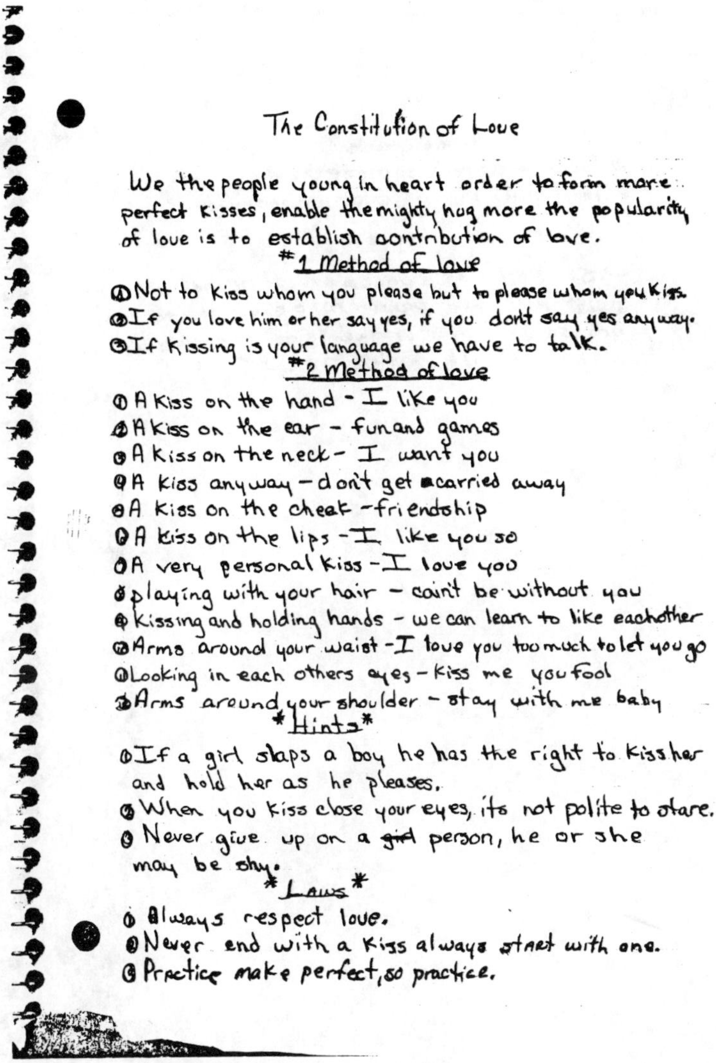

The Constitution of Love

We the people young in heart order to form more
perfect kisses, enable the mighty hug more the popularity
of love is to establish contribution of love.
    #1 Method of love

① Not to kiss whom you please but to please whom you kiss.
② If you love him or her say yes, if you don't say yes anyway.
③ If kissing is your language we have to talk.
    #2 method of love

① A kiss on the hand - I like you
② A kiss on the ear - fun and games
③ A kiss on the neck - I want you
④ A kiss anyway - don't get carried away
⑤ A kiss on the cheek - friendship
⑥ A kiss on the lips - I like you so
⑦ A very personal kiss - I love you
⑧ playing with your hair - cain't be without you
⑨ Kissing and holding hands - we can learn to like eachother
⑩ Arms around your waist - I love you too much to let you go
⑪ Looking in each others eyes - kiss me you fool
⑫ Arms around your shoulder - stay with me baby
    * Hints *

① If a girl slaps a boy he has the right to kiss her
and hold her as he pleases.
② When you kiss close your eyes, its not polite to stare.
③ Never give up on a girl person, he or she
may be shy.
    * Laws *

① Always respect love.
② Never end with a kiss always start with one.
③ Practice make perfect, so practice.

Figure 10.1(a) 'The Constitution of Love'.

naires (one was from a book by Ann Landers) to the lunchroom where
they copied the text and discussed and wrote down their answers. 'The
Constitution of Love and Amendments' (figures 10.1(a) and (b)) was also
written in the school lunchroom; one girl brought her handwritten copy
to the table, and a group of girls took turns reading the text to the girl who
made the copy shown here.

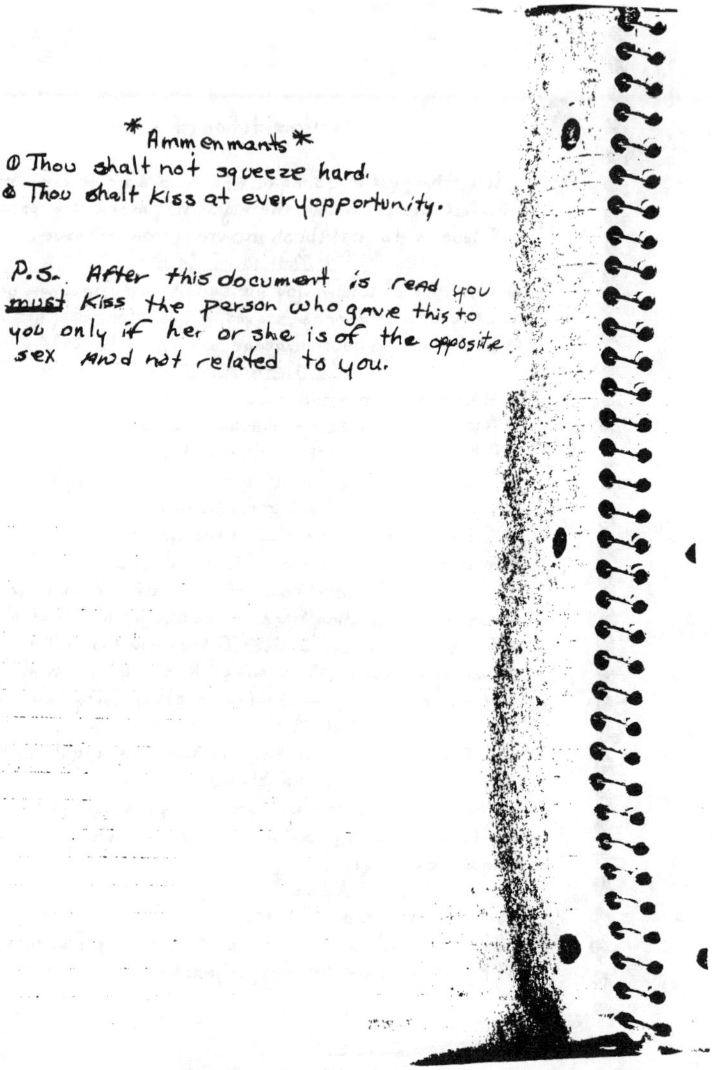

> * Ammenmants *
> ① Thou shalt not squeeze hard.
> ② Thou shalt kiss at every opportunity.
>
> P.S. After this document is read you
> ~~must~~ kiss the person who gave this to
> you only if her or she is of the opposite
> sex and not related to you.

Figure 10.1(b) 'Ammenmants'.

Most of the adolescents' collaborative playful writing involved a question followed by a reply. The Ann Landers questionnaires provided questions and the students replied. Signatures on The Constitution of Love could be seen as a variety of this sort of form plus response. Similarly, letter writing followed the request and response format.

Letter writing was, at its most playful, a collaborative endeavour in

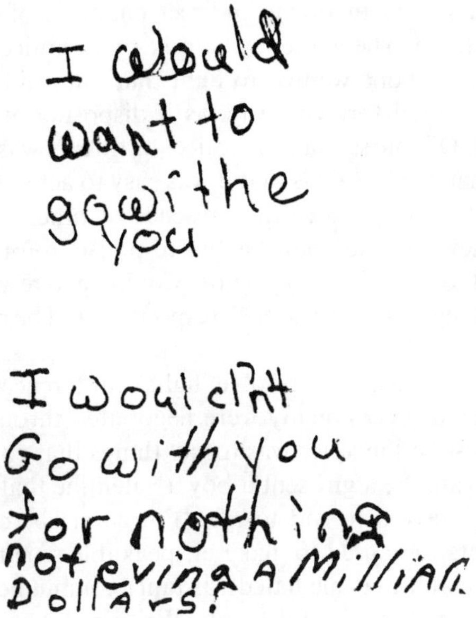

I would
want to
go with
you

I wouldn't
Go with you
for nothing
not eving a Million
Dollars?

Figure 10.2 Both sides of a scrap of paper.

which friends looked on as someone composed a message. The more obvious the collaboration of the letter, the less likely would a message be taken seriously, even if the boy and girl liked each other. For example, friends looked on as a boy in the class wrote 'I would want to go with you', on a scrap of paper (figure 10.2) and passed it to a girl in the class, who wrote on the other side 'I wouldn't go with you for nothing not eving [sic] a million dollars'.[5] Both sides of the paper were seen as competing acts of bravery. Letter writing followed a question and reply pattern whether the message was love or a fight challenge.

Writing things that could not be said

Written notes were sometimes used to send threatening messages and most often were stuffed anonymously into school lockers. The authors were not making challenges in their own names but instead were reporting on someone else's purported threats, in the form of so-and-so wants to fight you. The recipient rarely responded directly to such distanced communication and more often sent an indirect verbal response back through the rumour network. Even notes signed by the challenger were considered cowardly since they were not made face-to-face. Whereas written notes were discredited for their indirect channel of communication, verbal rumours, also involving indirect channels of communication, had great credence. The adolescents took more notice of a third party oral report that someone wanted to fight than they did of written notes. The notes were often thrown away, as if disposing of the paper disposed of the threat. Of course, 'taking notice' of threats was itself part of the event, and all that can be said is that it was easy to act as if one took no notice of written threats (read in the presence of others), but more difficult to have whatever would count as 'no response' to oral reports. The closest equivalent to throwing away a note would be to respond, 'So?' to the report of a challenge, and even a 'So?' response could be reported to the challenger.

While writing was not used to resolve fights, differences between boyfriends and girlfriends occasionally were negotiated through letters. In this case, the purpose of the letter was to say things that could not be said in person. (For example, a girl sent a boy a valentine that said, 'I'm sorry.' The boy who received it said to me, 'I'm gonna be cool about this.') Apologetic letters were used to make unspeakable remarks.

Face-to-face (proximate) and mediated (distant) communication had different consequences among the adolescents. Writing was one means to avoid the consequences of a face-to-face challenge. Using writing to say things that could not be said in person was a way of mediating communication and thereby minimising or deterring confrontations. This is not to say that writing was privileged or preferred; it simply played the role of go-between or mediator.[6] Mediation among the adolescents was quite literal, so that in orally transmitted messages, blame often shifted to the messenger; hostilities shifted from one of the disputants in a quarrel to a new quarrel about the entitlement of the message bearer to have transmitted the message. Similarly, in writing, the written message could become the target of hostilities, and the original problem could become subsumed by a new problem focused on writing as indirect and, usually, cowardly. I am suggesting that mediated communication of this kind is a form of collaboration, and although it makes collaboration look dangerous (one is always in danger of moving from the periphery, as message bearer, to the centre, as a target, of a dispute), we can see that for adolescents, anyway, collaboration was always about entitlement and participants were always responsible for, and potentially subject to, challenges about their participation.

The girls used writing to express things that could not be said, both in letters and in personal diaries. The letter writing, like the collaborative playful writing, was characterised by appropriations of, and adherence to, adult written forms. In contrast, the diary entries were closer to conversation.

The following letter, part of a National Letter Writing Week class assignment, was written by a seventh grade white girl to her white friend. It ended with a statement of affection that would not be conveyed face-to-face (Line breaks from original)

> Dear Josie,
> Hi, How are you doing. Do you go
> with John yet or are you
> still metting him he is cute
> what do you and John do
> do you go to his house yet
> aint his father Little when
> I first seen him I said who
> is he. and his mother said
> Tina this is you cousin John
> This is Tina and when he
> came up he said Look who
> I meet Mona. This bigger
> nurse came in chewing like
> a cow and he said Look
> at that cow. does he know
> your teacher is a nut. I
> hope you two go together. you
> and John will make a good
> match. I think Kitty likes
> you a lot. One day I want
> to hang with you. If
> you want to hang with me
> P.S.   Your Best
>
> write   Friend
>
> back   Tina
>
> Thomas

Tina's letter used many of the conventions of the white teenage girls' speech. Everything in the letter except the salutations and the last line could have been said as part of the daily conversation in the lunch room. The last two lines, 'One day I want to hang with you. If you want to hang with me', are statements of intimacy and betray the closing 'Your Best Friend' as a wish rather than a reality. 'Best friends' could be defined as people who said things to each other in confidence.

Tina's use of a spoken sentence structure in her letter could be attributed more to her lack of awareness of rules of standard written grammar than to a choice. Those students who did know how to use rules of standard written grammar made great efforts to use them in writing.

The writing activity that most closely reproduced speech in written form was the girls' diaries, an example of adolescent writing that did not involve face-to-face interaction, was not produced collaboratively, and was not read aloud. Many of the diary entries included quoted speech, and some, including Stacie's entry, reproduced below, used quotation marks for some reported speech. The entry is, in large part, the report of a conversation, and it provides the kind of detail one might expect in a he-said-she-said report of a dispute. At the same time, as a diary entry not intended for any audience, it was not part of the dispute, and though it may be governed by the conventions of conveying an argument, it was not part of an argument. In all of the other domains of written communication I was able to observe, writing and speaking were not only jointly constrained (that is that the conventions of one governed the other), but also jointly produced. Writing was produced in the cultural (conventional) context of what could or could not be said and often in the interaction context of a face-to-face oral collaboration.

The following diary entry, written by Stacie, a Black eighth grader, describes a dispute, but unlike orally told accounts of disputes, the diary entry was not written as part of an ongoing dispute. Whereas the oral accounts were often offered to provoke antagonists, to instigate or accelerate quarrels, or to resolve disputes, the private written diary account of what happened did not play a role in the interaction. In fact, Stacie rarely wrote about fights in her diary, and it seems that she considered diary writing to be far enough removed from her familiar contexts for discussing fights that she mentions that she had not been writing because her friends have been fighting.

> I think Marie and Linda
> is going to fight with Rose. I'll get
> back with you. Rose is going to get
> it bad. I'm only writing for a little
> while. Okay. Rose has scratches
> and they are realy red.
>
> I'm a little up set
> over Marie and Rose fighting
> That's why I haven't been writing.

Whereas fighting encouraged talking, and disputes did not 'count' for enhancing or discrediting reputation unless they were talked about, writing was not at all essential for disputes. Still, some of the adolescents' writing did concern fighting, especially in the form of threatening or warning notes.[7] Orally told fight stories were essential to fights, and in many cases they were more essential than a physical conflict. In other words, fighting words were enough to categorise an interaction as a fight.

Collaborative writing in the classroom

The written examples discussed above were produced primarily by adolescents for adolescents. The adolescents also did a great amount of writing that was intended for adults, and this writing followed different conventions to meet the expectations of another, yet familiar, audience. The adolescents demonstrated awareness of their audiences in non-classroom playful writing in which they often imitated adult forms. Playful use of adult-world genres, such as the questionnaire, demanded adherence to the conventions of the borrowed form. In contrast, the diaries and letters often reproduced, in written form, conventions of the adolescents' speech. In order to understand the constraints that characterised these different manners of writing and thus to see the writings as responding to different conventions appropriate to the different purposes, rather than as ill-formed or awkward in comparison to an adult standard, it is useful to investigate each genre of adolescent writing in terms of particular understanding (and demonstrated awareness) of the relationship between the sender and recipient. The writings exchanged between adolescents included the question-response, collaborative creations, playful documents read aloud to an audience of participant-listeners, and descriptions of actual occurrences. Generic and situational constraints varied most widely between those texts produced by and exchanged between adolescents and those texts either created by adults for adolescents or created by adolescents for adults.

The adolescents engaged in a great variety of writing for adults. It would be a mistake to see these writings as the prototype for all writing and thus to see the writings by adolescents for each other as take-offs or transformations of the system. According to such a perspective, the writings by adolescents for each other would always appear to be imitations of an established order. This producer-consumer model of literacy,[8] in which single authors write for other, distant, audiences more often than collaboratively or for familiar audiences, may provide the most pronounced forms of standardisation, but it is not necessarily the umbrella within which all textual exchanges should be considered.

The adolescents wrote for adults most often at school, and most of their classroom activities combined writing and speaking. Oral performances could not be submitted for evaluation and thus were rarely counted in the assessment of a student's 'work' for a class; nor was it clear what was expected of oral performance. A wrong oral answer

Figure 10.3 School classwork mimeo. (Copyright Scholastic Book Service. All rights reserved. Reproduction permission must be requested from original publishers.)

counted as class participation while a wrong written answer received no credit.

Much of the written work for teachers consisted of filling in forms. Teachers distributed 'worksheets' which usually consisted of sentences with blank spaces to be filled in by students (see figure 10.3). The teachers composed some of the worksheets themselves; many were supplied by the textbook companies which provided them already printed on mimeograph masters for duplication.

The teacher whom I observed most frequently used worksheets for almost every class, and most of his class time was devoted to filling in the worksheet as a collaborative effort. The teacher read the questions, and students raised their hands or were called upon to supply the answers. Many of his worksheets involved puzzles, and figuring out how to follow instructions was part of the work itself. Certain kinds of writing activities dominated classrooms, including writing sentences for spelling words, filling in blanks on worksheets, writing summaries of newspaper articles, writing specific answers to specific questions, answering true/false questions, and doing puzzles.

Fill-in forms teach a particular mode of writing and require not only an understanding of the genre but also a certain kind of interaction. The purpose of the worksheets, according to the teacher, was not so much to measure the students' understanding of the material as to ensure their participation in the lesson. The worksheet gave the students something to do and paced their participation throughout the lesson.

Worksheets controlled not only the subject of a lesson but also the time spent on each subject.[9] Like turn-taking, fill-in forms involved a measured relationship between participants, in this case a question and a response. However, in the classroom the response is pre-established not only in content but also in the space allowed. Each question on the worksheet represented a segment of time; the amount of time spent answering the question corresponded to the amount of time spent considering the subject. Further, the worksheets involved a logical progression from one point to the next. Although it was not always necessary to answer one question before proceeding to the next, the questions were organised according to the sequence of the lesson. One of the benefits of the worksheets, according to the teacher, was that they set up a situation in which individual students could offer oral answers to the teacher's questions and in which all of the students could participate by writing the answers on their own worksheets. Only a few people spoke; everyone wrote.

The teacher's preference for using worksheets was based on the quality of student participation rather than on the quality of writing demanded by the worksheet. The forms required the conceptualisation of answers in the form of single words or brief phrases rather than long explanations and the formation of answers rather than questions. The students' oral answers were treated as guesses, and guessing was always welcomed. In fact, the students described the enterprise as 'guessing an answer'. The wrong answers were simply acknowledged in the teacher's typical response: 'No, does anyone else have an answer?' Often, the teacher wrote the entire worksheet on the blackboard and filled in the answers along with the students as the lesson progressed. Students could participate by filling in answers on their own worksheets without attempting their own answers. In a classroom in which holding students' attention was a major challenge, the teacher found that he could encourage participation by all of the students by giving them the worksheet to fill in. Indeed, this teacher was clearly the most successful I observed in keeping the students' attention on the task. The teacher believed that if he could keep the students' attention, he was doing all he could to encourage the students to learn the material. Since he could not ensure attention to lecture-type lessons, he lectured through his worksheets. He made all of his statements into rhetorical questions in which students were asked to anticipate the correct answer to fill in the missing piece of a statement. He encouraged certain directions in the guessing by offering clues, and the students who gave correct answers had at least the pleasure of a correct guess and sometimes the knowledge that they had followed a line of reasoning to the answer. They learned by participating, and the teacher's method provided flexibility in degrees of participation.

A characteristic of fill-in forms is that the purpose of writing is to make an incomplete piece into a complete piece whose completeness is defined a priori by the form. The person who fills in the form is not the author but is instead an instrument of completion. Forms allow little room for equivocation or ambiguity; they discourage tangential questions. It is not possible to answer a question on a form with a question. In their own writing, in contrast to the writing produced for teachers, the adolescents were the authors of their forms, but the concept of the form as fixed and requiring responses to questions dominated much of their playful writing. The influence worked both ways, of course, and just as classroom forms seeped into play, play with forms contributed to the students' familiarity with use of forms in the classroom.

Collaborative writing in the family

Reading and writing tasks were not equally distributed in the adolescents' families, and responsibilities differed both according to an assessment of what was an appropriate way to spend one's time and in terms of who had the necessary skills. The adolescents did more reading and writing at home than people of other ages, and other age-groups were considered either too young or too busy with other things to spend time reading or writing. Many of the adolescents entered contests through the mail or participated in mail-order sales programmes in which they bought stationery and received cash or points toward prizes for selling the products. The mail-order sales programme offered one of the few opportunities for employment for the adolescents. (Other jobs included babysitting, doing neighbourhood errands, or selling pretzels or flowers on street corners.) Sometimes several members of a family participated in mail-order sales programmes, but the adolescents usually took responsibility for corresponding with the companies.

Many of the Puerto Rican girls took responsibility in their families and community for reading English and translating texts into spoken Spanish. They filled in forms for medical or governmental offices, and a few who could write in Spanish as well as English also wrote their own personal letters to relatives in Puerto Rico.

Adolescent uses of writing involved a hierarchical and complementary system in many of the collaborative writings with teachers and families and a duplicative system in collaborative writings of adolescents among themselves.[10] In writing with adults, the adolescents had a specific role determined by both deference to authority and the assignment of particular tasks. Particularly in their roles as interpreters, the Puerto Rican adolescents performed specialised tasks that were not duplicated by other members of the family. Ordinarily, teenage girls would not be involved in family business of this kind, and their participation as translators sometimes disrupted the social conventions for appropriate age behaviour. All of the teenage girls, black, white, and Puerto Rican, had responsibilities at home, but such assignments did not conflict, as did Puerto Rican translating tasks, with either one's social role in the family or attendance at school. Girls who stayed home to help when a parent was sick tended to be those who preferred not to go to school. The Puerto Rican girls whose skills were needed as translators were most often the best students who otherwise did not miss school and who saw their assistance with translation as a necessary choice between family and school responsibilities.

In duplicative collaborative literacy, including the playful collaborations among adolescents, the participants assumed that everyone had access to the skills necessary for both reading and interpreting texts. The adolescents assumed shared understanding at all levels, including the content of the message, the conventions of the forms, and entitlement and other social constraints on use.

Collaborative literacy activities do not necessarily imply the presence of the author. In hierarchical complementary reading and writing situations, involving relations between the adolescents and either teachers or family adults, the author of the text was distant or even anonymous, both socially and conceptually. To a certain extent, distant authored texts required collaboration, as if an intermediary helped to bridge the distance. The distance between authors and readers is created in many ways, in social status, time, or space, and temporal distance includes not only texts produced by one generation and read by another but also any text saved over time, even those written and later re-read by the author. Proximity similarly depends upon the constraints that shape the collaboration, and, of course, none of these relationships is based on texts themselves. Since distant relationships between readers and authors usually require that the text has been conserved in some way, the means for discarding or preserving texts is part of the ways distance and proximity are constructed. These constructions change, and, for example, a text created in proximity can later become part of distant communication.

Collaborative writing as resistance to authority

Collaboration provides an alternative to the situation in which a single author takes responsibility for the creation of a text, but multiple authorship does not in itself provide any guarantees of a change in the configuration of power relationships. The roles are negotiable in both oral and written communication. In oral exchanges, as Erving Goffman has put it, the 'animator', the person who speaks the words, is not necessarily the same as the author, and words can take their authority from the capacity assigned to the animator (1974: 518). In the discussion that follows, I will consider how the alignment between the authors and other participants, the tasks they manage, their access to knowledge, and the distribution of status among them, correspond to relations of power and authority.

I have described differences in the distribution of status and skills in terms of a distinction between duplicative and hierarchical collaboration. To examine this distinction further, I will now turn to a student petition, a genre of adolescent collaboration that combines many of the characteristics already discussed. Like much of the adolescent playful writing, the petition consisted of a formal message plus signatures. It was an example of duplicative collaboration, in which the participants assumed shared skills and shared understandings. The students appropriated an adult form to communicate with adults; petitions, by definition, involve a collaborative appeal made by a subordinate group to an authority.

Petitions require negotiation of both the rules of the collaborators and the rules of the authorities and thus are especially useful for understanding the ways in which collaboration can be an alternative to authoritative discourse.[11] Whether a petition reinstates or subverts the authoritative hierarchies depends not on the means of collaboration but on who successfully appropriates what.

The petition (figure 10.4(a) and (b)) was drafted to protest the principal's decision to exclude a particular act from the annual school talent show. The use of a collaborative process to disrupt hierarchical decision-making is one form of writing as resistance, but the non-hierarchical

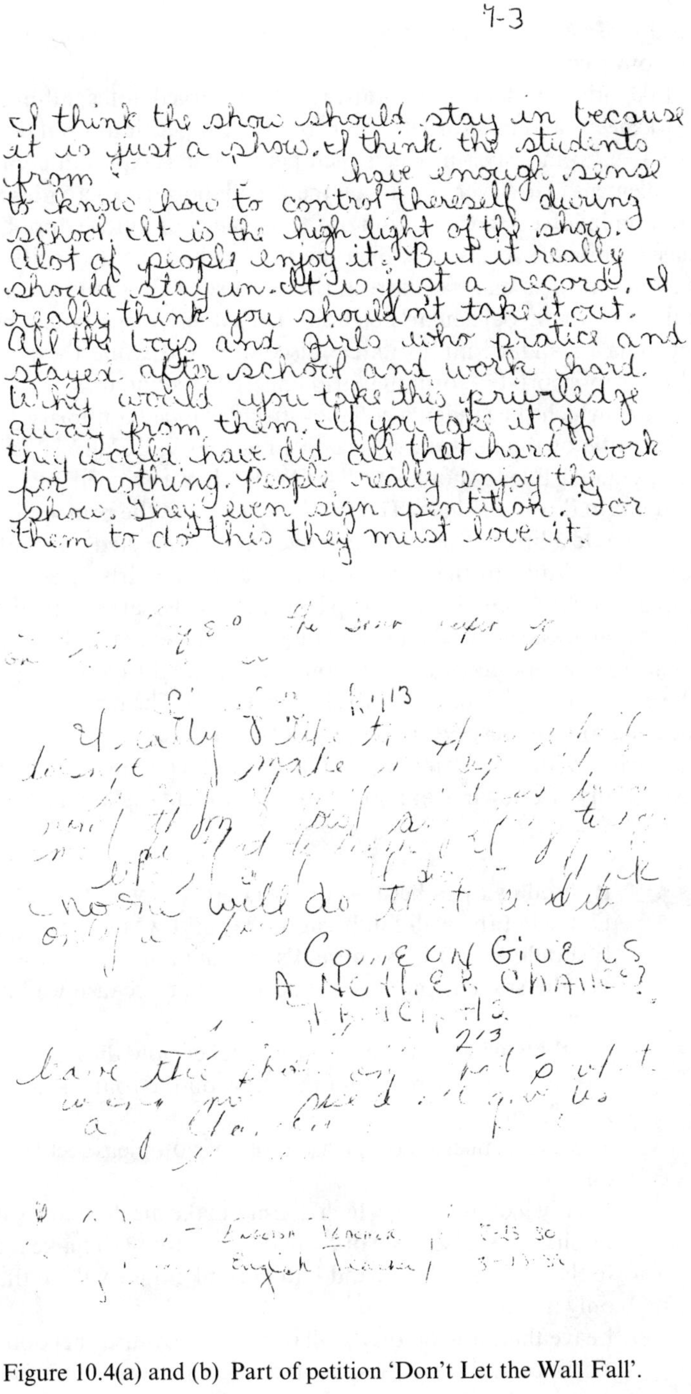
7-3

I think the show should stay in because it is just a show. I think the students from have enough sense to know how to control thereself during school. It is the high light of the show. Alot of people enjoy it. But it really should stay in. It is just a record. I really think you shouldn't take it out. All the boys and girls who pratice and stayed after school and work hard. Why would you take this priviledge away from them. If you take it off they would have did all that hard work for nothing. People really enjoy the show. They even sign pentition. For them to do this they must love it.

COME ON GIVE US A NOTHER CHANCE?

English Teacher

English Teacher

Figure 10.4(a) and (b) Part of petition 'Don't Let the Wall Fall'.

nature of petitions as a genre does not in itself provide any guarantee of empowerment for the participants.

Like other student collaborative writing (forged notes, fill-in classroom worksheets, and mail-order sales projects), the petition could be described as a central message in which each person's participation contributed a supplement. However, of all of these collaborative activities, only the petition involved the invention of the message, or authorship. Unlike the classroom worksheets, in which the teacher had the authority to decide whether the message was correct, the purpose of the petition was to claim authority for a particular position. The other forms could be said to reproduce standard authoritative discourse, and while the petition was also an appropriated form that also adhered to standards, it was the only genre in which the students collaboratively claimed authority.

The title of the petition was 'Don't Let the Wall Fall,' in reference to the excluded talent show act, 'The Wall'. It was signed by twenty-one students and two teachers. The protest concerned the principal's decision to eliminate a lip-sync act in which five white girls acted out Pink Floyd's song, 'The Wall'. In the performance, four of the girls, dressed in rolled up jeans, t-shirts, and baseball caps on backwards, sat with their feet up at classroom desks, chewed gum, and mouthed the words of the song, played on a cassette tape-recorder. The song is addressed to a teacher, who was played by a fifth girl, dressed in a skirt and heels. The principal considered the song to be disrespectful; the students countered that it was funny and that viewing the performance would not influence them to behave disrespectfully. Following are some of the students' statements from the petition:

> It should stay in because it was good, and won't affect the kids.
> Don't Let the wall fall because that part was good.
> It should be left in because it's the funniest in the show.
> We the student think is not a bad script because we know right from wrong.
> See thats whats wrong with the teacher now they don't give us a change [sic] they must put the show on the rold [sic].
> I'm all for you!
> The show must go on please I beg of you please let the show go on.
> I really like the show which doesn't make me do that to any of my teachers because none of them does anything to make me do that to them. I really like it and I don't think noone will do that and its only a show.
> Leave the show on that's whats wrong now use [sic] don't give us a chance and it won't affect the teachers either.

I think the show should stay in because it is just a show. I think the students from [name of school] have enough sense to know how to control thereself during school. It is the high light of the show. Alot of people enjoy it. But it really should stay in. It is just a record. I really think you shouldn't take it out. All the boys and girls who practice and stayed after school and work hard. Why would you take this priviledge away from them. If you take it off they would have did all that hard work for nothing. People really enjoy the show. They even sign pentition. For them to do this them must love it.

The petition and the excluded performance itself raise a number of issues. The text itself can be considered for the ways it presents its arguments. The statements demand a reader's familiarity with the situation and presume familiarity with the principal's reasoning. The text could be considered what has been termed a contextualised written text that provides too few cues to referents, or it could be seen as a cumulative statement in which individual entries were not meant to be understood apart from the text as a whole.[12]

The performance of 'The Wall', a collaborative act, was the only participation by white students in the talent show, and the act was one of very few possible roles for five white girls in a talent show dominated by very talented black and Puerto Rican dance groups. Until this incident arose, the only criterion for participation in the talent show was good academic standing, including adequate school attendance, and the talent show functioned as an incentive for many students to do their work and attend their classes. None of the five white girls had discipline records, and it was remarkable to everyone, both students and teachers, that they had so successfully integrated themselves in the event that black, white, and Puerto Rican students joined together to protest the principal's action.

The principal had several options for responding to the students, including: no response at all, since he had already stated his position; an oral statement on the public address system used for daily announcements and heard by everyone in the school; a written statement in the daily bulletin distributed to teachers (often including sections to be read to students); direct communication, either oral or written, separately or collaboratively, with the five girls or with the signers of the petition; and the method he chose, a letter to the teacher responsible for organising the talent show. This is the letter he sent:

Alice,
I appreciate the students' concern, but unfortunately, a principal at times must make decisions which are unpopular or even unjust in an effort to accommodate the general welfare.

I feel that this song is inappropriate at this time and in this place

I hope they can substitute another number.

M. L. O'Malley

The principal's letter, although addressed to a specific individual, was a formal statement that could have been made publicly. The content of his statement directly addressed the students' request for a reconsideration, but he made the statement not to them but through their teacher. Similarly, the students could have chosen an intermediary, including the teacher, to speak for them. They could have collaborated on a joint statement signed by all or submitted by a spokesperson. If they had chosen a student spokesperson, a likely choice would have been the person with the neatest handwriting or the best writing skills. The last entry on the petition, written on a separate piece of paper, could have served as a start for a collaborative statement. Instead, the students chose to submit all of their statements together, many with grammatical errors, and the teachers added their names near the end of the document. Presumably the teachers saw the grammatical errors and could have pointed them out or corrected them, but they too participated in the duplicative effort in which all signers wrote, as equals, to an authority.

What was at issue in the petition event was not whether or not certain voices were heard, but what those voices represented and whether those representations counted.[13] When the principal addressed his remarks to the teacher rather than to the students as a group, he was avoiding any possibility of a representative student group. The students were heard, in the sense that the petition was received, but by setting up an intermediary, a teacher, to receive the response to the petition, the principal ensured that the interests of what he called 'general welfare', rather than what he referred to as 'the students' concern' was represented. He purported to speak on behalf of the 'general welfare' and did so in his capacity as an authority representing the interests of the school. Collaborative documents, such as petitions, ostensibly represent a collective voice, but an authority also can make claims that represent a larger good.

The most important consideration in examining the effect of a collaboration (as resisting or complying with authority, or in this case, unsuccessfully resisting authority) is not the mode of interaction, whether democratic, dialogic, or hierarchical, but the claim for representation. Dialogic, or democratic, collaborations can make a claim to represent a consensus, and it is this claim, rather than the fact of collaboration, that is the issue. In the petition event, several representational concerns collided. At the core was a debate about whether a talent-show performance in which students were disrespectful to teachers represented some potential student-teacher interaction at the school. Though he did not put it in these terms, and though he was not suggesting that the song referred in any specific way to that particular school, the principal's argument was that the school could not tolerate a disrespectful representation of itself. The students' claim that the talent show performance did not represent them did not convince him. With the petition, the students claimed to represent themselves as a constituency. It was essential that they chose a collaborative form to make this claim. Unfortunately for them, the principal did not recognise this claim and chose instead to claim himself as authoritative representative for the best interests. Collaborative writing is no less interested, no less positioned, than single-authored writing. To the degree that collaborative writing gets away with the claim to 'naturally' represent a collective, rather than to speak for some contested (and thus disputable, non-natural, interest), it can appear that the collaboration, rather than the successful claim of interests, is subversive.

Collaboration as contextualized communication

Discussions of literacy invite us to consider questions of privileged access to exclusive domains: who claims what rights and who appropriates whose territories. When discussed as a skill, literacy is presented as an open channel of communication, a neutral ground accessible to all, and the only barrier is acquisition of skills. However, the discussion of literacy as a skill obscures the ways in which literacy is used to measure the adequacy of one's communication (as standard or deviant), the particular roles associated with those who claim the right to name the standard and judge the deviance, and the ways in which writers appropriate standard forms in order to communicate a message more persuasively.[14] One alternative to viewing literacy as skills is to view it in terms of genres, each with its own standards and conventions, determined by the kind of interaction between the participants involved in the exchange. Both the focus on skills and the focus on genres consider literacy in terms of interactions between participants, but the skills focus oversimplifies this relationship into a polarised battle between the gate-keepers and an excluded class of people. By focusing on literacy as interaction strategies, we are able to identify other authoritative claims involved in written exchanges.

Each of the genres of writing and speaking displays a different configuration of standardisation, entitlement, and appropriation. I found that much of the adolescent writing was characterised by the appropriation of adult standard forms and that the adolescents attempted to adhere to the standard in most cases as a way of legitimising their communications. This was the case in forged notes addressed to school authorities, in which the students hoped that adherence to the form would disguise the fact of forgery and in the case of the petition, in which students hoped that their message would be taken seriously if presented according to the conventions. In other words, they hoped that a forged note would be accepted as a note and that a petition would be treated as a petition. It is interesting, then, that the legitimacy of the notes was not challenged but that the principal failed to respond to the petition as a petition. One explanation for what happened here is that students and school authorities were complicit in their observation of the conventions of excuse-notes because students were not disrupting any power relationships. However, when the students appropriated the petition as a form of communication, they were also attempting to appropriate the authoritative power associated with the petitions (the right to protest), and this role was rejected.

I have considered the interactions involved in adolescent writing within the context of authoritative and face-saving activities in the adolescent community. Rather than begin with assumptions about the nature of writing as authoritative, I have instead identified the uses of writing in the context of authoritative relationships in everyday life.

Conclusion

The basic assumption about the value of collaborative writing is that it displaces the authority of single-authorship. Of course, not all single authorship is authoritative, but neither does multiple authorship necessarily undermine that authority.[15] Collaboration can involve a variety of possibilities for alignment and misalignment between participants. None of these relationships implicitly leads to either resistance or complicity with dominant authority.

The first collaborative arrangement examined here was the lack of correspondence in forged notes between message, signature, message, bearer, and the message-bearer's purpose. I observed that such notes often were produced collaboratively and that all of the participants were complicit in perpetuating both the lack of correspondences and the dominant system.

Second, in playful written collaborations, the students borrowed adult genres and played at being adults writing. This is not a misalignment but a dual alignment, an act of perpetuating two roles, accomplished in part through framing (Goffman 1974).

Borrowing adult standard forms for playful purposes could be considered a form of parody that undermines the original genre (Bakhtin 1981) or as a preparation for engaging in the adult and school world of filling in forms. (These are not mutually exclusive options.) Along with the third area of collaboration: collaborative classroom worksheets, and a fourth area: family collaborative business projects, fill-in collaborations depended upon the authority of the form, and like the forged notes, involved restricted control over the production of a message.

Playful collaborations fall into the category of what are sometimes called 'vernacular' or 'unofficial' writing (Camitta, this volume; Fiering 1980). Vernacular writing is defined by its adherence to local, rather than academic, standards. There is a presumed misalignment between the standards of a particular group, in this case, adolescents, and those of the institutional authority, in this case, the school. However, any binary opposition that suggests a necessary correspondence between types of alignment or participation and authoritative status is misleading.[16] The vernacular/official opposition can be particularly misleading by suggesting a correspondence between types of texts, types of participation, and the appropriation of power. Instead, vernacular writing is probably best understood in terms of choices of channel and genre of communication. In this case, the issue is the relationship between writing and speech and the questions are what one has the entitlement to say and what one is entitled to write. The issue is not only varieties of writing, standard and local, but also privileged channels and/or genres of communication.[17]

The appropriation of adult forms to engage in communication with adults involves a different sort of alignment problem. In the case of the petition, for example, the successful appropriation of the form depended upon whether or not the students could gain an audience with the principal. Unlike the use of vernacular writing among adolescents which involved a question of alignment between standards of communication, the use of the petition involved a question of alignment between participants in an exchange. By shifting attention to an addressee other than the petitioners, the addressor refused to recognise the student petitioners as participants in an exchange.

This sort of problem, in which a speaker or author redirects comments to someone other than the petitioner, may work out differently in writing than in speaking. In some speaking situations, the unaddressed or unrecognised petitioner might become unrecognisable or invisible. In written exchanges, such as the petition discussed here, it could be argued that although the dominant hierarchy was maintained, by putting themselves on record in writing, the students were able to deny participation in that authoritative hierarchy. They were excluded, but they appropriated the situation and excluded themselves from complicity in the authority's decision.

All of the genres of student writing discussed here involved appropriations of forms of writing. Sometimes that appropriation served to reaffirm the status of participants and in other cases it relocated authority.[18] Where people competed for authority in one domain from a position in another, the appropriation threatened to disrupt the social status of the participants. Appropriating adult forms for adolescent purposes did not necessarily empower the adolescents. What is appropriated can be just as easily, and sometimes more easily, reappropriated.[19] Moreover, in the case of student appropriations of adult genres, it is important not to fix a priori boundaries between the groups without examining the assumptions about age, class, racial, and other status categories that keep those boundaries in place, lest we too easily revel in 'representing the violation of the boundary' (Haraway 1992: 314).

Collaborative writing does not necessarily create different sorts of texts or different alignments between participants in communication. Multiple authorship does not necessarily undermine authority; vernacular writing is not necessarily empowering. Writing is a contemporary battleground for all sorts of issues, and writing itself, collaborative or authored, is one of the most appropriable grounds for disclosing or hiding other agendas.

Notes

1 This use of the 'everyday' in the sense of Wittgenstein's ordinary language contrasts with Henri Lefebvre's discussion of everyday life as a site of revolution. See Lefebvre 1971; Wittgenstein 1976.
2 The school population was composed of equal numbers of working-class black, white (predominantly Irish Catholic) and Puerto Rican students. Some of the white students who participated in my research attended the alternative high school where Miriam Camitta, a few years later, did her research, also included in this volume.
3 See Marjorie Harness Goodwin's chapter 'Talk as Social Action' in Goodwin 1990: 1–17.
4 See Susan Stewart's (1991) discussion of authenticity and forgery.
5 The participants gave me the scrap of paper when I told them I was collecting notes 'for my book'.
6 On writing the unspeakable, see Smith 1978: 110, 'Fictive discourse allows us to speak the unspeakable – but only if we agree not to *say* it'.
7 I discuss the relationship between disputes and writing further in Shuman 1986, chapter 4. See also, Roland Barthes, who writes, 'It is power or conflict which produces the purest types of writing' (1953: 20). See also Gossen 1976.
8 See John Szwed's (1981) discussion of this category.
9 It is interesting to consider the relationship between a writing task and the amount of time spent discussing a topic in the light of theoretical discussions of time in literature. I am not proposing a dual temporal model here in which there is some purported 'actual' time that is distorted or reshaped in representations (the worksheet) but instead suggesting that we view worksheets as representing time. See Genette who writes, '"reminiscence" is at the service of metaphor and not the reverse' (1980: 158).
10 These terms are borrowed from P. Van de Berghe's (1973: 959–78) discussion

of ethnic communities. I am grateful to Barbara Kirshenblatt-Gimblett for introducing this to me.

11 Andrea Lunsford and Lisa Ede distinguish between what they call 'hierarchical' and 'dialogic' collaboration. The hierarchical mode is 'carefully and often rigidly structured, driven by highly specific goals and carried out by people playing clearly delimited roles. The dialogic mode is loosely structured and the roles enacted within it are fluid ... the process of articulating goals is often as important as the goals themselves and sometimes even more important ... group effort is seen as an essential part of the production ... rather than the recovery of knowledge and as a means of individual satisfaction within the group. This mode of collaboration can in some circumstances be deeply subversive' (1990: 133). I would argue that the petition is hierarchical in terms of the structured social roles but that petitions can be subversive.

12 Perhaps what is lost in discussions that assume the virtues of decontextualisation is the larger context of differences between writing and speaking. For example, in formal oratory value is placed on 'adaptation of what is said to the character and the circumstances of the persons addressed' (Johnson 1991: 123). We could say that both writing and speaking require attention to context and that writing, in privileging the single-authored text for unfamiliar audiences, marks the collaborative cumulative statement as flawed.

13 Donna Haraway argues that discussions of representing the positions of those whose voices have not been heard only obscures the problem of the unrepresented by authorising the role of the scholar or activist who acts as a 'ventriloquist' for those who cannot represent themselves (1992: 312). I am grateful to Susan Ritchie for suggesting this reference.

14 James Gee similarly argues that literacy should be viewed as part of a discourse system (1988: 37).

15 See Michel Foucault for discussions of both authorship and what he calls 'an insurrection of subjugated knowledges' (1972: 81).

16 See Richard Terdiman's discussion of binarisms in terms of the 'competing messages of social groups' (1985: 36).

17 For discussions of writing in the context of spoken communication, see Tannen 1982; on entitlement, see Shuman 1993.

18 See Louis Althusser's (1971: 171–6) discussion of interpellation. My use of the term appropriation should not be confused with the post-modern concept of mixing genres. To the contrary, I am concerned with the appropriation of genres as an act of either complicity or defiance. For discussions of writing and empowerment and the related topic of resisting dominance, see Giroux 1983, Aronowitz and Giroux 1985, and Clark and Ede 1990.

19 As Eliot Wiggington has pointed out, although his *Foxfire* programme of working with high school students to collect and publish folklore was invented to derail an oppressive educational system, it can be used to provide students with a tame and seemingly innocuous topic that prevents them from investigating more politically sensitive adolescent issues. When the students in a Foxfire-based programme in Zanesville, Ohio decided to interview other teenagers about date rape rather than interview elderly members of the community about traditional crafts, the school administration protested. (Discussion by

students from Zanesville at the 'Rekindling Foxfire' conference, Ohio Historical Society, Columbus, Ohio, 6 February 1988.)

References

Althusser, L. 1971. 'Ideology and ideological apparatuses (Notes towards an investigation)', in *Lenin and Philosophy and other essays*. Trans. B. Brewster. New York: Monthly Review.

Aronowitz, S. and Giroux, H. A. 1985. *Education under siege: the conservative, liberal, and radical debate over schooling*. South Hadley: Bergin.

Bakhtin, M. M. [1934] 1981. *The dialogue imagination*, ed. M. Holquist. Trans. C. Emerson and M. Holquist. Austin: University of Texas Press.

Baron, N. 1981. *Speech, writing and sign: a functional view of linguistic representation*. Bloomington: Indiana University Press.

Barthes, R. 1953. *Writing degree zero*. Trans. A. Lavers and C. Smith. New York: Hill and Wang.

Bernstein, B. 1971. *Class, codes and control*, vol. 1, London: Paladin.

Brown, A. L. 1975. 'The development of memory: knowing, knowing about knowing, and knowing how to know', in H. W. Reese (ed.), *Advances in child development and behavior, vol. 10*. New York: Academic Press.

Clark, S. and Ede, L. 1990. 'Collaboration, resistance, and the teaching of writing', in A. A. Lunsford, H. Moglen and J. Sleven (eds.), *The right to literacy*, pp. 276–85. New York: Modern Languages Association of America.

Dundes, A. and Roger, C. R. 1978. *Work hard and you shall be rewarded: urban folklore from the paperwork empire*. Bloomington: Indian University Press.

Fiering, S. 1980. 'Unofficial writing in the classroom and the community'. Unpublished in-house report, Center for Urban Ethnography, University of Pennsylvania Graduate School of Education.

Foucault, M. 1977. 'What is an author?', in *Language, counter-memory, practice: selected essays and interviews*. Trans. D. F. Bouchard. New York: Cornell University Press.

1980. *Power/knowledge: selected interviews and other writings*, ed. C. Gordon. Trans. C. Gordon, L. Marshall, J. Mepham, K. Soper. New York: Pantheon. (First published 1972.)

Gee J. P. 1988. 'Discourse systems and aspirin bottles: on literacy', *Journal of Education*, 170 (1): 27–40.

1989. 'Literacies and tradition', *Journal of Education*, 171: 26–38.

Genette, G. 1980. *Narrative discourse: an essay in method*. Trans. J. E. Lewin. Ithaca, NY: Cornell University Press.

Giroux, H. A. 1983. *Theory and resistance in education: a pedagogy for the opposition*. South Hadley: Bergin.

Goffman, E. 1974. *Frame analysis: an essay on the organization of experience*. New York: Harper and Row.

1983. 'Footing', in *Forms of talk*, pp. 124–59. Philadelphia: University of Pennsylvania Press.

Goodwin, M. H. 1990. *He-said-she-said: talk as social organization among black children*. Bloomington: Indiana University Press.

Gossen, G. 1976. 'Verbal dueling in chamula', in B. Kirshenblatt-Gimblett (ed.), *Speech play: research and resources for the study of linguistic creativity*, pp. 121–48. Philadelphia: University of Pennsylvania Press.

Haraway, D. 1992. 'The promises of monsters: a regenerative politics for inappropriate/d others', in L. Grossberg, C. Nelson and P. Treichler (eds.), *Cultural Studies*. New York: Routledge.

Heath, S. B. 1983. *Ways with words: language, life and work in communities and classrooms*. Cambridge: Cambridge University Press.

Hymes, D. 1972. 'Models of the interaction of language and social life', in J. J. Gumperz and D. Hymes (eds.), *Directions in sociolinguistics*. New York: Holt, Rinehart and Winston.

Johnson, N. 1991. *Nineteenth-century rhetoric in North America*. Carbondale: Southern Illinois University Press.

Lefebvre, H. 1971. *'Everyday' life in the modern world*. Trans. S. Rabinovitch. Harmondsworth: Penguin.

Lunsford, A. and Ede, L. 1990. *Singular text, plural authors: perspectives on collaborative writing*. Carbondale: Southern Illinois University Press.

Mishler, E. G. 1979. 'Meaning in context: is there any other kind?', *Harvard Educational Review*, 49: 1–19.

Pedraza, P. 1980. 'Rethinking diglossia', *Centro Working Papers*, 9: 1–45.

Scollon, R. and Scollon, S. B. K. 1981. *Narrative, literacy and face in interethnic communication*. Norwood, NJ: Ablex.

Shuman, Amy. 1986. *Storytelling rights: the uses of oral and written texts among urban adolescents*. Cambridge: Cambridge University Press.

  forthcoming. 'Gender and genre', in L. Pershing, S. Hollis and M. J. Young (eds.), *Feminist theory and the study of folklore*.

  1993. '"Get outa my face": entitlement and authoritative discourse', in J. T. Irvine and J. H. Hill (eds.), *Responsibility and evidence in oral discourse*. Cambridge: Cambridge University Press.

Smith, B. H. 1978. *On the margins of discourse*. Chicago: University of Chicago Press.

Stewart, S. 1991. *Crimes of writing*. Oxford: Oxford University Press.

Street, B. V. 1984. *Literacy in theory and practice*. Cambridge: Cambridge University Press.

Stubbs, M. 1980. 'Initial literacy and explanation of educational failure', in *Language and literacy: the sociolinguistics of reading and writing*. London: Routledge and Kegan Paul.

Szwed, J. F. 1981. 'The ethnography of literacy', in M. F. Whiteman and C. H. Frederikson (eds.), *Variations in writing functional and linguistic-cultural differences*. Hillsdale, NJ: Erlbaum.

Tannen, D. (ed.), 1981. *Spoken and written language: exploring orality and literacy*. Norwood, NJ: Ablex.

Terdiman, R. 1985. *Discourse/counter-discourse*. Ithaca: Cornell University Press.

Van den Berghe, P. 1973. 'Pluralism', in J. J. Honigman (ed.), *Handbook of social and cultural anthropology*. Chicago: Rand-McNally.

Wiggington, E. 1986. *Sometimes a shining moment: the foxfire experience*. Garden City, NY: Anchor Doubleday.

Wittgenstein, L. 1976. *Philosophical investigations*. Oxford: Blackwell.

11

LITERACY AND SOCIAL PROCESS: A COMMUNITY IN TRANSITION

GAIL WEINSTEIN-SHR

Introduction

'AT THE MERCY OF AMERICA', shouts the cover page headline of *The Philadelphia Inquirer Magazine* (21 October 1984). 'SHOCK AND CON-FUSION WHEN WORLDS COLLIDE' reads a later news headline from the same paper (20 March 1985). 'THE PRIMITIVE PARADISE OF THE HMONG' heads a third (9 June 1985). Hmong refugees from Laos are often portrayed in the American media as helpless peasants who have been thrust empty-handed into the brutal realities of civilisation.

In fact, if Hmong refugees had not been resourceful they would not be here; they would be dead. In the ten years before arriving in the United States, these mountain farmers moved their families through dangerous jungle, seeking temporary refuge in secret camps, living on the run. The Hmong have been enormously resourceful in adjusting to drastic changes and dangerous conditions over extended periods of time.

The Hmong are a hilltribe who trace their origins to China. For about 150 years, the Hmong have been on the move, beginning with migration into South-east Asian countries including Burma, Thailand, Vietnam and Laos (Geddes 1976). Explanations for the migrations range from pressure by hostile neighbours to searches for land for farming and livestock. Throughout the nineteenth century, Hmong migration caused little objection in host countries, because of their preference for establishing villages high in the mountains, a niche for which few others were interested in competing (Barney 1981).

Known for their strongly developed clan organisation and fierce resistance to rule (Dunnigan 1982b), many Hmong in Laos were hired by the United States government in the 1970s to fight under the leadership of General Vang Pao against the Pathet Lao Communist movement. When the Pathet Lao gained power in 1975, those Hmong who had been hired by the Americans had to flee the country (Yang 1972). Those closest to Vang Pao were airlifted by helicopter, while the more fortunate of those remaining made their way across the Mekong River into Thailand.

After a period ranging from months to several years in Thai refugee camps, approximately 70,000 of these survivors were resettled in the United States (Office of Refugee Resettlement 1983). Media articles like those cited above are unaware of some resources such as kinship ties that Hmong bring to life in America, while they report primarily those areas that would seem to pose difficulty for living in the United States.

The same clan organisation that strengthened their resources as fighters operates today as the Hmong struggle with adjustment to western urban life. While strong kinship structures play an important role in Hmong adaptation strategies, also significant is a resource that they do not traditionally possess: native language literacy. As subsistence farmers in Laos, the Hmong had little use for literacy or formal schooling. Although missionaries developed writing systems for the Hmong language in the late 1950s (Smalley 1976), only a minority of Hmong learned to use them. Inexperience with literacy poses various kinds of problems for the Hmong as they grapple with life in American cities, and it shapes the kinds of strategies that they employ as they solve the problems of daily living in their new environment.

While cross-cultural studies of literacy were often aimed at discovering cognitive consequences (for example Olson 1977; Goody and Watt 1968; Ong 1982), increasing attention has been given to the variety of literacies and the social context in which reading and writing take on communicative meaning by historians (for example Schofield 1968; Graff 1979), psychologists (for example Scribner and Cole 1981), and social scientists (for example Street 1984; Heath 1983). With a shift in focus, new questions become interesting. How does life in a literate environment affect or change social relationships? How do social relationships influence the way that literacy is acquired and used? The Hmong from Laos who have come to the United States provide an exciting opportunity to look into the relationship of literacy and social process. Because literacy is a relatively recent innovation for the Hmong, it is possible to observe rapid changes as this mode of communication is introduced into their repertoire of communicative resources. The experience of the Hmong as they adapt to their new environment provides an opportunity for gaining insight into the interaction of communicative technology and social organisation.

Hmong refugees began arriving in Philadelphia in 1979. Over the next six years, I was to have the opportunity to observe at close range the strategies and struggles of my new neighbours as they brought their enormous resources to bear in their transition from the mountaintops of Laos to the streets of Philadelphia. During this time, I surveyed each household in the city, to discover the kinds of social resources available for adapting to life in the United States. In addition, I developed several in-depth 'portraits' of Hmong adults in the city to document language and literacy use in daily life, as well as patterns of interaction with kin and non-kin, both within and across ethnic boundaries.[1]

In this chapter, first, information is provided about kinship and literacy as they existed for the Hmong historically and as they operate in their new lives in urban Philadelphia. Next, the role of kinship and literacy in two men's lives is presented. The contrasts between these two men, their ways of using literacy and their ways of maintaining/making relationships are placed in context of Philadelphia's wider community in a general discussion of literacy and social process. My aim is to illustrate the point that the study of the functions and uses of literacy in specific people's lives can provide insights into human organisation and social process. Finally, I will argue here that anthropologists have an important contribution to make in informing literacy instruction and educational practice as urban society becomes increasingly culturally diverse.

Old and new resources

Traditional resources: kinship

In the Hmong community, kinship relations are the primary features of a person's identity in the social order. The patrilineal clan system dominates Hmong social organisation, as well as serving as a primary integrating factor in Hmong culture as a whole (Barney 1980). Altogether there are 20 clans, known as *xeem*, each of which traces its origin to a common mythological ancestor.

It is impossible to talk about Hmong families in Philadelphia without referring to the clans to which they belong. Among the twenty Hmong clans that exist, eleven are represented in Philadelphia by male household heads. These include Chang, Hang, Kue, Lee, Lo(r), Moua, Thao, Vang, Vue, Xiong and Yang. Attempts to take a census of Hmong families in Philadelphia confront the researcher with the contradictions in Hmong and American ways of reckoning family units. The term 'household', or *tsev neeg*, for the Hmong, need not refer only to those who live in one house, but rather includes any persons under the authority of the householder.

The American social welfare system, in contrast, is organised around the notion of nuclear families. A list compiled by the Hmong Association, in its role as liaison to the American bureaucracy, lists 'families' which are headed by any married man or by women who are divorced or widowed.[2] This is to facilitate the distribution of welfare and social security benefits. In 1985, the list included, for example, nine Kue families. Any Kue who was asked for the number of Kue families in Philadelphia, however, would have replied three. In fact, these nine 'families' were under the authority of three household heads.

The Hmong list officially divided the Hmong in Philadelphia as living in 'Weston' and 'Norton' (not the real neighbourhood names). In a survey of September 1985, I found that Philadelphia's Hmong community consisted of fifty-eight nuclear families comprising approximately twenty-eight households (*tsev neeg*, that is). Nuclear families tend to live in clusters, sometimes with entire households occupying the same building. Geographical cohesiveness is the general rule for clans in Philadelphia. The division between Norton and Weston, reflected by residence patterns, is characterised by other features which will be discussed below.

Counting on kin in America

Life in Laos was characterised by the comfort of knowing that the mountains were webbed with a haven of kin, known and unknown. If a man made a long journey, he could be sure that in any village, as long as he found a clansman, he would be housed and fed along the way. Likewise, this web of kin connections still operates for some Hmong in urban America. Hang Chou describes his experience attending a conference in San Francisco. Upon arriving at the airport, he simply opened the phone book to the 'H's, calling the first Hang listed. He was then picked up, housed and fed for the duration of the conference by a family he had never before met.

Resettlement efforts that recognise the continuing operation of traditional kinship structures such as the clan and 'family' (*tsev neeg*) have a better chance of success. Doctors, for example, who need permission for certain medical procedures are more likely to get cooperation (that is, the necessary signatures) if members of the appropriate sub-group or lineage are included as information is given and decisions are made (Dunnigan 1982a). Health clinics in Minneapolis, among other cities, have found substantial improvements in patient cooperation when treatment took into account the operation of kinship networks and the ways in which these affect decision-making and action (Dunnigan 1982b).

While categories of kinship may have remained the same, ways of reckoning the members of those categories have gained enormous flexibility in the face of the drastic changes entailed by resettlement. While *pawg neeg* translates technically as 'sub-lineage', for some it has come to mean 'helping group' in a much broader sense. War orphan Ying Lo now counts among members of his *pawg neeg* members of the Hmong student club at the local community college (who study together and plan special events), as well as other orphan bachelors who collectively lend money to one another for the bride price in turn as they get married. Even the *tsev neeg* (literally 'house people') has become fluid enough to begin healing gaps left by the terrible losses of war. While Ying reports living with his 'blood brother', neither of the men can identify the point of connection on their respective genealogical charts.

These flexible ways of reckoning kin have made it possible for some Hmong people in Philadelphia to continue relying on traditional kinds of relationships for support while adapting to the realities of the social decimation caused by death and diaspora in the wake of a decade of war and flight.

New resources: literacy and schooling

History of Hmong schooling and literacy
While the Hmong have a history of well-developed clan organisation, they have a very short history of experience with formal schooling. Because of their isolation in Laos, virtually no Hmong in the mountains had any formal education before the Second World War. The first village school in the high mountain region was set up in 1939 (Barney 1967). Even after the number of village schools grew, children had to go to larger towns if they were to study beyond the third year. Although schools became more accessible after the war, there was a high dropout rate as Hmong children became older, had to travel further to secondary schools in larger towns and take on more responsibility for family farm activities. In addition, classes were taught exclusively in Lao, creating yet more of an obstacle to success for Hmong children who only speak the Hmong language (Yang 1972).

The Hmong in Philadelphia have brought with them educational resources consistent with this history. I found that of the 167 adults in Philadelphia, only 16 per cent report having more than three years of schooling in Laos. It is interesting to note the distribution of education by clan. Among the nine clans in Philadelphia with members who have more than six years of education in Laos, all of the larger Philadelphia clans are represented (2 Hangs, 3 Kues, 2 Los, 2 Mouas, 1 Vang, 1 Xiong, 1 Yang). This suggests that schooling was not the domain of any particular clan. Rather, it was a rare commodity for which lineage groups had to pool their resources to invest in the eldest or brightest boy. The low percentage of women in the figures is consistent with this explanation.

Traditional Hmong society might be characterised as 'non-literate'. Smalley (1976: 2) describes such a culture as one in which:

> a child can be born and grow up, an adult can live and die, without a strong need to read and write. He can live a normal existence within his own community without a feeling that he is in any way culturally deprived by lack of ability to communicate through marks made on paper. Life as he knows it does not include reading and writing as a major component.

Indeed, until the early 1950s, the Hmong of Laos did not have a system for writing their spoken language. Smalley (quoted above) is one of the missionaries who developed the Romanised Popular Alphabet (RPA) at that time, for purposes of religious teaching. The RPA was easy to learn; Hmong in Philadelphia report learning it informally from friends or relatives, or by studying a primer on their own. They report mastering the system in time periods ranging from one afternoon to four weeks.

Within ten years, use of the RPA began to spread for purposes such as newsletters and the recording of history and oral literature (Reder 1985). In the late 1960s, missionaries created another Hmong writing system based on the Lao script to accommodate the Lao government, with their concern for unity in Laos and control over ethnic minorities. Hence, while uses for literacy were extremely limited, there were three varieties available to some Hmong people in Laos:

(1) Lao script for Lao language (schooled literacy)
(2) Lao script allied to Hmong language (government created literacy)
(3) RPA for the Hmong language (introduced by missionaries)

For those who became literate, the choice of script was a political one. The choice of RPA was a signal of allegiance with Western literacies and a recognition of authority from that cultural source.

Literacy today: Philadelphia's Hmong
In Philadelphia, the number of Hmong who report being literate in Lao corresponds exactly with those who report having received formal schooling in Laos. Thus, Lao literacy and formal schooling are inextricably bound. In contrast, many who never had experience with formal schooling have at least some literacy skills in Hmong. Most, knowing of their impending resettlement in the West, learned RPA informally after their flight from Laos, either in Thai refugee camps or here in the United States. Self-reports of household heads for themselves and their families indicate that 60 per cent of those between twenty and forty-five years old are now able to read and write Hmong, despite the very low rate of formal schooling in Laos. Because literacy has become a resource that is spread by non-institutional means that do not require setting aside lineage resources, women have caught up with men in their acquisition. The mode of transmission has changed the possibilities for acquisition and for use.

How do old and new resources affect one another? Does coming to a literate environment change who depends on whom? Do kinship relationships have any effect on who learns to read and write and for what purposes? Both educators and social scientists can profit from understanding the interaction of kinship and literacy, two kinds of social resources. In the next section, this interaction is examined in the lives of two men and in their communities.

Literacy and changing lives

In order to see at close range the ways that kinship connections and literacy figure in real people's everyday lives, it is useful to focus on individuals and their families. What kinds of problems do people have to solve? How do they go about solving them? More specifically, how do people use literacy and solve literacy-related problems? How are kinship ties used in context of radically changed circumstances? What other kinds of social resources are being developed in adapting to a new setting?

This section examines the lives of two men who have selected very different strategies for adapting to life in the United States, including the functions and uses of literacy in each man's life, as well as in terms of kinship relationships. Chou Chang[3] was a young man of twenty-five who successfully completed his high school equivalency diploma during the time of the research. The son of a town merchant, he had had the opportunity to become literate in Lao during four years of schooling before becoming a soldier at the age of twelve. I watched with awe as Chou and his wife grappled with an impossible bureaucracy that had immediate power over their survival and sustenance. I suggest below that for Chou Chang, literacy can be seen as an addition as well as an agent of change in the communicative economy, with profound effects on his relationships with others.

Pao Youa Lo, on the other hand, was a failing student in my community college classroom. He never spoke, never completed an assignment, and never passed an exam. I had no idea at the time that this mysterious older gentleman had experience with education and literacy that most of his Hmong contemporaries did not have. He learned Lao literacy in military camp and taught himself to read and write in Hmong. It wasn't until several years after he flunked out of school that I would learn about his power in the community and his considerable resources for solving problems.

As I learned more about Pao Youa Lo, the things I knew about Chou Chang became more interesting. The contrasts were striking in the two men's ways of using literacy, the other kinds of resources, their desires and their ways of making meaning in their new lives in the United States. The contrast between these two men illuminates revealing contrasts in Philadelphia's wider Hmong community.

Literacy and changing relationships: Chou Chang's story[4]

I first met Chou in a Lutheran church service. In his role as assistant, he sat patiently beside the pastor until it was time to give a reading from a Lao bible to the mixed Hmong and American congregation. After the service, I was introduced to Chou as an English teacher who was interested in the neighbourhood refugees. Characteristic of his interest in Americans, Chou invited me to his home without hesitation.

When I arrived at the fire-gutted row in Weston, I was welcomed into the end house, the only one intact. The second-floor apartment was clean and uncluttered, with two babies sleeping in a heap of blankets, and a table full of Thai herbs growing in plastic pots by the window.

Chou invited me to stay for dinner. Having heard that Americans prefer bread to rice, Chou's wife Sai placed half a loaf of Wonderbread on my dinner bowl. They were anxious to please, in contrast to what I would later experience in Pao Youa Lo's house, where my presence was tolerated with unhostile indifference.

In order to learn the Hmong language and to observe the functions and uses of literacy for one family, I arranged to move in with Chou and Sai for four weeks in the winter of 1981. During these weeks I came to see Chou Chang as a literacy and culture broker who used his language skills for surviving urban bureaucracy, as well as for creating new roles and relationships for himself in this new setting. The data presented here are drawn primarily from that homestay.

Literacy as a tool for negotiating with new institutions

Adult literacy teachers are often sensitised to the extent to which managing life in urban America entails dealing with literacy. Students often bring in their baffling documents, important-looking letters, insurmountable forms and questions about what they see around them. Life in the Chang household provided a sampling of some of the problems to be solved that required literacy skills.

One Tuesday afternoon, Chou received a letter from his caseworker instructing him to report to her office Friday morning, or his 'case' would be 'closed'. He was to bring four documents with him, including one which had to be stamped by an agency several miles away (and not easily accessible by public transportation), and others which required picking up various forms with signatures from different places. That evening, Chou spent his homework time fixing his bicycle, knowing that it would be impossible to complete the tasks on foot in one day. He called his English teacher to tell her he would be absent.

On Friday, Chou reported to his caseworker with all of the forms that he had gathered. Both his signature and Sai's were required, and both had to be made in the presence of the caseworker. When Chou got home at about midday, he took over the child care so that Sai could repeat the journey. Sai did not yet know how to use the subway, how to distinguish the North from the Southbound platform, nor how to read the sign for the Springgarden stop. Unsure if I would be able to accompany her, Chou memorised the location of the correct platform and counted the stops to report to Sai for her journey.

Chou felt lucky to have his then-current caseworker because 'she help us everything', in contrast to a previous caseworker: 'Window broken, he don't care. No heat, he not do anything. New baby born, he don't help extra money'. Some neighbours did not find the new one as 'lucky'. An older Hmong woman living one floor below who did not know how to decipher forms, letters or bills found the preparation of the required documents to be an insurmountable task. In exchange for Chou's help on procuring gas money through the caseworker, the woman allowed Chou to use her oven to save on his own gas bills.

When the old woman was unable to solve a literacy-related problem, she sometimes brought it to Chou. When Chou was stymied by bills or difficult homework, for example, he turned to me or to another American in his church. Sometimes favours were returned in kind, as illustrated above with the story of the gas money. Other requests for help caused conflict.

Chou had been complaining for a couple of days about a man who wanted him to write a fraudulent letter to welfare. The man, who lived six blocks away, had asked Chou to claim that he lived with him so that he could pick up a welfare check at Chou's address. Chou complained: 'He want me to cheat for him ... he not my relative, he never help me anything. He just make trouble for me'. Chou felt that the request was inappropriate, and that it jeopardised his own standing with welfare. The visitor was neither a neighbour nor a clan member. He called upon Chou for this favour because Chou was among the few literate household heads who would be able to perform the task.

Chou later received a call from a Hmong leader. As in many other cities, social service agencies hired the earlier Hmong arrivals who became bilingual to work in the resettlement process. These people have become the prime mediators between American caseworkers and the Hmong population in the area. Not coincidentally, Chou reports, the members of some clans seem to fare best in matters that require attention from the social service system. For example, Chou said that when he first arrived, the leader called the police when Sai was in labour, rather than taking the time to accompany the couple to the hospital as he did for some families. Because Chou spoke very little English at the time, he felt helpless when the doctors decided to perform a Caesarean section on Sai. He is sure that it could have been avoided with the right advocacy. In Laos, this leader would appropriately be expected to aid members of his own clan. As a caseworker in Philadelphia, however, he is seen by Americans as a representative of 'the Hmong' and is asked to be an advocate for members of many clans. The old and new expectations do not always harmonise.

The leader, then, called Chou asking him to write the fraudulent letter to welfare while several Americans persuaded him not to do it. As the phone continued to ring, and Chou's homework lay neglected, he shouted in exasperation, 'Too many calls! Too many questions!' With that, he pulled the phone wires out of the wall and sat down to do his homework, complaining, 'Everybody want something from me!'

In these examples, decoding and composing documents play an important role in economic survival. For Chou Chang, ability to decode bureaucratic messages in a timely way meant the difference between keeping and losing government support. Relatives and neighbours also turned to Chou (with or without success) to help them negotiate the maze of literacy-based channels to gain access to resources. Those who have literacy skills must use them to gain and maintain benefits, and those who don't must often rely on those who do. The homestay with Chou Chang made evident that who may rely on whom had become problematic. Whereas dependence relationships once resided wholly with families and clans, new categories such as caseworker/client, co-tenant or urban neighbour pose new possibilities and pressures for different kinds of interaction in this new setting.

Literacy as a tool for mediating between culture groups
Members of Chou's church grappled with how to effectively accommodate the large new population of refugees. Incorporating the Hmong into religious life was a priority. On any given Sunday, one or more Hmong couples were baptised, becoming full members of the 'church family', a term used by one of the Sunday school teachers. Chou used to spend several hours each Saturday studying the Bible with the pastor. Thus prepared, he led Sunday school Bible lessons in Hmong for new arrivals and others who could not understand English. When Chou did his short Bible reading in Lao for the whole congregation, on the other hand, he introduced some Hmong culture to Americans. His seat next to the pastor during the service and his name printed in the service programme legitimised both the task and Chou himself as mediator in the exchange.

Chou's role as mediator extended past the boundaries of the church. During the homestay, a social worker from a neighbouring church who had heard of Chou's writing skills called, asking him to translate a sign from English to Hmong for a clothing room. That evening he put aside his homework to write and rewrite the message until he was satisfied that it was well done, and invited the woman to call on his help any time. Thus, Chou also conveyed information to Hmong people outside of his church, and in so doing, became a mediator for the wider neighbourhood.

Chou spent time deliberately cultivating relationships with Americans. Before I moved in with his family, Chou would often call me on the phone to chat. One afternoon during my four-week stay, when I returned to his apartment, Chou was going systematically through his memo-pad phone directory calling each American on his list, one by one. The content of each conversation was more or less the same, as he asked each person what was 'up' and told his own news. It seemed clear that Chou made efforts to connect with American friends, teachers, and church members. The decision he and Sai made to let me live with them for a month was another daring move to allow an American into their world.

For Chou Chang, literacy skills are resources that enabled him to take the role of culture broker. Hmong compatriots like those in his church relied on Chou to bring them information and access to participation in American institutions. The pastor and the social worker cited above are among many Americans who called on Chou effectively to reach members of the Hmong community. While Chou actively sought to incorporate Americans into his network, he cultivated his role in linking these two cultural worlds. What are the rewards for this role? Why did Chou Chang devote so much energy to this difficult task? These questions are explored below.

Literacy and new social status in a changing social order
Returning to Chou and Sai's apartment in the afternoons, I would often find Sai sewing decorative squares with tiny precise stitches and stunning colours while she rocked her youngest child on her back in a brightly embroidered baby carrier. Sai often worked with her sister and mother, as well as several neighbours. All chatted or sat quietly as I joined them with my clumsy crochet hook and yarn. At just such a gathering, I thought of inviting friends and neighbours to a party at which the women could display their pieces for sale. The event was planned, resulting in $700 of collective sales. The money was distributed to the individual artists whose pieces were sold.

I suggested to Chou and Sai that each woman contribute one or two dollars for a kitty to cover refreshments for the party, and to start some collective savings for renting craft tables or even eventually saving for a storefront. Chou spoke out: 'Hmong people can pay for food at the party, [to reimburse an American helper] but not to save money together. My name Chang, I help Chang. We don't trust money together'.

There were the divisions: family helps within family, clan helps with clan. Cooperation was only possible to repay the American authority. An interesting conflict then arose. By miscommunication between myself and another American who was keeping books, money was not collected for reimbursing me for the refreshments as we had agreed originally. I brought it to Chou's attention. 'Don't worry', he comforted me. He would collect the money from those seamstresses who were also members of Sunday school. Because of Chou Chang's language and literacy skills, in this setting he had a new kind of authority. He could not collect from the other sale participants. 'They not obey me', he said. 'But people in my church, I think we can help you'. A new unit of cooperation was being formed – members of a congregation who could be influenced to act by a young man who may or may not share their clan name.

Chou once commented to me, 'I don't have family here – I have my church. People help me, give me a desk, dresser, chair ... ' Indeed, the church has been a source of furniture and clothing for Chou and Sai. During my short stay at their home, individual congregation members lent a space heater when the heat was broken and moved to investigate the delay in bringing Chou's brother over from Thailand, among other things. They provided those things for which, in the past, Chou could only turn to 'family' or clan.

In sum, for Chou and Sai, literacy was a critical tool for navigating through educational and social service bureaucracies. It was a tool which enabled them to mediate between culture groups. As this new mode of communication has entered the social fabric, for people like Chou Chang, the use of literacy has accompanied important changes in their relationships with others. Without strong kinship connections, cultivating new relationships and becoming a literacy broker provided a strategy for managing life in a difficult new setting.

Pao Youa Lo: community newskeeper

Here I bring the reader's attention to a man with entirely different circumstances and strategies for getting along in urban Philadelphia. Two years after the homestay in the Chang household, when I expressed interest in getting to know another Hmong family, my Hmong teacher offered to introduce me to his (clan) brother, a man of 51. Having heard that this man had declined the nomination for President of the Hmong Association because of his poor English skills, I prepared to offer English lessons in order to have a chance to observe life in another household. The man was none other than Pao Youa Lo, the hopeless student from my community college classroom several years earlier. Oddly, I felt embarrassed as if I had been the one who failed![5] He showed no such discomfort. Pao Youa was not interested in the tutoring sessions I offered. His wife and daughters, however, were delighted by the prospect, and agreed to have me come to see them twice a week.

Entering Pao Youa's Norton row house I was immediately struck by the portraits framed and hung on each wall of the front room. On the first wall was an austere photograph of a balding man staring resolutely ahead, with a heavy silver necklace prominent on his chest indicating he was a man of means. Pao Youa explained that this was his uncle, a brave and respected fighter who died in Laos. On the same wall was a photo of Pao Youa himself in combat fatigues, standing with the General Vang Pao, under whose leadership the Hmong fought and fled to America. On an opposite wall hung a family photograph of all the Lo men, with occasional children filling fathers' laps. Each photograph had a slip of paper taped at the bottom with an explanation typed in Hmong, as well as the date of the photograph. While the enjoyment of family photographs is typical among the Hmong, the carefully typed embellishments are not. Centred over the false fireplace was a certificate with Lao writing, declaring Pao Youa's courage and his contribution as a soldier to the war.

What was going on here? How could it be that my most pathetic and helpless student was pictured beside the Hmong community's greatest leader? Who was this man and how did he manage? Over the next year, I was to learn about resources that are simply not visible to a Community College English teacher.

Kin connections, leadership roles

On any given day, when Pao Youa is home, he usually sits by the large window, where he has arranged a u-shaped cluster of tables stacked with pads and notebooks, his chair nestled inside. There is rarely a morning or afternoon that goes by without a visit – usually from a clan brother. On one typical afternoon Pao Youa chatted with several of these brothers, carefully pouring arrowroot he had bought in Chinatown into a bottle of Dubonnet, altering proportions by pouring contents back and forth between two bottles. The men took small tastes, until they were all satisfied that the medicine was correctly mixed to help 'weak men' regain their strength. The chatter during the project was typical of these frequent visits in which the men talked, among other things, of fishing, of prospects for income during the new blueberry-picking season, of their own travels, or of the impressions their sons had got of life in other states.

It is at gatherings like these that the need for help is voiced, and cooperative strategies agreed upon. Cheng Mao Lo had just moved into his new home. The purchase was made possible by pooling of money for the down payment. When the mortgage payments were under control, Cheng Mao would return the funds to be made available for the next cooperative approach to individual problems.

Gatherings of kin are not always small or informal. Pao Youa's house is arranged, like many other Hmong people's rowhouses, with furniture easy to push aside. Pao Youa hosted several parties over the period of my regular visits. He was often invited to parties of others as well. I rarely attended a party in Norton in which Pao Youa was not present. Part of Pao Youa's position in Philadelphia is created and supported by the alliances his family has made with other Philadelphia families. Pao Youa's eldest daughter married the son of Hmong Association President Hang Chou in 1984. The wedding was an event that created a bond between the Los and the Hangs, two of Philadelphia's more powerful families. Such a bond strengthens and perpetuates existing alliances.

Pao Youa's popularity is not limited to Philadelphia, however. During the New Year season, Pao Youa travelled to Boston and Rhode Island among other cities to attend New Year Festivities, indicating that his support network is wide and strong. Pao Youa's eldest daughter married a clan 'nephew' of the number one Hmong leader in the United States, General Vang Pao. This continues the alliance formed when Pao Youa himself married Lee Vang, another member of the clan.

The invitation to run for the presidency of the Hmong Association in 1983 was a clear signal of Pao Youa's high regard in Philadelphia's Hmong community. His absence on the official slate, evidently, did not interfere with his leadership role. Nine household heads reported going to him for help with family and other problems. People go to Pao Youa 'because he know how to find the middle way' when there is conflict, reported one man. Pao Youa's son Fue says that it is good not to have the wisest leaders at the top (referring to his father). 'Our Hmong president need to be spokesman, like secretary of state Schultz. Then if we have problem with him, we can go higher, to the wisest man. If top man, he is president, then there is nowhere to go if there is a problem'.

Indeed, the list of those who go to Pao Youa for advice or help is impressive. Three of his clan brothers reported coming to him, including the community's paid job counsellor. Those from other clans who reported turning to Pao Youa all play leadership roles in Philadelphia, such as two *mej koob* (marriage go-betweens) and the deacon to the community's beloved Father Avery. Finally, elected president Hang Chou himself, as well as his aged father, both reported turning to Pao Youa when they want advice about important decisions or when there is a conflict within the household.

Pao Youa's role as leader raises a host of interesting questions about the nature of leadership. While his younger affinal kinsman was elected as spokesperson of the Hmong community, elders are, in some cases, maintaining traditional roles of authority. While certain kinds of problems, such as negotiating with English-speaking institutions, require new solutions, other age-old conflicts such as marital discord persist, requiring the intervention of traditional experts with traditional solutions. Old and new forms of authority coexist as different sorts of problems require the wisdom of different kinds of experts.

Literacy activities

Pao Youa does not have a job. Because of a leg wound suffered in the seventies he cannot be long on his feet. Nevertheless, he was rarely idle. In his window niche, I often found him reading, browsing, jotting notes or cutting and pasting. Behind him stood a tall cabinet filled with books and albums that he himself created.

The first thing an observer notes when Pao Youa has a book or magazine in his hand, is that he leafs through with an obvious goal. It becomes clear that he is drawn to photographs of powerful leaders. If a picture of Reagan or Thatcher appears on the page, for example, he studies the picture. If the caption is brief, he follows it with his finger, trying to reach each word. 'Reagan very good man', he smiles. 'Very strong against Communism'. Pao Youa showed me a scrap book made from a 1979 desk diary. Each page was covered with pictures of world leaders and accompanying text, or by pictures alone. His fascination with powerful leaders is in keeping with his own stature as a soldier and a military strategist.

Pao Youa has also used his literacy skills in the creation of elaborate personal chronicles. In a typical document, the reader opens the first page to find a photograph of Pao Youa in combat fatigues with several other men. At the top of the page is a neatly typed slip of paper that reads (in Hmong): 'The first person here is Pao Youa Lo. The second person is . . . ' The next page translates: 'This is Mrs. Pao Youa's book 9/28/85'. The reader meanders through images of family members and friends, some posing solemnly in traditional Hmong clothing, some gathered in ragged groups at the Thai refugee camps, and others smiling from behind their sunglasses near their American inner city apartments.

Other chronicles include Pao Youa's life story, with a detailed account of his days as a soldier in Laos, particularly during the war. Britannica Books of the Year for 1971, 1972 and 1974 are highlighted in yellow marker in the sections that provide the historical context for the story. One steno pad is filled with Pao Youa's version, in careful Lao lists, of the history of French and American intervention in Laos. Fue explains that his father is the history 'expert', and that people come to him with any questions they have about history.

With albums, scrapbooks, reference materials and personal journals, Pao Youa has created a rich and varied chronicle. He is satisfied to think that his efforts will help his children to understand the country from which they came, and the events leading to their flight and relocation in their new home. They will surely also come to gain some understanding of their father's role in the historic saga.

Pao Youa's interests are not confined to the distant past, nor are his efforts solely a family affair. His interest in current news events has become integral to his role in the community as an expert on world events, both past and present. During a party in Pao Youa's home, as is the custom, the children and women scattered after the meal, and the adult men gathered around the freshly cleaned table for beer and talk. Pao Youa passed three letters written in Lao around the table, where the literate men read them aloud to their kin who were unable to read. From a California-based organisation, these letters discussed plans for guerrilla warfare against the government of Laos. Fue explained an article about the soldiers missing in action and military activity in Laos from that morning's American newspaper to the whole group.

Each day, Pao Youa monitors the media for news of the United States, of the world powers, of individual heroes and of leaders. His findings are often the topic of discussion when kin come to call. Pao Youa is also the focal point for information about Laos. Members of the community depend on him for information, and at times, for analysis. A great deal of Pao Youa's time and creative energy is given to activities that support his role as newskeeper and newssharer.

New technologies, old ties
One of the ironies of dislocation is that new technologies made possible the maintenance of old ties in novel ways. This is illustrated by some of Pao Youa's activities. Pao Youa keeps a notebook in which he is carefully compiling (in Lao) a list of every Lo family in Philadelphia with members' names, sexes, birth dates and relations to the householder. He is collecting these, he explains, to contribute to the effort of identifying the Lo families worldwide. The information will be forwarded to an elder Lo, at 'Lo headquarters', in Omaha, Nebraska. The site has been chosen deliberately because of its centrality to Los on both coasts and between in the United States.

The clan operates as a corporate group beyond geographic boundaries. Pao Youa attended a Lo clan meeting in Wisconsin in spring 1987 where talks went on all day and night, non-stop for three days. Among the topics covered were the spelling of the clan name (there are now three variations that were created during the time of immigration) and whether or not steps should be taken to make the spellings uniform, thus reflecting clan solidarity; the laws of the United States and how to carry on with Hmong tradition without breaking American laws[6]; and finally, how to encourage children to succeed in their education. As one result of this meeting, Pao Youa made plans with local clan members to hold a party where they could reward each Lo child with fifty cents for each 'A' earned on the report card during the school year. What is interesting here is that education of the children and good citizenship are still seen as issues that are the domain of the clan as a whole, rather than the domain of a local geographic community.

It is ironic that literacy has provided Pao Youa and his family with a tool for studying Hmong oral tradition. Over the last couple of years, I have heard complaints from elders that the young people don't know the love songs anymore. They don't know the appropriate courtship, marriage and funeral songs. In 1985, under new leadership, the Hmong Association created 'culture classes'. Every Saturday, for three hours, four *mej koob* (marriage go-betweens) were paid out of a grant raised by the Association to teach the old customs and appropriate songs to younger men. The old men complain that they are getting too old to travel so often and to drink so much (as is required in the negotiation of marriages), and they are relieved that younger men are learning how to take over their role.

The students, including Pao Youa, are predominantly Los. The younger students take turns spending Friday nights with the teacher for that particular week, helping to prepare notes and written aids. They then assist in the actual class as well. Fue says that he sometimes takes notes in Hmong when the exact words are required, but that for general information it is faster to write Lao. With the help of young mediators, then, the old men are teaching oral traditions in a classroom format, which has become the most efficient and comfortable setting in which the young men have become accustomed to learning. It will not be surprising, if, in a few years, a traditional marriage is desired, one of the Lo men will be called to negotiate the terms and aid in preparation for the wedding. In their newly learned traditional roles, these young men will use literacy tools, for better or worse, that were not available to their mentors.

In sum, Pao Youa is a professional soldier who has created for himself the roles of history- and newskeeper. Members of the community see him as an expert, and depend on him for information about the past and about the current state of affairs in the world. In these pages literacy is presented as a way of celebrating powerful people, and a means through which to tell the story of what is happening. In addition, for Pao Youa, literacy provides a way of keeping himself and his community informed and connected with one another, with their traditions, and with their past and present.

Literacy and social relations: two men in context

Pao Youa Lo and Chou Chang use literacy skills for very different ends with different consequences. Just as literacy plays a different role in the life of each, so each individual plays a distinct role in the life of the community.

The literacy activities of these two men are characterised by striking differences. Pao Youa's literacy activities are directed inward to his family and clan, reinforcing his connection with his tradition and with his history. The documentation he engages in affirms old ties and keeps old connections vital to kin, to the past, and to Laos. Chou, on the other hand, uses literacy to reach outward, connecting with new kinds of resources, creating new relationships in a social world of Americans that Chou takes risks to explore.

The conditions under which Pao Youa and Chou interact with print are vastly different. When Chou comes home, he and Sai open mail. They both read out loud as they slowly process the correspondence. A letter can mean the difference between continuing or losing their welfare benefits. One afternoon I watched first Sai, then Chou read aloud through a long computerised luggage advertisement before deciding, in the end, that it did not interest them. They did not have the mechanisms yet for quickly screening important documents from 'junk' mail. Pao Youa, on the other hand, need not concern himself when screening mail. His son can perform a second screening, and Hang Chou, his affinal kin, can tackle the more difficult problems. Pao Youa is free from the responsibilities of solving bureaucratic problems or of coping with enigmatic English-language documents.

These two men differ in the degree to which they must solve problems themselves. Pao Youa's strong kin network permits a division of labour which enables him to delegate English literacy tasks to others (while he retains prestigious responsibility not derived from Western literacy for a wide range of problem-solving). Chou must perform most of his own literacy-related tasks himself or turn to an American with whom he has an institutional relationship. This is often a last resort since there is little way of reciprocating the favour to Americans who, apart from anthropologists, have little use for Chou's resources. The men also differ in the ends for which they use literacy. These uses are obviously constrained and affected by the kinds of problems which they must solve.

The data from the in-depth studies are representative of patterns found in the sub-communities to which these two men belong. While there are some individual deviations, in general Norton and Weston are characterised by different clusters of features including different religious preferences, social networks, and literacy needs and practices. As one Hmong articulate woman[7] once explained to me:

> Hmong people we have Weston way and Norton way. Not the same. Some things the same, like language, like some custom. But Norton Hmong people they still have *ua neeg* [shaman], play *qeeg* [talking reeds], want to learn old song, keep old custom. Weston

> culture not the same. Weston Hmong very want to be Christian, not dance or sing. They think that bad. They want to forget old way, maybe they afraid the Hell. They think the new way, that's better.   (Bao Xiong, 5 January 1986)

The relation among these features is not incidental. The most obvious relationship is that between religious conviction and literacy – as in Weston, where the explicit motivation for learning to read, and the prime literacy activity thereafter, is reading the Bible. The relationship between literacy activity and the nature of social network in both communities is less obvious but equally compelling. A person whose social network is comprised of kin is likely to have a rich pool of resources that will be at his/her disposal. When many kin are involved, the relationships are multiplex, assuring a variety of means of reciprocity. In the case of Norton Hmong, dense and multiplex networks permit a division of labour in which specialists can be relied upon for negotiation with institutions, or for solving other literacy-related problems. Services can be repaid with cooking at special occasions, with contributions toward bride price, or in any number of ways that kin support one another.

In Weston, networks are less dense, relationships are singular, and people like Chou have to work harder to get a particular problem solved. Problems cannot be casually brought up while fishing, but rather must be addressed in a telephone call specifically for that purpose. Such a person has less means at his/her disposal to reciprocate, and therefore must turn to institutional relationships to get things done. The costs can be considerable for depending on people with whom one does not have a trusting or long-term relationship. In situations where networks are less dense and multiplex, relationships may be less stable.

As a result of the instability of helping groups, literacy becomes a commodity which is needed by each family that is faced with solving its own problems. Without specialists in advocacy positions, literacy is a critical tool for survival in a dangerous world of bureaucracy. It is not surprising that the troubled summer of 1981 resulted in the exodus and dispersion of most of Weston, while Norton remained intact.

Conclusions

In this study, the uses and meanings of literacy for the Hmong in Philadelphia were examined in context of other modes of communication, while their kinship ties were looked at along with other kinds of helping relationships. Both of these were viewed as social resources which were drawn on to solve various problems in adapting to life in the United States. I have compared the social networks of two people as well as the differences in how literacy is used in their lives. Pao Youa uses literacy to connect to the past and to Hmong tradition, while Chou uses literacy to make new relationships. These men were then placed in the context of the larger community. It is shown here that there are really two sub-communities of Hmong in Philadelphia in which the members engage in very different kinds of meaning-making activities involving different kinds of literacy events.

Differences in literacy use both reflect and create differences in social relationships. For Chou Chang and Pao Youa Lo, uses of literacy both reflected their aspirations while also creating new roles for them in their respective communities. Anthropologists who are interested in models of kinship and social interaction have much to gain by taking into account the communicative means by which social relationships are maintained or developed, and through which they are mobilised. As in the case for the two men described above, differences in literacy use can provide a lens through which to gain an understanding of important community patterns and social process.

When I first met Pao Youa in the classroom, I could only see him as a dismally failing student with no hope for making it. Chou Chang, on the other hand, plodded through, allocated the time and resources necessary to complete enigmatic grammar exercises, learned the rules of classroom behaviour, and came out with his high school equivalency degree. A teacher who met these two men in the classroom would have missed much – she could not have imagined the kinds of resources at the command of the older student, nor could she have imagined the difficulties of the star pupil, who would eventually leave Philadelphia in despair of his social isolation.

Anthropologists who study literacy and social process have much to offer educational policy and practice. By helping to make explicit what social as well as educational resources adults bring with them, anthropologists can help educators to build on resources that adults already have. By discovering the meanings and uses of literacy for members of diverse cultural communities, anthropologists can help educational planners take into account what adults want literacy to do for them.

By recognising the resources that students bring to education, we make it possible for them to build on what they have, and to therefore have more successful and productive learning experiences. By encouraging adults to develop resources for their own ends, we encourage the development of diverse cultural treasures that can enrich us all.

Notes

1 For more on research design and results of the study, see Weinstein-Shr 1986.
2 I count widows and their families among their husbands' clan, as do the Hmong themselves. However, the unpredictability of residence choice casts doubts on the completeness of transfer of a woman's membership after her husband's death.
3 All names have been changed to protect privacy.
4 Some of the material on Chou Chang appears in 'Investigating literacy: approaches, tools and their consequences for inquiry', in Downing and Olney (eds.) 1985.
5 My relationship to these men and their families and my role in the community over the six years of the research include that of language teacher, language learner, community activist and enthographic researcher. For more on these roles and the inherent conflict between them, see Weinstein-Shr 1990.
6 A frequent complaint that Hmong have about adjusting to life in the United States concerns the laws that govern every aspect of living. Hmong are perplexed, for example, that zoning laws prohibit the keeping/killing of animals such as pigs and chickens in their own homes, that there are all sorts of rules about where you can live and how many people can live in the house, and especially that the rules even dictate where you are allowed to bury your dead.
7 Bao Xiong is a remarkable entrepreneur who has developed a prosperous craft business, enabling her to live in a middle class suburb outside of Weston. For more on her success story, see Weinstein-Shr 1989.

References

Barney, G. L. 1967. 'The Meo of Xieng Khoung Province, Laos', in Kundstadter (ed.), *Southeast Asian tribes, minorities and nations*, II. Princeton, NJ: Princeton University Press.
    1981. 'Hmong of Northern Laos', in *Glimpses of Hmong history and culture*. Washington, DC: Center for Applied Linguistics.
Downing, B. and Olney, D. (eds.) 1985. *The Hmong in transition*. New York: Center for Migration Studies.
Dunnigan, T. 1982a. 'The importance of kinship in Hmong community development.' Unpublished manuscript, University of Michigan.
    1982b. 'Segmentary kinship in an urban society: the Hmong of St Paul-Minneapolis', *Anthropological Quarterly*, 55(3): 126–35.
Geddes, W. R. 1976. *Migrants of the mountains*. Oxford: Clarendon Press.
Goody, J. and Watt, I. 1968. 'The consequences of literacy', in J. Goody (ed.), *Literacy in traditional societies*. Cambridge: Cambridge University Press.
Graff, H. 1979. *The literacy myth: literacy and social structure in the nineteenth-century city*. New York: Academic Press.
Heath, S. B. 1983. *Ways with words: language, life and work in communities and classrooms*. New York: Cambridge University Press.
Office of Refugee Resettlement 1983. 'Report to Congress: refugee resettlement'. Washington, DC: Department of Health and Human Services.

Olson, D. 1977. 'From utterance to text: the bias of language in speech and writing', *Harvard Educational Review*, 47.

Ong, W. 1982. *Orality and literacy*. London: Methuen.

Reder, S. 1985. *The Hmong resettlement study. Vol. I*, Final report. Literacy and Language Program, Northwest Regional Laboratory, for Office of Refugee Resettlement, Oregon.

Schofield, R. S. 1968. 'The measurement of literacy in pre-industrial England', in J. Goody (ed.), *Literacy in traditional societies*. Cambridge: Cambridge University Press.

Scribner, S. and Cole, M. 1981. *The psychology of literacy*. Cambridge, MA: Harvard University Press.

Smalley, W. A. (ed.) 1976. *Phonemes and orthography: language planning in ten minority languages of Thailand*, Pacific Linguistic Series, no. 43. Canberra, Australia: Linguistic Circle of Canberra.

Street, B. 1984. *Literacy in theory and practice*. Cambridge: Cambridge University Press.

Weinstein-Shr, G. 1986. 'From mountain tops to city streets: an ethnographic investigation of literacy and social process among the Hmong of Philadelphia.' Ph.D. dissertation, University of Pennsylvania.

1989. 'Survival resources: a Hmong woman's story.' Unpublished manuscript.

1990. 'From problem-solving to celebration: discovering and creating meanings through literacy,' *TESL Talk*, special issue on literacy, 20, 1.

1991. 'People, process and paradox: qualitative research as journey', *Qualitative Studies in Education*, 3(4): 345–67.

Yang, D. 1972. *Les Hmong du Laos au face du développment*. Vientiane, Laos: Siosavath Publishers.

12

CODE SWITCHING AND MODE SWITCHING: COMMUNITY INTERPRETERS AND MEDIATORS OF LITERACY

MIKE BAYNHAM

Introduction

Recent trends in literacy research, represented by the contributions to this volume, as well as, for example, Street (1984), Heath (1983), Shuman (1986) and Baynham (1987 and 1988a), have stressed the need to study literacy practices in specific social contexts, avoiding the grandiose generalisations of earlier generations of literacy researchers, concerning the cognitive consequences of becoming literate and the 'great divide' between oral and literate modes of communication.

Much of this new research has focused on the theoretical construct of the 'literacy event', defined by Anderson, Teale and Estrada (1980) as 'any sequence, involving one or more person, in which the production and/or comprehension of print plays a role'. Heath suggests that 'literacy events have social interactional rules which regulate the type and amount of *talk* about what is written, and define ways in which oral language reinforces, denies, extends, or sets aside the written material'.

In this chapter I will examine the interaction of orality and literacy in the communicative practices of the Moroccan community settled in the Ladbroke Grove area of London, UK. I will focus in particular on two distinctive, if often interrelated, communicative practices: the enlistment of *interpreters*, formally or informally, to accomplish interaction bilingually and the use of *mediators of literacy* (see Wagner, Messick and Spratt 1986), formally and informally, to accomplish literacy purposes. As we shall see, in multilingual settings like London, or for that matter Morocco, the accomplishment of literacy events may routinely involve bilingual or trilingual interaction, but for clarity of exposition, we will begin by presenting these two communicative practices separately, while noting a number of similarities between them. I will suggest that interaction accomplished by the use of interpreters typically involves a distinctive kind of 'code-switching' (see Gumperz 1982). I will also suggest that the typical interactional patterns of the literacy event, involving text and talk about text, the joint reconstruction of meaning and the collaborative construction of texts can be described with the term 'mode-switching', switching from activities focused on reading and writing to talk about these activities and back again, within the moment to moment development of the interaction.

Since literacy practices in multilingual settings are likely in themselves to involve cross-linguistic work, for the purposes of this presentation I will characterise interactions round texts in multilingual settings as potentially involving both code-switching *and* mode-switching: participants strategically deploy their competences in oral and literate modes as well as their abilities to communicate in the relevant languages (here Moroccan Arabic, Standard Arabic, Spanish, French, English) to accomplish literacy work.

Methodology of the study and theoretical context

The data on which the present discussion is based were gathered as part of a study of the oral communicative practices of the Moroccan community in the London setting (written up in Baynham 1988b). Although initially gathered as part of a study on oral language, the data also proved to be relatively rich in information about the literacy practices of the community (Baynham 1987, 1988a). These attempts to characterise the oral and literate practices of the community draw on theory and method derived from both anthropology and linguistics, most notably ethnography and discourse analysis, in ways that have been advocated by Street (see Street 1988a, and introduction to this volume). They are also, however, influenced by an oral history approach to the gathering of data about literacy practices (see Baynham unpublished, and the work of Barton et al on the Lancaster *Literacy in the community project*). The findings of the Morocco Literacy Project (see Wagner, Messick, and Spratt 1986) provide an opportunity to relate the communicative practices observed in the London community to those studied by the project in Morocco. In particular, their description of the function of the 'mediator of literacy' has proved to be a valuable explanatory construct in making sense of the London data and discerning patterns in the interactions observed. If it is possible to establish connections between communicative practices 'back home' in Morocco (and the data I will cite as oral history testimony in extract 1 below provide evidence of this) and communicative practices in the London setting, it is also of interest to establish whether the interactional patterns described are typical of this community alone or are more general. The work of Shuman in Philadelphia (see Shuman this volume, and 1986) with Puerto Rican groups does in fact provide evidence that these communicative practices may be quite widespread in what the Linguistic Minorities Project (1985) calls 'multilingual settings characterized by immigrant bilingualism'.

Before considering the interaction of the oral and the literate in literacy practices and the strategic use of bilingual interaction to accomplish literacy work, I will look at a range of types of oral interpreting in interaction and will further argue that interpreting can be regarded as a specialised form of code-switching.

The interpreter strategy

I have argued (Baynham 1988b) that one of the typical communicative strategies employed by adult members of the Moroccan community, in particular those whose competence in English is restricted, is the enlistment of an interpreter to accomplish a communicative purpose. The 'interpreter strategy' seems to have much in common with the use of mediators of literacy, described in the Morocco Literacy Project and, as we shall see, is also a commonplace in the London setting. The theoretical relevance of these similarities to our understanding of the interactional characteristics of literacy events will be drawn out later in this chapter. Firstly I will give a brief account of the function of the mediator of literacy in the Moroccan context.

Wagner and his associates (1986) point to the use of mediators of literacy as a typical strategy for the accomplishment of literacy tasks. These mediators can be formal or informal. An example of a formal mediator of literacy is the 'écrivain publique' who will, for a fee, write official letters, while educated neighbours and relatives, often a literate younger family member (see Shuman 1986), will act as informal mediators of literacy. Baynham (1987) gives a case study of a literacy event involving the use of a mediator of literacy and I shall be examining some of the data cited therein from a slightly different theoretical perspective in this chapter. The use of a mediator of literacy to accomplish a 'joint literacy event' in which more than one person participates, is seen as a typical strategy in Morocco, as it is among community members in the London context.

Here is an example, taken from field notes, of an incident in which I was informally enlisted as a mediator of literacy to accomplish a literacy purpose:

> I am standing in the visa office of the French Consulate in London, waiting while my wife, who is an Australian citizen, queues to obtain a visa for a forthcoming visit to France. A Moroccan comes up to me, holding the application form, and asks me, in English, to help him to complete it. This involves explaining what is required in each of the boxes into which the form is divided.

The categories: SURNAME
                 FORENAMES
                 OTHER NAMES: maiden, professional, religious,
                 pseudonym
                 DATE OF BIRTH
                 PLACE OF BIRTH: town, country
                 CIVIL STATUS: married, single, widow(er),
                 divorced, separated
are relatively unproblematic, as are NATIONALITY and HOME
ADDRESS. I explain to him what is required at each point and he
fills it in. There are a number of questions relating to his travel
document, a Moroccan passport, in which information is presented in both French and Arabic. I locate the information asked
for:
                 KIND OF TRAVEL DOCUMENT
                 NUMBER
                 PLACE OF ISSUE: town, country
                 DATE OF ISSUE
                 DATE OF EXPIRY
I indicate what information should go where and again he fills it
in. There are a number of questions relating to reasons for
entering France, length of stay, dates of arrival and departure. In
order to fill these in, we need to have quite a lengthy conversation. Once the form is completed, he thanks me for my help and
moves off to join the queue.

Although the interaction was entirely in English, the texts we were
working on were in English and French (the form), and French and
Arabic (the passport). We find in this episode the typical mix of oral and
literate activities characteristic of the literacy event, as well as the
multilingual dimension of working with text in three languages. In
addition we see how a stranger (myself) can be enlisted to accomplish a
literacy task.

   In addition to the role of mediators of literacy in the London based
Moroccan community, there is a similarly patterned use of interpreters to
accomplish communicative work. Again there is a formal/informal dimension. I distinguish three sources of interpreters: (1) interpreters
obtained *informally* 'on the network', that is relatives, friends, accessible
others; (2) interpreters obtained through the Moroccan community
organizations; and (3) interpreters obtained through official channels
(that is through statutory or voluntary agencies). Examples from my
fieldwork will illustrate these three types of interpreting situations.

(a) Informal interpreters

During the course of the fieldwork, there were a number of instances when the person being interviewed called on another person present to interpret informally. This extract from the interview with Mr el Gh can serve as an illustration:

I:	which hospital do you go to now?
Mr el Gh:	eh Reina Sofia
F:	he goes to Hammersmith
?:	*la daba* (no, now)
Mr el Gh:	*daba* Hammersmith (now Hammersmith)

The topic of conversation is a car accident which Mr el Gh sustained in Spain, resulting in hospitalisation in the Reina Sofia hospital. Back in London, he is receiving treatment at the Hammersmith Hospital. F., who is Mr el Gh's daughter, intervenes to clarify his misunderstanding of the interviewer's question and answers for him. Another member of his family (?) unidentified on the tape, points out his misunderstanding in Moroccan Arabic.

When Mr el Gh doesn't understand a question, he turns to a member of his family, asking *šnu qal* (What did he say?) and they translate. For example:

I:	how did you come to England why did you come to England?
Mr el Gh:	*šnu qal* (What did he say?)
F:	*ma: žti landan* (Why did you come to London?)
Mr el Gh:	*žit nxdm* (I came to work)
F:	to work
I:	yeah
Mr el Gh:	to work yeah

Mrs Tar in her narratives is very concerned to get the family relationship of protagonists right. In the following extract, she fails to elicit the correct term from the interviewer through the medium of Spanish and turns to her son for a translation, switching into Moroccan Arabic:

Mrs Tar:	well I'm come one day I'm sleep ( ) well she have him n *como te quiere decir en español mm eh sobrino* (How do you say in Spanish like nephew?)
I:	*sobrino erm* (nephew term)
Mrs Tar:	*sobrino como se dice ǎs kayaqulu bil ingliza bhal awlad hbibek* (nephew how do you say SWITCHES TO MOROCCAN ARABIC how do you say in English like your cousin's children?)

A: auntie
Mrs Tar: nephew
I: nephew
Mrs Tar: no my nephew de my cousin

In this extract we see three languages at work, Moroccan Arabic, a non-standard non-native speaker variety of Spanish and a non-standard non-native speaker variety of English, as well as the standard English of the interviewer and the interviewer's non-native speaker's competence in Spanish. We see very clearly the informal interpreter strategy operating within informal conversation, as a way of managing communicative difficulty.

Early on in an interview with Z.A., the topic is her desire to be rehoused. The interviewer enquires what Z.A. has said on previous visits to the Housing Office and Z.A. replies, 'I dunno because no speak English well well for tell him something bad or good tomorrow I'm take my Aisha with me'. She plans to take her daughter Aisha to interpret for her, drawing on a family member to interpret for her in the public setting of the Housing Office.

(b) Interpreters from the community

One of the voluntary activities of those active in the public life of the community, via participation in one or other of the Moroccan community organisations, is interpreting for other community members whose level of English requires it. In the following extract, M.S. describes his involvement as an interpreter:

I: did you have any specific skills, professional skills that
          you could bring to the work itself?
M.S.:   not really just I think maybe linguistic because I speak
          French I speak Arabic little bit of Spanish and I can
          write them and so on and I think that was really the
          main thing because eh doesn't really need because by
          going and interpreting for people and so on I go ( ) I
          represent people in courts and go with them to
          industrial tribunals and so on

(c) Official interpreters

In her narrative describing her arrival in the UK and successful challenge to the immigration officials who wished to refuse her entry, Mrs Tar narrates an interaction which is facilitated through interpreting: 'He told me what you speak French I'm tell him no I'm no I'm speak Spanish he told me *mira que dice la policia hoy no puede entrar ya muy tarde l ultima dia* (listen the police say you can't enter today, it's too late, the last day)'. The communicative events referred to in (b) and (c) involve both oral and literate practices. M.S. cites his useful language skills as both oral (multilingual) and literate (multiliterate): 'because I speak French I speak Arabic little bit of Spanish and I can write them and so on'. We see that in particular key individuals, interpreting and literacy mediating functions can overlap and do occur. There are structural similarities between the interpreter strategy and the use of mediators of literacy, but they are also related in that the same people tend to be enlisted for both. The interpreting situation which Mrs Tar describes is one that involves a literacy dimension: the immigration officer is trying to deny her entry into the country on the grounds that her visa has expired. The oral negotiation is round a written text. Mrs Tar, who is completely unable to read and write, successfully challenges the official on the grounds that the visa still has not expired, that she has arrived on the last day before it expires.

It seems that, in this data, it is quite hard to keep the oral and the literate dimensions apart, and find instances of interpreting situations in which the interaction is purely oral. We do however have two such instances in (a) and I will now examine them to substantiate the claim that interpreting as an activity can be thought of as a type of *code-switching*, as the term is used in Gumperz, for example. Gumperz (1982: 59) writes: 'Conversational code-switching can be defined as the juxtaposition within the same speech exchange of passages of speech belonging to two different grammatical systems or subsystems'. Now of course, Gumperz is interested in code-switching as a stylistic feature of bilingual interaction, encoding information relating to speaker identity, relationship with other participants and other subtle instances of a speaker's footing in relation to his/her own speech and the speech of others. In the example above, code-switching serves a more obvious, or at least apparently obvious function: to further the course of a conversational interaction where one or more participants have, think they have, or wish to present themselves as having, insufficient command of a given language to engage in interaction by themselves.

Let us take, for example, the interaction that results when the interviewer asks Mr el Gh, 'Which hospital do you go to now?' (Mr el Gh is receiving treatment following a car accident in Spain which resulted in his hospitalisation there). Mr el Gh misunderstands the question and answers with the name of the Spanish hospital where he was treated. His daughter intervenes to answer the interviewer's question, another speaker (unidentified) switches into Arabic (*daba* = 'now' in Moroccan Arabic) and Mr el Gh corrects himself in a two word utterance (Moroccan Arabic *daba* + English place name Hammersmith).

The conversation is being interactionally constructed, using switches into Moroccan Arabic at key moments to clarify utterances or part of utterances that are not understood. While the code-switching that Gumperz considers frequently takes place within a participant's turn at speaking, here we have code-switching that is inter-turn and clearly motivated by functional considerations like misunderstanding.

In the next example there is a typical strategy used by the speaker when he cannot understand an utterance. Mr el Gh turns to his daughter asking in Moroccan Arabic *šnu qal*: ('What did he say?'). In this example F. gives him a literal translation of the question, he replies in Moroccan Arabic to F., who relays the reply to the interviewer in English. The interviewer acknowledges the response (yeah) at which point Mr el Gh, switching into English, repeats the response to the question, affirming F.'s response on his behalf.

We may perhaps note here a similarity with the joint accomplishment of literacy events, documented in the literature cited above. The similarity lies in the ways in which participants jointly work together to achieve understanding in an interaction where at least one participant does not have access to the means of communication. In the literacy event it is differential access to communication in the written mode, in the interpreting event it is differential access to the dominant language.

The next example demonstrates that it is not just in order to clarify the meanings of others that participants resort to the interpreter strategy. Mrs Tar switches into Spanish because a particular kinship term is not available to her in English. She fails to raise the term from the interviewer, who is momentarily blank about the translation equivalent of *sobrino*, and she therefore switches in mid utterance to Moroccan Arabic to address her son. Interestingly, she is aware that his offering of auntie is incorrect, so she prompts him further, using him something like a human dictionary. This strip of interaction provides an example of trilingual switching.

To sum up, these examples show how communicative purposes can be achieved in situations where one or more participants lack code knowledge to participate. The switching is functionally motivated. Structural similarities can be discerned with the joint achievement of literacy work in situations where one or more participants lack aspects of 'mode knowledge' to participate. The other examples of the interpreter strategy cited above illustrate the social contexts and strategies for getting interpreting done: either by drawing on a family member, or by using a prominent community member, or else when an interpreter is provided by a government ministry, like the Home Office, or some other agency. Again, interactional and contextual similarities can be observed between interpreting events and literacy events.

Literacy events

I have already looked at one example of a literacy event: the episode in the French Consulate, in which the oral interaction was conducted in English, French and Arabic. In terms of the code-switching/mode-switching distinction, this literacy event involved mode-switching, but not oral code-switching (the fact that the texts of the literacy event were in English, French and Arabic, however, already introduces a multilingual dimension into the literacy event). Before we go on to consider data where code-switching and mode-switching are featured, I will cite some data from Heath's work, where the oral interaction is conducted in one language (English).

In *Ways with words*, Heath writes that 'in almost every situation in Trackton in which a piece of writing is integral to the nature of participants' interaction and their interpretation of meaning, talk is a necessary component'. She goes on to point out that 'for Trackton adults, reading is a social activity; when something is read in Trackton, it almost always provokes narratives, jokes, sidetracking talk and active negotiation of the meaning of written texts among listeners.' She describes the way that the evening newspaper is read:

> The evening newspaper is read on the front porch for most months of the year. The obituaries on the back page are usually read first, followed by employment listings, advertisements for grocery and department store sales, and captions beneath pictures and headlines. An obituary is read for some trace of an acquaintance with either the deceased, his relatives, place of birth, church, or school; active discussion follows about who the individual was and who he might have known. Circulars or letters to individuals regarding the neighbourhood centre and its recreational or medical services are read aloud and their meanings jointly negotiated by those who have had experience with such activities or know about the forms to be filled out to be eligible for such services. Neighbours share stories of what they did or what happened to them in similar circumstances.
>
> (Heath 1983: 196)

She describes how Lillie Mae, a Trackton resident, receives an official letter about a daycare project and how neighbours are drawn into a discussion that lasts nearly an hour, pooling their experience of such projects, discussing the pros and cons. Reading leads naturally to narrative and the pooling of experience. 'Lillie Mae, reading aloud, decoded the written text, but her friends and neighbours interpreted the text's meaning through their own experiences' (Heath 1983: 197).

These examples give ample evidence of the mix of the oral and the literate in situated interactions around text. Lillie Mae's aloud reading is accompanied by the oral interpretations of her friends and neighbours. This is what I have called mode-switching. One of the problems in deepening our analysis at this point is the nature of the data: ethnographic data tend towards summarising and generalising interactions; rarely do they present the reader with transcripts of situated interactions, from which information about the fine grain of detailed interactional patterns can be derived. We know what Lillie Mae and her friends and neighbours were engaged in, but we don't know exactly *how* they were engaged in it: were they indeed code-switching between different varieties of English? We can guess that they may have been, but the ethnographic vignette does not yield sufficient linguistic detail for the sociolinguistic analysis of strips of discourse. It seems to be that, at the point that good ethnographic descriptions of literacy practices can be achieved, the role of linguistic analysis must be to pinpoint the communicative resources available to speakers/readers/writers and provide good descriptions of the social interactional rules that constitute the literacy event and its embedding in specific social contexts.

Hornberger (1988: 15) has suggested that, 'just as the oral/literate dichotomy fades under scrutiny, so too does the monolingual/bilingual dichotomy, at both the societal and individual levels'. Code-switching is not just a cross-linguistic phenomenon, but also exists between varieties of the same language. It may well be that, when literacy events involving speakers of the same language are analysed using both the methods of ethnography and discourse analysis, we will find that literacy events typically involve both code-switching and mode-switching, whether they are 'bilingual' or 'monolingual'. Whether this is the case or not, we need to know more about the oral language component of literacy events.

In the final section of this chapter, I will examine data from the London study which provide evidence of code-switching and mode-switching in literacy practices. The first extract is of a narrative, in which the speaker describes how she and some friends of hers managed to get their permits to work in London. This can be seen as an oral history testimony, which provides us with evidence of the type of literacy practices involved, but does not permit insight into the fine grain of linguistic detail which could tell us how these communicative practices are achieved in discourse.

The second sequence of extracts is from a real-time tape recording of a literacy event, involving oral interaction in English, Spanish and Moroccan Arabic. These data permit us some insight into the finer grained detail of the interaction, involving both code-switching and mode-switching. These data have already been considered from the point of view of the literacy event and the role of the mediator of literacy (Baynham 1987).

I will here re-analyse it, focusing more on the types of oral interaction and the types of 'work with text' involved, in line with the theoretical perspective developed in this chapter.

Extract 1. Literacy in a multilingual setting: code-switching and mode-switching

Z.T. describes how, after quitting school in Morocco she couldn't find a job and decides to emigrate:

I: what made you decide to come to England

Z: erm well really not eh to England but somewhere abroad

I: yeah

Y: and eh of course emm I quit my high school and I was looking for a job actually

I: yeah

Z: I couldn't find any so erm we had eh local whaddyoucallit eh the man who does eh typewr- erm whaddyoucallit I forget now who does writing by the machine you know for the public

I: ah hah

Z: and I think because he told me that someone in England came to Meknes

Z: and he knew this man but he's very very very nice very educated and he gave him the address of Grand Metropolitan Hotel

I: ah hah

Z: so friend of mine know him and she said I wanted to go to see Mr N. so and so and can you go with me says all right so we we went

I: yeah

Z: and erm we were talking and he said do you want to go abroad said oh yes I'd love to but how well I have got the address and you can write to them yourself

I: uh huh

Z: and send them two picture of yours but you're going to get reply in English so who's going to read it for me (LAUGHTER) I don't know English at all so erm we really did it is erm eh not a seriously

I: yeah

Z: but just through our luck maybe yes or no

I: uh huh

Z: so I did and I wrote a letter for my friend as well

I: yeah because you could write in

Z: yes I wrote in eh in eh in French and we send two picture of each and then in four weeks we get a reply

I: yeah

Z: in English but I and a friend of mine very old woman she's French and she works at the co- uh French consulate so I took it to her and she told me that you're going to get your work permit within four to six weeks but didn't ... I know I I wasn't lucky but eh I didn't take it eh that much so I waited

I: yeah

Z: well that time three of us wrote letters already myself and Fatima then another Fatima which I told her to do so and she did but when we did get work permit the last one was the first my friend was the second and I was three days behind them

I: yeah

Z: so I says well I know my luck is my sign is good go to work so um so it did so I get my work permit

In her account of how she went about migrating to England, Z.T. provides us with an interesting insight into the accomplishment of literacy purposes in the Moroccan context, which is, in many ways, similar to the practices described in the Morocco Literacy Project. Z. struggles to find the right word in English for the 'écrivain publique': 'whaddyoucallit eh the man who does eh typewr-erm whaddyoucallit I forget now who does writing by the machine you know for the public'.

It is through a chain of network contacts that Z. gets to hear of the opportunity of contacting the Grand Metropolitan Hotel chain who, at that time, were recruiting hotel staff in Morocco. Her contact tells her how to go about writing the letter, including the requirement of sending two photographs with the letter. A linguistic problem appears here, since the reply to her letter will be in English, a language she does not speak. Z. however has been educated to secondary school leaving level and is able to write a letter in French. She serves as a mediator for another friend, for whom she writes a letter. When the reply arrives, Z. is again able to make use of a network contact to achieve her literacy purpose: getting the letters read. She takes the letter to her friend who provides her with the gist of the letter: 'you're going to get your work permit within four to six weeks'. The outcome is the arrival of another text: the work permit.

We see in this account how Z. is involved in chains of network contacts to achieve her literacy purposes and is herself a mediator and facilitator for others. The account is informative, but also somehow tantalising to the discourse analyst. How did Z. go about writing the original letters? When her French friend told her the content of the reply in English, did she translate word for word, or summarise the gist of the letter? How, precisely, was the activity of aloud or silent reading, of relaying content, related to the other oral activities which constituted the literacy event (querying, commenting, asking for repetition or clarification)? These are the sort of questions that the discourse analyst wants to ask and which may indeed hold the key to the social interactional rules that constitute the literacy event, as Heath suggests.

In the next extracts I will look at some real-time strips of interaction of a 'literacy-event-in-progress' to see how discourse analysis can complement the dimensions of ethnographic and oral history enquiry into literacy practices.

The literacy event in question (reported in Baynham 1987) arose during an interview carried out as part of the fieldwork for the study of oral communication in the London based community, referred to above (Baynham 1988b). The scene is the sitting room of Touria's flat. I have arrived, armed with a tape recorder, to interview her. Menana, Touria's aunt is also visiting. Menana has received a letter from the DHSS (Department of Health and Social Security) and asks me to tell her what it says. In extract 2(a) I read the letter and tell her the gist of it. In extract 2(b) Menana successfully challenges my suggestion that she should take the letter to a Moroccan worker at the Citizen's Advice Bureau and I agree to write a letter of appeal for her. In extract 2(c) I attempt to reconstruct the story of what actually happened, in order to write the letter of appeal. In extract 2(d) I read back the reply that I have written.

Extract 2. A letter from the Department of Health and Social Security: extracts from the data

M = Menana, T = Touria, I = Interviewer
(a) Paraphrasing the DHSS letter for Menana
    Her response to it
    My strategy for responding: go and see Souad

  I: department of health and social security
  M: yeah what's happen
  I: supplementary benefit ... oh dear ...
  M: what's happen Mike
  I: it says they've given you too much supplementary benefit too much money
  M: social security no much give it to me because I'm pay the rent twenty-six pounds twenty-four pounds for the rent still to me twenty only give me this ...

T: *šnu 'andhum*   (What's wrong?)
I: it says they've given you ninety-six pounds too much
M: nooh never give me ninety-six ... give me every week
I: yeah
M: the book I'm give him the book straight
I: it says they wanted you to give the book back when you
    started work
M: yeah I'm give him the book back when me start work ...
    straight ...
I: mmm ... do you know what I think you ought to do
M: yeah
I: is a problem like this is a bit difficult you know is a
    difficult problem you ought to erm do you know Souad
    who works in the office there
T: yeah Souad
M: yeah Souad yeah
I: if you go and see her and then ask her to write a letter cos
    you have to you have to write a letter to say this is wrong
M: is a wrong
T: mm
I: it's called an appeal you have to make an appeal ... let me
    just tell you I'll tell you exactly what the letter says it says
    dear madam I'm sorry to tell you that you have been paid
    ninety-six pounds too much because of you didn't give the
    book back when you started work
M: yeah I'm give him straight
I: straight away
M: yeah
T: yes
I: it says you can (.........)
M: no I'm give him straight the book
T: straight on when she (.........) she give him straight on
M: (.........) give him straight away the lady take with me cut
    the book
I: straight away
T: yes
M: yeah straight away
I: because they say that you didn't they say here that you
    didn't do it
M: nooh do it straight first week call first week after give him
    me collect the money Friday I'm give him Monday
T: Monday (.........)

M: no no no no take the money Monday I'm leave the money
     in the book I'm give him
T: because she off Monday and she start work
M: yeah
T: she start work
M: no
T: (.........) she get first week for her work the first week is
     Friday
M: yeah
T: she get her money and then (.........)
M: (..............)
T: and Monday she go straight away she don't go to post
     office to take money she go straight on to give him his
     book because she have money now

The first phase of this extract involves my silent reading of the letter, with the oral accompaniment of reading out loud two key phrases from the letter, 'Department of Health and Social Security', followed by 'Supplementary Benefit' and 'oh dear'. The function of this is to alert Menana to the type of news she should expect from the letter and inform her of where the letter is from and what it concerns. The formula here is:

SILENT READING OF TEXT + OUT LOUD READING AS COMMENT OR
GLOSS

The out loud reading keys Menana in to the bad news to come.

My third utterance is an example of a different kind of switching, which we could perhaps call *register switching*. I switch from the register of official letters 'supplementary benefit' to a simplified paraphrase: 'too much money'. My understanding of that particular switch is that it involved a kind of amplification of the initial utterance, designed to make absolutely clear to Menana the implication of being given too much Supplementary Benefit. The switch is from the technical to the everyday. Supplementary Benefit is of course a term which is also in everyday use, so it may well be that the register switch employed here was redundant, but there clearly is a switch here, motivated by the interaction around the text.

Further on in the interaction, we find a register switch in the opposite direction, from the everyday paraphrase equivalent of a technical term to the term itself: 'you have to write a letter to say this is wrong it's called an appeal you have to make an appeal'. Here we start with the simplified form and then switch to the technical expression. The interaction is punctuated by utterances in which I, the interviewer, provide paraphrases of what the letter says, carefully attributing them (it says ....) at each point. In the final utterance in this extract, I provide a paraphrase of the whole letter, preceded by the phrase: 'I'll tell you exactly what the letter says ...' Throughout this strip of interaction I, as reader, am providing paraphrase equivalents of the original text, carefully attributed, so that it is clear that the accusation is contained in the letter and is not one that I am personally responsible for.

We can understand the function of IT SAYS + PARAPHRASE on the analogy of direct and indirect speech. Direct speech claims to report the utterance, or in this case text, both in its surface form and in its content. Indirect speech, however, always involves the reporting not of surface form but of propositional content. The utterance 'I'll tell you exactly what the letter says', followed by a telling that patently isn't an exact reading but a paraphrase seems in some ways problematic. We can perhaps suggest that the utterance 'I'll tell you exactly' can be glossed as 'this paraphrase will give you exactly the propositional content of the letter, what it *means*'. We begin to see that an interaction which at first glance seemed like a fairly simple mix of 'the oral' and 'the literate' contains in fact some rather complex shifts and switches of footing in the ways that the text is related orally. It is not far-fetched to see in the interpretative paraphrase which I provide of the text something akin to cross-linguistic interpretation, except in this case it is a question of mode (spoken/written) and register (technical/non technical).

(b) Menana challenges my strategy and I offer to write a response for her myself

> I: well what you should do you have to write a letter saying
>
> M: this letter look (.........) send me this letter look this (.........)
>
> I: I think it's much better Menana if you take erm take this to see Souad because she understands all the problems
>
> T: yes
>
> I: and what you'll have to do is write a letter saying I returned
>
> M: what this write letter this letter (.........) fill this form small
>
> I: yeah
>
> T: (...........)
>
> M: what she tell him *qué quiere decir*   (What does that say?)
>
> I: *pues* ...(...........) do you want me to write the letter
>
> M: yeah please
>
> I: can you tell me I'll start the letter and you can tell me
>
> M: *empieza a trabajar el día cinco de abril*   (I start work on 5 April)

In the earlier part of this interaction strip, I am trying to suggest to Menana the form that her response should take, without committing myself to actually writing it, since my opinion is that she should take it to the CAB so that someone experienced in these matters could deal with it. What Menana is doing throughout the interaction, is challenging my advice in a very explicit way, by drawing my attention to the fact, which had escaped me, that there was a section on the form to complete if you wished to appeal. The letter, if such it be, can be written on the form in the space provided. In the middle of this, we find an example of Menana code-switching from English to Spanish in a way much closer to the type of code-switching described by Gumperz (1982: 78), specifically the type he calls *reiteration*: 'Frequently a message in one code is repeated in the other code, either literally or in somewhat modified form. In some cases such repetition may serve to clarify what is said, but often they simply amplify or emphasize a message'. It is at this point that I give in and offer to write the letter myself.

(c) Reconstructing the story of what actually happened

> I: where where did you give *dónde eh dónde trajiste el libro este*   (where did you take the book?)
> M: social security
> I: dónde en westbourne grove   (Where? In Westbourne Grove?)
> T: yeah Westbourne Grove
> M: yeah westbourne grove . . . no no this westbourne grove here no no
> I: *el otro*   (the other one)
> M: *el otro*   (the other one)
> I: *cómo se llama*   (what's it called)
> M: *no sé como se llama*   (I don't know what it's called)
> T: *măsi dyel hinaya*   (not the one round here?)
> M: nooh the rounjit baker street
> I: lisson grove
> M: yeah this one nearly in baker street
> I: yeah
> M: yeah . . . look the letter where she come from

Once I have agreed to write the letter, an extended stretch of oral interaction is dedicated to getting clear the actual event sequence, the location of events, prior to writing the response to the DHSS letter. This has similarities to a jointly reconstructed story, although its purpose is not to tell the story, but to serve as information for drafting a response. The story genre is embedded in the letter genre. We note that the oral interaction, which elicits 'the facts' is conducted in English, Spanish and Moroccan Arabic.

(d) Reading the letter back to Menana and her evaluation of the incident

    I: *espera un momentito que yo voy a yo voy a* (wait a
        moment I'm going to I'm going to)
    M: *bueno* (OK)
    I: *le voy a leer* (I'm going to read) I wish to appeal against
        your demand of ninety-six pound ninety-six I returned the
        book to the office in Lisson Grove on 13 April I started
        work on 5 April I cashed the cheque for the week of the
        fifth
    M: yeah
    I: because I did not have the money to pay me rent
    M: yeah
    I: to buy food for myself and my daughter
    M: that's it
    I: I did not cash it after that
    M: nothing no eat one penny him
    I: uh
    M: no eat one *no deja a mi* (I didn't keep) one penny s crazy
        locos (mad)

After the process of reconstructing the event sequence, I read the letter back to Menana. The reading is embedded in oral interaction in Spanish, indeed the phrase which introduces the reading back, '*le voy a leer*', is in Spanish, followed immediately by a switch into English. This is the category of code-switching which Gumperz (1982: 75–6) calls *quotational*: 'In many instances the code switched passages are clearly identifiable either as direct quotations or as reported speech'. This quotational code-switching is very different from the quoting clauses we noted in extract 1, which were followed by a verbal paraphrase of the text of the letter. The format in extract 1 was:

IT SAYS + PARAPHRASE

The paraphrase involved a kind of translating of the formal technical language of the letter into a more informal everyday language:

too much supplementary benefit + too much money

as well as translating back from the everyday to the technical:

you have to write a letter to say it's wrong
it's called an appeal you have to make an appeal

The paraphrasing activity in extract 1 seems to involve *making texts talk*, providing a reading that is in itself a switch from literate to oral, what we have called a mode-switch. In contrast the out loud reading of the reply to the DHSS in extract 2(d) gives a clearer example of both code-switching and mode-switching at work. The initial clause is in Spanish, but the text read out is in English. '*Le voy a leer*' is an oral marker for a strip of 'reading' and a clear instance of mode-switch.

Conclusion

In this chapter I have examined two sets of communicative practices used by adult members of the Moroccan community in the London setting: the interpreter strategy and the use of mediators of literacy. We have seen how literacy events in multilingual settings typically have an oral dimension that involves shifting or switching between the languages available to speakers, for some of the purposes indicated in Gumperz (1982), but also to avoid misunderstanding when one or more participant has limited access not only to written language but also to the oral forms of the dominant language.

We have also seen, however, that in strips of interaction without language-switching, for example extract 1 above, there were interesting kinds of switching at work in the oral interaction in which the literacy activity was embedded.

It may well be that the study of literacy events in multilingual contexts simply makes salient a characteristic of all literacy events, which is masked when they take place (apparently) in one language. This characteristic is that the embedding talk, which surrounds and enacts the literacy event, will typically involve complex shifts and switching in the sociolinguistic repertoire available to participants. In this chapter I have chosen to theorise this in terms of code-switching and mode-switching, and could perhaps have examined the data in terms of shifts of footing in Goffman's sense. It should be apparent that, for effective literacy research, ethnographic and oral history methodologies need to be complemented with methods derived from sociolinguistics and discourse analysis.

Finally, we must ask to what extent the issues raised in this chapter can be generalised to other settings, other day-to-day uses of literacy in multilingual environments. The following quotation from Shuman (1986: 101), in which she discusses the communicative practices around literacy of Puerto Ricans in Philadelphia provides many parallels with the issues we have been discussing:

> In the visits to public offices, in some cases, the adolescents read English and translated texts into spoken Spanish. In other cases, they read the English aloud. The parents usually responded in Spanish, and the adolescents often used both English and

Spanish in their interpretations. The choice of language was determined by both necessity and propriety, although necessity was often the overriding factor.

Similarly, when M. talks of her intention of going to the Housing Office, she says: 'I dunno because no speak English well well for to tell something bad or good tomorrow I'm take my Aisha with me'. It may be that these practices will turn out to be common in many communicative settings, multilingual and otherwise, where individuals and groups struggle to make texts speak and work for them, struggle to make and exchange meanings.

References

Anderson, A. B., Teale, W. B. and Estrada, E. 1980. 'Low-income children's preschool literacy experience: some naturalistic observations', *The Quarterly Newsletter of the Laboratory of Comparative Human Cognition*, 2 (3): 59–65.
Barton, D. and Ivanič, R. (eds.). 1991. *Writing in the community*. Written Communication Annual, vol. 6. Beverly Hills: Sage.
Baynham, M. J. 1986. 'The oral dimensions of literacy events.' Unpublished paper given at the Annual Meeting of the British Association for Applied Linguistics, University of Reading, 1986.
1987. 'The oral dimensions of literacy events: a letter from the DHSS', in T. Bloor and J. Norrish (eds.), *Written language*. British Studies in Applied Linguistics 2. London: Centre for Information on Language Teaching and Research.
1988a. 'Literate, biliterate, multiliterate: some issues in literacy research', in J. McCaffrey and B. Street (eds.), *Literacy research in the UK: adult and school perspectives*. RaPAL Occasional Papers no. 1. Lancaster: RaPAL.
1988b. 'Narrative and narrativity in the English of a first generation migrant community'. Unpublished Ph.D. thesis, University of Reading.
Goffman, E. 1981. *Forms of talk*. Oxford: Blackwell.
Gumperz, J. J. 1982. *Discourse strategies*. Cambridge: Cambridge University Press.
Heath, S. B. 1983. *Ways with words*. Cambridge: Cambridge University Press.
Hornberger, N. H. 1988. 'Becoming biliterate: what do we know?' Unpublished paper presented at the 'Right to Literacy' Conference sponsored by the Modern Language Association, Ohio State University, and the Federation of State Humanities Councils.
Linguistic Minorities Project (LMP). 1985. *The other languages of England*. London: Routledge and Kegan Paul.
Shuman, A. 1986. *Storytelling rights: the uses of oral and written texts by urban adolescents*. Cambridge: Cambridge University Press.
Street, B. V. 1984. *Literacy in theory and practice*. Cambridge: Cambridge University Press.
1988a. 'Literacy practices and literacy myths', in R. Saljo (ed.), *The written*

world, Springer Series in Language and Communication, vol. 13. Springer Press.

1988b. 'A critical look at Walter Ong and "the Great Divide"', in *Literacy Research Centre Newsletter*, 1. University of Pennsylvania.

Wagner, D. A., Messick, B. M. and Spratt, J. 1986. 'Studying literacy in Morocco', in B. B. Shieffelin and P. Gilmore (eds.), *The acquisition of literacy: ethnographic perspectives*. New York: Ablex.

INDEX

admonitory function of letters, 78–9, 80
affect/affection
   and letters, 2, 26, 67–82, 252–4
   and speech, 63–4, 69–70
   and written communication, 63–5
age, and knowledge, 101, 103, 104–5, 186
   and see elders, maturation concepts
Aiarpa, Kruni, 34–5
Aladura movement, 141, 200–3, 213–15
   and religious literature, 210, 212–13
   study outline, 6, 141–2, 198–200
   and see Church of the Lord, Nigeria, Oshitelu
Alaska *see* Seal Bay
Alien Law, USA, 161
Ambohivohitra, 89
Ambositra, 89
Amhara people, 144–6, 154
animator, 260
anthropology, and linguistics, 12–17
Arabic
   education, 120–6, 147
   in Sierra Leone, 114, 115–17
   in Somalia, 147–8
   and written language, 122
   and see Islam
archives, 236–7
authority
   and collaborative writing, 260–5, 266, 267–8
   and education, 101–2, 103
   and literacy, 27
autonomous model of literacy, 5–7, 10–12, 111

Baptists, at Seal Bay, 181–6
Bemba religion, Zambia, 213–14
Bible, 36, 39, 127–8
big men, 43
blessings, 119, 120–1, 125, 126
Bogia, Papua New Guinea, 35
books, 39, 286
   and see Glory of Kings, Iwe ABD,
   Moses' Book, printed matter, religious literature
bureaucracy

and Hispanic people, 165
and Hmong people, 274–5, 279–81, 282, 283
and Moroccan people, 304–12
and see village governance

Cargo cult, 35–6, 39–41, 55
Catholicism and literacy, 25–6, 34–6, 90
   and see Christianity
Chang, Chou, 226, 278, 279–83, 288–91
   and see Hmong people
Christianity and literacy
   in Gapun, 25–6, 30–1, 34, 36–41, 55
   in Nigeria, 200–3, 210–13, 215
   in Nukulaelae, 65
   in Seal Bay, 180–6
   in Sierra Leone, 127–9
   Yoruba, 200–3
   and see Aladura movement, Baptists, Catholicism, Church of the Lord, Jehovah's Witnesses, Lutheran church, religion, religious literature, Russian Orthodox religion
Church of the Lord, 205, 210–13, 214–15
   and see Holy Script, Oshitelu
City High School, Philadelphia, 229–30
   collaborative writing, 231, 236, 237–9
   letters, 237–8, 241
   poetry, 236, 241, 242
   rap, 236, 238–9
   religious feeling, 241–2
   satire, 236
   students, 235–7, 240–1, 243
   study outline, 223–4, 230–2
   and see vernacular writing
clerks, Nigeria, 202
code-switching, 300, 303, 304–12
collaborative writing, 265–8
   and authority, 260–5, 266, 267–8
   City High School, 231, 236, 237–9
   in the classroom, 255–8
   in the family, 258–60
   forged notes, 248
   junior high school, 248–68
   letters, 237–8, 250–1
   mail-order sales, 258–9